PEARSON   ALWAYS LEARNING

Philip McCaskey

Selected Topics in United States History, 1783–1877

Seventh Custom Edition for Cape Fear Community College

Pearson Learning Solutions, 501 Boylston Street, Suite 900, Boston, MA 02116
A Pearson Education Company
www.pearsoned.com

Printed in the United States of America

1 2 3 4 5 6 7 8 9 10 V0ZN 18 17 16 15

000200010271960855

AL

ISBN 10: 1-323-08218-2
ISBN 13: 978-1-323-08218-8

Selected Topics In United States History

1763–1877

Seventh Edition

By
Philip McCaskey

Acknowledgements

This book would have been impossible to complete without the invaluable assistance of my colleagues at Cape Fear Community College. In particular, I would like to thank the following persons: Bob Brennan, Jason McCoy, Julie Lee, Genevieve Feliu, Ben Billingsley, Frank Carter, Robert Puckett, Deborah Basket, Ronnie Kirkland, and Thomas Massey.

For
God, my beloved family, Jenny, friends, animals, and my country.

Chapter 1

Introduction: The Beginnings – Colonization to 1763

<u>Colonization of the "New World"* and the Development of the</u>
<u>Trans-Atlantic Slave Trade 1450–1775</u>

The colonization of the Western Hemisphere by Europeans and Africans between the 15th and 19th centuries is truly one of the epochal developments in world history. There are several important questions to consider when studying and assessing this period. Interestingly, many of the answers are surprisingly blunt and simple.

<u>1 - Who?</u> – Although the Vikings explored North America as early as 1000 A.D., the first major western explorers were the Spanish and Portuguese who dominated European colonization of the Americas from approximately 1500 to 1600. The British, French, and Dutch subsequently took the lead after 1600.

<u>2 – Personalities Involved?</u>

A. <u>Spanish</u>
   - Christopher Columbus – the Italian explorer commissioned by the Spanish monarchs, Ferdinand and Isabella, to pursue a western route to India and China in 1492. Instead, he encountered the Americas (dubbed the "New World") and landed on the island of San Salvador in the Bahamas. Although not the first European to discover the Americas, and perhaps not even the greatest of the explorers (consider the individuals subsequently listed) Columbus remains the most recognized symbol of European exploration and colonization of the Western Hemisphere.
   - Amerigo Vespucci
   - Ferdinand Magellan
B. <u>Portuguese</u>
   - Prince Henry the Navigator
   - Pedro Alvarez Cabral
   - Gaspar Corte Real
C. <u>British</u>
   - John Cabot
   - Sir Francis Drake
   - Henry Hudson (Henry Hudson also hired out to the Dutch for journeys of exploration)
D. <u>French</u>
   - Giovanni de Verrazano
   - Jacques Cartier

<u>3 – Where?</u> - Coastal Africa (1450s), South and Central America including Mexico, Florida, the Caribbean Sea and the Gulf of Mexico (1450s–1560s), coastal North America (1498–1620), and Canada (1501–1642).

*Think the categorization of the Western Hemisphere as the "New World" seems a little exaggerated and overblown? Think again. The first Spanish and Portuguese explorers to the region encountered animals and plants which, at the very least, appeared exotic if not bizarre; for example, corn, peanuts, chocolate, vanilla, squash, pumpkins, rattlesnakes, armadillos, and possums. For their part, the Europeans brought with them animals which stunned, and in some cases, terrified the natives of the Americas; for instance, cattle, sheep, goats, pigs, and horses. They also introduced the important staple crops of rice, wheat, barley, and surprisingly, bananas!

4 - <u>Why</u>? - think about the three big "Gs," "God, gold, and glory." This statement is sometimes attributed to the Spanish conquistador Hernando Cortes in reference to his explorations and military campaigns in Central America during the early 1500s. This does not reflect the real significance of the statement however. "God, gold, and glory" concisely expresses some of the primary reasons people explore and extend frontiers and limits, then and now. Consider this:

> "God" could be the desire to spread and bolster one's faith whatever it may be (in the case of the Europeans, Christianity), to worship without fear of persecution, or to pursue and explore the creations of the Creator. "Gold" is and has always been a universally accepted symbol of wealth, and without question, voyages to the New World were strongly motivated by the desire to accumulate wealth. (The legend of *El Dorado*, the "City of Gold," comes to mind.) It is quite reasonable to assume that if gold, diamonds, oil, or any other valuable material were discovered just beneath the surface of Mars, the space program would dramatically accelerate!* Finally, "glory" is a term synonymous with great or heroic effort. Americans John Glenn, Neil Armstrong, Charles Lindbergh, Chuck Yeager, and many others all fit the description of heroes. Why? Courage, devotion, rigor, achievement, and the will to breach the unknown are attributes which heartily deserve the acclaim and respect of human beings everywhere, not just the United States.

5 - <u>How</u>? A. Political Centralization and economic growth gave Europeans both the sense of national interest and the finance capital necessary to spur exploration and colonization. These forces continued to heavily influence Europeans until the post-World War II era.
B. Technological improvement—such as the <u>Caravel</u>—and better navigational devices—such as the <u>Magnetic Compass</u> and <u>Astrolabe</u>—gave Europeans the ability to explore profitably. Militarily, primitive firearms (especially the <u>Harquebus)</u>, steel swords (<u>Rapiers</u>), the horse, and ship mounted cannon gave the Europeans a decisive advantage in force, incalculably facilitating their conquests.

The Development of the Trans-Atlantic Slave Trade
Unfortunately for human history, the institution of slavery has always existed as punishment for a crime, from kidnapping, for indebtedness, as a condition of birth, and a variety of other reasons, but it has always paralleled warfare. War, then and now, produces a victor and a vanquished. The reality of this situation is quite stark:

the defeated become subject to the will of the winner, whatever that disposition may be.

*By 1650 the amount of gold introduced into Europe had increased by 20%, silver 300%. Also exploration is exceptionally expensive. For example, Columbus' voyage which consisted of 3 ships and 90 men and boys cost approximately $14,000, an exorbitant amount for the era. Closer to the present, the Moon mission in 1969 cost $25.4 billion (1970 dollar value). Adjusted for inflation, this amounts to about $135 billion today.

In other words, if you surrender you surrender your identity, your freedom, even your life if that suits the interests of the victors. In addition, war is a universal phenomenon waged by every race, religion, and ethnic group, with the consequence that slavery is a universal phenomenon.* Why then does slavery in the modern era evolve in such a manner that slaves become exclusively African? What caused the explosive development of both the African slave trade and the plantation style of slavery in the "New World," first in South and Central America and subsequently in North America? Finally, how does this transformation affect racial perceptions today?

1) Prior to 1453, two primary sources existed for slaves, one in Europe and one in Africa. Both of these sources had been established for at least 1700 years. The first had its base in Trans-Saharan Africa stretching from Egypt across North Africa (the sub-Saharan route). The second stemmed from the Baltic Sea region in northern Europe running southward to the Black Sea and then through the Dardanelles into the Aegean and then Mediterranean Seas (the Slavic route, consider the term!).

    In 1453, the Ottoman Empire (a Muslim empire, based in Turkey, which controlled large areas in North Africa) captured the vital port city of Constantinople. Constantinople controlled the outlet from the Black Sea to the Mediterranean Sea. As the Ottomans held a monopoly of the sub-Saharan slave route, they gradually blocked the exportation of white slaves from the Baltic Sea region. Subsequently, Mediterranean merchants increasingly turned to Africa for slaves. As a result, white slavery began to disappear in Europe.

2) Sugar- the demand for sugar in Europe grew tremendously after the 15th Century. Areas in South and Central America colonized by the Spanish and Portuguese were ideal for cultivating sugar, a crop most profitably suited to plantation labor, which almost immediately meant slave labor. The Europeans however had enslaved native South and Central American Indians at that time and for such purposes. Why would they need to import Africans?

3) Smallpox and other diseases devastated the native populations in apocalyptic numbers. (Smallpox was allegedly introduced in 1520 by an African slave carried to Mexico on a Spanish ship.) Consider these statistics:

In 1519, the native population of the Mexico-Guatemala region consisted of perhaps 25 million people. By the 1650s approximately 1.5 million remained. Similarly, the island of Hispaniola in 1492 contained an estimated 100,000 natives. By 1570, that number had dropped to 300. In Central and South America, the entire population declined from perhaps 75 million before Columbus' arrival to about 10 million in 1555, a loss greater than 85%!

Why the mortality rates? Indians had never been in contact with Europeans or Africans and thus had no physical resistance to their diseases, not only smallpox, but typhoid, measles, diphtheria, influenza, mumps, and a host of additional

*For example, an excellent documentary on the subject was released in 2010 by filmmaker Mimi Chakarova "The Price of Sex," and a report titled, "Human Trafficking In The Port City," aired on Wilmington, NC television station WWAY on May 23rd 2012. More recently, a human trafficking story was reported on the front page of the Wilmington *Morning Star* on Aug. 14, 2014, involving two alleged traffickers, aged 19 and 28, and their reported victims, two girls, 15 and 16, and two boys, 18!

killer maladies. The same held true for the Europeans and Africans who were (according to some pathologists) introduced to the dreadful and deadly disease, Syphilis.

A very interesting aspect of the slave trade is the destinations for the slaves. Most Americans wrongfully assume that the U.S. received the most African slaves, but the facts do not support such a conclusion.

    1)-The climate precluded the growing of sugar in the North American colonies, and sugar brought plantation style slavery into the "New World."

    2)-African slaves were brought to South America as early as 1503. The first African slaves brought to the British North American colonies did not arrive until 1619—116 years later! Where did they land? Jamestown, Virginia Colony.

    Where then did the slaves go, and in what numbers?

British North America (to 1790)	- 274,000
The United States (to 1786)	- 124,000

Approximately 5%
of the total trans-Atlantic
slave trade

British Caribbean	- 1,665,000
French Caribbean	- 1,600,000
Dutch Caribbean	- 500,000
Spanish America	- 1,552,000
Brazil	- 3,646,800
Total	- 9,362,800

Tragically, those numbers reflect only a fraction of the total. Approximately 20 million Africans were enslaved by Africans and transported across Africa for sale to European slavers on the coast. Of these, only about 11 million persons survived. Once on the coast, they were put on board European and American vessels (mostly British) and sent to the Americas. This hellish journey became known as the "Middle Passage," and on average about 15% of the slaves died while in transit, hence the lesser total arrivals to the Americas previously cited. Of all the general regions listed above, only one saw the imported African population demonstrate positive demographic growth (that is, Africans had babies and their numbers grew).

From the beginning, the 13 British North American Colonies (later the United States) had a positive demographic growth in Africans despite being the recipient of the least number of slaves. Why? Several factors contributed, such as the <u>relatively</u> less disease ridden climate than in the tropics, the <u>relatively</u> less arduous tasks assigned to the slaves than the cultivation of sugar, at least initially, and the slow evolution of the institution from its introduction at Jamestown, Virginia Colony in 1619. Slavery was much less defined and more malleable in the 13 colonies than in the Caribbean and Central and South America. In brief, slavery had to find a place in the colonial economy and society. In the Southern Colonies, that place came in agriculture; first with tobacco, then with rice. In the Northern Colonies, slaves were employed in much more diverse vocations (such as domestic servants, drivers, laborers, and artisans), but without the climate to produce the aforementioned staples, the institution was financially less viable, a vital factor in its eventual disappearance from the region. Finally, it must be noted that in all phases of American history to 1865, there existed a free black population, North and South, concomitant with the enslaved black population, also imbued with the universal human desire to procreate.

<u>Colonial Economic Patterns—Colonialism and Mercantilism</u>

After the initial colonization efforts by the Spanish and Portuguese in the 15th and 16th centuries, the Dutch, British, and French assumed the initiative. The Dutch established colonies in Guiana, Malacca, the Malay Peninsula, Ceylon, the Celebes Islands, and the Cape of Good Hope. The British and French were vigorous rivals in North America, the West Indies, West Africa, India, and the Far East. The British established heavily populated colonies on the east coast of North America, while the French set up widely scattered trading posts throughout the hinterland and Canada. Quebec, the most important of the French settlements, lay on the northern bank of the St. Lawrence River. The British and French implemented different strategies in regards to colonialism, each reflective of their home governments. The French colonial pattern was based on absolutism and centralism with rigid, across the board standardization, while the British pattern stressed independence and flexibility (later referred to as "Salutary or Benign Neglect"). Economically however both nations practiced <u>mercantilism</u>, a system designed to provide a favorable balance of trade and an influx of gold and silver to the mother country. An ultra-protectionist system, the mechanics of mercantilism were quite simple. The colonies provided the mother country with raw materials, while the mother country produced more expensive finished goods which the colonies would have to purchase. Obviously there were items desired by the colonists which their respective mother countries did not produce, for instance, French champagnes, British woolens, or colonial products such as tobacco, cotton, sugar, and indigo. In such cases the mother country would simply impose taxes on imports (a.k.a. duties or <u>tariffs</u>) on such items. For both Britain and France, mercantilism proved fabulously profitable. Colonial commerce accounted for 1/3 of British and French foreign trade. Listed below are two examples of a colonial trade triangle.

#1- From Britain—pots, blankets, paper—to North America—picks up fish oil, fish, beef, timber—to the West Indies (Jamaica for example) where sugar is picked up.

#2- From Providence, RI— Rum—to West Africa—for slaves—to the West Indies—for molasses.

Slavery was the lynchpin for colonization with the British acting as the main agents. During the slave trading era, a yearly average of 88,000 Africans were sold out of Africa to the Western Hemisphere. The British accounted for 50% of the slave trade, the French 25%, while the Spanish, Dutch, Portuguese, Danish, and Americans made up the other 25%.

 British Colonial Population, Exports and Slave Trading Data

Overall Population	Slave Population
1,700 – 250,000	1,700 – 25,000
1,750 – 1,000,000	1,760 – 250,000
1,775 – 2,500,000	1,790 – 698,000
1,790 – 4,000,000	1,800 – 857,000

In 1672, The Royal African Company obtained its charter and slave importation to North America began to slowly increase. However, the slave trade exploded after 1697 when the Company's monopoly expired and the overseas slave trade expanded rapidly.

Hubs of the North American Slave Trade

The first American slave trading ships (slavers) disembarked from Boston in 1645; by 1700, Boston had become the principal slave trading port in the 13 Colonies. Between 1700–1750, 155 British slavers were registered, most out of Bristol and Liverpool, while 20 were registered in the American colonies. After 1770, however, 150 ships were based out of Rhode Island alone and 192 hailed from Britain. The two major crops which utilized plantation style slavery in the North American colonies were tobacco and rice.

Tobacco Exports To Britain	Rice Exports To Britain
1,700 – 37,840,000 lbs.	1,700 – 304,000 lbs.
1,725 – 21,046,000 lbs.	1,725 – 5,367,000 lbs.
1,750 – 51,339,000 lbs.	1,750 – 16,667,000 lbs.
1,775 – 55,968,000 lbs.	1,775 – 57,692,000 lbs.

Virginia Colony – established as a royal charter of the London Company in 1606. Its **primary purpose** was to make money.

   After the failure of the colonization attempt on Roanoke Island in 1587*, the prospects for success at Jamestown seemed dubious. Nonetheless, British colonists set foot on Virginia soil in 1607. Their first year proved nightmarish. Starvation, insect borne diseases, salt water poisoning, and Indian attacks rendered the colony nearly useless and helpless. For example, in 1608 only 53 out of 120 colonists remained alive, and only 1,132 colonists out of 14,000 survived or remained by 1624. Ruthless, if not dictatorial, leadership beginning with Capt. John Smith and continuing with Lord Delaware, Thomas Gates, and Thomas Dale precariously stabilized the colony. Tobacco made it pay however. John Rolfe, after observing

*The 117 "Lost Colonists" had disappeared without a trace when a relief expedition arrived in 1590.

Chesapeake region Indians, began his tobacco growing and curing experiments with the harsh Virginia plants in 1612. These experiments were aided by Rolfe's importation of seeds of a sweeter tobacco from Trinidad. In 1613, he perfected a new variety, and by 1616 Virginia tobacconists exported 2,500 lbs. to England. By 1619, tobacco provided the economic stimulant vital to the survival of VA and then MD, and NC.

New England Colonies – In general, these colonies were settled by persons desiring to escape religious persecution. In their new homes in North America, they set about establishing functional theocracies.

Separatist Pilgrims in Plymouth
Non-Separatist Puritans in Mass. Bay Colony

Colonial Organization and Settlement

Colony	Settlement Date	Founders – Motivation	Main Figure
Virginia	1607	London Co. – Profit	John Smith
Plymouth	1620*	London Co. – Profit, Religion	William Bradford
New Amsterdam	1624@	West India Co. (Dutch)-Profit	Gov. Peter Minuit
New York	1664@	Royal Colony (England)-Profit	Duke of York
New Hampshire	1629	Royal Colony – 1679 Profit, Religion	Capt. John Mason
Mass. Bay	1630*	Mass. Bay Co. – Religion	John Winthrop
Maryland	1634	Proprietary Grant – Religion	George Calvert (L. Balt)
Rhode Island	1636	Puritan Charter – 1644	R. Williams, A. Hutchinson
Connecticut	1636	Council of New England Charter	Thomas Hooker
North Carolina	1654#	Proprietary Grant – Profit	W. Berkeley, G. Carteret
New Jersey	1664	Proprietary Grant – Profit	J. Berkeley, G. Carteret
South Carolina	1670#	Proprietary Grant – Profit	Anthony Ashley-Cooper
Pennsylvania- (Originally united)	1681	Proprietary Grant – Religion	William Penn
Delaware-	1681	Separate Assembly from Penn. after 1701	
Georgia	1733	Proprietary Grant – Debtor's Haven	James Ogelthorpe

*Became Massachusetts
@ Became the English colony of New York
# Originally united as Carolina in 1663, South Carolina became a royal colony in 1719, North Carolina became a royal colony in 1729.

Colonial Status
By 1775, Virginia, Massachusetts, Connecticut, New Hampshire, New York, New Jersey, North Carolina, South Carolina, and Georgia were, by designation, royal colonies. Pennsylvania, Delaware, and Maryland were proprietary colonies, and Rhode Island remained self-governing, continuing its long tradition of independence.

Important Facts- In 1619, a tobacco curing boom increased Virginia's financial viability; the first black slaves* (or indentured servants) numbering 20 arrive at

*15 of these Africans were subsequently indentured to the Governor of Virginia, Sir George Yardley, who owned a 1,000 acre Plantation, *Flowerdew Hundred.*

Jamestown aboard a Dutch man-of-war, and the General Assembly of Virginia consisting of the governor, six counselors, and twenty-two burgesses convene for five days. It is the first representative assembly in the history of English North America.

Population Characteristics Within The 13 Colonies With Dominant Immigrant Groups By Colony To 1775

Massachusetts	-English	**New England or Northern Colonies**
Connecticut	-English	(In 1790 – English – 82%, Scottish,
Rhode Island	-English	Scots-Irish, and Irish – 11.9%,
New Hampshire	-English	Free Blacks – 1.3%, Slaves - .04%)

New York	-English, Dutch, German, Swiss	**Middle Colonies**
Pennsylvania	-English, German, Scots-Irish	(In 1790 - English – 36.9%,
New Jersey	-English, Dutch	Germans – 20.9%,
Delaware	-English	Scots-Irish – 10.7%, Dutch
		– 9.3%, Free Black – 3.8%,
		Slaves – 1.5%)

Maryland	-English	**Southern Colonies**
Virginia	-English, African	(In 1790 – English – 35.7%,
	Scots-Irish*	Slaves – 34.6%, Scottish,
North Carolina	-English, African, Scots-Irish,	Irish, and Scots-Irish –
	Highland Scots	16.9%)
South Carolina	-English, African	
Georgia	-English, African	

*(various tribes – see below)

Selected African Tribes—Geographic Origin In Africa

Tribe
Asante
Benin
Coromantees
Dahomey   Central West Coast, known as the "Slave Coast"
Foulah
Oyo
Popows
Whydah

Angolas, Eboes, Gaboons, Senegalese   Southwest Coast - Angola-Congo Region

Amerindian (a.k.a Indian or Native American) Affairs- Perhaps 10 to 15 million Amerindians lived in North America circa 1500. Major tribes first encountered by the English along the East Coast would list as follows:

<u>Pennsylvania to Maine</u> – **Susquehanna, Pequot, Iroquois, Massachusett, Mahican, Abnaki**
<u>Delaware to South Carolina</u> – **Delaware, Nanticoke, Powhatan, Tuscarora, Catawba**
<u>South Carolina and Georgia</u> – **Cherokee, Cusabo, Yamasee, Yuchi**

Explaining colonial and Indian interaction is brutally simple. The Indians either assimilated and accommodated or were pushed west until there was no longer any west available. One of the reasons for this were the conflicting and ultimately irreconcilable belief systems concerning land ownership held by the Europeans and the various Native American peoples. Bluntly stated, <u>in general</u> the European/American (and indeed, our) concept of land ownership can be summarized as, "It belongs to me," whereas for Amerindians, it was, "We belong to the land." The two are as incompatible in regards to land as was the reality of humans being humans "and yet objects of profit" in reference to slavery. The inability of the Amerindians to effectively unite against the ever more powerful Europeans, and then Americans, was another critical factor, as were the sheer numbers and technological and organizational superiority the newcomers ultimately brought to bear against the natives.

   Throughout our history, various Amerindian tribes and charismatic leaders stubbornly resisted this reality with temporary success. In 1622, the Pamunkey chief Massatamohtnock forged an alliance with 24 tribes and massacred 347 English colonists in Virginia. In 1644, he "orchestrated" another attack which claimed as many as 500 lives. In <u>The Pequot War of 1637</u>, Massachusetts and Connecticut colonists alongside their allies basically eradicated the Pequot tribe. In 1675, the Wampanoag tribe under the leadership of Metacom (a.k.a. King Philip) declared war on Massachusetts and Rhode Island colonists because of Christian missionary activities and land disputes. The war lasted for 3 years with Metacom's forces destroying 20 New England towns, marching within 20 miles of Boston, and killing perhaps 1,000 colonists. However, 4,000 Amerindians perished (25% of the total), Metacom was killed, and the remainder were subjugated, a scenario which would be repeated many times over the next 200 years. Yet another example occurred in coastal North Carolina beginning in 1711, when Tuscarora warriors nearly wiped out the new settlement of German and Swiss immigrants in New Berne. The conflict raged for 2 more years until the Tuscarora were defeated.
(See Addendum II, page 256)

<u>British Mercantile Policies and Navigation Acts- 1607–1763</u>
British economic policies towards the colonies for nearly 150 years can be described as "benign" or "salutary neglect." Under prime ministers such as Sir Robert Walpole (1720–1742), the colonies were largely left to their own devices developing strong traditions and institutions of self-government. The British

reasons for allowing such autonomy were quite simple:
1. Logistics (3,000 miles of physical separation)
2. The immense profits reaped from the colonies
   ("Leave well enough alone" syndrome)

As such, Americans felt themselves both British citizens, and self-sufficient, mindsets which would eventually come into conflict. Americans also were quite adept at getting around royal trade restrictions, such as the Navigation Acts, which were designed to restrict legitimate trade with other nations and curb illegal smuggling. Psychologically, the British made fundamental errors in adopting this policy of benign neglect. For instance, when dealing with an adolescent you initially impose strict rules and then relax them as the "child" becomes more responsible. The British did just the opposite in their relations with the colonies creating an atmosphere of consternation and resentment, especially after 1763. Secondly, British enforcement of the Navigation Acts was lax until 1740, when the expenses of the wars with France were becoming a critical concern. The colonists reacted quite unhappily to this new stringent enforcement of navigation laws. The analogies between parents and children are appropriate for describing the colonial relationship between Britain and America, or "mother country" and colonies!

The Navigation Acts

1. 1651—goods bought in Britain could only be transported to the colonies on British ships.
2. 1660—foreign goods could only be shipped to the colonies on British or colonial vessels.
3. 1663—all foreign goods had to be brought to Britain first and then exported to the colonies. Also, colonial exports to other nations were restricted.
4. 1670—export duties imposed on American captains.

Colonial Wars 1689–1763

1. **King William's War** 1689–1697

2. **Queen Anne's War** 1702–1713 (European name - War of the Spanish Succession)

3. **War of Jenkin's Ear** 1739–1744

   Note: 37 Years of Intermittent Warfare left Great Britain 140 million pounds in debt.

4. **King George's War** 1744–1748 (European name -War of the Austrian Succession)

5. **French and Indian War** 1754–1763 (European name -The Seven Years War)

The French and Indian War was actually initiated in the North American colonies due to land rivalries between the British and French in the trans-Appalachian region. French fort construction from Ft. St. Pierre (west of Lake Superior) to a second Ft. St. Pierre (north of Natchez) was threatening to hem in eager Virginia land speculators. In the spring of 1754, Major George Washington, detached by Virginia Governor Dinwiddie "to warn off the French" along the Ohio River (present day West Virginia Pennsylvania border), skirmished with French troops and ultimately was forced to surrender (on July 4) after a siege at Ft. Necessity. This action signaled the beginning of the war which would determine who controlled North America. Various Indian tribes (including most of the Algonquian tribes) such as the Ottawa (led by Pontiac), Delaware, Potawatomie, and Huron, allied with the French for 2 general reasons:

1. French colonists in North America only numbered about 60,000 and were scattered across the mid-continent. British colonists by contrast numbered over 1 million. In addition, many of the French colonists were trappers and fur traders, professions the Indians both practiced and felt far less intrusive than British colonists farming operations.

2. There existed a great deal of resentment among Amerindians towards the British and their ally, the powerful Iroquois Confederation, for land encroachments, treaty violations, tribal rivalries, and conflicts. Interestingly, the Iroquois remained largely neutral during the war, "impressed by early French victories."

   For the first 4 years of the war, the French scored victory after victory, punctuated by successes such as Ft. Duquesne in July 1755, where the French and their Indian allies surprised British and American troops under General Edward Braddock killing or wounding 977 out of 1,459 men. By 1757, William Pitt became Prime Minister, "humbly" though accurately stating, "I know that I can save England and no one else can." Invigorating the war effort, Pitt's policies turned the tide of battle. In 1758, Ft. Louisbourg surrendered to British and American forces. Ft. Niagara fell in 1759, and after a brilliant two-month campaign, British land and sea forces commanded by 33-year-old General James Wolfe defeated General Louis Joseph de Montcalm and seized Quebec on Sept. 13, 1759. Though Wolfe perished during the fighting, Quebec proved the decisive battle of the war. By 1760, Montreal fell, and despite sporadic Indian fighting along the frontier and the entry of the Spanish into the war in 1761 (owing to their Bourbon monarchy connections with the French), the war was essentially over. Peace efforts commenced in 1760 when George III ascended to the throne after the death of his grandfather, George II. The Peace of Paris concluded the war in 1763. (see p. 14)

Chapter 2

The American Revolution: Origins to the Treaty of Paris

The American Revolution – Specific Causation

A series of acts which taxed and regulated the colonists to an unacceptable degree. The British viewed these actions as necessary to defray the costs of the several wars with the French, especially the French and Indian War.

1. The colonists considered themselves British citizens. As such, they were justified when they claimed to be denied just representation in Parliament on matters such as taxation and westward expansion.
2. The British failed to appreciate the effects produced by the Atlantic separation. Local self-rule was enhanced by the colonists adapting to exigencies such as Indian affairs and the different American environment, both unknown in England.
3. The colonists themselves tended to have an independent mindset. They emigrated for a variety of reasons (religion, fortune, freedom) and were allowed to put down roots in a land where success did not primarily rely on birth, station, or tradition. Economic success translated quickly into higher social status in the colonies.
4. "Benign Neglect" allowed the colonists extraordinary freedom to govern themselves.
5. The ideas of the philosophers John Locke, Rousseau, and Montesquieu, found fertile intellectual ground in the colonies. The concepts of "government by the consent of the governed" and natural rights influenced the colonists in their perceptions of popular sovereignty and proper government.

The British Prime Minister between 1757–1763 was William Pitt.

1763 – Peace of Paris – Britain receives Canada and Florida. France retains Haiti, and French Catholics in Canada (Quebec) are granted religious toleration. Spain receives Louisiana and New Orleans.

British Actions Towards The American Colonists After 1763

Proclamation Line of 1763, proposed by the Earl of Shelburne, prohibits American settlement west of the Appalachian Mountains.* Reasons:

> A. Prevent renewed and protracted conflicts with the Indian tribes in the region, especially the bloody rebellion led by Pontiac between 1763–66.
> B. Reduce defense expenditures such as fort construction and troop deployments which would be necessary to protect new American settlements.

Result: Estrangement
British Prime Minister 1763–1765 – George Grenville

1764 – 1. Currency Act – Parliament prohibits the colonies from printing paper money. The colonists resorted to this practice as they had few banks and a very limited supply of specie (gold and silver).

* The Line would be adjusted to the colonists advantage in 1764 and 1768 .

2. Sugar Act – Although this act reduced taxes on molasses by 50%, it increased duties on sugar, indigo, coffee, wine, and woven cloth. Enforcement was to be very strict, with lengthy documents for colonial ship owners, Admiralty courts adjudicated by a royally appointed judge, not a colonial jury, and a presumption of guilt in suits. The Sugar Act especially hurt New England rum distillers.

1765 – 1. Stamp Act – a direct tax on all paper products which seriously called into question colonial rights in Parliament. The result was a colonial uproar. Widespread boycotts of British goods were implemented, and the "Sons of Liberty," scattered groups of anti-Stamp Act protesters, sprang up in New York, Boston, Charleston, Wilmington, and in cities and towns throughout the colonies. More significantly, a Stamp Act Congress convened in New York from Oct. 7–24, 1765. Attending were 27 delegates representing 9 colonies (NH, VA, NC, and GA. Did not send delegates). It was the first inter-colonial Congress assembled for the purpose of appealing common grievances to Britain. The delegates drafted petitions to the King and Parliament to repeal the Sugar and Stamp Acts and also included a "Declaration of the Rights and Grievances of the Colonies." The crisis lasted only a short period however as Grenville lost his position to Lord Rockingham (1765–1766), a Whig politician whose policies were more conciliatory towards the colonists. In March 1766, the Stamp Act was repealed and the Sugar Act's duties were reduced from 3 pence to 1 pence. But on the same day, Parliament overwhelmingly passed, the Declaratory Act appeared which asserted Parliament's full authority over the colonies "in all cases whatsoever." The Declaratory Act clearly refuted the colonists arguments that they were equal to other British subjects in regards to rights and representation.

British Prime Minister 1766–68 – William Pitt
Chancellor of the Exchequer (Treasury) 1767 – Charles Townshend
1766 – The Townshend Acts – earlier Quartering Acts (housing of British troops) enforced in New York, duties on paint, glass, tea, and lead expanded to pay for royal judges, anti-smuggling Board of Commissioners established in Boston, and the Admiralty Courts were expanded. In addition, more British regiments would be sent to Boston in 1768. In response, the Sons of Liberty in Boston, led by Samuel Adams, began to intensify the anti-British rhetoric. Although most of the Townshend Acts were eliminated (the tax on tea remained) by 1768, tensions, recriminations, and suspicions between Britain and the American colonies heightened.

1768 – Originating in Massachusetts, a "Circular Letter" denouncing "taxation without representation" was distributed throughout the colonies. The British Prime Minister (1769–1782) – Lord North

1770 – March 5th - The Boston "Massacre" occurs, killing 5 Americans.
– April 12 – Townshend Act duties repealed on all items except tea.

1772 1. The British schooner *Gaspee* was burned to the waterline off Providence, Rhode Island by angry Americans on June 9.

2. **Samuel Adams, James Otis, and other irate New Englanders set up the first "Committee of Correspondence" in November reporting on British actions in the colonies and suggesting coordinated action throughout the colonies. Similar "Committees" spring up all over New England and spread to Virginia and South Carolina by 1773.**

<u>1773</u> – By the 1770s, the British East India Company neared bankruptcy. Factors such as colonial smuggling of less expensive Dutch tea had driven the company to the wall despite its 175 year monopoly on tea exportation. Lord North thought he had the solution when he engineered the passage of the <u>Tea Act</u> in 1773. Even though the $.3 a pound tax on tea stipulated by the Townshend Acts remained in force, the Tea Act actually lowered prices on tea. But how? Provisions included:

a) - The removal of duties on tea brought into England, and the elimination of storage taxes in British East India Company warehouses.

b) - Direct export of tea to America to selected agents and consignees. Once the tea tax was paid, it would be sold to American merchants and retailers who had not participated in boycotts of British goods resulting from the Townshend Acts.

Instead of being an economic boon for the British East India Company and the British government, the Tea Act precipitated angry, and sometimes, violent reactions in America. Americans were infuriated by the law as it excluded many American merchants from handling and selling the tea, but more importantly, the act appeared to many as nothing more than a thinly-veiled and cynical bribe designed to persuade Americans to sheepishly acquiesce, pay the tax, and drink British tea. Below are some of the colonial responses to the new law:

- In Charleston, SC, all the official tea consignees were forced to resign rather than try to distribute and sell the tea.
- In Edenton, NC, American women burned their household supplies of tea to protest British policy.
- In Annapolis, MD the British tea schooner *Peggy Stewart* was burned to the waterline.

Not surprisingly, the most dramatic and significant of the colonial reactions to the Tea Act occurred in Boston. In Massachusetts, the Royal Governor Thomas Hutchinson was immovable in his determination to have the tea tax paid and the tea unloaded, undoubtedly in large part due to his loyalty to the King and Parliament.* His insistence however produced an inevitable collision with the protesters which occurred on Dec. 16, 1773 – the Boston "Tea Party," in which 340 chests containing 23,000 pounds of tea were thrown overboard from 3 ships anchored in the harbor. There were 115 participants, some of whom were disguised as Mohawk Indians. (By the way, the "Tea Party" was planned at the Green Dragon Inn in Boston.)

<u>The British Reaction</u> – April 1774 – The British responded to the Boston Tea Party with the Coercive or "Intolerable" Acts, specifically designed to punish

*The fact that Hutchinson had 2 sons and a nephew who were tea consignees may have had something to do with his zeal to enforce the Tea Act!

Massachusetts, but also to send an intimidating message to the other colonies. The opposite effect occurred as the other colonies rallied to support Massachusetts. New Yorkers sent 125 sheep to feed Boston's poor, and the Virginia House of Burgesses at the behest of Thomas Jefferson declared June 1 a day of fasting and prayer in Virginia, a propaganda measure designed to raise popular support for the Bostonians. But what actually were the Intolerable Acts?

1. Massachusetts governors were now to be appointed by the King, in addition to the colonial judges. All were on the royal payroll.
2. Boston Harbor closed until the tea was paid for ($800,000 in today's money).
3. Town meetings limited to one a year.
4. The Justice Act, which allowed British soldiers charged with crimes in Massachusetts to be tried in Britain.
5. The Quartering Act extended to unoccupied private dwellings in addition to boarding houses, taverns, and inns.

In addition, Parliament passed the Quebec Act which expanded Quebec's territory south to the Ohio River and west to the Mississippi River, established a permanent government without a representative assembly, and provided that Catholicism would be the official tax supported religion. Protestant colonial land speculators, especially from Virginia, Pennsylvania, and Connecticut, were horrified.

Colonial Reactions

At the behest of the Virginia Legislature, the First Continental Congress convened at Philadelphia's Carpenter's Hall on Sept. 5, 1774. 55 delegates from every colony except Georgia (perhaps owing to its frontier status) sent representatives. The Congress resolved to raise troops, suspend trade with Great Britain, send petitions asserting the colonists rights as British citizens to the King, and established Colonial Associations to enforce the embargo. Parliament's mood however was anything but conciliatory and responded to the Congress' petitions by declaring Massachusetts in a state of rebellion and sending secret orders to the Mass. Royal Governor and the British General Gage to strike at the rebels. Gage ordered Major John Pitcairn and 700 British regulars to leave Boston and seize the arsenal at Concord, about 20 miles west of the city. On April 19, 1775, British troops and American "Minutemen" clashed near Lexington leaving 8 patriots dead and 10 wounded. The American Revolution had begun. As the British proceeded towards Concord, they were targeted by American snipers hiding everywhere. As a result, the British retreated back to the safety of Boston. On this first day of the Revolution, the British lost 273 men, the Americans 95.

Advantages:	The Combatants (*indicates the advantage)	
	British	American
Population	*11 million	2.5 million
Troop Strength	*50,000	perhaps 20,000
Foreign Troops	30,000 Hessians	8,000 French soldiers and sailors

	British	American
Local Support	30–50,000 Tories who supported Britain, 1/3 of Americans indifferent to the Revolution, and thousands of slaves sided with the British who promised freedom if they fought against their former owners.	1/4 to 1/3 popular support, lack of support for the War in Britain by the end of the Revolution, 5,000 black Patriots.

(Massachusetts provided more soldiers for the Continental Army than all 5 Southern colonies!)

	British	American
Military Staff	*Trained professionals	Limited capable military staff at the outset of the war.
Navy	*Best in the world	Irregular naval forces at first, French fleet in 1781 proved critical
Finances	*Well established imperial economy with a sound currency and taxation structure. Strained to critical levels due to pre-War debts and the expenses of a protracted and expanding conflict.	No set currency or specie, financed the War through $8 million in bonds, $8 million in foreign loans, $5.5 million in loans from the States, and $240 million in paper money of fluctuating value.
Logistics	*Lack of good roads and transportation facilities severely hindered British interior movements.	Americans enjoyed "home field" advantage. In addition, the capture of any single American city would not prove decisive for the British.
Tactics		*American hit-and run and guerilla tactics frustrated the British regulars accustomed to

	British	American
		conventional European style warfare. British blunders in New York also proved critical.
Alliances		*The French alliance after 1778 gave the Americans invaluable assistance and expanded the Revolution into a global conflict. Dutch and Spanish assistance exacerbated Britain's problems.
Strategies	British strategy was 2-pronged: 1) Sever New England from the other colonies (1775–1778). 2) Invade the South and secure the assistance of Southern loyalists, thereby cutting off the Northern colonies from Southern support (1778–1781).	*Maintain the Continental Army and resist the British protracting the War and making it unpopular in Britain. Secure foreign alliances.

In the wake of Lexington-Concord, a Second Continental Congress convened in May 1775. Urgently preparing for war while simultaneously attempting one last peace overture, the Congress resolved to absorb the Minutemen into a new Continental Army with <u>Virginian</u> George Washington appointed as Commander-In-Chief. Its first task was to protect Boston. Also, on July 5-6 an "Olive Branch" Petition was sent to King George III pledging the loyalty of the colonists and pleading with the King to show restraint and avoid expanding the hostilities. When the petition reached the King in mid-August, he read it with contempt, and on August 23, he declared that a state of insurrection existed in the colonies which would be crushed by military force. On Nov. 9, 1775, the Congress learned of George III's rejection of their reconciliation proposal, and that 20,000 British troops were in route to the colonies to quash the rebellion and hang the Congressmen as traitors. By then however, military actions at Bunker Hill had pushed the Revolution almost to the point of no return.

<u>The Push for Independence</u> – On January 9th 1776, Thomas Paine, an English expatriate who had only resided in the colonies for a year, published *Common Sense*. Referring to King George as "a royal brute" and proclaiming that "of more worth is one honest man to society and in the sight of God than all the crowned ruffians who ever lived," Paine effectively ridiculed monarchy in general and engendered the idea of complete American independence from England. Within a matter of months *Common Sense* sold over 150,000 copies, an extraordinary number considering that

the American population was approximately 2.5 million. *Common Sense* remains one of the most effective pieces of social and political propaganda in U.S. history. *The Declaration of Independence* – In June 1776, Richard Henry Lee of Virginia introduced a resolution for independence from England to the Continental Congress. The resolution proposed to the Congress on June 7, 1776 stated:

> *That these United Colonies are, and of right ought to be, free and independent states, that they are absolved from all allegiance to the British crown, and that all political connection between them and the state of Great Britain is, and ought to be, totally dissolved.*

Also in June, a committee consisting of Benjamin Franklin, John Adams, Robert Livingston, Roger Sherman, and chairman Thomas Jefferson were charged with creating a document which would outline and describe the motives behind the independence movement. Thomas Jefferson became the primary author of this document, *The Declaration of Independence,* and John Adams acted as its main advocate in the Continental Congress. The *Declaration* consists of four primary sections:

1) Preamble – outline of purpose and intentions
2) Political Ideals – "All men are created equal…"
   - "unalienable Rights of Life, Liberty, and the Pursuit of Happiness" (John Locke)
3) Complaints – "imposing taxes on us without our consent"
4) Resolution – to be "Free and Independent States" (This came directly from Lee's resolution).

On July 2, Congress (with the exception of New York which abstained; its delegation affirmed the *Declaration* on July 13th however) approved *The Declaration of Independence.* Two days later it went into print as "*The Unanimous Declaration of the Thirteen United States of America.*"

<u>Battles and Campaigns</u>
1) June 17, 1775 –(Outside Boston) <u>Bunker Hill</u> (in reality Breeds Hill)– After 3 successive assaults on American patriots atop the Hill, the British finally secure the area, losing 1,054 out of 2,200 soldiers. The American losses amounted to about 400.
2) July – Sept. 1776 – <u>New York City Campaign</u> –British General William Howe commanding 34,000 regular troops, 10,000 sailors, with 400 troop transports and 30 ships sails to New York intent on seizing the city and capturing or defeating Washington's 19,000 ill-equipped and poorly trained troops. New York was seized and Washington barely escaped with his army into New Jersey and then Pennsylvania (due in part to Howe's sluggishness and a timely thunderstorm). During the retreat, volunteer Thomas Paine composed *The Crisis*, a stirring set of papers designed to steel the resolve of demoralized patriots:
   > *These are the times that try men's souls: The summer soldier and the sunshine patriot will, in this crisis, shrink from the service of his*

country; but he that stands it NOW deserves the love and thanks of man and woman. Tyranny, like Hell, is not easily conquered. Yet we have this consolation with us, that the harder the conflict, the more glorious the triumph.

Dec. 25, 1776 —Washington surprises and defeats Hessian mercenaries at Trenton, NJ

Jan. 3, 1777 – Follow up victory at Princeton, NJ Both of these victories were morale boosters for the Americans, though not militarily decisive. Subsequent winter quarters at Morristown, NJ were so harsh for the American army that only about a thousand regulars stayed true to the cause. By springtime however, new incentives of cash and land raised troop strength to about 9,000.

Oct. 17, 1777 – In an ambitious 3-pronged plan, the British attempted to militarily sever New England from the rest of the colonies by seizing control of the Hudson River. The operation called for General St. Leger to advance southwest down the St. Lawrence River then proceed east from Ft. Oswego on Lake Ontario. Simultaneously, General Howe was to proceed from New York City, north up the Hudson River, while General John ("Gentleman Johnny") Burgoyne moved south from Montreal to Lake Champlain. All the British forces were to link up at Albany, thus sealing off New England. It failed utterly due to the slow pace at which St. Leger, Howe, and Burgoyne pursued their objectives, and the brilliant and determined resistance offered by the Americans, especially under Benedict Arnold and John Stark. (Burgoyne covered only about a mile a day. His "military supplies" included 30 carts of "personal baggage!") Howe foolishly diverted his troops to capture Philadelphia. His rendezvous with Burgoyne was prevented by Washington's forces at Germantown. Arnold stopped St. Leger at Fort Stanwix on the Mohawk River, and in Bennington, VT, Stark and his "Green Mountain Boys" killed or wounded 700 of Burgoyne's troops who were foraging for food in the countryside. Burgoyne limped into Saratoga which was now fortified by American troops under General Horatio Gates. After two futile attacks, Burgoyne realized his entrapment and surrendered his entire army of nearly 5,500 men. This was a major turning point of the war because the French, upon hearing the news of the surrender on Dec. 2, decided to conclude an alliance with the Americans, finalized in Feb. 1778. As a consequence of the defeat, a deeply humiliated General Howe resigned his command.

There is also a very interesting footnote to Saratoga concerning Benedict Arnold, the "Great American Traitor." Arnold's career was a strange combination of heroism and selfish ambition. Arnold's treachery began with his command at Philadelphia between 1778–1780. He and his wife Peggy Shipman (whose parents were Loyalists) entertained lavishly, and with Loyalists. Two stern reprimands were issued by Washington, but in 1780 Arnold persuaded Washington to give him command of the American garrison at West Point, NY Washington had always been fond of Arnold and respected his abilities and sacrifices for the cause. Arnold had boldly removed cannon from Ft. Ticonderoga to be used against the British in Boston, been severely wounded in the ill-fated attack on Quebec in 1775, and fought decisively at Saratoga. All the while however, he sought to embellish his finances with dubious expense claims and constantly felt his successive promotions from Colonel, to Brigadier General, to Major General were insufficient. Arnold set his traitorous schemes in motion in Sept. 1780. Communicating through British Major John Andre, Arnold proposed to hand over West Point to the British commander Sir Henry Clinton for 20,000 pounds ($1,000,000 today). Major Andre, en route to Clinton with Arnold's notes and plans, was captured by American troops on Sept. 13, 1780. Arnold, upon hearing the news, fled south to British lines. Ironically, West Point was saved on the same day when Washington discovered the treasonable plot while traveling to visit Arnold, who had just escaped! The British subsequently rewarded Benedict Arnold with 6,000 pounds and a Brigadier General's commission. His campaigns in Virginia and Connecticut were of no real consequence to the outcome of the Revolution. After the war, Arnold emigrated to England and two of his sons would become British officers. He however would be coldly received and treated with indifference and contempt for the rest of his life, a fitting fate for the "Great American Traitor."

Although Saratoga ultimately proved to be a critical American victory, the immediate aftermath for the Americans was quite dismal. The Continental Army established winter quarters at Valley Forge, Penn. in 1777–78. Food shortages were appalling, especially considering that nearby American farms bustled with produce and livestock. Many <u>American</u> farmers refused to accept the devalued Continental dollar; some even opted to sell to the British! Washington finally had to resort to commandeering food and supplies for his dwindling and demoralized army. Freezing, ill-clad, and barely surviving on rancid provisions, nearly 2,000 of Washington's troops deserted. Washington's force of personality and commitment to his men most likely prevented the complete collapse of the army and the Revolution itself. In addition, if General Howe had come out of retirement and led an army against Washington at that moment, he may well have achieved the same outcome. Howe, however, contented himself in the comforts of Philadelphia, refusing to re-engage. Benjamin Franklin remarked that Philadelphia had taken Howe! In the West (western Virginia, Kentucky, and the Ohio River region) however, George Rogers Clark had some success in clearing the area of the British and their Indian allies.

In 1778, the British decided to turn their attention to the South, hoping to rally the Tories (a.k.a. "Loyalists")* and perhaps raise the prospect of a race war to cripple revolutionary sentiment in the region. Sir Henry Clinton, Howe's successor, sent troops by sea from New York to Georgia and South Carolina to commence the campaign. For nearly two years the British would score victory after victory, but were unable to win "the hearts and minds" of southerners, nor could they control their Tory allies who were primarily interested in settling

*Concentrated west of the Atlantic Coast.

personal grudges with the Tidewater aristocracy. In addition, the swamps and backcountry of the colonial South proved ideal for guerilla warriors such as Thomas Sumter and Francis Marion, the "Swamp Fox." Finally, a servile war never materialized, even though many slaves fled their owners heeding British promises of emancipation. As a result, American commanders began to offer slaves (with their owners' permission) similar guarantees of freedom for patriotic service. Approximately 5,000 black Americans, mostly freemen, served in the American army during the war out of a total of perhaps 300,000 Americans who served at various times throughout the Revolution. Several thousand slaves were manumitted by supporting the British, many emigrating to Canada or to British possessions in the Caribbean, but many more were dealt a tragic betrayal.

Battles – Dec. 29, 1778 – Savannah, GA falls to the British. The rest of Georgia will capitulate within weeks.

– May 12, 1780 – After a 3-month siege, Charleston, S.C, defended by 5,500 Americans under the command of General Benjamin Lincoln, surrenders to Clinton and General Lord Charles Cornwallis. It is akin to Saratoga in reverse. A desperately alarmed Congress decides to dispatch General Gates south, despite Washington's firm objections.

– On Aug. 16, 1780, General Cornwallis routs Gates and his forces at Camden, SC, justifying Washington's dire warnings. Gates revealed himself as incompetent, if not a coward, as he fled ahead of his retreating army. The army finally stopped running at Hillsborough, NC, 160 miles from Camden. Subsequently, Gates lost his command to "the fighting Quaker" Nathaniel Greene of Rhode Island. Greene possessed the complete confidence of Washington and the course of the war changed decisively in the South.

– Oct. 7, 1780 – Kings Mountain, NC- SC – Frontier patriots destroy a British – Tory force of 1,100, killing 157 soldiers, including the British commander Major Patrick Ferguson, wounding about 150 and capturing the remaining 800.

– Jan. 17, 1781 – Backwoods leader, General Daniel Morgan routed Lt. Col. Banastre Tarleton at Cowpens SC, killing 100 and capturing 700, nearly 90% of Tarleton's forces.

– March 15, 1781 – Guilford Court House, NC – Nathaniel Greene "loses" to Cornwallis and effects a strategic retreat. Cornwallis suffered 532 casualties, including 150 killed. His "victory" left him in no position to effectively pursue Greene. British member of Parliament Charles James Fox said of the battle, "Another such victory and we are undone." Cornwallis subsequently moved his troops to Wilmington, NC for supplies, and then headed north into Virginia setting the stage for the final battle at Yorktown.

<u>Yorktown, Virginia</u> (August 30 - Oct. 17, 1781)

After Cornwallis rendezvoused with Arnold at Petersburg, he headed for the coast with an army of about 8,000 intending to re-establish contact with the British Navy. He arrived on the York Peninsula on Aug. 1 encountering a small American force under the command of the Marquis de Lafayette. Cornwallis subsequently established a base at Yorktown. Washington and the French commander Rochambeau were positioned outside New York City when they received word that the French West Indies fleet, under the able command of the Admiral Comte de Grasse, would be available for coastal action for about 3 weeks, and had been given orders to sail to the Virginia Capes with 30 ships and 3,000 soldiers. Immediately seizing the opportunity, Washington and Rochambeau moved their forces south to link with Lafayette and set the trap. Cornwallis' position would prove indefensible if he did not have access to the Atlantic Ocean via the Chesapeake Bay. Comte de Grasse arrived near Cape Henry on Sept. 5 and battled the British fleet under Admiral Thomas Graves the next day. Graves could not break through and withdrew on Sept. 10 leaving Cornwallis trapped. The siege of Yorktown began on Sept. 28 with American and French troops totaling more than 16,000, twice Cornwallis' number. Cornwallis' defenses began to give way on Oct. 14, and a British counterattack failed on Oct. 16. On Oct. 17, 1781, Cornwallis surrendered at Yorktown ending the American Revolution with the Americans victorious.

<u>Total American War Dead</u> – 10,623 (estimated)

<u>The Treaty of Paris</u>

<u>Participants</u>	<u>United States</u>	<u>Great Britain</u>
	John Adams	Lord Shelburne
	Benjamin Franklin	Richard Oswald
	John Jay	

The U.S. and Great Britain bypassed the French and entered into secret negotiations in 1782. Why? Because the French and their Spanish allies desired a small, weak coastal United States which the Americans obviously did not want, and the British wanted a quick, small-scale settlement which would not award any territorial concessions to the French. When the secret negotiations concluded in November 1782, the American and British delegates simply handed the French (represented by Charles Gravier, the Comte de Vergennes), the Spanish, and the Dutch a *fait accompli* ("accomplished fact") known to history as the Treaty of Paris which all parties signed in 1783.

<u>Provisions of the Treaty of Paris</u>

<u>For the United States</u>

1) The United States gains its independence.

2) The boundaries of the United States run south from the Great Lakes to Florida, and west to the Mississippi River.

3) The U.S. gains fishing rights in the Atlantic Ocean off Newfoundland.

4) The British agree to evacuate their forts in the northwest U.S.

For the United States and Great Britain

1) Both nations and Spain have navigational rights on the Mississippi River.

For Great Britain

1) The United States agrees to recommend compensation for the Loyalists.

2) American merchants are to pay their pre-Revolutionary debts of nearly 4,000,000 pounds to their British creditors.

The unwillingness of both the United States and Great Britain to uphold some of the provisions of the treaty will have serious ramifications in the 1790s.

Chapter 3

The First United States: The Articles of Confederation

The United States Under The Articles of Confederation – 1781–1787

The Articles of Confederation served as the <u>original</u> governing document for the United States prior to the ratification of the Constitution of the United States of America between 1787 and 1790. Originally drafted in 1777, it was not formally adopted until 1781. Its structure provided for a <u>loose</u> union of the 13 original states with a <u>very weak and limited</u> central government. Most powers were reserved to the individual states. Below is a partial list of what the national government <u>could not</u> do under the Articles.

Structural Weaknesses of The Articles of Confederation

1) It could not tax. (It relied on the States for money!)

2) It could not regulate commerce between the States.

3) It had no significant executive branch. (No powerful President; in fact, there were 14 presidents between 1774–1789, when Washington was sworn in. The first of these was Peyton Randolph; the last Cyrus Griffin, both Virginians.)

4) It had no judicial branch. (No Supreme Court!)

5) It had no permanent capital city. (5 different capitals between 1777 and 1787 – see p. 28)

6) To pass any significant legislation, the Congress needed a 2/3 majority vote. (Our Congress only needs a simple majority, 1 more than 50%)

7) To add an amendment to the Articles, the Congress needed a unanimous vote. (Today, the requirement is approval by 3/4 (38) of the States)

8) Inability to raise a 9-State quorum to conduct official business

9) Congressmen elected for 1-year terms and only permitted to hold office 3 years out of 6.

The national government under the Articles however <u>could</u> perform 3 very important functions:

1) It could organize western lands. Refer to the Land Ordinance of 1785 and the Northwest Ordinance of 1787.
2) It could negotiate treaties with foreign powers. In fact, the Treaty of Paris which ended the Revolution was concluded under the auspices of the Articles.

3) It maintained at least a sense of union. The alternative could have been 13 different nations.

American Capitals 1774–1865

Philadelphia, Penn. 1774–1777

Lancaster, Penn. 1777

Philadelphia 1778–1783
(The French alliance prompted the British to leave.)

Annapolis, MD 1783–1785

New York City, NY 1785–1790

Philadelphia 1790–1801

Washington, DC 1801–present

Montgomery, Ala. 1861
(First capital of the Confederate States of America)

Richmond, VA 1861–1865
(Second capital of the Confederacy)

Danville, VA 1865
(Last capital of the Confederacy)

Land Policies Under The Articles of Confederation

The conflicting land claims of the 13 states may have destroyed the nascent United States had it not been for the Virginia Legislature acting at the behest of congressman and former governor Thomas Jefferson. Virginia ceded its extensive land claims to the Old Northwest in 1784 to the Confederation government, with the stipulation that these territories eventually be organized into "distinct republican states" equal with the original 13. This set into motion similar cessions by other states. Massachusetts ceded its western claims in 1785, Connecticut in 1786, South Carolina (to Georgia) in 1787, North Carolina in 1790, and finally Georgia in 1802. An interesting footnote to these cessions concerns Jefferson's proposal within the Land Ordinance of 1784 that slavery be prohibited in the entire Mississippi Valley region after 1800. This measure failed in Congress by 1 vote, prompting Jefferson to comment, "Thus we see the fate of millions unborn hanging on the tongue of one man, and Heaven was silent in that awful moment!"*

Land Ordinance of 1785 – provided for the survey of public lands, and the establishment of townships of 36 square miles divided into one square mile sections with revenues from one of the sections (#16) devoted to public education.

Northwest Ordinance of 1787 – provided a three-stage process (see below) for territories to become states, included a Bill of Rights of sorts for inhabitants, and prohibited slavery in the Northwest Territory. Thomas Jefferson envisioned the Northwest Territory organized into 14 separate states, of which he suggested an assortment of interesting names including Cherronesus, Michigania, Saratoga, Sylvania, Illinoia, Polypotamia, Metropotamia, Assenisipia, Pelisipia, and Washington!

Territorial Process

Stage One – Congress appoints a governor, secretary, and three judges to oversee the territory. When 5,000 men over the age of 25 settle in the territory, Stage Two begins.

Stage Two – A two-house legislature is established. Representatives in the lower house are elected by property owners holding 50 or more acres. A 5-man upper house would be selected by Congress. The legislature also sent a non-voting delegate to Congress.

Stage Three – When the territorial population reached 60,000 inhabitants, the territorial legislature or special constitutional convention could draft a state constitution, submit it to Congress, and upon approval, become a state within the Union.

State Governments Under The Articles

During the Confederation period, the 13 former British Colonies had little difficulty in their transition to independent States. In most instances, their individual colonial charters provided an excellent framework for their new state

*John Beatty of New Jersey was ill and did not attend the critical committee meeting regarding the prohibition of slavery in the western territories. His absence doomed the measure to failure, hence Jefferson's prescient and mournful quote. It is also interesting to note that Jefferson himself owned 135 slaves!

constitutions. Due to the inherent weakness of the Confederation government, the States also retained a great deal of legislative, judicial, and social authority within their respective boundaries. The States did not attempt to create overbearing or oppressive governments however. Most of the States' constitutions contained both civil rights guarantees for their citizens, and provisions for amendment. In the social and political arenas, the Confederation era featured a concomitant decline in elitism and aristocratic privilege, and a gradual reduction in property qualifications for voting and holding office. The exodus of 100,000 Tories from America, the redistribution of their lands to Patriots, and the collective egalitarian experience of the Revolution all spurred social change, and nurtured a nascent suspicion of rank and privilege. Over the next 200 years, this attitude gradually spread throughout all facets of American culture.

An unexpected and unfortunately bitter "reward" awaited many of the American slaves who had fled to the British expecting protection, freedom, and acceptance. When the war ended, thousands (approximately 100,000) of slaves were recaptured by their former owners. Some were retained in the United States, but large numbers were transported to the Caribbean region and sold to sugar plantation owners. For their part, the British were scarcely more compassionate to the slaves they had promised freedom. Although some 16,000 former slaves were transported by the British from Charleston and Savannah, in many cases black loyalists were denied passage on evacuating British ships leaving American ports, and in some instances, wounded or killed as they attempted to board. Some were even resold into slavery. One of the more benevolent and honorable British officers, General Samuel Birch, refused to abandon black loyalists to these tragic fates. He compiled a list of approximately 4,000 persons in *The Book of Negroes* and provided them safe passage and freedom from New York City to Great Britain, Jamaica, Nova Scotia, and Sierra Leone. The narrative of Boston King provides a rare view of the experiences of black loyalists during and after the Revolution. (Some of the above information comes from the film series *Africans in America: Part 2 -1750–1805.*)

Social Developments During the Period 1781–1800
1) Church-State ties loosen
  a. Church of England loses its financial support from the 13 states.
      Taxes continued to be paid to support churches, but taxpayers now determined which church they would attend and financially support. In 1786, the Virginia Legislature passed "The Statute for Religious Freedom" which abolished religious qualifications as a criteria for voting or holding office. After 1800, only 4 New England States* maintained tax support for churches. Several states also continued to require various professions of faith as political prerequisites briefly into the 19th century. (For example, North Carolina officeholders were required to be Protestants.) Despite this seeming retreat of government support for organized religion, most (but not all) of the Founding Fathers believed religion, and Christianity specifically, was indispensable to the creation and survival of republics. George Washington and John Adams minced no words in stating that conviction.

      * Religious qualifications removed - NH (1817), Conn. (1818), Maine (1820), and Mass. (1833).

b. The Methodist and Baptist denominations expanded rapidly. Their relatively informal organizations characterized by lay preachers and circuit riders, attracted an increasing number of Americans, especially on the Southern and Western frontier.

2)- Women are virtually excluded from the political process (no voting, and property holding and inheritance restrictions). New Jersey provided the only exception to the rule. In that state, women who held property valued at 50 pounds (50 pounds today is worth approximately $87 U.S. dollars) or more could vote from 1776 to 1807. Social privileges also remain largely limited to adult males. Interestingly, divorce became <u>slightly</u> easier for both men and women.

Abigail Adams, the dynamic and outspoken wife of Founding Father and future president John Adams, cautioned her husband about excluding women from the political process in a letter dated March 31st 1776:

> …and by the way in the new code of laws which I suppose it will be necessary for you to make, I desire you would remember the ladies, and be more favorable to them than your ancestors. Do not put such unlimited power in the hands of husbands.
>
> If particular care and attention is not paid to the ladies we are determined to foment a rebellion, and will not hold ourselves bound by any laws in which we have no representation.
>
> That your sex are naturally tyrannical is a truth so thoroughly established as to admit of no dispute, but such of yours as wish to be happy will willingly give up the harsh title of master for the more tender and endearing one of friend….

Abigail Adams entreaties were almost completely ignored however. As mentioned previously, only New Jersey gave women even a semblance of political power.

3)- Decline in aristocratic sensibilities. During and after the Revolution, there was a notable decrease in popular acceptance of aristocratic (elitist) distinctions.* The British notions and recognition of "Gentlemen" and "Commoner" began to erode as evidenced by the marked reduction of <u>white</u> servants, and provisions within state constitutions prohibiting aristocratic inheritance practices such as <u>primogeniture</u> ("the right of the first-born son to inherit the property, title, etc., of a parent to the exclusion of all other children") and <u>entail</u> ("To restrict the inheritance of lands to a particular class"). This trend continued into the Constitutional Convention as evidenced by Article I, Sec. 9, Cl. 8 which prohibits the United States from granting Titles of Nobility. Finally, it is entrenched in our electoral process which over 181 years continually expanded suffrage rights through state action, federal laws and constitutional amendments (15th, 19th, and 26th).

*John Adams claimed "The Five Pillars of Aristocracy are Beauty, Wealth, Birth, Genius, and Virtues."

4)- Anti-slavery movements develop in all regions of the United States.
   <u>Abolition Of The Slave Trade In The United States - By State Action</u>

1)-Delaware (1776)

5)-South Carolina-temporarily stopped in the 1780s, reopened in 1803

2)-Virginia (1778)

6)-North Carolina-heavy taxation imposed

3)-Pennsylvania (1780)

7)-Georgia (1798)

4)-Maryland (1783)

<u>Slavery Abolished Outright or Prohibited From the Outset</u>

- Vermont (1777)
Vermont did not become a state
until 1791, hence it cannot be
considered one of the original 13 states.

- Massachusetts (1782) – Slavery was
abolished by adjudication, most notably
in court challenges brought by two
slaves, Quock Walker in 1781 and
Elizabeth Freeman in 1782. In both
cases, the plaintiffs contended that
Article I of the Massachusetts state
constitution which asserted that "all
men are born free and equal" proscribed
slavery. The Massachusetts Supreme
Court agreed.
- New Hampshire (1784)

- Northwest Territory (1787)

<u>Slave Trade Abolished By National Action –1808</u>

<u>States Abolishing Slavery By Gradual Emancipation</u>

- Pennsylvania (1780)

- Connecticut (1784)

- Rhode Island (1784)

- New York (1799)
   (All remaining slaves freed
   on July 4, 1827)

- New Jersey (1804)

International Abolition Of Slavery

Date Of Abolition	Country, Colony, Or State
1777	Vermont
1794	French Colonies (reestablished by Napoleon in 1801)
1807	Great Britain abolishes slave trade
1808	U.S. abolishes slave trade
1823	Chile
1824	Central America
1829	Mexico
1831	Bolivia
1833	British Empire
1848	French Colonies Danish West Indies
1854	Venezuela
1863	Dutch Colonies
1865	United States
1873	Puerto Rico
1880	Cuba
1888	Brazil

Between 1780 and 1800, slavery came under increased attack for a variety of humanitarian, ideological, and economic reasons. Religious groups such as the Quakers denounced the institution as an affront to God. Others lamented the inherent cruelty in owning another human being, and being able to possess or sell their offspring akin to a farm animal or chattel. Some contemporary political leaders, especially Benjamin Franklin, also found it difficult to reconcile the continued existence of slavery in the wake of a political revolution based on freedom and self-determination. (As a matter of fact, Quaker sponsored abolition petitions were introduced to the First Congress under the Constitution in Feb. 1790 prompting ferocious debate. However, the petitions failed, and the Congress declared itself powerless to "interfere in the emancipation of slaves, or in the treatment of them within any of the States; it remaining with the several States alone to provide any regulation therein....") Although all of the Northern states had permitted slavery, the region had never been economically reliant on the system. The cold climate prevented the cultivation of staples such as rice or tobacco, hence plantation style slavery and the commensurate large numbers of slaves never became a fixture in the North, although New York City had one of the largest urban slave populations on the eve of the Revolution. Thus, the main financial interest Northerners held towards slavery involved the lucrative overseas slave trade, not slavery itself. Beginning in the 1780s, nearly all of the Northern states ended slavery through a process of gradual emancipation. Gradual emancipation however ensured that the owners would not lose the productive capabilities of their slaves in any hurried manner. New Jersey's law, a fairly typical gradual emancipation statute, provided that the freed slave would have to be born on or after Jan. 1, 1804 and remain a slave until the age of 21. If they were born prior to that date, they would remain slaves for life. As a result of these stipulations, slavery persisted for decades in the North. In 1800, New York had 20,000 slaves, New Jersey 12,000, and Pennsylvania 1,700. In 1810, there were still 30,000 enslaved Americans in the "free" states. There were slaves in Pennsylvania as late as 1847, and in 1851, there were 236 slaves for life residing in New Jersey. Slavery in the North under such a system would have continued at least until 1875, if it had not been destroyed by the War Between the States (a.k.a. the Civil War).

By 1790, slavery appeared to be a dying institution in the South as well as the North. For example, Virginia, the state with the most slaves from colonization to the end of the War Between the States (the Civil War) passed a law in 1782 which allowed Virginians to manumit their slaves, a practice which had been made practically impossible by British laws enacted in <u>1660</u> and <u>1667</u>. (Unfortunately the manumission law was reversed in 1805.) By 1790, at least 10,000 slaves had been freed in the Southern States. This trend began to disappear after the invention of the cotton gin in 1793 by Eli Whitney, a native of Connecticut. Whitney had stopped off in Georgia to visit the widow of Nathaniel Greene, Catherine, at her Mulberry Hill plantation en route to a tutoring assignment in South Carolina. They became acquainted through her overseer Phineas Miller, a fellow Yale graduate, while traveling aboard a South bound ship. Upon viewing the utterly inefficient methods used in picking and seeding cotton, 27 year old Whitney invented the first cotton gin (or engine) after just ten days of experimentation. An incredibly simple wire spooled device, a gin could process 50 times the cotton a single worker could pick and seed in a day—only about a pound! This single invention drastically expanded both cotton cultivation and production and the institution of slavery, which <u>may</u> have died out in the South without it. Ironically, the simplicity of the machine's design made it incredibly easy to duplicate, and despite his 1794 patent, Whitney never made much money from the cotton gin! In the North cotton could not grow, but profits from textile mills full of slave-picked cotton could and did. So while slavery dwindled out of existence in that region due to the environmental and economic limitations to its profitability, Northern businesses reaped the boon of agricultural staples produced in the South in large part by enslaved former Africans!

<u>Northern Policies Towards Free Blacks 1780–1850</u>

In the Northern states, free blacks, mulattos, and Indians were treated in many cases with social and legal contempt. For example, Massachusetts enacted a law in 1788 which ordered the whipping of any black, mulatto, or Indian who entered the state and remained for more than 2 months with provisions for repeat punishment. This law remained on the books until 1834. Additionally, in varying degrees, all the Northern states restricted or prohibited blacks from testifying against whites in court, and strict segregation by custom existed in schools,* residences, public establishments, and even graveyards! Blacks also found themselves severely limited in their vocational opportunities, and beginning in 1804, laws providing for their disenfranchisement and exclusion appeared in several Northern and Northwestern states.

---

*In 1849 the Massachusetts Supreme Court ruled in *Roberts v. City of Boston* that segregated schools were legal as long as they were separate but equal, a precedent for *Plessy.*

A list of these includes:

Disenfranchisement

New Jersey – 1804 (Process completed by 1807)

Connecticut – 1814

Rhode Island – 1822

Pennsylvania – 1838

Exclusion

Ohio – No admittance until 1849

Illinois – 1853

Indiana – 1853

Oregon – no new black residents after 1857

Kansas – 1861

Within the slaveholding South, harsh discriminatory and disenfranchisement laws were the rule for free blacks. However, unexpected contradictions to such policies existed. For example, free blacks enjoyed both the right of jury trial and the right to sue in open court. In addition, Tennessee did not disenfranchise free black males until 1834, and North Carolina did not follow suit until 1835. In the North Carolina state Constitutional Convention, the vote to disenfranchise was 66 for and 61 against! Population statistics for the period reveal some additional surprises. In the Upper South between 1790 and 1850, the free black populations' proportional growth was greater than either the white or slave population. Finally, in 1860 the free black population of Virginia owned more property in the state than the entire black population possessed in 1890!

Problems Under the Articles of Confederation

International

A. British
  1.-Credit problems
  2.-The issue of Loyalist restitution
  3.-British occupation of forts along the Great Lakes (U.S. Soil)
  4.-British intrigue in Vermont. The British attempt to persuade influential
     Vermonters, including Levi and Ethan Allen, to join the independent

republic Vermont with Canada. They offer considerable territorial, economic and military incentives. NY, Mass., and NH, all had territorial claims in Vermont, and were obviously dismayed by this prospect.

B. Spanish
    1.-Claimed southern portions of the Mississippi River region, vital to southeastern settlers. In 1784, the Spanish closed the Mississippi to all foreign traffic. It was reopened in 1788, but with high tolls.
    2.-Spanish incitement of the Indians to raid American towns, while simultaneously promising to accept American repatriates, providing land grants, religious toleration, and Mississippi River rights if they transferred their allegiance to Spain. This would cement Spanish claims to the area.
    3.- The Spanish made overtures to New England for increased trading rights with Spain and her American colonies in exchange for the U.S. abandoning its use of the Mississippi River for 25 years (an appealing prospect to New Englanders as the Mississippi was of no immediate commercial value, and for fear of losing New England emigrants to cheap lands in the West). John Jay representing commercial interests in Boston, New York, Newport, and Philadelphia agreed with the terms and attempted to pass a treaty with Spain, the so-called Jay-Gardoqui Treaty. Outraged Southerners killed the treaty.

Domestic

A. Foreign Trade Imbalance, especially with Great Britain (imported three times as much as we exported)
    1.-Tariff legislation defeated in the Confederation by 1 vote, and uniform navigation acts were defeated by 2 states, NC and RI. These commercial reforms were intended to boost struggling American businesses, and provide needed tax revenue for the government.

B. Economic Woes
    1.- Currency problems, each state printed its own currency.
    2.- Debtor farmers who in response to bankruptcy and foreclosure, demanded the implementation of stay (grace period) and tender (produce) laws in repayment of debts. They also pushed for more paper money to be circulated which would devalue currency, create inflation, and make it easier for the farmers to pay their creditors. Although seven states yielded to various farmers demands, these monetary schemes were condemned by creditors and fiscal conservatives, who felt their loans would not be paid back in full value.

C. <u>Shays' Rebellion</u> – In Jan. 1787, Captain Daniel Shays was frustrated by unfair taxation, economic hard times, tight money, debtor's prison, etc., and led a rebellion of about 1,000 western Massachusetts farmers against state tax collectors and mortgage courts. When Shays and his followers threatened to seize an arsenal at Springfield, the Mass. state militia led by General Benjamin Lincoln dispersed Shays' forces killing 4 rebels in the process. The, rebellion ended in Feb. 1787. George Washington, Samuel Adams, and others, were horrified and demanded action, although Thomas Jefferson declared from France, "The tree of liberty must be refreshed from time to time with the blood of patriots and tyrants." Even before Shays' Rebellion, calls for revision of the Articles had been issued, most notably from VA and MD In the Spring of 1785, the VA Legislature invited all 13 states to send delegates to Annapolis, MD for this purpose. Only 5 states were represented at the Annapolis Convention in Sept. 1786, but at the behest of New York delegate Alexander Hamilton and Virginian James Madison, a new conference would be scheduled for a later date. Shays' Rebellion hastened the process and by May 14, 1787 a rump convention began at Philadelphia with only the Virginia and Pennsylvania delegates attending. By May 25, the Constitutional Convention began in earnest with 29 delegates from 9 states represented. Eventually 55 "Founding Fathers" from 12 states (Rhode Island never took part) participated, with 39 signing the finished document, *The Constitution of the United States of America* on Sept. 17, 1787. The process of ratification of *The Constitution* by the individual states began on Sept. 28, 1787.

Chapter 4

The Constitutional Convention: The Birth of the Second United States (1787–1800)

The Constitutional Convention –Philadelphia, Penn.
May 14-Sept 17 1787

The Constitutional Convention brought together some of the most diverse and talented Americans in the history of the United States. Consisting primarily of lawyers, planters, and merchants, the "Founders" were remarkable in their ability to compromise on incredibly difficult issues, and with the speed in which they constructed the Constitution. It took them just three months to create the longest lasting written constitution in the history of the world.

Procedures

Although the Convention began on May 14, the important work did not commence until May 25, when a functional quorum of delegates had been assembled. The Virginia delegation, led by Edmund Randolph and James Madison, prompted the first serious action taken at the Convention. On May 29, Randolph suggested discarding the Articles, not revising them as originally planned. The Articles were to be replaced by an entirely new structure of government designed by the 36-year-old Madison. The delegates agreed to scrap the Articles the next day and consider Madison's plan. The Constitutional Revolution had begun.

1) – Structure of the Government
   A. Madison's "Virginia Plan"- Three-Branch (Executive, Legislative, Judicial) federal government with the Legislature being the most important branch as it selected the members of the Executive and Judicial branches. This arrangement is described as "separation of powers." The Legislature would be <u>bicameral</u> (2-House), not <u>unicameral</u> (1-House) as the Congress under the Articles had been. Each state's representation would be based on <u>population</u>, inherently favoring the largest states. In terms of population, the largest state by far was Virginia.

Congress

Lower House (House of Representatives)	Upper House (The Senate)
-The Lower House would be elected by the voters of each state and would serve 2-year terms.	- The Upper House would be elected by the Lower House, from nominees by each state's legislatures and serve 6-year terms.

Delegates of the smaller states loudly objected to this plan as they complained with some justification of becoming powerless against a combination of large states, which with ample western lands would become even more populated and more powerful. William Patterson of New Jersey countered the Virginia Plan with the much more conservative New Jersey Plan which retained the unicameral legislature, but gave it the power to tax and regulate commerce. In addition, each state would continue to have one vote in the Congress regardless of the size of the state's delegation. The state legislatures would select representatives to Congress, which would be given the power to choose a plural executive and a judicial branch. By July, the questions of structure and representation threatened to derail the Convention, and Benjamin Franklin proposed the issues be settled in committee. Roger Sherman suggested to the committee that Connecticut delegate John Dickinson's alternative plan be adopted. This came to be known as the "Great Compromise" or the "Connecticut Compromise." The structure incorporated much of Madison's Virginia Plan, a three-branch federal government with more power given to the Executive and Judicial branches, and a bicameral Congress with a popularly elected House of Representatives based on population. In the Senate however, each state would have 2 Senators, thereby assuring the smaller states equality in that house. 5 States, Connecticut, Delaware, Maryland, New Jersey and North Carolina supported the Compromise; Georgia, Pennsylvania, South Carolina, and Virginia rejected it. It came down to the Massachusetts delegation which split its vote. This allowed the Compromise to narrowly pass by a 5 to 4 margin.

The 3/5 Compromise

The 3/5 Compromise resulted from the impasse over how to count slaves for representation and taxation purposes. Southerners wanted slaves to be counted in determining each state's representation in Congress, but not for taxation purposes. Northerners wanted slaves to be counted for taxation but not for representation. Some Northerners proposed that slaves be counted for both. The issue went to a committee again chaired by Benjamin Franklin. Utilizing a proposal first introduced in the Confederation Congress, the committee suggested that slaves be counted as 3/5 of a person for both. This ratio came in part from the dubious proposition that slaves were only 3/5 as productive as free persons. The 3/5 Compromise passed with little opposition.

Compromises Over Federal Regulation of Commerce

Northern states favored federal regulation of commerce because this would allow the creation of tariffs which would provide protection for nascent industries in the region. Southerners were concerned that strong federal laws in regards to commerce would hurt their export based economy. The delegates were alarmed that the federal government might impose high export taxes, or interfere with the slave trade. As such, they insisted that federal laws dealing with commerce be passed by a supermajority of 2/3 of Congress. The resulting compromise included the following:

1) – Federal regulation of commerce by simple majority vote
2) – No export taxes (Article I, Section 9, Clause 5)
3) – No federal regulations abolishing the slave trade for 20 years (Article I, Section 9, Clause 1)
4) – A fugitive slave provision to return runaway slaves to their owners (Article IV, Section 2, Clause 3)

Upon completion of their work, the delegates were not overly enthused with their creation, essentially a compendium of compromises. As Benjamin Franklin wrote to George Washington, "I consent, Sir, to this Constitution, because I expect no better, and because I am not sure it is not the best. The opinions I have had of its errors, I sacrifice to the public good." On Sept. 28th, the Constitution went to the individual states for ratification or rejection. (See Ratification Sheets for the votes on p. 42)

<u>Struggle for Ratification</u>

Between 1787 and 1788, fierce campaigning ensued between supporters of the new Constitution (Federalists) and opponents (Anti-Federalists). Supporters tended to be coastal dwellers who felt the Constitution offered an acceptable balance between economic opportunity and individual freedom. Opponents, who generally lived 50 miles or more from the coast, disagreed with the new Constitution for a variety of reasons. Some felt that the Constitution would do little to promote their particular economic interests, others viewed it as an agent to destroy the autonomy of the States. Additionally, there were criticisms towards the structure of the new government with its strong presidency and its lack of a bill of rights for citizens. Finally, some Anti-Federalists felt the country was simply too large to be a republic. Anti-Federalist leaders included George Clinton of New York, Luther Martin of Maryland, Sam Adams and Elbridge Gerry of Massachusetts, Richard Henry Lee, Patrick Henry, and initially, Gov. Edmund Randolph of Virginia. According to Henry, "The question turns, sir, on that poor little thing—the expression, We the *people*, instead of the *states*, of America." (A states' rights perspective.) Henry also warned that, "Your President may easily become your king. Your Senate is so imperfectly constructed that your dearest rights may be sacrificed by what may be a small minority: and a very small minority may continue forever unchangeably this government, although horribly defective." Less prominent Anti-Federalists reasonably assumed that only wealthy aristocrats and lawyers would be elected to the Congress. Once in office, they would use their political position to perpetually maintain their own power and interests. Amos Singletary, an irate Massachusetts farmer put it this way:

> These lawyers, and men of learning, and moneyed men, they talk so
> finely, and gloss over matters so smoothly, to make us poor illiterate
> people to swallow down the pill expect to get into Congress themselves;
> they expect to be managers of this Constitution, and get the power and
> all the money into their own hands, and then they will swallow up all of us
> little folks, like the great Leviathan, Mr. President, yes, just as the
> whale swallowed up Jonah.

Although the Anti-Federalists arguments were compelling and in some cases accurate, the Federalists were better organized and prepared, having participated in the Convention and thus familiar with the aforementioned contentions. Even their name suggested a positive program, while Anti-Federalist sounded reactionary. Also, the Federalists included in their ranks such luminaries as George Washington, John Adams, Benjamin Franklin, John Jay, Alexander Hamilton, and James

Madison. The last three acted as the chief propagandists for the Constitution, composing 85 essays known collectively as The Federalist Papers in 1787–88. 77 appeared in book form on May 28, 1788; the remaining 8 were published between June 14 - Aug. 16, 1788, critical dates for the VA and New York Constitutional Conventions. 51 of the essays were composed by Hamilton, 29 by Madison, and the remaining 5 by Jay. Essay #10, written by Madison, proved one of the most important and persuasive of the Federalist arguments.* Madison refuted Anti-Federalist claims that the size of the country precluded republican government. Instead, the very expanse and diversity of interests within the country would prevent any one group, interest, or "faction," from taking singular control of the government. The government would operate according to shifting, temporary majorities which, in order to achieve their objectives, would be compelled to compromise. Between Dec. 7, 1787 and June 21, 9 states ratified the Constitution, the quorum necessary to put the Constitution into effect.

Ratification Of The U.S. Constitution and Populations Of The 13 Original States At The Time Of Ratification

State	Date of Ratification	Vote (for-against)	Population
Delaware	December 7, 1787	30–0	59,096
Pennsylvania	December 12, 1787	46–23	434,373
New Jersey	December 18, 1787	38–0	184,139
Georgia	January 2, 1788	26–0	82,548
Connecticut	January 9, 1788	128–40	237,946
Massachusetts	February 6, 1788	187–168	475,327
Maryland	April 28, 1788	63–11	319,728
South Carolina	May 23, 1788	149–73	249,073
New Hampshire	June 21, 1788	57–47	141,885
Virginia**	June 25, 1788	89–79	747,610
New York**	July 26, 1788	30–27	340,120
North Carolina	November 21, 1789	194–77	393,751
Rhode Island**	May 29, 1790	34–32	68,825

*The Anti-Federalist Papers, a collection of 85 essays against the Constitution, was drafted by least 23 writers during the debates over ratification as a counter to The Federalist Papers.

**These states included "escape clauses" within their ratification documents, asserting their right to withdraw from the Union if it became harmful or destructive to their interests.

Without the ratification of VA and New York however, the prospects for the new nation were dubious to say the least. In VA Government, Randolph proved crucial. Anti-Federalists in the state demanded a national bill of rights be included in the Constitution and Randolph concurred. James Madison complained that recalling the Convention would undo all of their previous work, and promised that a Bill of Rights would be added <u>after</u> the Constitution went into effect. Randolph acquiesced, proclaiming "I am a friend of the Constitution." Virginia ratified by 10 votes, 89 to 79. New York ratified a month later by a 3 vote margin, and then only after New York City threatened to secede from the state and join New Jersey! Madison kept his word and worked on a <u>very comprehensive</u> list of protections for citizens. 210 amendments were proposed, 17 were adopted by the House of Representatives, 12 were approved by the Senate, and the states ratified 10, our Bill of Rights, effective Dec. 15, 1791. An 11th proposed by Madison in 1789, became the 27th Amendment in 1992. It states that while the Congress can raise its own pay, the raise will not go into effect until a new election of Representatives has occurred.

The First National Period 1789–1801

After the ratification of the Constitution by Virginia and New York, the Second United States began operations, despite the omission of NC and RI which would be pressured into the Union by 1790. In 1789, George Washington became President (by unanimous consent) with John Adams as his Vice President. Washington was the first of the "Virginia Dynasty" of American presidents. 4 of the first 5 presidents were Virginians, and Virginia holds the distinction of being the birthplace of more American presidents, 8, than any other state. Washington's first cabinet consisted of Attorney General Edmund Randolph, Secretary of War Henry Knox, Secretary of Treasury Alexander Hamilton, and Secretary of State Thomas Jefferson. Hamilton and Jefferson dominated the cabinet and also served as the spokespersons for an immediately emergent Two-Party System, which featured the pro-central government Federalists and the pro-state governments Anti-Federalists. Hamilton, upon assessing the nation's finances, proposed an ambitious but quite controversial scheme. In his 1790 *Report on the Public Credit,* he called for the national assumption of all official debts, which totaled approximately $75 million (Domestic debt owed to citizens - $42.4 million, State indebtedness - $21.5 million, and Foreign debt - $11.7 million). This debt would be paid by a variety of taxes, including excise taxes on products and <u>tariffs</u> (taxes on imports). Also, old Revolutionary and Articles of Confederation bonds would be exchanged for new United States government bonds. Finally, a privately owned Bank of the United States would be chartered with assets totaling $10 million, including $2 million in government money. Hamilton reasoned that the Bank would provide a uniform paper currency, a safe depository for government revenues, a stimulant for investments, and a convenient depository for tax collection. The entire program appeared extraordinary and quite possibly unconstitutional, but Hamilton stubbornly insisted that the Constitution in Article I, Section 8, Clause 18 (The "Elastic" or "Necessary and Proper" Clause) basically supported his belief that "the end justifies the means," a phrase associated with Hamilton himself. In this manner, he applied "loose constructionist" reasoning towards the Constitution. Simply stated, "loose construction" means that unless the Constitution specifically prohibits an action, the federal government has considerable flexibility in implementing policies.

However, Secretary of State Thomas Jefferson and his able lieutenant, Speaker of the House James Madison, provided forceful objections to his plans on a variety of grounds. First, considering the assumption of state debts, several Southern states (including Virginia) had already substantially paid down their debts. Should national taxes be levied on those states to pay a debt which they already paid, and was it fair that citizens in solvent states be taxed to pay off the debts of insolvent states?! Secondly, most of the old bonds had been sold at a fraction of their price to speculators who would reap enormous profits upon exchange for the new U.S. bonds. Was this fair to the original bondholders? Finally, what section of the Constitution provides for the establishment of a national bank, which would obviously wield a great deal of power, both wanted and unwanted? Conversely, the 10th Amendment reserves powers not delegated to the federal government to the States and the people respectively. According to Jefferson, interpreting the Constitution loosely would allow Congress to "take possession of a boundless field of power, no longer susceptible to any definition." In this statement, Jefferson encapsulated the "strict constructionist" view of the Constitution. In other words, the Constitution specifically granted certain limited powers to the federal government. Beyond these "expressed" powers, the federal government has very little flexibility in formulating laws and creating new government institutions.

Hamilton knew President Washington would be the key to this debate, and he acquitted himself admirably. Responding to the touchy issue of assuming state debts, Hamilton successfully argued that this would improve the nation's credit rating as a whole (he was correct), and as a compromise, he agreed that partial compensation should be given to the citizens of solvent states. More importantly, he accepted Jefferson's demand that a new national capital be created in the South. According to Jefferson, Hamilton, Jefferson, and Madison concluded this arrangement during an informal dinner at Jefferson's New York residence. Jefferson erroneously believed that locating the capital in the South would give Southerners greater influence in national affairs. The bond proposal passed with much less difficulty. It basically came down to the simple fact that the speculators had made a wise investment, and the original bondholders had sold out too soon. Finally, Hamilton convinced Washington despite his serious reservations that the Bank of the United States would be efficacious to the nation's financial interests. He suggested that "a bank has a natural relation to the power of collecting taxes—to that of providing for the common defense." In short, Hamilton's entire scheme was enacted, and it succeeded brilliantly.

Domestic Affairs

In keeping with the Hamiltonian financial plan, a protective tariff, a series of excise taxes (most notably on whiskey), and the Bank of the United States were enacted by 1792. In addition, the Judiciary Act of 1789 gave additional powers to the federal courts. The nation expanded as well, adding Vermont in 1791 and Kentucky in 1792. Washington's first term seemed an unmitigated success and his reelection in 1792 came very easily. However, there seems to be, starting with

Washington, a curse on every President who wins a second term, and problems at home and abroad surfaced almost immediately (the "second term curse"). In the West, Little Turtle, leader of the Miami Confederacy terrorized the frontier. His ultimate defeat did not occur until Aug. 4, 1794 at the Battle of Fallen Timbers south of Detroit, when American forces under the command of General "Mad Anthony" Wayne destroyed his army and laid waste to the countryside. The subsequent Treaty of Greenville gave the United States large tracts of Indian land in present day Ohio and Indiana.

Simultaneously, in Pennsylvania, outraged farmers rebelled against what they perceived as an exorbitant tax on whiskey—$.25 on the dollar. The farmers, hindered in selling their crops down the Mississippi River by the Spanish, sold and exchanged whiskey for other goods on a regular basis. In addition to its obvious appeal, whiskey found its way into apothecary shops and doctors' prescriptions. Much easier to transport than corn or grain, whiskey played a significant role in both American society and in the economic welfare of countless western farmers. In the summer of 1794, the "Whiskey Boys" tarred and feathered tax collectors and disrupted federal court proceedings greatly alarming President Washington, who called up the militia of several states (VA, MD, PENN, and NJ) to deal with the disgruntled farmers. With General "Lighthorse Harry" Lee commanding and Hamilton supervising, 13,000 men marched and quickly routed the "Whiskey Boys." Twenty of the rebels were rounded up, and 2 were convicted of treason. Washington pardoned both, proclaiming one man "insane" and the other a "simpleton." While many Federalists applauded the action as a positive measure demonstrating the power of the new federal government, some western farmers and Anti-Federalists denounced this use of force as a dangerous precedent for the abuse of executive power. The episode further strengthened partisanship in the United States.

Foreign Affairs

If domestic affairs proved vexing for Washington between 1793–1797, foreign relations were at least equally problematic. Diplomatic tensions grew between the U.S. and both Great Britain and France primarily due to the French Revolution and subsequent European wars. These conflicts impaired our commerce, and displayed the United States inability to obtain foreign recognition of its neutral rights. Despite its idealistic beginnings in 1789, by 1792 the French Revolution degenerated into a bloody conflagration complete with foreign intervention, class and religious warfare, regicide, massacres, and demagoguery. Most Americans initially supported the Revolution as another popular movement to replace monarchy with representative government. Eventually, the atrocities and radicalism of the French Revolution cooled American enthusiasm towards the French cause, especially among Federalists. New England Federalists were suspicious of the French revolutionaries' social and religious radicalism. Also, their trading relationship with Great Britain, now at war with France, seemed to be increasingly threatened by actions on the high seas. Anti-Federalists including Thomas Jefferson remained sympathetic due to their more egalitarian and decentralized political philosophy. However, by 1794, events such as Citizen Genet's visit to the U.S., and the "Reign of

Terror" in France diminished even their ardor. To many Americans' horror, the "Reign of Terror" featured the incarceration of half a million people, and the execution of 30,000. During this period, the French government increasingly attempted to rekindle the American - French alliance of 1778, still technically in effect, and were infuriated when Washington declared that the U.S. would remain neutral.*

Citizen Genet

In an attempt to re-initiate this alliance, the French Revolutionary government dispatched Citizen Edmond Charles Genet to the U.S. Upon arrival in Charleston in Jan. 1793, Genet immediately antagonized his American hosts. He outfitted American privateers for use against British shipping, set up French courts on American soil, and encouraged southern frontiersmen to attack Spanish settlements in Florida and Louisiana. In addition, he attempted to arouse class animosity by organizing anti-privilege clubs, and even made disparaging remarks concerning President Washington's age, a diplomatic faux pas. By August, the American government demanded his recall to France. The new French ambassador, Citizen Fauchet, arrived carrying arrest warrants for Genet. Realizing the guillotine most likely awaited him, Genet pleaded for and received asylum, ultimately marrying the daughter of New York's Gov. George Clinton and quietly fading away.

Abuses of U.S. Neutrality

Neither the French nor the British respected our neutrality and seized our ships at will when we attempted to trade with either country. (A total of 600 ships between 1793–1794.) In addition, in Dec. 1793 the British began impressing sailors off American vessels either claiming that the kidnapped seamen were deserters or English citizens. Thomas Jefferson resigned as Sec. of State partly due to his disgust with the increasingly pro-British slant adopted by the Federalists. Simultaneously, the British refused to evacuate six forts they held in the American Northwest, a violation of the Treaty of Paris. From these garrisons the British were strongly suspected of arming and inciting various Indian tribes to attack American settlements in the region. By the fall of 1794, France's navy had been so decimated by the British that French seizures of American ships and cargo declined significantly. Consequently, the French courted American trade and supplies, emphasizing profits not piracy, a much more attractive policy for the U.S. This change further strained Anglo-American relations. The British responded by increasing their kidnappings and seizures. For example, during the Summer and Fall of 1794, the British seized some 250 American ships attempting to trade in the French West Indies alone! Even pro-British Federalists such as Hamilton were finding it difficult to countenance British naval actions. War seemed increasingly imminent, and the Federalists desperately sought a peaceful solution. They recognized both the impotent state of the American military and the dire consequences for Hamilton's financial program should formal hostilities commence with Britain. In April 1794, Washington dispatched Supreme Court Chief Justice Jay to London to seek a comprehensive settlement of all the outstanding issues.

*Washington claimed that the treaty had been between the U.S. and the French King Louis XVI. When he was deposed and executed in 1793, the treaty was therefore nullified.

Jay's Treaty

In lengthy negotiations lasting until November, Jay and the British foreign minister Lord Grenville finally concluded the Treaty of London, also infamously known as "Jay's Treaty." The Americans, "bargaining" from a position of weakness, gained very little from the British.

Provisions

For the United States:

1) – the British will evacuate the forts by 1796, but reserve the right to keep trading with the Indians. Also, the British agree not to incite the Indians against Americans.
2) - the British will compensate American shipping losses at a future date through arbitration.
3) - the British and Americans both respect each others right to utilize waterways on the American continent.
4) - U.S. gains limited trade concessions in the British East Indies and India.
5) - U.S. obtains extremely limited trade concessions with the much more profitable British West Indies. No ships larger than 70 tons could engage in trade, and Americans were forbidden from re-exporting goods (cocoa, molasses, sugar, etc…) purchased from West Indies ports to other world ports.

For the British:

1) – the Americans concede the British definition of contraband. Roughly stated, any product sold to an enemy is subject to seizure.
2) - the British refuse to respect our neutral rights.
3) - the British reserve the right to continue impressments.
4) – the Americans must pay their pre-Revolutionary debts to British merchants, the amount to be determined through arbitration.

Some Treaty!

Washington reacted to Jay's Treaty with shock and dismay, but ultimately sent it to the Senate for consideration. Many Senators immediately denounced the treaty and, when the Anti-Federalist newspaper the *Philadelphia Aurora* publicly revealed its contents, Washington noted that the citizenry reacted "like a mad dog." John Jay lamented that he could walk from Philadelphia to New York by the light of his caricature burning in effigy. Newspapers referred to him derisively as "Sir John Jay," and Congressman Andrew Jackson declared that Washington should be impeached on the grounds of cowardice for signing the treaty. Below are samples of anti-Jay rhetoric:

1) "John Jay, ah, the arch traitor—seize him, drown him, hang him, burn him, flay him alive!"

2) "Damn John Jay! Damn every one that won't damn John Jay!! Damn every one that won't put lights in his windows and sit up all night damning John Jay!!"

Nevertheless, the Senate, concluding that they could not obtain better treatment from the British, ratified the treaty by the bare minimum 2/3 majority, 20 senators for, 10 against. However, there were positive ramifications from Jay's Treaty. One, the United States and Britain did not go to war, and it also paved the way for future treaties with other European nations, such as Spain. In 1795, U.S. Foreign Minister Thomas Pinckney successfully concluded the Treaty of San Lorenzo with Spain. This time, the U.S. negotiated from a position of strength as Spanish designs in the West had gone awry. Better known as Pinckney's Treaty, the United States won every point in dispute.

1)-The U.S. gained all of the disputed territory north of the 31st parallel.

2)-The U.S obtained the right of deposit for American goods in New Orleans for 3 years.

3)-Spain gave the U.S. unrestricted access to the Mississippi River.

4)-A commission would be established to assess damage claims of U.S. citizens against Spain with Spain promising to abide by their findings.

5)-The Spanish agreed to stop inciting the Indians against American settlements.

Despite the success of Pinckney's Treaty and the addition of Tennessee as the 15th state in 1796, Washington suffered merciless attacks during his second term. According to the Anti-Federalist newspaper the *Philadelphia Aurora*, Washington acted as "a supercilious tyrant in his political dotage." On the day before he left office the same newspaper declared that "this day ought to be a jubilee in the United States for if ever a nation was debauched by a man, the American Nation has been debauched by Washington." Nevertheless, another Federalist, Vice President John Adams, would serve as Washington's successor. Adam's defeated Thomas Jefferson in the Election of 1796, 71 to 68. The first partisan election had the unanticipated and undesired effect of putting members of the two opposing political parties as president and vice president respectively (remedied by the 12th Amendment ratified Sept. 25th, 1804).

The Adams Years 1797–1801

John Adams' career puts him squarely in the front rank of the Founding Fathers, although he has often been overshadowed by Washington and Jefferson. He had been a pivotal figure during the Revolution, nominating Washington for command of the Continental Army. He was an invaluable member of the committee charged with drafting the Declaration of Independence. In the Continental Congress, he spoke so convincingly for its adoption that Jefferson referred to him as "the Atlas who carried American independence on his shoulders." After the War, he served ably as minister to Holland and became the first American ambassador to be received by King George III. He also became the first Vice President of the U.S., a position he lamented to his spirited and intelligent wife Abigail as "the most insignificant office that ever the invention of man contrived or his imagination conceived." Adams was a man of great devotion to his country and to his own principles. However, he possessed an explosive temper and lashed out at his enemies, especially in his private life. Like the other Founders, he produced volumes of letters both expounding his political views and denouncing many of his colleagues. For example, he loathed Alexander Hamilton who had tried to unseat him as the Federalist nominee for president in 1796, once referring to him as "the bastard brat of a Scotch peddler." Adams' one term in office witnessed a series of dramatic events; a successful naval war with France, the continuing success of Hamiltonian fiscal policy, the passage of the highly unpopular Alien and Sedition Acts, the drafting of the influential Virginia and Kentucky Resolutions in response, and finally, the peaceful transfer of power to the Anti-Federalist party in the Election of 1800. (By 1800, they changed their name to the Democratic-Republican Party.)

Problems With France

During the election of 1796, the French government, having identified the Federalists as inherently hostile to their regime (due in no small part to Jay's Treaty), threatened to sever diplomatic relations with the U.S. if a Federalist candidate were elected president. With Adams' election, the 5 man Directory which governed France made good on their promise. Adams wished to prevent war between the U.S. and France, and subsequently dispatched South Carolinian Charles Cotesworth Pinckney to France to repair relations. The French refused to receive Pinckney and ordered him back to the U.S. Adams, although angry by this diplomatic affront, still felt compelled to effect a rapprochement and sent Pinckney, Elbridge Gerry, and John Marshall to Paris to try again. The French foreign minister Talleyrand kept the American envoys waiting for 3 months, and then granted them an informal audience of just 15 minutes! Days later, three low-level clerks in the French foreign ministry known historically as "X,Y, and Z" ("X" was Jean-Conrad Hottinguer, "Y" was Pierre Bellamy, and "Z" was Lucien Hauteval) met with the Americans. There were no negotiations; the French simply demanded an immediate $250,000 bribe for Talleyrand and the Directory, a $12 million loan, and an apology for American policy from the president just to start negotiations! The Americans were furious, and Pinckney responded with the statement, "No; No; not a sixpence!" which the American press later altered to "Millions for defense but not one cent for tribute!" Outraged at French insults and contempt, Adams mobilized the fledgling American navy to carry on war with France on the high seas. Construction of new naval vessels commenced with 33 ships being commissioned by 1799. Some of these ships including the U.S.S. Constellation, the U.S.S United States, and the U.S.S Constitution ("Old Ironsides") went on to earn heroic if not legendary status. The Department of the Navy came into existence in 1798 as a result of this quasi-war, and American vessels were authorized to attack any French warship or privateer on site. Even George Washington offered to come out of retirement to lead an army against Spanish Florida and Louisiana. (Spain allied itself loosely with France.) When Adams and the newly installed Napoleon began peace talks in March 1799, some radical Federalists became enraged. (While Adams took a brief respite at his home in Massachusetts, Federalist Congressman Robert G. Harper publicly mused that he hoped Adams' horses would throw him and break his neck, a violation of the Alien and Sedition Acts of 1798. Harper was never charged.) The naval campaign was an unmitigated success with French losses at 85 ships, the U.S., only 1! Peace negotiations concluded in 1800. Adams had safely steered the country through a successful limited war, but domestic defeat would be pulled from the jaws of foreign victory.

The Alien and Sedition Acts

During the naval war with France, Adams and other Federalists looked warily at the growing number of small farmers and immigrants who were joining the Democratic-Republicans. They foolishly decided to misuse wartime fervor to suppress their political opponents. To accomplish this, the Federalists pushed through the Alien and Sedition Acts in June and July of 1798. The Alien Act extended the length of time for becoming a naturalized citizen from 5 to 14 years and gave the president authority to expel "dangerous" aliens. The Sedition Act made it a "high misdemeanor to engage in any conspiracy or combination against legal measures of the government, including interference with federal officers, and insurrection or riot." In addition, it forbade anyone to "write, print, utter, or publish anything false, scandalous, or malicious against the government, the Congress, or the president." Violators could be punished by up to 5 years in jail and a $5,000 fine! The first prosecuted case occurred in Newark, NJ at a cannon salute for a recent naval victory. A critic of Adams stated, "I wish the cannons wadding would be lodged in the President's backside!" For this he incurred a $100 fine. On the floor of Congress itself, a fight broke out between the Dem.-Rep. Matthew Lyon and Federalist Roger Griswold. Federalist rhymesters referred to Lyon as "a strange, offensive brute, too wild to tame, to base to shoot." Lyon was convicted of sedition and sentenced to four months in jail and a $1,000 fine (paid by Vice President Jefferson) for writing a letter which characterized Adams as having, "an unbounded thirst for ridiculous pomp, foolish adulation, and selfish avarice." Another episode involved pro-Jefferson pamphleteer James Callender. In 1800, Callender wrote and published a lengthy and scathing attack on Adams entitled *The Prospect Before Us*, for which he was sentenced to 9 months in jail. (However in a bitter irony, once Jefferson became president, Callender turned on him. Jefferson refused to appoint Callender the postmaster of Richmond, VA and Callender responded by disclosing Jefferson's alleged sexual relationship with one of his slaves, Sally Hemings. The controversy concerning Hemings, Jefferson, and their offspring was hotly debated for 200 years before DNA evidence seemingly removed all doubt.)

In all, 25 persons (all Democratic-Republicans) were arrested, 14 indicted, and 10 convicted of violating the Sedition Acts. The backlash against these acts and the Federalist Party in general helped secure the presidency for the Democratic-Republicans in 1800.

The Virginia and Kentucky Resolutions of 1798

In response to the Alien and Sedition Acts, James Madison writing for the Virginia legislature and Thomas Jefferson writing for Kentucky, drafted the Virginia and Kentucky Resolutions. The Resolutions denounced both of the acts as contrary to the Constitution. The Sedition Act specifically was singled out as a violation of the First Amendment of the Bill of Rights, added to the Constitution only seven years earlier. Also, Jefferson contended that the state legislatures collectively could nullify (void), within their respective borders, federal laws deemed unconstitutional. Furthermore, the states had never surrendered their sovereignty (self-rule or autonomy), and that the Union itself was a compact between the states and the federal government, with the Constitution acting as a binding contract explicitly detailing the rights and limitations applicable to both the state and federal governments. The Resolutions were non-binding and neither the VA or KY legislatures attempted to nullify the Alien and Sedition Acts. However, the Resolutions became extremely influential documents in the states' rights interpretation of the Constitution and the overall nature of the Union. The importance of these documents is due in no small measure to the Founding Fathers' status of the authors. Along with the ratification and amendment processes outlined in the Constitution, the provisions for the Senate and the Electoral College, and the 10th Amendment, the VA and KY Resolutions give considerable creditability to states' rights theory.

Elections 1788–1800	Party	Electoral Vote	Popular Vote
1788 – George Washington*	None	69 (Unanimous)	None
1792 – George Washington	None	132	None
1796 – John Adams	Federalist	71	None
– Thomas Jefferson	Anti-Federalist (Democratic-Republicans)	68	
1800 – Thomas Jefferson	Dem.-Rep.	73	None
– John Adams	Federalist	65	

*Washington is the only president to both be elected and re-elected unanimously.

Chapter 5

The Virginia Dynasty Continued:
Jefferson to The "Era of Good Feelings"

The Election of 1800

The election of 1800 proved to be one of the more significant contests in American history for a number of reasons. One, it demonstrated that the U.S. could have a peaceful transition of power from one political party to another, in this case from the Federalists to the Democratic-Republicans. Two, the election showed that holding different political interpretations of the Constitution and the role of the federal government did not necessarily mean counter-revolution or civil war. Instead, the important political tradition of the "loyal opposition" would take firm root in American politics. Finally, the election served notice that the Founders had committed an error when they originally designed the presidential electoral procedures. Specifically, the provision at fault allowed the candidate who came in second, invariably a political opponent, to become vice president. Also, the electors' preference for who would become president and who would become vice president was not distinguished. All of this would be remedied with the passage of the 12th Amendment on Sept. 25, 1804, which provided for vote by separate "ballot for president and vice president." What occurred in this election to trigger these reforms?

To avoid the unwanted scenario of having Jefferson win the election with John Adams becoming his vice president, the Democratic-Republicans attempted to maneuver New York lawyer Aaron Burr into second place in the election thus ensuring that Dem-Reps. would hold both the presidency and vice presidency, but the plan succeeded too well. Suspiciously, electors in NY and SC expected to either abstain from voting, or vote for another candidate, voted for Burr nonetheless. When the electoral vote was tallied, Jefferson had 73 votes and Burr had 73 votes. (Before the the votes were counted, Burr promised Jefferson in a written statement that he would defer to Jefferson in the event of a tie!) According to the Constitution, if no candidate receives a majority in the Electoral College, the contest is thrown into the House of Representatives for resolution. (See Appendix #2 for more information about the Electoral College.) In order for either candidate to win the presidency, they would have to win in a majority of the states—at the time 9 states out of 16. (Today a candidate would have to win 26.) For 35 ballots, no candidate won a majority with Jefferson carrying 8 states, Burr holding 6 states, and 2 states unable to reach a consensus. In the interim, Jefferson made conciliatory promises to Federalists in important states, but the key figure in resolving the dispute turned out to be Jefferson's old nemesis, Alexander Hamilton. Hamilton had been rendered unelectable as president due to publications revealing a sordid extra-marital affair with a certain Mrs. Maria Reynolds of Philadelphia, and subsequent demands for blackmail payments to her husband to keep the affair quiet. Ironically, Hamilton published the damning letters himself! Despite this, Hamilton still possessed formidable political power which he decided to wield against Burr in a series of letters sent to important Congressmen. Consider the following portion of one of these letters:

> *If there be a man in this world I ought to hate, it is Jefferson,*
> *but the public good must be paramount to every private*
> *consideration. Burr however is a cold-blooded Catiline (an*
> *ancient Roman conspirator denounced by Cicero), decidedly*

> *profligate (having no decency or virtue), selfish to a degree which*
> *which excludes all social affections, a voluptuary (obsessed with*
> *sensual pleasures)...without doubt insolvent. (bankrupt) For*
> *Heaven's sake, let not the federal party be responsible for the*
> *elevation of this man!*

Such attacks swayed the House of Representatives as Federalist James Bayard of Delaware withheld his vote for Burr on the 36th ballot, and persuaded his Federalist allies in Vermont and Maryland to follow suit. This action gave the election to Jefferson, 10 states to 4 on Feb. 17, 1801. Burr, became Jefferson's vice president for 1-term only, but the career of the "Great American Scoundrel" continued in intrigue after intrigue.

Marbury v. *Madison* (1803)

  John Adams still had one option left to play to ensure that the Federalists, defeated in the presidential and congressional elections, would not simply vanish from the nation's body politic. In the winter, Congress passed the Judiciary Act of 1801 which allowed Adams to appoint staunch federalists to the federal judiciary for life. 23 so-called "midnight justices" were appointed, ranging from the Chief Justice of the Supreme Court (John Marshall) down to the position of Justice of the Peace for Washington, D.C., William Marbury. Adams apparently did not finish his appointments until late into the evening of March 3rd 1801, shortly before Jefferson's inauguration on March 4th. (Which Adams did not attend by the way!) Despite his best efforts, not all of the official contracts had been delivered to the appointees, and upon assuming office Jefferson instructed his Secretary of State James Madison to withhold all of the remaining confirmation letters from the recipients. William Marbury reacted furiously when Madison would not issue his contract and decided to sue the Secretary of State for his commission.* Marbury contended that the relatively obscure Judicial Act of 1789 gave the Supreme Court the power to issue a *writ of mandamus* commanding Madison to give him his official commission. In addition to the pending case, the new Dem.-Rep. controlled Congress passed the Judicial Act of 1802, a law of dubious constitutionality which in effect repealed the previous act and would presumably remove the so-called "Midnight Justices."

  The stage was now set for a major showdown between the Executive and Judicial branches which would have ramifications to the present day. In 1803, the case *Marbury* v. *Madison* would be adjudicated by the Supreme Court, under the strong Federalist leadership of Virginian John Marshall. Marshall, a personal enemy of Jefferson, faced a daunting challenge. The Supreme Court had issued only one truly important ruling in the short history of the nation, *Chisholm* vs. *Georgia* (1793), which led to the passage of the 11th Amendment in 1798. Did it have the power or the right to challenge the Executive Branch? If the Marshall court ruled for Marbury, it would enrage Jefferson. In addition, could the Supreme Court <u>actually</u>

---

*Federal Justices of the Peace served for 5 year terms, not life, which further bolstered Jefferson's conviction to withhold
  Marbury's commission.

force Madison to give Marbury his writ? If it voted to uphold Madison, the court would appear weak and subordinate to the other branches of the federal government. What then could Marshall do? Using an analogy from football, he executed the political equivalent of an end around. Marshall stated, that while the Court concurred that Marbury should receive his appointment, the Court lacked the constitutional authority to force Madison to issue it. The reason? The Supreme Court ruled the Judicial Act of 1789 <u>unconstitutional</u> on the basis that the power to issue writs of mandamus was not mentioned in Article II of the Constitution, and thus was not part of the Court's original jurisdiction. (The Constitution's supremacy as law is spelled out in Article VI, Sec.2.) Marshall denied an individual a minor appointment, but gave the Supreme Court the immense power of <u>judicial review</u> over federal laws, that is, the power to determine for itself if an act of Congress signed into law by the president was valid or not in the context of the Constitution.* This marked the beginning of the Marshall Court's expansion of federal power at the expense of the states, a process of <u>judicial nationalism</u> which continued for 35 years.

Jefferson, angered by this maneuver, attempted to remove Federalist judges by having them impeached. New Hampshire District Judge John Pickering, strongly suspected of being insane and given to drunken and vulgar outbursts in court, was easily removed on March 14, 1804. Associate Supreme Court Justice Samuel Chase proved a harder target. A bitter critic of Jefferson and his supporters, Chase dismissed Democratic-Republicans from jury service in sedition cases and denounced the state of Maryland for allowing universal white male suffrage which he claimed would lead to "mobocracy." While Chase was arrogant, distasteful, and insulting, the prosecutor John Randolph could not obtain the required 2/3 majority of the Senate to convict him of "high crimes and misdemeanors." Chase was acquitted on March 1, 1805. As a result, Jefferson dismissed the whole process as farcical and ceased impeachment as a political tactic. Since 1805, only 16 federal officials have been subject to impeachment with only 6 being removed from office. (see p. 56)

The Jefferson Administration 1801–1809

Key Figures   - Sec. of State James Madison
                     - Sec. of Treasury Albert Gallatin

Despite Federalist fears to the contrary, Jefferson did not engage in the wholesale dismissal of Federalist officials appointed by John Adams (he removed 109 out of 433 Federalist officeholders), nor did he dismantle Hamilton's creations. Instead, under the effective counsel of Albert Gallatin, Jefferson reduced the size of the federal government and scaled back its budget, expenditures, and debt. In managing the nation's fiscal affairs the two men proved quite adept. The excise taxes on whiskey were abolished, and tariffs, land sales, and postal services were bolstered. Public land sales policy became much more flexible and accessible for ordinary Americans after 1800. Consider the following land acts:

* It should be noted however that the Supreme Court had previously upheld the constitutionality of a federal law in *Hylton v. U.S* (1796), and ironically, *Stuart v. Laird* (1803), a concurrent case specifically concerning judicial review was next on the Supreme Court's docket.

Land Act of - 1800 – 320 acres at $2.00 an acre
- 1804 – 164 acres at $1.64 an acre

By 1807, all federal bonds had been redeemed and the federal debt had been reduced from $83 million in 1801 to $57 million in 1807. One of the methods (see p. 57)

Impeachment of Federal Officials 1799–1999

The Senate has sat as a court of impeachment in the following cases:

1. William Blount, Senator from Tennessee; charges dismissed for want of jurisdiction, Jan. 14, 1799.
2. John Pickering, Judge of the U.S. District Court for New Hampshire removed from office March 12, 1804.
3. Samuel Chase, Associate Justice of the Supreme Court; acquitted March 1, 1805.
4. James H. Peck, Judge of the U.S. District Court for Missouri; acquitted Jan. 31, 1831.
5. West H. Humphreys, Judge of the U.S. District Court for the eastern, middle, and western districts of Tennessee; removed from office 1862.
6. Andrew Johnson, President of the United States; acquitted May 26, 1868.
7. William W. Belknap, Secretary of War; acquitted August 1, 1876.
8. Charles Swayne, Judge of the U.S. District Court for the northern district of Florida; acquitted Feb. 27, 1905.
9. Robert W. Archbald, Associate Judge, U.S. Commerce Court; removed Jan. 13, 1913.
10. George W. English, Judge of the U.S. District Court for the eastern district of Illinois; resigned Nov. 4, 1926; proceedings dismissed.
11. Harold Louderback, Judge of the U.S. District Court for the northern district of California; acquitted May 24, 1933.
12. Halsted L. Ritter, Judge of the U.S. District Court for the southern district of Florida; removed from office April 17, 1936.
13. Harry E. Claiborne, Judge of the U.S. District Court for the district of Nevada; removed from office Oct. 9, 1986.
14. Alcee L. Hastings, Judge of the U.S. District Court for the southern district of Florida; removed from office Oct. 20, 1988.
15. Walter L. Nixon, Judge of the U.S. District Court for Mississippi; removed from office Nov. 3, 1989.
16. William Jefferson Clinton, President of the United States; acquitted Feb. 12, 1999.

Totals
16 officials impeached
8 acquitted
7 removed
1 resignation
Source: *Congressional Directory*

Jefferson used to reduce public expenditures involved drastically cutting back the armed forces. The army shrank from 4,000 regulars to 2,500, and naval expenditures were reduced from $3.5 million to $1 million, which scaled down the U.S Navy from 25 ships to 7. These cuts would leave the nation quite vulnerable when, in 1805 tensions increased between the U.S. and the north African based Barbary Pirates, and the Napoleonic Wars entered an ominous new phase. (This seems quite ironic considering the U.S. Military Academy located at West Point began classes in 1802 during Jefferson's first term!)

Jefferson proved successful in other domestic matters as well. The Alien and Sedition Acts were allowed to expire in 1801, and Jefferson granted amnesty to all persons imprisoned under the acts and refunded their fines. Citizenship requirements were also restored to their original 5-year levels. Another Jeffersonian reform came with the abolition of the African slave trade effective Jan. 1, 1808. Great Britain and the U.S. were the first western nations to do so. Jefferson's greatest domestic achievement occurred in 1803 when the United States peacefully acquired the Louisiana Purchase which nearly doubled the size of the country.

The Louisiana Purchase - Background

In 1763, as a result of their defeat in the French and Indian War, the French had been driven off the North American mainland, ceding Quebec to the British and Louisiana to their Spanish allies. The French retained only the West Indian colony of Haiti on the island of Santo Domingo. In 1791, rebellious slaves led by Toussaint L'Ouverture overthrew French colonial rule in Haiti, the only successful slave uprising to occur in the Western Hemisphere. However, when Napoleon seized power in Nov. 1799, he committed to the re-establishment of a French empire in North America. In the secret Treaty of San Ildefonso, he tricked the Spanish government into returning Louisiana to French control. (He did so by falsely promising to place a Spanish princess and her husband on the throne of Tuscany in northern Italy.) In May 1801, Jefferson learned of the treaty and wrote to the American ambassador in France, Robert Livingston, that there was "on the globe one single spot, the possessor of which is our natural and habitual enemy. It is New Orleans, through which the produce of 3/8 of our territory must pass to market....The day that France takes possession of New Orleans we must marry ourselves to the British fleet and nation....," certainly not a sanguine prospect for Jefferson. In 1802, Napoleon dispatched General Leclerc and a huge French forced to Haiti to recapture the colony and use it as a base for future operations. Again, L'Ouverture, the "black Napoleon," resisted Leclerc's forces using guerilla tactics reminiscent of the "Swamp Fox" Francis Marion in the American Revolution. However, an exhausted L'Ouverture surrendered to Leclerc, who sent him to France. It seemed inevitable that Napoleon would re-establish control over Haiti, but his determination to re-establish slavery spurred the Haitians to fierce and desperate resistance. Ultimately, Leclerc's army proved utterly unable to subdue the guerillas or withstand the ravages of yellow fever carried by mosquitoes (Leclerc himself succumbed to the disease), and the French withdrew from Haiti. Nevertheless, Napoleon, at least for the moment, refused to abandon his plan. On Oct. 16th 1802, Napoleon pressured the Spanish to close New Orleans to American vessels. This action precipitated a crisis for the U.S. In Dec. 1802, Jefferson dispatched James Monroe to France to collaborate with Livingston and attempt to purchase New Orleans and the Floridas for up to $10 million. By the time Livingston and Monroe met with French Foreign Minister Talleyrand in April 1803, Napoleon had changed his mind concerning his New World empire and instructed Talleyrand to sell <u>all of Louisiana</u> (the boundaries of which were not entirely clear) to the United States. Why? Failure to pacify Haiti and the imminent prospect of renewed conflict with Britain undoubtedly were factors in his decision. (On a humorous note, his brothers Lucien and Joseph attempted to dissuade him from selling Louisiana while he was enjoying a perfumed bubble bath. Napoleon became so outraged that he literally splashed them out of the room!) When Talleyrand made the proposal, the American ambassadors were flabbergasted but quickly offered to pay $10 million, which Talleyrand rejected as not quite sufficient. Without explicit authority or instructions, Monroe and Livingston nonetheless recognized their outstanding opportunity and were determined not to let it slip away. They subsequently offered Talleyrand $15 million ($11.25 million for the land and $3.75 million to settle American claims against France). Talleyrand agreed to the terms, stating that the Americans had made a "noble bargain" for themselves, and on April 30, 1803 France ceded Louisiana to the U.S.

When the ambassadors returned to the U.S. in the summer of 1803, Jefferson reacted with astonishment. A strict constructionist, he wondered if he even had the authority to approve such a gigantic addition to the U.S., but the promise of the vast lands in the West proved irresistible. He consulted with James Madison about approving the purchase through a series of amendments to the Constitution, but Madison warned him that Federalist opposition in New England would doom that tactic. (Many Federalists in New England were quite concerned about losing inhabitants to the West which would diminish their population and political power, as well as damage their economy. They also feared the entire Louisiana region would follow current political trends and become Democratic-Republican.) Instead, Jefferson sent the Louisiana Purchase to the Senate as a treaty where it easily passed 26 to 6 in Oct. 1803. In New Orleans on Dec. 20, 1803, the United States, represented by Gov. William C.C. Claiborne and General. James Wilkinson, assumed formal control over Louisiana. With the Louisiana Purchase the Americans gained some 822,000 square miles of territory for roughly about $15 per square mile, or $1.8 cents an acre! Jefferson dispatched intrepid explorers to map and describe the newly acquired Louisiana Territory, the most notable, army officers Meriwether Lewis, William Clark, and Zebulon Pike. Beginning in 1804, the Lewis and Clark Expedition trekked west from St. Louis ("the Gateway to the West") towards the Pacific Ocean, invaluably aided by Sacajawea, the Shoshone wife of a French explorer. They arrived at the Pacific near the mouth of the Columbia River (in present day Washington state). They did not return to St. Louis until 1806, after a journey covering approximately 7,000 miles, bringing journals and illustration books which became wildly popular with the American public. Not surprisingly, their monumental achievement accorded them heroic status and is comparable to the 20th century feats of Lindbergh flying solo across the Atlantic in 1927, or the Apollo Moon Landing of 1969. Zebulon Pike's explorations were hardly less fantastic. Starting from St. Louis in 1805, Pike reached the northernmost point of the Mississippi River in present day Minnesota. In 1806–1807, Pike traveled west from St. Louis to present day Colorado, where he mapped the 14,110 foot mountain aptly named Pike's Peak. He then ventured south into present day north-central Mexico before moving northeast and ultimately reaching Natchitoches in present day Louisiana. Along the journey, he mapped the headwaters of the Arkansas and Red Rivers.

For the United States, the Louisiana Purchase marked just the first in a series of incredibly lucrative land purchases from European nations. The successes of Jefferson's first administration ensured easy re-election. However, there were ominous portents in 1804 that the "second term curse" for presidents would reveal itself again.

Election of 1804	Party	Electoral Vote	Popular Vote
- T. Jefferson	Dem.-Rep.	162	None
- Charles Pinckney	Federalist	14	

The Essex Junto

James Madison's warnings of Federalist disapproval of the Louisiana Purchase quickly surfaced in the early months of 1804. Sen. Timothy Pickering of Mass. became convinced that New England's only hope of avoiding domination by the hated Dem.-Reps. lay in seceding from the Union and forming a new northern nation consisting of New England, Newfoundland (in Canada), Pennsylvania, and most importantly, New York. Pickering and his co-conspirators originally attempted to enlist the support of Alexander Hamilton. Hamilton, whose own political fortunes were on the decline, had made disparaging remarks about democracy and American society in general. He remarked to a friend in 1804 that, "every day proves to me more and more that this American world was not made for me." Of women and children, he declared that, "(they) are rendered more useful, and the latter more early useful, by manufacturing establishments, than they would otherwise be." The day before he died he wrote to Theodore Sedgwick that "our real disease…is democracy…." (the context of his statement interestingly was against disunion, which Hamilton actually thought would spread and strengthen democracy!) Hamilton however had no interest in the secession plot, and Pickering turned to Aaron Burr who had been disavowed by Jefferson. Burr, realizing he would be dropped from the Dem.-Rep. ticket in 1804 decided to run for governor of New York. During the campaign, Pickering promised Burr the junta's support if he agreed upon election to bring New York into the new nation. In April however, Burr suffered an overwhelming defeat at the polls to Dem-Rep. Lewis Morgan due in part to blistering attacks leveled upon him by Hamilton. Hamilton once again thwarted Burr's political ambitions, and in May, Burr decided to seek satisfaction by challenging Hamilton to a duel. New York state law prohibited dueling, so arrangements were made for the confrontation to take place at Weehawken, NJ at just past 7:00 A.M. on July 11, 1804. Hamilton loathed the practice of dueling; one of his sons had previously been killed in a duel. Accounts vary, but when a "second" (an assistant at a duel) proclaimed "Present!", Hamilton likely fired first, which missed Burr. A few seconds later, Burr shot Hamilton in the abdomen. The bullet passed through his liver and smashed into his spine, inflicting an agonizing and mortal wound. Hamilton, aged 47, expired 31 hours later, survived by his widow Elizabeth and 7 children. The man who virtually created the nation's financial structure died nearly $55,000 in debt. Nonetheless, a few days after his death he regained all of his lost fame and more. Daniel Webster wrote of him, "He smote the rock of the natural resources and abundant streams of revenue gushed forth; he touched the dead corpse of Public Credit and it sprang to its feet."

The "Great American Scoundrel"

Burr however was not so fortunate. His life from that point on became a series of treasonable misadventures, sordid extramarital affairs, and personal tragedies. Indicted for soliciting to duel and murder in New York and New Jersey, Burr fled to Philadelphia where he consorted with a woman named Celeste.* He subsequently headed to South Carolina and Georgia. Strangely enough, he returned to Washington in January to finish out his term as vice president! In 1805, Burr set out for the West and New Orleans planning to create some form of southwest empire in Mexico, Texas, Louisiana, or Florida. He enlisted the aid of another unscrupulous opportunist General James Wilkinson (now the American governor of Louisiana, but still on the Spanish payroll!), and began to make overtures to British and Spanish officials. According to one account, Burr told a British ambassador that for $500,000 he would overthrow the American government, or perhaps create a separate nation in Louisiana and forge a military alliance with the British. Simultaneously, he began recruiting volunteers for his treacherous plans. By 1806, he journeyed north to Lexington, KY to continue eliciting support. Ostensibly, Burr and some 60 men were to rendezvous in Arkansas, where Burr had recently purchased land. However, the plot began to unravel in the Fall of 1806 as rumors and ominous reports of conspiracy and treason reached the White House. Additionally, in Nov. 1806 Jefferson received a letter from Gov. Wilkinson (who sensed the time had come to abandon Burr and avoid possible indictment and arrest) confirming the existence of a plot. In early 1807, Burr discovered Wilkinson's betrayal and attempted to escape from Natchez, Miss. into Spanish Florida. Burr never made it however and upon capture he was transported to Richmond, VA to stand trial for treason and conspiracy. The trial convened in Aug. 1807 with Chief Justice John Marshall (acting in his capacity as circuit judge) presiding. The trial featured disgraceful bias and partisanship on both sides. President Jefferson instructed prosecutors how to proceed against Burr, and offered pardons to material witnesses who would aid in Burr's conviction. Marshall blatantly sided with Burr, even accepting a dinner invitation offered by Burr's lead attorney John Wickham, with Burr in attendance! Not surprisingly, Burr gained acquittal as Marshall applied an extremely strict definition of treason. According to Marshall, treason consists of physical acts against the government, with at least 2 corroborating witnesses. Words alone are not sufficient grounds for conviction. This precedent holds great importance to the present day. (Only 7 convictions from less

*Dueling became so stigmatized in the North that a person killed in a duel might be buried without a coffin with a stake driven through their body, or their corpse hung up in public to rot, or worse still, donated to medical students for research!

than 40 indictments!)

What came next for Aaron Burr? He emigrated to Europe where he spent the next 5 years. On occasion, Burr met with Napoleon, offering to overthrow the U.S. government for large sums of money. His gestures were utterly futile. He returned to New York in 1812 (his indictment for murder had been dropped) and quietly resumed his legal practice. In later years, he constantly mourned the loss of his beloved daughter Theodosia who had disappeared at sea. He walked along New York's Battery for years looking out at the ocean vainly hoping for her return. Eventually, he married his wealthy longtime mistress Betsy Bowen Jumel at the ripe old age of 77, but she soon became disgusted with his extra-marital dalliances and divorced him for adultery. He died alone at the age of 80 wailing to his doctor, "I can't die! I won't die!" Burr's doctor is alleged to have responded, "Mr. Burr, you are already dying." In 1800, Aaron Burr missed becoming president by 1 vote, and for 4 years was a heartbeat away from the presidency.

Jefferson's Second Term

Jefferson had more than just the plots and schemes of Aaron Burr to worry about when his second term began on March 4, 1805. Domestic criticism and foreign crisis made his last 4 years in office extraordinarily difficult. In domestic affairs, Jefferson faced the troubling dilemma of division within his own party. John Randolph, one of Jefferson's staunchest and most effective allies in Congress, began to turn against him in 1804. Randolph, an extreme states' rights advocate, feared both the growth of the United States and the expansion of the federal government. He vowed never to support a new state's admission to the Union because it would infringe upon the rights of the original 13. He proclaimed, "Asking one of the States to surrender part of her sovereignty is like asking a lady to surrender part of her chastity!" A clash with Jefferson over the Yazoo Land Frauds in Georgia (see *Fletcher* vs. *Peck* in Chapter 6) triggered the break in 1804. By 1806, he opposed Jefferson at every turn. What made John Randolph such a formidable opponent?

A descendant of Powhatan and Pocahontas, John Randolph of Roanoke was born into one of the "First Families" of Virginia on June 2, 1773. At age 19, he fell ill to a unknown disease which left him with a soprano voice and without facial hair, giving him a strange adolescent appearance throughout his adult life. However, he possessed a brilliant mind and a gift for savage invective which made him the terror of Congress, which he entered in 1799. An 1854 biographer described Randolph thusly, "Mr. Randolph ever remained a bachelor, and his naturally unamiable temper often became perfectly intolerable, becoming exceedingly abusive in debate....But no man was listened to with more attentive silence in the House or Senate than he." Personally fearless, he fought and won several duels. One of the most notable occurred in 1826 between he and Henry Clay over Randolph's claim that a "corrupt bargain" between Clay and John Quincy Adams had given Adams the presidency in 1824. Randolph also became legendary as a horseman and breeder, once riding nearly non-stop from Charleston, VA (now West Virginia) to Savannah, GA, a distance of about 1,800 miles (one of his horses died during the journey and had to be replaced). When he died, he possessed 180 horses, including 120 "blood-horses." Randolph, often wearing riding boots with spurs and carrying whips, enjoyed attending Congress accompanied by his favorite dogs! Listed below are a few examples of his biting and acidic comments:

On Democracy: "I am an aristocrat. I love liberty, I hate equality."

On the Armed Forces: "Ragamuffins (bums) and mercenaries." When two soldiers tried to provoke him into a fight, he contemptuously referred to them as "puppies" and they retreated. He demanded that President Adams personally apologize for the incident!

On Jefferson's Embargo Policy: "What is it? A milk and water bill…! a dose of chicken broth…." (It is) "attempting to cure corns by cutting off the toes."

On A Proposed Bribe: "I found I might cooperate or be an honest man—I have therefore opposed and will oppose them.

In A Street Confrontation With Henry Clay (1810): While Randolph was walking his dogs on a Washington sidewalk, Henry Clay approached him from the other direction. Upon meeting face to face, Clay taunted Randolph, "I don't make way for dogs." Randolph replied dryly, "I always do," and stepped aside.

Responding to Edward Livingston In Congress: "He shines and stinks like rotten mackerel by moonlight!"

On Politics: "With a superficial and defective education, I commenced a politician."

Responding to a Congressman's statement who declared his "manhood" suspect: "You pride yourself upon an animal faculty, in respect to which the Negro is your equal and the jackass infinitely your superior!"

Responding to another Congressman's statement: "You Sir (referring to Randolph), will die of a terrible venereal disease, or will be hung like a criminal!" Randolph replied, "That depends Sir, on whether I embrace your mistress or your morals."

Randolph in future years denounced both the War of 1812 and military preparedness, and declared that Virginia should immediately leave the Union rather than compromise during the Missouri Crisis of 1820. Randolph degenerated into insanity and died on May 24, 1833. Ironically, Randolph, an ardent defender of state rights in regards to slavery as an institution, never bought or sold slaves. Also, in his will he freed the 383 slaves he had inherited and provided 10 acre lots in Ohio for them. When asked who was the greatest speaker <u>he</u> had ever heard, Randolph responded, "A slave, Sir. She was a mother and her rostrum was the auction block."

The Napoleonic Wars

By 1805, war once again raged through Europe with its concomitant impact on American trade. On Oct. 21, 1805 Napoleon's plans to invade Great Britain were destroyed during the critical naval battle of Trafalgar off the Spanish coast. Six weeks later, Napoleon defeated the combined Austrian and Russian armies at Austerlitz near the city of Vienna. The cumulative result of both battles left Great Britain in control of the sea, and Napoleon in control of large portions of Europe. Disrupting foreign trade and crippling the economy became the only means for either country to inflict damage on the other. To achieve this objective, Napoleon instituted "The Continental System" through the Berlin and Milan Decrees in 1806 and 1807 respectively. This system prohibited any European nation allied with France from trading with Britain, and stipulated that neutral nations attempting to trade with Britain did so at their own risk. Great Britain responded in 1807 with the reciprocating "Orders–In–Council" which forbade neutral nations from trading with France and her allies.

The big losers in this economic war would be neutral countries such as the United States which wished to stay out of the conflict, but to continue trading with the combatants. From 1805 on, the British and French responded just as they had in the 1790s. Both nations seized American ships, and the British impressed American sailors. Between 1805 and 1812, the British and French seized some 1,475 American vessels and confiscated their cargoes. During the same period 42,000 British sailors deserted attempting to escape the hellish conditions of British naval service. (Consider "keelhauling"!) Many of these deserters attempted to become American citizens, and the British responded by impressing 10,000 American sailors into the British Navy. Drastically weakened by Jefferson's cost cutting measures during his first term, the American military and the navy in particular lacked the capability to stop such blatant violations of our neutrality. Negotiations between Britain and the United States in the summer and fall proved utterly fruitless, and American anger and resentment towards the British increased with each reported seizure and kidnapping, culminating with the *Chesapeake* Incident of 1807.

The *Chesapeake* Incident of 1807

On June 22, 1807 the British frigate H.M.S. *Leopard* sailed up to the U.S.S. *Chesapeake* about ten miles off Cape Henry on the Virginia coast. The British vessel commanded by Captain Salusbury Humphrey sent a signal message to the American Captain James Barron demanding that British sailors be allowed to come aboard to search for deserters, specifically a sailor by the name of Jenkin Ratford. Barron refused to allow the search, and subsequently the *Leopard* unleashed a broadside on the *Chesapeake*. The attack killed 3 American sailors, injured 18 (one of the injured Robert MacDonald died on June 27), and seriously damaged the ship. Most of the *Chesapeake's* guns were sealed as she was en route to the Mediterranean Sea on a peaceful assignment. The only shot fired from the *Chesapeake* came as the result of a heroic, though futile gesture by U.S. Lieutenant William Allen. Due to a lack of matches, he hand lit the fuse of a cannon with a piece of burning coal, but the cannonball missed the *Leopard*. Commodore Barron hauled down the U.S. flag, the British boarded at gunpoint, and 3 American sailors and Jenkin Ratford (Ratford's presence was unknown to Barron) were removed. One of the Americans seized was a free black from Massachusetts, David Martin, who presented his U.S. citizenship papers to no avail. Signifying his defeat in the battle, Barron offered Humphrey's his sword. Humphrey's added insult to injury by contemptuously refusing the gesture and departed the *Chesapeake*. When the event became known to the public, American cries for war according to Jefferson rivaled those heard immediately after the confrontations at Lexington and Concord in 1775. Jefferson however did not want war knowing full well the weakness of the American military. He opted instead for an ill-conceived, ineffective, and politically disastrous policy known as "peaceful coercion," with its initial policy of a total embargo of American foreign trade!

Aspects of "Peaceful Coercion" - The Embargo Act of 1807 – Passed on Dec. 22, 1807, this literally prohibited all U.S. trade with foreign nations. Any American vessels still in American ports would by law be stuck there for the duration of the law's existence, in actuality 14 months. The embargo proved disastrous. Although

U.S. imports fell from $138 million to $57 million benefiting native industries, exports fell even more drastically, from $108 million to $22 million. The reason for the remaining revenues could be found in "loopholes" in the law pertaining to "coastal trade" and the retrieval of American goods in foreign ports. Ports were idle, sailors, stevedores, and longshoremen were put out of work, and raw materials rotted unsold in warehouses. As the editor of *The Norfolk Gazette* lamented, "Better, far better would it have been for the nation to have incurred a debt of $100,000,000 or more, for military and naval preparations, than to pursue a policy which leads to national bankruptcy, and to the destruction of all public spirit." Enforcement of the embargo was both lax and next to impossible leading to a huge increase in black market and smuggling operations, especially from New England, America's shipping center. Consequently, the British and French, the chief targets of the embargo were only marginally affected. Finally, the Embargo Act of 1807 gave the dying Federalist party in New England a new lease on life as they could rally support against the ruinous policies of the Dem.-Reps. Like national prohibition over a century later, this act created problems instead of solving them. Repeal of the embargo came in March 1809, just before President-Elect James Madison assumed office. Jefferson now exited the "splendid misery" of the presidency and retired from public life just as John Adams had done.*

   A fitting epilogue to the lives and careers awaited the two former presidents. Adams and Jefferson would repair and rekindle their long friendship which had been strained by intrigue and party politics. They commiserated through a series of remarkable letters beginning in 1812 and lasting until both their deaths on July 4th 1826, the fiftieth anniversary of independence. How appropriate for these two Founding Fathers!

Election of 1808	Party	Electoral Vote	Popular Vote
- James Madison	Dem.-Reps.	122	None
- Charles Pinckney	Federalist	47	

2)– <u>The Non-Intercourse Act (1809)</u> – This act replaced the embargo but was just as objectionable and ineffective. It provided for the reopening of trade between the U.S. and every nation <u>except</u> Britain and France. Trade could be restored to those nations however, if they agreed to respect our rights. Due to Napoleon's stranglehold over Europe, and the extensive colonial empires of both the British and French, there were very few unaffiliated countries or colonies the U.S. could trade with. The British and French scoffed at the act and continued their objectionable practices, receiving all the American goods they needed through smugglers. In addition, Madison briefly reopened trade with the British on June 10, 1809 after assurances were given by the British Foreign Minister David Erskine that the Orders-In-Council would be repealed unconditionally. Erskine had exceeded his instructions however and his superior George Canning recalled him to Britain, the Orders-In-Council still very much in effect. Because Madison had jumped the gun, British warehouses were able to stockpile American goods which made our bargaining position even weaker.

*Jefferson remarked, "Never did a prisoner in chains feel such relief as I shall on shaking off the shackles of power."

Madison ineffectually reinstated non-intercourse towards Britain on Aug. 10th 1810, but was forced to concede failure and repealed the law later that year. It was subsequently replaced by Macon's Bill #2.

3) - <u>Macon's Bill #2</u> (May 1, 1810) – Congress passed this measure which restored trade with all British and French vessels except warships with the provision that the U.S. would boycott France if Britain respected our rights, or the U.S. would boycott Britain if France respected our rights. Napoleon immediately accepted the proposal, agreeing "on paper" to cease the harassment of American shipping, while in reality continuing the confiscations. Seized American vessels were kept in port under "protective custody!" His goal of outmaneuvering the British succeeded as Anglo-American tensions mounted due to restive Indians on the frontier, and continuing maritime clashes. Ironically, Macon's Bill probably would have succeeded if imposed earlier, perhaps even in 1807. Why? By 1811–1812, Britain's economy had been so disrupted by Napoleon's Continental System, that attempts were being made to normalize trade relations with the U.S. In fact, the British rescinded the Orders-In-Council in the Summer of 1812, but by then it was too late. (See "Strange Facts" section on the following page.)

Other Causes of The War of 1812

In addition to British practices on the high seas, there were other significant factors pulling the U.S. into war, especially on the western frontier. The American population continued to grow rapidly, from 3,929,214 in 1790 to 7,239,881 in 1810. Continuing the trend starting in 1607, Americans moved west, establishing 5 states in the Mississippi River region by 1812. Just as in 1607 however, various Indian tribes inhabiting those lands did not react kindly to their displacement. Since the defeat of Little Turtle in 1794, no major Indian leader had emerged to slow American westward expansion. A charismatic Shawnee Indian, Tecumseh, would change that circumstance, albeit briefly.

Tecumseh and Tenskwatawa- "the Prophet"

Tecumseh, the son of a Shawnee brave, assumed the mantle of leadership of the Shawnee in the Ohio region in the first decade of the 1800s. The governor of the Indiana Territory William Henry Harrison once referred to Tecumseh as an "uncommon genius." A dynamic military leader, he aimed to repel the Americans from Shawnee lands. He was greatly aided by a spiritual revival kindled by his half-brother Tenskwatawa, "the Prophet." Tenskwatawa spent most of his youth consumed by alcohol and decadent pursuits, but at age 30 he experienced a revelation which drastically altered his outlook on life. In his visions, he witnessed glimpses of both paradise and perdition along with instructions for redemption. According to "the Prophet," the white man with his alcohol, religion, and institutions had corrupted Indian culture almost to the point of destruction. If allowed to continue, the Indians and their lands would be overrun by the Americans. The only chance for survival lay in returning to the virtues of the past, rejecting and separating themselves from all facets of American culture. Above all, the various Indian tribes needed to establish some form of union, and coordinate military resistance to the American western expansion. In 1811, Tecumseh attempted to facilitate this vision by proposing a confederation of the Shawnee, Chickasaw, Choctaw, Creek, and Cherokee tribes, and purchasing arms from the British in Canada. In the fall of 1811, he left the Shawnee village, "Prophet's Town," on the Tippecanoe River in northwest Indiana, and traveled south to secure the alliance. Before departing however, he warned against attacking the Americans in his absence, fearing a disastrous outcome. 1,100 Americans commanded by Harrison occupied a precarious position near the mouth of the Tippecanoe near the village. Encouraged by their foes apparent weakness, the Indians attacked on Nov. 7, 1811. By day's end nearly 190 of Harrison's men lay dead or wounded, while Shawnee casualties numbered about 130. However, the warriors became disillusioned due to the carnage and retreated into the countryside and Canada. Harrison pressed his advantage and burned Prophet's Town and confiscated its arms, many found to be British made.

The battle proved significant for two main reasons. First, Tecumseh's dream of a Mississippi Indian Confederacy evaporated due to the defeat. Tecumseh would go to Canada only to die at the Battle of the Thames (Oct. 1813) during the War of 1812. The prospect of a united and independent Indian homeland east of the Mississippi River died with him. Unfortunately for the American Indians as a whole, their inability to unify against an ever more powerful and ambitious enemy doomed them to ultimate defeat by 1890. Second, Harrison's seizure of British made weapons after the battle convinced many Americans of British complicity in Indian resistance in the West. War with Britain became ever more likely. What of Tenskwatawa? He fled to Canada, but returned to the United States in 1824 and died ignominiously on a reservation in eastern Kansas in 1836. (See Addendum II, page 256.)

The "War Hawks"

Elected to Congress in 1810, a group of young, fiercely nationalistic individuals derisively nicknamed the "War Hawks" (by John Randolph, who else!) assumed leading roles in steering the country into war. Primarily from the South and West, Congressmen such as Felix Grundy of TN Langdon Cheves of SC, Richard M. Johnson and Henry Clay of KY and John C. Calhoun of SC (Calhoun and Clay would play pivotal roles in American history for the next 40 years) constantly clamored for war on the basis of upholding national honor, obtaining western lands and Canada, and "pacifying" the Indians on the frontier. Their efforts succeeded in the late spring of 1812.

Strange Facts About the War of 1812

The War of 1812, which nearly wrecked the United States, most likely would have been avoided had communication capabilities been more advanced. Consider this:

- On June 16, 1812, the British repealed The Orders-In-Council, though not impressments. Even so, the Orders had been a major point of contention between the two nations.
- On June 18, 1812, Congress declared war, ignorant of the British action. Considering the rather narrow margin with which war was declared (79 to 49 in the House, 19 to 13 in the Senate), knowledge of the repeal of the Orders may have proved decisive.

- The Treaty of Ghent which ended the War on Dec. 24, 1814 stipulated the terms *Status Quo Ante Bellum*, meaning "State of Things Before the War." Nothing which caused the War had been resolved, and no boundaries changed. Other than the costs and casualties involved, it was as if the War that never happened!
- The largest battle of the War, the Battle of New Orleans, took place on Jan. 8, 1815, two weeks after the peace treaty had been signed! The combatants were unaware the conflict was over.

Regardless of the deteriorating international conditions, the United States once again held its quadrennial presidential contest. The Federalists regained some ground politically, almost certainly due to the hardships inflicted upon the U.S. by the Napoleonic Wars and consequent Democratic-Republican enactments and policies. Still, President Madison would be re-elected by a comfortable margin, perhaps owing to a reluctance of the electors to change leaders in the face of the deepening crisis with Great Britain.

Election of 1812	Party	Electoral Vote	Popular Vote
James Madison	Dem.-Rep.	128	None
De Witt Clinton	Federalist	89	

Synopsis of the War of 1812

Strategies	Britain	United States
	1) – Blockade U.S. ports	1) – Invade Canada
	2) – Secure the Great Lakes and invade the Northwest	2) – Secure the Great Lakes and protect the Northwest
	3) – Detach New England from the rest of the U.S.	3) – Repel the British from the Hudson River region
	4) – Invade coastal cities in the Southern U.S.	4) – Repel British invasions in the Southern U.S.

Additionally, the ongoing wars with Napoleon were of the utmost importance to the British during the War of 1812. Indeed, the War of 1812 could be regarded as a costly diversion for Great Britain until Napoleon's initial defeat in the late winter of 1814. The United States for its part entered the War with a tiny army of 6,700 recruits lacking both adequate training and equipment. The officer corps at the onset consisted primarily of old and ill-prepared Revolutionary War veterans, some of whom would give new definition to incompetence. The U.S. Navy by contrast, was reasonably prepared for war, although the entire fleet consisted of only 16 seaworthy vessels. However, three of these ships, the heavy frigates *Constitution*, *President*, and *United States*, would prove more than a match for their British counterparts.

Cowards and Heroes

   Despite the grand plans of the "War Hawks" and other American enthusiasts for the war, very little went according to plan during the first year of the conflict. Indeed, American attempts to invade and conquer Canada met with humiliating defeat due in no small part to the ineptitude, selfishness and perhaps cowardice of certain American commanders and militia units. The War of 1812 without question produced genuine American military heroes, two of whom would later become presidents, but it also produced characters whose conduct in battle could best be characterized as contemptuous. Consider the following incidents:

1) In August 1812 American General William Hull, an old Revolutionary War veteran, commanded 2,000 troops in Detroit. He had marched into Canada but fell back to Detroit citing the "unfriendliness" of the Canadians, and the failure of the Navy to secure Lake Erie. The British forces in the region were led by the intrepid General Isaac Brock (one of the best soldiers the war produced on either side) who immediately rushed to confront Hull. Although outnumbered by the Americans, Brock, surmising the skittishness of his opponent, demanded that Hull surrender. He also hinted that his Indian allies could not be controlled if a battle ensued, and a wholesale massacre of women and children might result if Hull did not capitulate. For hours a terrified Hull sat in camp nervously spattering tobacco juice all over his uniform before deciding to surrender his entire army and the city on Aug. 16, 1812, without firing a shot! By the way, the Indian threat insinuated by Brock was primarily a bluff! Hull was subsequently tried and convicted of cowardice!

2) On Oct. 13, 1812, an American force consisting of U.S. Army regulars and N.Y. state militia was positioned just across the U.S.-Canada border in New York. The American commander General Van Rensselaer ordered an attack on adjacent British positions at Queenston Heights. 600 U.S. Army regulars led by Capt. John E. Wool were initially successful, but when the militia was ordered to reinforce the regulars they refused to budge, claiming they were not obligated to invade a foreign country! The American forces were ripped to pieces while their countrymen looked on obliviously. The battle concluded with the capture of some 900 American troops.

3) In Nov. 1812, 2,000 American troops stationed along the Niagara River were ordered by General Alexander Smyth to board small cockboats on the river for no apparent reason. They were quickly ordered off again. He repeated these orders 3 days later, but this time the soldiers balked at his commands and took potshots at his tent! He fled back to his home in Virginia and was relieved of all military duty.

4) During the invasion of Washington in Aug. 1814, 1,500 British regulars routed 5,000 Virginia and Maryland militia who fled in such haste that only 8 were killed. The only bright spot for the Americans was the performance of 600 U.S. Navy seamen who fired their naval guns until being surrounded. On Aug. 24 the British Admiral Sir John Cockburn and his soldiers occupied the

White House and ate a banquet meal which had been prepared for President Madison and 40 guests, still hot on the spit! Madison and his wife Dolly had fled the building carrying portraits, documents, china, and a parrot! After the meal, the British torched the White House and Washington.

Such disgraceful actions are not recounted to impugn the reputation of American fighting forces. Rather, they provide a useful and necessary contrast to the truly heroic actions of other American soldiers and sailors during the War of 1812. Consider the actions of the following war <u>heroes</u>:

1) On Sept. 10, 1813, Captain Oliver Hazard Perry and his personally designed squadron of ships confronted the British at Lake Put-In-Bay on Lake Erie. Despite his flagship the U.S.S. *Lawrence* losing 80% of its raw recruits killed or wounded, and having all his guns knocked out of operation, Perry and his men refused to quit. They boarded another American vessel and continued the fight, finally bludgeoning the British into surrender. In a famous dispatch, he reported to General William Henry Harrison, "We have met the enemy and he is ours." The victory opened up Upper Canada to an American invasion. Subsequently, on Oct. 5, 1813 at The Battle of the Thames River, General Harrison defeated the British and eliminated the threat to the American northwest frontier. The battle also resulted in the death of Tecumseh, and the disintegration of the Indian alliance in the region.

2) Throughout 1812 and 1813, the U.S. Navy scored a series of stunning victories over their British adversaries in the Atlantic, who since Trafalgar considered themselves invincible. Notable among these include the defeat of the H.M.S. *Guerriere* by the U.S.S. *Constitution* in two and a half hours, the destruction of the H.M.S. *Frolic* by the U.S.S. *Wasp* in less than an hour, and the capture of the H.M.S. *Macedonian* by the U.S.S. *United States*. The *United States* was commanded by Captain Stephen Decatur, a truly heroic commander who first distinguished himself in the campaigns against the Barbary Pirates of North Africa in 1804.

3) On Sept. 11. 1814 Commodore Thomas Macdonough defeated Sir George Prevost commanding over 10,000 British veterans at the Battle of Lake Champlain. A crucial and decisive victory, Macdonough's forces captured 7 British ships and thwarted the British plan to detach New York and New England from the Union.

By 1814, the war had ground into a stalemate. The British were out of the United States, but the Americans had been defeated in Canada. In the summer and fall, the British decided to take advantage of their numerical majority in ships and attack coastal villages and cities. They established themselves in coastal Maine all the way to the Penobscot River, and set up a naval base on Cape Cod. As mentioned previously, they successfully attacked and laid waste to Washington, D.C. and headed up the Chesapeake Bay to attack Baltimore. In addition, American reports suggested (correctly as it turned out) that the British were dispatching an expeditionary force to capture New Orleans. Peace initiatives begun in January had wrought nothing of substance, and the U.S government was running out of money to continue the war. Finally, ominous undercurrents of secession in New England, long opposed to the war, were surfacing.

The fall of 1814 proved the darkest days of the conflict for the U.S. During this period, the most encouraging development took place in Baltimore on Sept. 14–15. Maryland militia units angered by the destruction of Washington and determined to protect the city drove the British out of Baltimore Harbor after a two-day bombardment. The British General Ross, who had boasted to his men that Baltimore would serve as his winter quarters, was killed by an American sharpshooter in front of his troops. An American lawyer, Francis Scott Key, imprisoned on one of the British ships pounding Fort McHenry, patriotically penned "The Star Spangled Banner" which became our national anthem in 1931. Ironically, the music of The Star Spangled Banner was adapted from an old British drinking song "Anacreon In Heaven!" Despite success at Baltimore, the situation remained desperate. Between December 1814 and January 1815, however three events simultaneously took place which would not only end the war but have far reaching political implications for the future.

1) The Hartford Convention - Dec.15, 1814 – Jan. 5, 1815

On Oct. 5, 1814 a group of Massachusetts Federalists disaffected by both the war and Democratic-Republican policies called for the New England states to meet in convention to discuss grievances and demand constitutional changes which would benefit the region. 22 delegates from Mass., Conn., NH VT and RI convened at Hartford, Conn. on Dec. 15, 1814. Delegates included Timothy Pickering, an advocate of secession, and Harrison Gray Otis who led the moderate wing of the Federalists. By Jan. 5, 1815 the delegates had completed their deliberations and set off to Washington with their proposals which consisted of seven proposed amendments to the Constitution.

1)- repeal the 3/5 Compromise and apportion taxes and representation only among freepersons (a policy which would reduce the power of the slave states)
2)- new states could only be admitted to the Union by 2/3 majority vote in both houses of Congress (an attempt to block the admission of new Western states)
3)- embargoes on U.S. ports and citizens could only be imposed for 60 days
4)- a 2/3 majority in Congress would be necessary to suspend trade between the U.S. and foreign nations
5)- with the exception of a foreign invasion of the U.S., a 2/3 majority in Congress would be required to declare war
6)- no naturalized citizen would be permitted to hold any civil office within the

U.S. government (a measure designed to severely limit the political power of immigrants)

7)- no person could serve a second term as president, "nor shall the President be elected from the same state in succession" (an obvious attack on the "Virginia Dynasty")

If these measures were not approved, the New England states reserved the right to hold another convention to consider their alternatives, most likely secession! Three Massachusetts delegates were dispatched to Washington to present the proposals, but they arrived only to find that both a peace treaty had been signed, and American forces under Andrew Jackson had scored a decisive victory over the British at New Orleans. President Madison ignored the delegates and the American press viewed the entire convention as not only ill-conceived but perhaps treasonable. The Federalist party was discredited and virtually destroyed as a result.

2) The Treaty of Ghent

On Dec. 24th 1814 the United States and Great Britain concluded a peace treaty which simply ended the war. The U.S. sent a distinguished set of negotiators, Henry Clay, John Quincy Adams, and Albert Gallatin to Ghent, Belgium, while the British delegation consisted of minor level officials, William Adams, Lord Gambier, and Henry Goulburn. The treaty failed to settle any points of contention concerning neutral rights or impressments, two major causes of the war, and no territorial changes were effected. In fact, the peace agreement seemed to suggest that the conflict had never occurred! Nonetheless, the war was over.

3) The Battle of New Orleans (Jan. 8, 1815)

On Dec. 18, 1814, 8,000 British veterans under the command of Sir Edwin Pakenham arrived off the coast near New Orleans. Pakenham was unaware of the imminent peace treaty and was under orders to seize New Orleans. However, he delayed his attack and wasted valuable time reconnoitering the city and its outskirts. This postponement of battle was due in no small part to arrogance and overconfidence. After all, these troops were battle tested in the Napoleonic Wars. What could a motley crew of Americans do against such an army?! Plenty. The American commander General Andrew Jackson, a proven fighter, mobilized some 7,000 American regular soldiers, militia units, frontiersmen, free blacks, slaves, and pirates to defend the city. Entrenched behind fortifications constructed of dirt, wood, and cotton bales, they awaited Pakenham's assault which finally came on the morning of Jan. 8, 1815. The Americans watched the British march towards them in perfect formation. When they came into range, the Americans unleashed a murderous volley of artillery and rifle shot. By the end of the day the British had 2,000 dead or wounded, including Pakenham, who would be sent back to England in a keg of rum to preserve his body. American casualties were 13 killed, 8 wounded—one of the most one-sided victories in U.S. history! As peace had already been negotiated, the battle had no military consequence. However, victory at New

Orleans made Jackson a great war hero and an attractive political candidate. It also confirmed American independence and provided a great boost to national pride in the wake of a rather unsuccessful war. Finally, it characterized the Hartford Convention as cowardly and treacherous by contrast.

Chapter 6

The "Era of Good Feelings" to the Election of 1828

The Era of Good Feelings 1817–1823

After the war, a wave of nationalism swept the country most notably evidenced in five distinct aspects:

1) - The brief absence of a two-party system
2) - Significant developments in American art and literature
3) - Financial and infrastructure policies beneficial to national economic development
4) - Judicial decisions which strengthened the federal government
5) - Foreign treaties which expanded American borders and interests

Politics

James Monroe, the last of the "Virginia Dynasty," loyally served the U.S. in an impressive succession of positions prior to his election as president. Revolutionary War general, governor of Virginia, senator, diplomat, Sec. of War, and Sec. of State, Monroe was easily selected by the Democratic-Republicans at James Madison's behest. The election, considering the baneful effects of the Hartford Convention on the Federalists, was a foregone conclusion. Although Monroe did not possess the intellectual brilliance of Madison, Jefferson, or Adams, his personality and character seemed perfectly tailored to the mood of the country.

As Jefferson once remarked, "You could turn his (Monroe's) skin inside out and yet not find a blemish on his character." On a post-war goodwill tour of New England, not the friendliest territory for Democratic-Republicans, Monroe impressed and soothed the residents to such an extent that the Federalist newspaper, the *Boston Sentinel*, proclaimed that Monroe's presidency would usher in "an Era of Good Feelings" for the country.

Election of 1816	Party	Electoral Vote	Popular Vote
- James Monroe	Dem.-Reps.	183	None
- Rufus King	Federalist	34	

Fittingly, Monroe reduced partisan tensions by appointing able Federalists and Democratic-Republicans to cabinet positions. Monroe's selection of John Quincy Adams from Massachusetts as Secretary of State (a position which would likely result in Adams becoming the next president) and John C. Calhoun of South Carolina as Secretary of War proved particularly important for two reasons:

1)-It demonstrated Monroe's determination to create a sectional balance within his Cabinet.
2)-Both men accomplished significant feats in their secretarial capacities.

Additionally, Monroe supported moderate policies agreeable to both the remnants of the Federalist Party and the Democratic-Republicans. Preceding Monroe's inauguration, Congress passed two very important financial initiatives. In 1816, it chartered the Second Bank of the United States for the next 20 years. This new bank was capitalized with $35 million, including $7 million provided by the federal government. In return for these government funds, the bank provided several important services such as loans, cash bonuses, and free transactions for the federal government. Like its predecessor, the second B.U.S. (Bank of the United States official abbreviation) was expected to provide a consistent national paper currency, create branches of the B.U.S. throughout the several states, and act as the sole depository for government revenues. The bank acted as a powerful stimulant to nationalism, especially after 1823.

Additionally, the government enacted the Tariff of 1816 which taxed imported items at an average rate of between 20 and 25%. This moderate tariff encountered some opposition from New England shipping interests still mindful of the negative effects of the Embargo of 1807. Some Southerners also protested to the tariff on the grounds that protective tariffs had not been specifically provided for in the Constitution ("strict construction"). Protective tariffs provide different tax rates for different imported items. A high tariff has a strong tendency to discourage a consumer from purchasing a particular imported item due to its price, while making its domestically produced counterpart more affordable. A tariff for revenue would simply tax all imports at the same rate. Finally, as the South imported most of its finished goods, the region would pay the lion's share of the tariff. Nonetheless, the tariff passed largely as the result of post-war patriotism. As South Carolina Rep. John C. Calhoun stated:

> Such, then, being the obvious advantages of internal improvements
> (which tariffs would help pay for), why should the House hesitate
> to commence the system? I understand there are, with some members,
> constitutional objections....I am no advocate for refined arguments on the
> Constitution... It ought to be construed with plain, good sense;"

The Tariff Question

Ironically, John C. Calhoun became a staunch opponent of tariffs by 1828. From that point on Calhoun directed his efforts towards Southern rights. To defend the South, Calhoun became the greatest and most influential proponent of strict construction of the Constitution and states rights. In short, his sentiments changed from nationalism to sectionalism. Why? What changed his mind about tariffs?

By the end of the 1820s, the economy of the Atlantic Coast South (VA, NC, SC, and GA) was in serious decline due to a variety of factors. Most Southerners however blamed tariff policies. They became convinced that high tariffs were detrimental to their export based economy. As the agricultural South possessed very few factories, Southerners purchased manufactured goods from the Northern States or Europe. As such, they desired inexpensive, high quality items from any available source, domestic or foreign. For example, if an iron plow blade manufactured in Great Britain sold for less than a similar quality blade produced in Massachusetts, Southerners would usually purchase the British product. Protective tariffs however drove up prices for imported manufactured goods. (See next page)

Example

British Plow Blade - Without Tariff - $10.00   **Massachusetts Plow Blade - $11.50**
- With 25% Tariff - $12.50

Thus, tariffs forced Southern customers into paying higher prices, regardless of whether they purchased imports or American made products. Southerners also believed that tariffs discouraged foreign nations from purchasing the agricultural staples produced in the South such as tobacco, rice, and especially cotton. Northern manufacturers conversely felt that tariffs were necessary to protect them from a massive influx of cheap overseas goods which could destroy their businesses. Disputes over tariff policy divided the sections all the way to the War Between The States (the Civil War) in 1861. Indeed, the tariff issue carried well into the 20th Century!

Art and Literature

During the "Era of Good Feelings," American authors produced significant works of art and literature which reflected American themes and topics. James Fennimore Cooper's *The Last of the Mohicans* and Washington Irving's *Rip Van Winkle* are good examples of this nationalistic trend. While written in styles nearly identical to contemporary European authors, the subject matter of both stories (Indians and a sleepy American respectively) is purely American. Cooper and Irving both conveyed that America topics were worthy of serious literary effort.

In art, most American painters and artists adhered to European neoclassicism, the predominant style of the period. However in the 1820s, a new, more romantic trend in American art developed. Known as the Hudson River School, artists such as Thomas Cole concentrated on landscapes attempting to capture the unique beauty and expanse of the American wilderness.

Infrastructure Developments

The War of 1812 exposed the inadequate and dilapidated condition of many American roads, canals, and harbor structures. Underscoring these deficiencies, the federal government initiated its "Third System" of coastal fortifications in 1816. (Construction of the First System began in 1794; the Second System in 1807.) Ultimately, 38 new or improved forts were planned for this Third System, stretching from Ft. Knox in Maine to Ft. Alcatraz in California (ironically not even American territory in 1816). The most famous fort in the Third System was (is) Ft. Sumter in South Carolina, constructed from 1829 to 1860. In North Carolina, Third System fortifications include Ft. Caswell on Oak Island (built 1826–1838), and the beautifully restored Ft. Macon near Atlantic Beach (built 1826–1834).

Also, in the 1810s and especially the 1820s, various states and private companies undertook projects to improve the nation's infrastructure. The federal government, despite the urgings of Henry Clay of Kentucky (the architect of the proposed "American System") and John C. Calhoun, only timidly sponsored major construction projects. The most significant federal project was the National Road begun in 1811 at Cumberland, MD. It extended westward to Wheeling, VA (now West Virginia) by 1818. Major improvements and additions to the road resumed in 1825, and by 1838 it reached well into Illinois, terminating in Vandalia, Ill. Existing major roads, such as the First Post Road (today U.S. 17) which ran north-south down the east coast were also upgraded. State sponsored canal construction began in earnest in 1817 when the state of New York began the Erie Canal project which would link the Hudson River to Buffalo, a distance of 363 miles. Prior to this date, less than 100 miles of canals existed in the entire nation! Its completion in 1825 was marked by a ceremony in which Gov. Dewitt Clinton poured 5 gallons of water from Lake Erie into the Atlantic to symbolize the connection between New York City and the West. The subsequent profitability of the Erie Canal sparked a canal building boom, especially in the North. Other notable canal projects included the Ohio and Erie (completed in 1832), the Wabash and Erie and Miami and Erie (18450, and the Illinois and Michigan (1848). The South, with its ample navigable rivers connected to ocean ports such as Charleston, Savannah, Wilmington, and Norfolk, had <u>relatively</u> little interest in major canals (although the Great Dismal Swamp Canal, opened in 1805 and deepened in 1829, linking southeastern VA with northeastern North Carolina had a significant economic impact on both regions). By 1840, 3,326 miles of canals had been constructed. After 1840 however, railroads would begin to surpass canals in commercial importance. (By the way, in 1840 the world's longest railroad at 161 ½ miles was just completed linking Wilmington, NC and Weldon, NC) Finally, on the coast, numerous lighthouses were constructed or improved upon for both navigation and defense purposes. The Smith Island Light ("Old Baldy") was constructed in 1817 (for $16,000) to protect ships entering the Cape Fear River. It is the oldest standing lighthouse in North Carolina The second oldest lighthouse still in service on the East Coast was constructed on Ocracoke Island, NC in 1823. Both structures are prime examples of early 19th century "internal improvements."

Judicial Nationalism Under The Marshall Court

During John Marshall's tenure as Chief Justice of the Supreme Court (1801–1835), the power of the federal government and the rights of individual citizens were consistently expanded at the expense of the states. Decisions rendered during this period have had an enormous impact on social and political issues to the present day. Why?

1) - The authority of the Supreme Court has continuously increased. (Consider the presidential election of 2000 for instance.)

2) - The federal government's influence in the states has greatly increased. (Consider federal regulations concerning religious exercises, social and sexual activities, commerce, school practices, speed limits, and hundreds of other examples.)

3) - States' rights doctrines (especially after 1865) have been consistently refuted, usually by Supreme Court actions, though recently the Court has sided with the states in a few decisions.

4) - There is no practicable check on a Supreme Court decision once it is rendered. In effect, such rulings can only be voided by subsequent Supreme Court decisions, or by amending the Constitution itself.

Notable Court Cases 1803–1824

1) - *Marbury* v. *Madison* (1803) - Marshall establishes the precedent of <u>judicial review</u> (the ability to determine a law's constitutionality) of <u>federal</u> laws.

2) - *Fletcher* v. *Peck* (1810) - The Court orders that states cannot renege on contractual obligations with citizens, in this case, a contested land sale in Georgia. In <u>Peck</u>, the Court asserted the right of judicial review over <u>state laws</u>.*

3) - *McCulloch* v. *Maryland* (1819) – After the state of Maryland passed a law to tax transactions conducted by branches of the B.U.S within its borders, a self-interested and rather unethical bank official, James McCulloch, at the Baltimore branch refused to pay the tax and brought suit to the Supreme Court. The Court ruled that the B.U.S was constitutional under the "Necessary and Proper" clause, but more significantly, the Court declared the federal government and its creations are supreme to the states. (Article VI, Cl. 2) As such the B.U.S could not be taxed by Maryland because as Marshall stated, "the power to tax is the power to destroy."

4) - *Cohens* v. *Virginia* (1821) - The case emanated from Cohen's attempt to establish a privately run lottery in Virginia. Virginia rejected his plan, and even though Marshall upheld Virginia in the case, the Court extended its power of judicial review to the decisions of <u>state courts</u>.

5) - *Gibbons* v. *Ogden* (1824) - This case involved a dispute between two ferry operators in New York Harbor. Aaron Ogden possessed a N.Y. state license to run his service, while Thomas Gibbons obtained a coasting license issued by the government.** The Court held in favor of Gibbons and asserted that the federal government had the sole authority to regulate interstate commerce. (Think of how broadly that power can be expanded! The Federal Communications Commission is a good example. It regulates television and radio programming based on air waves broadcast over state lines!)

In summary, John Marshall was committed to strengthening the federal government, and fostering nationalism. According to Marshall:

> That the United States form, for many, and for most important purposes, a single nation, has not been denied. In war, we are one people. In making peace, we are one people. In all commercial relations, we are one and the same people. In many other respects, the American people are one; and the government which is alone capable of controlling and managing their interests in all these respects, is the government of the Union.

Marshall exerted extraordinary influence over his fellow jurors. In 34 years as Chief Justice, Marshall wrote 519 of the 1,106 majority opinions issued by the Supreme Court. He found himself in opposition to the majority on <u>only 8 occasions</u>!

Foreign Affairs 1816–1824

Prior to 1820, the attention of the United States in foreign affairs centered on Florida, her mother country Spain, and the Western Hemisphere in general. The situation in Florida had become increasingly compelling after West Florida (coastal

*A precedent for this ruling had actually been issued by the Supreme Court in the case *Ware v. Hilton* (1796).

**Interestingly, Gibbons and Ogden had started out as partners but had become estranged due to Ogden's treatment of Gibbon's married daughter. After the case, Gibbons became a millionaire, while Ogden languished for a while near bankruptcy, eventually becoming a customs collector in New Jersey.

Mississippi and Alabama) rebelled against Spanish rule and proclaimed independence in 1810. West Florida subsequently joined the U.S. in 1813. Additionally, Florida had long been a haven for Seminole Indians (Seminole is a Creek word meaning "renegade" or "runaway"), pirates, renegades, runaway slaves, hostile Spaniards, and British plotters who periodically raided American frontier settlements along the southeast coast. In late 1816, the Seminoles, with the unofficial blessing of a Scottish trader Alexander Arbuthnot, declared that treaties ceding Creek lands to the U.S. in 1814 were void. (Similar contentions had been made in 1815 by a British veteran of the Battle of New Orleans, Lt. Colonel Nicholls.) Concurrently, a former soldier under Nicholls, Robert Ambrister, arrived in Florida eager for fortune and adventure. He joined up with a contingent of Seminoles under the leadership of Chief Billy Bowlegs with the intention of establishing some sort of settlement with the backing of both the Seminole Indians, and a group of pirates located on Amelia Island on Florida's east coast.

By 1817 various Seminole groups began to settle on former Creek lands inside U.S. territory. Angry American settlers clashed with Seminoles and President Monroe authorized Sec. of War John C. Calhoun to send General Andrew Jackson into Florida to subdue the Seminoles and their allies, but not to attack any Spanish outpost. Jackson resented any such restriction and asked for unofficial permission to exceed his orders. He may have received authorization through a mysterious communiqué, the Rhea Letter, named for Rep. John Rhea of TN In the meantime however, two Seminole chieftains, Himollemico and Hillis Hago, ambushed a detachment of Jackson's troops, prompting a furious pursuit and reprisal by Jackson. Jackson chased the Seminoles to the Spanish outpost of St. Marks. He quickly occupied the Spanish installation, lowered the Spanish flag, and hanged the two chiefs. In addition, Jackson captured Arbuthnot as he was attempting to flee St. Marks, and held him for questioning. Jackson's next move was to push east to capture Billy Bowlegs at the Suwanee River. Jackson failed, but managed to capture Ambrister who wandered into Jackson's encampment. Unfortunately for Ambrister, a letter from Arbuthnot was discovered on one of his aides. The letter, intended for Billy Bowlegs, included information concerning Jackson's plans, and an offering of gunpowder for military use against Jackson.

Returning to St. Marks, Jackson convened a court martial for both men, charging Arbuthnot with espionage and incitement, and Ambrister with conducting war against the United States. Both were ultimately executed, Ambrister by firing squad and Arbuthnot by hanging. Predictably, the Spanish were outraged as were the British (though they would not react in such a way as to seriously jeopardize Anglo-American trade), and certain prominent government figures such as Speaker of the House Henry Clay, Sec. of Treasury William Crawford, and Sec. of War Calhoun contemplated reprimanding Jackson. Calhoun had the most legitimate grievance as Jackson had exceeded his official instructions. Sec. of State John Quincy Adams (John Adams' son) wisely resisted such actions as he saw an opportunity to compel the Spanish to sell Florida to the U.S. He subsequently blamed the Spanish for failing to maintain order in Florida, stating to the Spanish foreign minister Luis de Onís y González that the U.S. would do so if the Spanish could not. The result was the Adams-Onís Treaty of 1819, a resounding success for American diplomacy.

The treaty had 5 major provisions:

1) The U.S. pays American citizens $5 million in damage claims held against Spain.
2) Florida becomes U.S. territory.
3) The western boundary of the Louisiana Purchase extends to the Pacific at the 42nd Parallel.
4) The U.S. relinquishes its claims to Texas.
5) Spain gives up its claims to the Oregon Territory.

Relations with the British were more amicable due in part to the prudent leadership exhibited by Foreign Secretary Lord Castlereagh. As a result, new treaties between the U.S. and Britain were concluded.

1) The Rush-Bagot Treaty of 1817 demilitarized the Great Lakes. By 1872, the U.S. and Canada would share the longest demilitarized border in the world.

2) The Convention of 1818 set the U.S.-Canada border at the 49th Parallel from Lake of the Woods (near 95 degrees longitude) to the eastern slopes of the Rocky Mountains, and provided for joint Anglo-British occupation of the Oregon Territory for 10 years. This treaty would be renewed in 1827.

The Monroe-Adams Doctrine

The fate of newly independent South American republics became an important international issue in the early 1820s. In rapid succession, Spain lost all her American colonies except Cuba between 1811 and 1822. In their efforts to undue the revolutionary fervor caused by Napoleon, the major European powers of Austria, Prussia, and especially Russia (the "Holy Alliance") largely supported Spain's desire to restore her colonial empire, even to the point of possible joint military action within the Western Hemisphere. The British were strongly opposed to such a policy as the new republics were becoming excellent customers for British products. If they were once again placed under Spanish rule, these commercial opportunities might vanish. The United States opposed the reassertion of Spanish authority for the same reason. Also, the U.S. feared any massive new European intervention in the hemisphere, as such actions might jeopardize our national security. In the early 1820s, this appeared a real possibility. On Sept. 4, 1821, Czar Alexander I of Russia claimed the 51st Parallel—Russian Alaska's southern border, an area which overlapped into the Oregon Territory. Secretary of State J.Q. Adams strongly protested to the Russian foreign minister in 1823, that, "the American continents were no longer subject for any new European colonial establishments."

Much more ominously, encouraged by the Holy Alliance the French invaded Spain in 1823 to re-establish royal rule. They easily restored the traditional powers of the Spanish King, Ferdinand VII. Would they restore his control over South America? The prospect alarmed the new British Foreign Minister George Canning and his American counterpart John Quincy Adams. Canning proposed to Richard Rush, the American minister to London, that the U.S. and Great Britain issue a joint declaration condemning any European attempt to reclaim Spain's former colonies. Although on the surface Canning's overture seemed reasonable (indeed, former Presidents Madison and Jefferson supported it), Sec. Adams strongly advised against a joint statement. Why? Adams knew that regardless of any official statement, the British Navy would prevent any such reclamation. Also, Adams felt that a joint declaration would make the U.S. appear a junior partner to Great Britain, damaging our prestige in the Americas and virtually tying us to British foreign policy initiatives in the future. Adams proclaimed on Nov. 7, 1823, that, "It would be more candid, as well as more dignified, to avow _our_ principles explicitly to Great Britain and France, than to come in as a cockboat in the wake of the British man-of-war." On Dec. 2, 1823, Pres. Monroe delivered his annual message to Congress and outlined the foreign policy principles now referred to as the Monroe-Adams Doctrine. It contained 4 basic points:

1) No further European colonization in the Western Hemisphere
2) The U.S. will not intervene in European affairs
3) The U.S. will not interfere with existing European colonies in this hemisphere
4) No European intervention in this hemisphere, as this would threaten our national security

The Monroe-Adams Doctrine in 1823 proved largely symbolic as the U.S. possessed no enforcement power. However, by the late 1800s, the doctrine became a cornerstone in our foreign policy in the Western Hemisphere which continues to the present.*

Domestic Affairs 1819–1824
James Monroe's tenure as president witnessed a great degree of political and regional harmony. Consider the absence of the Two-Party System in the Election of 1820:

Election of 1820	Party	Electoral Vote	Popular Vote
James Monroe	Dem.-Rep.	231	None
John Quincy Adams	Independent-Rep.	1**	

However, 2 events occurred in 1819 which revealed the sectional tensions just beneath the surface of the nation's cultural landscape. The issues raised at this time presented themselves repeatedly, and with ever increasing intensity over the next 4 decades.

The Panic of 1819
During the 19th century the economy of the United States entered into periods of both expansion ("boom") and contraction ("bust"). After the War of 1812, the economy grew at a rapid pace due to land sales in the West and the artificially high importation of American agricultural goods by various European nations. It would

*For example, as early as 1842, President John Tyler invoked the Monroe –Adams Doctrine to the Hawaiian Islands, claiming that they were an independent nation in the Western Hemisphere and thus off limits to European colonization!
** It was agreed that 1 electoral vote should go to JQ Adams so that George Washington would be the only president elected unanimously! That vote came from a New Hampshire elector.

take time for Europe's agricultural production to recover in the wake of the Napoleonic Wars. This recovery occurred by 1819, and both agricultural prices (especially in wheat and cotton) and European purchases of American staples began to decline. There were also crop failures in the mid-teens, the most exceptional of which took place in 1816, the "Year of No Summer."*

Additionally, the booming land sale market rapidly collapsed. It had been fueled by land speculation, that is the purchase of land by investors for the purpose of resale at considerable profit. This process is nearly identical to investing in the stock market today. Furthermore, many speculators borrowed the money to purchase land from banks eager to collect interest payments. Many of these banks recklessly issued loans in excess of their actual assets which put them at considerable risk of bankruptcy. The B.U.S. was heavily involved in such perilous loans, both to individuals and to smaller state banks.

The problem with land speculation lay in the relative lack of settlers to purchase property from the speculators. In other words, westward settlement, though rapid, was not swift enough to suit the speculators designs, and they were left with property but few buyers. Speculators could not pay back their loans to the banks resulting in bank failures which ruined thousands of depositors. To make matters worse, the B.U.S. to avert bankruptcy began calling in its loans, foreclosing on farms, businesses, and state banks which owed it money. It found itself the unwilling owner of dozens of businesses, from motels to livery stables, while the previous owners sank into financial collapse. Finally, the entire problem was exacerbated by the Land Act of 1804 which required purchases of large parcels (164 acres) of public land thus requiring relatively large sums of money. The Land Act of 1820 attempted to remedy this situation by lowering the price of land, reducing to 80 acres the minimum acreage for purchase, and abolishing the installment payment plan. Business slowdowns inevitably produce frictions between both groups and regions. In the case of the latter, Southerners and Westerners blamed the North for supporting tariffs, which they believed caused the decline in European purchases of American agricultural goods. The B.U.S. was also singled out as a "monster" which contracted credit at the precise time it was needed most. Northerners blamed the South and West for blocking increased tariffs, a measure which Northern manufacturers felt vital to slow down the importation of inexpensive British goods. Although the Panic of 1819 abated by the mid-1820s, sectional resentment persisted for years afterwards.

The Missouri Crisis of 1820

In the period between 1791 and 1819, the population of the free states gradually surpassed that of the slave states. By 1819, the free states' population stood at 5,152,000, while the slave states' population numbered 4,485,000. This difference manifested itself in the growing power of the North in the House of Representatives. The North had 105 Representatives, while the South had 81. Sectional balance was maintained in the Senate however, as there were 11 free states and 11 slave states. Sectional tensions erupted in Feb. 1819 when Missouri petitioned for admission to the Union having met the 60,000 inhabitant requirement. It seemed entirely predictable that Missouri, bordering the slave states Kentucky and Tennessee and

*This climate anomaly, most keenly felt in New England, was caused by a massive volcanic eruption (Mt. Tambora) in Indonesia on April 10th, 1815.

including some 10,000 slaves, would encounter little difficulty in entering the Union as a slave state. However, a little known, though earnestly anti-slavery representative from NY, James Tallmadge, added an amendment to Missouri's petition calling for the gradual abolition of slavery as a condition for statehood. The Tallmadge Amendment stipulated that no additional slaves could be brought into Missouri, and those born in Missouri after statehood would be emancipated at age 25. The vote was cast almost exclusively on sectional lines, with the amendment passing in the Northern controlled House but failing in the evenly balanced Senate where Southerners exerted slightly greater influence. Congress adjourned with the matter unresolved, reconvening in Dec. 1819.

The debates, reflecting sectional interests and constitutional issues, grew increasingly heated and bitter. Northern Congressmen denounced Southerners as entrepreneurs of human chattel, "raised like black cattle and horses on plantations," while Southerners warned of possible civil war. Howell Cobb of Georgia declared, "You are kindling a fire which all the waters of the ocean cannot extinguish. It can only be extinguished in blood!" Both sides threatened secession if their demands were not met. Most of the arguments centered on constitutional grounds however. Northerners vented their continuing resentment at the 3/5 Compromise, and Rufus King of NY correctly asserted that the Congress in 1787 prohibited slavery in the Northwest Territory. Southerners countered that in 1787, the United States was governed under the Articles of Confederation; in 1819, the Constitution acted as the supreme law of the U.S., and the 5th Amendment stated that no person "shall be deprived of life, liberty, or property (such as slaves) without due process of law." Southerners claimed they could carry their slaves as property into the western territories. In addition, William Pinckney of Maryland declared that Congress did not possess the right to place additional restrictions or qualifications on new states entering the Union.

In 1819, the District of Maine petitioned to detach itself from Massachusetts and be admitted to the Union as a free state, possibly providing a solution to the impasse. "Mainers" had long resented the Massachusetts legislature's neglect, if not contempt, for the northern district, exemplified by the apparent willingness to abandon Maine to British invaders during the War of 1812. The admittance of slave state Missouri and free state Maine became politically linked and much more acceptable to all parties as the balance in the Senate would be maintained. In addition to Missouri and Maine becoming states, southern born Sen. Jesse Thomas of Ill. proposed that in the future, slavery be forever prohibited in that portion of the Louisiana Purchase north of the 36 degree, 30 minute line, but permitted south of that line. Henry Clay threw his considerable influence behind the "Missouri Compromise," and it passed in the spring of 1820. (The intractable John Randolph declared that no compromise was acceptable, and that the South should immediately leave the Union!) Maine became a state on March 15, 1820, and Missouri followed on Aug. 10, 1821. Seemingly, the crisis had been solved, but consider the following questions. What would happen if the United States were to expand beyond the Louisiana Purchase? Would the 36 degree 30 minute line also be extended? In regards to Congress' role in territorial settlement, which side held the stronger constitutional position? The aging Virginian Thomas Jefferson wrote congressman John Holmes presciently, "This momentous question, like a fire-bell in the night , awakened and filled me with terror. I considered it at once as the knell of the Union. It is hushed, indeed, for the moment. But this is a reprieve only, not a final sentence." (See p. 84 for the admission dates for states prior to 1861.)

Free States – Slave States Entering the Union 1790–1861

Free States – Entry Date		Slave States – Entry Date	
Vermont	1791	Kentucky	1792
Ohio	1803	Tennessee	1796
Indiana	1816	Louisiana	1812
Illinois	1818	Mississippi	1817
Maine	1820	Alabama	1819
Michigan	1837	Missouri	1821
Iowa	1846	Arkansas	1836
Wisconsin	1848	Florida	1845
		Texas	1845

In 1849, there were <u>15 Free States</u> and <u>15 Slave States</u> comprising the Union.

California	1850	
Minnesota	1858	
Oregon	1859	No new Slave States admitted
Kansas	1861	

Politics 1824–1829 – The Election of 1824

The Election of 1824 proved to be one of the more interesting in U.S. history due to the number of candidates and the controversial nature of the outcome. Also, all of the candidates were members of the same party, the Democratic-Republicans, making this the first and only single party presidential election in American history. The issues however were not particularly riveting. The following list outlines these issues, the candidates respective positions, and the region where each candidate enjoyed the most support.

Candidates	Internal Improvements	Tariffs	Caucus System*
-John Q. Adams (New England)	Supported	Supported	Opposed
-Andrew Jackson (The West)	Unknown	Unknown	Opposed
-William Crawford (Georgia)	Opposed	Opposed	Supported
-Henry Clay (The West)	Supported	Supported	Opposed
-John C. Calhoun (Vice Presidential candidate on both the Adams and Jackson tickets. As such, it was very likely that he would become Vice President.)	Supported	Supported	Opposed

*The caucus system was an early method for the selection of presidential candidates. A good definition of a caucus is provided in the 2001 edition of Webster's II New College Dictionary. A caucus is "a closed meeting of the members of a political party to make policy decisions and select candidates for office."

The Initial Results	Electoral Vote	Popular Vote
Andrew Jackson	99 (38%)	154,544 (43%)
John Quincy Adams	84 (32%)	108,740 (31%)
William Crawford	41 (16%)	46,618 (13%)
Henry Clay	37 (14%)	47,136 (13%)

Andrew Jackson possessed a plurality (the largest number) in both the popular and electoral vote. (Note - This is the first presidential election in U.S. history which featured the popular vote.) However, Jackson did not possess the necessary majority (1 more than 50%) of the electoral vote. Similar to the Election of 1800, the contest now devolved to the House of Representatives. Unlike that previous election, three candidates, Jackson, Adams, and Crawford, would vie for the presidency instead of two. (The 12th Amendment to the Constitution provides that only the top three candidates according to the electoral vote be considered.) However, William Crawford's health eliminated him from serious consideration; in 1823, he suffered a debilitating stroke from which he never fully recovered.

Though disqualified himself, Henry Clay proved the key to the election. Clay wielded decisive influence as the sitting Speaker of the House. He subsequently threw his support to Adams. Why? He viewed Jackson as his political rival in the West, and also felt that Adams was more supportive of his "American System" of moderate tariffs and internal improvements. On Feb. 9, 1825, John Quincy Adams carried 13 states, Jackson 7, and Crawford 4, and thus became the sixth president much to the disgust of Jackson and his followers who claimed that the election had been stolen from the American people. When Adams subsequently chose Clay as his Sec. of State, the "Jacksonians" howled "Corrupt Bargain!", an unsubstantiated charge which nonetheless seriously damaged the Adams Administration over the next 4 years. According to Jackson, "the Judas of the West (Clay) closed the contract and will receive the 30 pieces of silver. His end will be the same." John Randolph was particularly damning in his attacks, claiming Adams and Clay were "the coalition of Blifil and Black George (villains from Henry Fielding's novel *Tom Jones*) – the combination, unheard of till then, of the puritan with the black-leg." Angered over such insults, Clay challenged Randolph to a duel which took place on April 8, 1826 at Pimmit Run, VA However, neither man was injured in the duel. Why? Clay's shot at Randolph went through the folds of Randolph's ridiculously oversized white morning gown, and Randolph, who had no intention of hurting his adversary, deliberately shot over Clay's shoulder!

President John Quincy Adams - 1825–1829

John Quincy Adams spent nearly his entire adult life in the service of his country, as a diplomat, Congressman, and most brilliantly as Monroe's Secretary of State. Although erudite, extraordinarily intelligent, and hardworking, he possessed little personal charm, humor, or warmth. While many of his contemporaries respected his abilities and accomplishments, he nevertheless was considered distant if not unfriendly. Adams seemed to confirm these observations when he described himself as "…a man of reserved, cold, austere, and forbidding manners." Additionally, Adams seemed almost belligerently out of touch with the changing political and social realities in the nation. At the precise time when voting rights were being extended to nearly all white males, Adams proclaimed that government and its officials should not be "palsied by the will of our constituents." (In other words, pass legislation that may be good for the country regardless of what the voters say!) Adams also refused to countenance political patronage, the dispensing of government jobs based simply on party support. Throughout his presidency, only 12 government officials lost their positions. Last but not least, Adams introduced a comprehensive plan to Congress in December 1825 for tariff increases, road construction and other internal improvements, a Department of the Interior to rationally manage public lands, Indian removal on a voluntary basis with compensation, and the establishment of a naval academy, a national university, and, national observatories, conservatories, and science centers!

Although Adam's ideas would have considerable merit in the future, contemporary Americans and most of their representatives in Congress could neither conceive of or find desirable a plan which would so drastically increase the size and authority of the federal government. It is important to note that Adam's proposals were aimed at Congress only; he made no serious effort to enlist the support of the American people. Apart from his infrequent visits with his wife and children, Adam's would spend his White House years for the most part lonely and friendless. His daily routine usually consisted of nude swims in the Potomac River between 4 and 6 A.M.,pre-breakfast Bible and newspaper readings, daily diary entries, and intense labor at his presidential duties. Once, while Adam's was enjoying one of his morning swims an intrepid female reporter sat on his clothes in order to force an interview out of the reluctant president!

Indian Affairs

Adams was somewhat sympathetic to the various Indian tribes and sought to deal with them in an honorable manner. As a result, he aroused considerable political opposition for this position. In 1826, he had a showdown with Georgia Governor George Troup over a treaty (the Treaty of Indian Springs) with the Creeks in that state. The treaty stipulated that the Creeks would cede over 4.5 million acres of land in Georgia. Adams signed this treaty in accordance with the 1802 agreement between the federal government and Georgia. In that agreement ,Georgia gave up its western lands in exchange for title to Indian lands within the state. However, the Treaty of Indian Springs was concluded under extremely dubious pretenses, and Adams rescinded his approval in order to negotiate a more equitable agreement; the result was the Treaty of Washington. An outraged Gov. Troup mobilized the state militia and threatened military action if the federal government attempted to abrogate the earlier treaty. Adams backed down and the Creeks were expelled. The incident made Adams appear weak, and had the practical effect of a state nullifying a federal treaty.

The Panama Congress of 1826

Adams responded favorably to an invitation by the newly independent South American republics for the United States to attend a conference in Panama to discuss mutual economic interests, and agreed to send two delegates. Seeking to embarrass Adams, pro-Jackson forces in Congress objected to U.S. involvement, denouncing "entangling alliances", and claiming that participation may block the possible future annexation of Cuba by the U.S. In addition, Southerners disapproved of U.S. officials meeting with the black representatives from Haiti. Eventually, the two delegates were dispatched. One died en route, and the conference had adjourned by the time the other delegate arrived!

The West Indies

Adams attempted to negotiate with the British to reopen American commerce with the West Indies (Bermuda, the Bahamas, Jamaica, and other islands). The U.S. had virtually been excluded from the lucrative island trade since 1776. However, the British foreign minister Lord Canning, embittered over the Monroe-Adams Doctrine, rebuffed Adams gestures. This especially humiliated Adams, as he was best known for his expertise in foreign affairs.

The "Tariff of Abominations"

In 1828 New England textile manufacturers proposed a new, much higher tariff bill seeking protection from European competitors. To bypass Southern opposition, the New Englanders courted various Northern and Western states by supporting exorbitant duties on goods produced in those regions.

Region	Items For Tariff Protection
Northeast	Factory Products
New Hampshire	Silk
New York	Wool
West	Fur, Lead
Kentucky	Hemp

Tariff rates averaged between 45% and 60%, or $.45 to $.60 added to every $1.00! Southern congressmen were predictably outraged at this tariff proposal for a variety of reasons. As mentioned previously, they knew that as the South was the primary customer for imported goods, the region's inhabitants would supply a disproportionate share of the proposed tariff's revenues. They also objected to the measure as they construed (correctly as it turned out), that most of the proceeds of the tariff would be diverted to infrastructure projects in the Northern states;* and again, many Southern leaders, most importantly John C. Calhoun, contended that protective tariffs were unconstitutional. Tariffs are authorized in Article I, Sec. 8, Cl. 2 of the Constitution ("The Congress shall have Power To lay and collect Taxes, Duties, Imposts, and Excises to pay the Debts and provide for the common Defence and general Welfare of the United States;") However, protective tariffs, that is tariffs which have different rates for different products to deter Americans from purchasing certain imported items, are not mentioned. (For example, imposing a 25% tariff on the British plow blade, but no tariff at all on British plows.) Calhoun and other detractors of protective tariffs claimed that tariffs for revenue alone were legally sanctioned by the Constitution. The difference? A tariff designed specifically for revenue purposes would impose a singular rate on all imported items.

In Congress, Southern opponents of the bill felt the tariff would never be passed as proposed, and thus decided to resist any attempt to lower tariff rates on any specific items. To the South's horror, the tariff was approved due to Daniel Webster's lobbying efforts and Pres. Adam's reluctant support. Flags in the South were flown at half-mast and Vice President Calhoun anonymously wrote "The South Carolina Exposition and Protest" which proposed nullification as a possible remedy. This doctrine would later be refined by Calhoun, and utilized by South Carolina in 1832, prompting a national crisis.

*For example, between 1789 and 1845, only 20% of the projects (roads, lighthouses, forts, etc...) paid for by the tariff were allocated for the Southern States, and yet by 1860, Southerners paid 75% of the nation's tariff bill!

Chapter 7

Andrew Jackson and the Rise of Sectionalism

The Election of 1828

This election, pitting Pres. Adams against Andrew Jackson, stands as one of the most bitter and rudely fought political contests in American history, marked by character assassination on both sides. Although there were significant political differences between the candidates, the main issue in the election seemed to be the candidates' personalities. Jackson, whose <u>1792</u> marriage* to Rachel Robards was tainted due to her failure to obtain official divorce papers, was attacked as a "whore-monger", "a paramour, and a consort to a common prostitute." His mother likewise was libeled as a whore catering to British soldiers during the Revolution! He was also referred to as a plotter in league with Aaron Burr, and an ignorant brute prone to murdering American soldiers, political opponents, and innocent civilians alike. (These actions were propagandized in the "Coffin Handbills.") The "Jacksonians" responded in kind however, claiming that Adams was a corrupt career politician (the "Corrupt Bargain"), a misanthrope (hater of humanity), and a pimp who delivered a beautiful young American girl to Russian Tsar Alexander I for sexual purposes in exchange for diplomatic favors!

The outcome was not particularly close as Jackson carried the South, West, Pennsylvania, and most of New York, while Adams carried only New England, New Jersey, Delaware, and most of Maryland. An interesting footnote to the election was the action of John C. Calhoun, Adam's Vice President, who switched over to Jackson and became <u>his</u> Vice President. More significantly, the country was rapidly extending suffrage rights to nearly all adult white males. This extension of the vote also seemed to usher in a celebration of the "common" American, and political office no longer appeared the singular domain of American aristocrats. Beginning in the 1810's, states began removing their property and taxation qualifications for voting. By 1830, only Louisiana, Rhode Island, and Virginia had not adopted universal white male suffrage. Jackson, a man of humble Carolina <u>origins</u>, the first president who lived west of the Appalachian Mountains, embodied this trend; he however could hardly be described as the typical American. After all, Jackson had been a celebrated general, and was also a wealthy, slave-owning planter in Tennessee.

Election of 1828	Party	Electoral Vote	Popular Vote
-Andrew Jackson	Dem.– Rep.	178	647,286
-John Q. Adams	National Republican	83	508,064

"Jacksonian Democracy"	Major Issues
First Term	Second Term
1) The Peggy Eaton Affair	1) The Tariff and Sectionalism
2) Western Settlement	2) Western Settlement
3) The Webster-Hayne Debate	3) The Nullification Crisis
4) The Split with Calhoun	4) The Bank War –Whig Party Forms
	5) Foreign Affairs (including the Indians)

*Andrew Jackson and Rachel both believed her divorce from Lewis Robards had been finalized when they wed in Natchez in 1792. They lived together as husband and wife for nearly 2 years before they realized the divorce was flawed by an interesting "technicality", Lewis had not divorced Rachel for abandonment. He did however divorce her for adultery, after which Andrew and Rachel married for a second time in 1794. Jackson was so embittered and enraged by these personal attacks that part of the inscription on Rachel's tombstone (she died on Dec. 22, 1828 from a heart attack) reads "A being so gentle and so virtuous, slander might wound but could not dishonor."

Andrew Jackson can best be described as a fearless, honest, hot-tempered, intolerant reactionary. These strengths and weaknesses were already evident in his youth. During the American Revolution, a British officer ordered 14 year-old Jackson to shine his boots. Jackson defiantly refused and the officer struck him in the head with a sword. Bleeding and scarred, Jackson nonetheless continued to resist. (The Revolution was tragic for Jackson as he lost his home, his mother to cholera, and his two brothers - one in combat, the other to smallpox while a POW.) Jackson also demonstrated this stubborn courage in several Indian conflicts and the War of 1812. Additionally, "Old Hickory" (Jackson's nickname) possessed a razor sharp sense of personal honor as evidenced by his participation in several duels.* This quality proved somewhat dubious throughout his public career, as Jackson transformed political disagreements into personal affronts to his character, which in turn affected the entire nation. Medical complications from these duels may partially explain Jackson's tempestuous and intransigent manner. Jackson had 2 bullets lodged in his body which caused him incessant pain. To relieve this discomfort, his doctor prescribed him teaspoons of <u>milk of lead</u>, inadvertently poisoning Jackson and perhaps contributing to mental disorders!

During his two terms in office, Andrew Jackson extended presidential authority to an unprecedented degree. Jackson exercised the veto power (12 times) more than all of his predecessors combined (9), not including pocket vetoes. He also ignored Supreme Court decisions which ran counter to his very eclectic and personal interpretations of the Constitution, and forcefully intervened on behalf of the federal government during the nullification crisis. Finally in stark contrast to Adams, he embraced the "Spoils System" in regards to political appointments, replacing about 20% of federal employees during his 8 year tenure, often reflecting personal conflicts and party considerations as opposed to actual job qualifications.

The Inauguration

On March 4th 1829, Jackson, 62 and in poor health, prepared for inauguration as the nation's seventh president. It would prove to be unlike any other inauguration in the country's short history. Jackson delivered a somber and uneventful inaugural speech and proceeded to the White House followed by a drunken and riotous crowd estimated at 20,000 people. They followed Jackson into the White House, cheerfully tearing off pieces of his clothing as souvenirs of their hero. The mob broke the White House china, and muddied the carpets and furniture. At one point, they pressed Jackson so tightly against a wall that he may have been killed if aides had not ushered him out a window! The crowd was subsequently enticed back onto the White House lawn with tubs of lemonade, punch, and hard cider.

The Peggy Eaton Affair

If this incident did not have such serious political consequences, it would have made an excellent tabloid cover story. After Jackson's election, his beloved wife Rachel died which he believed to be the result of the malicious assaults on her character during the campaign. Enter the new Sec. of War John Eaton and his new wife Mrs. Margaret (Peggy) O' Neale Timberlake Eaton. Eaton and Jackson had been friends in the Army and in the Senate. The new Mrs. Eaton was the beautiful and outgoing daughter of a Washington bar owner, and the widow of a navy purser

*Including a future Governor of TN John Sevier, Thomas Hart Benton, a future Missouri congressman, and
  Charles Dickinson, who put the bullet in Jackson's chest!

John Timberlake who died mysteriously while deployed. (Rumors held that he committed suicide after a drunken debacle.) She and Mr. Eaton met in 1818 and quickly became close friends. When O' Neale's first husband was away at sea (many Washington insiders felt Eaton used his political influence to keep him out of the country, and he), she lived in the boardinghouse owned by her father. In 1818 Eaton took up residence at the same boardinghouse, and it was at this point that the couple most likely began an extramarital affair. After Timberlake's death, it did not take too long for the couple to formally cement their relationship. They married on Jan. 1, 1829! Mrs. Eaton had long been the subject of scandalous gossip; she was suspected of having many lovers, perhaps driving 2 men to suicide, and one rumor suggested she fell to induce the miscarriage of a baby fathered by Eaton while her first husband was still alive! However, marrying into Washington society elevated the question of her character to the highest levels of government.

The "White House Wives" led by Vice President John C. Calhoun's wife Floride would not receive Peggy socially, even refusing to speak to her at official functions. Jackson's niece and White House hostess, Emily Donelson, also participated in the social boycott. When he requested she treat Peggy more graciously, she moved out of the White House! Jackson, who met Peggy in 1823, began to draw similarities between the attacks on the young wife, and the slanderous treatment suffered by his deceased wife Rachel during the campaign. He thundered to his friends, "I tell you, I had rather have live vermin on my back than the tongue of one of these Washington women on my reputation!" Jackson demanded that the husbands stop their wives in their campaign against Peggy. He even held a Cabinet meeting to determine her virtue and chastity, and subsequently declared "she is a chaste as a virgin." All of his efforts were fruitless however and the so-called "Eaton Malaria" dragged on into 1830.

Jackson's opportunistic Sec. of State, Martin Van Buren, a widower with no daughters, saw a political advantage in defending Mrs. Eaton. "The Little Magician", one of Van Buren's many nicknames denoting his cleverness, sought to curry favor with Jackson in order to succeed him as president, a goal shared by his rival Vice President Calhoun. (According to John Randolph, "Van Buren rowed to his objective with muffled oars.") Van Buren suggested to Jackson that he defuse the controversy by dismissing his cabinet (which consisted primarily of Calhoun supporters), including Van Buren himself. Such contrived self-sacrifice was designed to ingratiate Van Buren to Jackson, and it worked perfectly. The entire Cabinet was dismissed and Van Buren became Jackson's most trusted advisor. Van Buren also attempted to estrange Jackson from Vice President Calhoun. Using subtle hints, he convinced Jackson that Calhoun actually supported his wife's crusade against Peggy and a serious rift between Jackson and Calhoun emerged. Van Buren succeeded in posturing himself to become Jackson's successor to the presidency. As for Peggy, the wives never wavered in their snobbish contempt for her, and she withdrew from Washington society, an interesting footnote in American history.

The Webster-Hayne Debate and Nullification Theory

In late 1829, a debate arose over the settlement of Western lands. On Dec. 29, 1829 Senator Samuel Foote of Connecticut proposed a bill which would temporarily halt survey of Western territory thus slowing emigration to the region. The reason behind this proposal lay in New England's continuing fear of losing population and political power to the West. Western senators such as Missouri's Thomas Hart Benton condemned Foote's Resolution and worked for an alliance with the South to block its passage. Senator Robert Hayne of South Carolina took up the cause and attempted to link the South and West against New England on both the issues of cheap Western land and low tariffs. South Carolina and the other Atlantic Coast Southern States had indeed suffered under the "Tariff of Abominations" given their reliance on manufactured goods produced outside the region. As such, they blamed nearly all of their economic misfortunes on it. Ironically however, these old states were hurt just as much (if not more) by westward expansion to the new states of Alabama, Mississippi, and Louisiana and their rich Mississippi River soil. The soils of Virginia, the Carolinas, and to an extent, Georgia were exhausted by decades of intense planting without the benefit of modern fertilizers and more efficient crop rotation practices. Many young men and their families simply left their native states to pursue "greener pastures" along the Mississippi River. This decline in population weakened the old states politically and economically, which was precisely the reason Foote had made his proposals for New England! However, the leaders of the Atlantic Coast South continued to view the Tariff as the main source for their region's misery.

In Jan. 1830, Hayne spoke to a packed Senate gallery denouncing Northern land policies, and warning of the dangers to the states posed by a strong central government made rich by retaining all of the profits rendered by land sales. Senator Daniel Webster of Massachusetts defended New England and deftly shifted the focus of the debate from Western lands to the issue of states' rights vs. federal authority. Hayne responded with a well reasoned defense of state sovereignty basing his arguments on the Constitution, the Virginia and Kentucky Resolutions of 1798, and Calhoun's Theory of Nullification which had initially been proposed in the "South Carolina Exposition and Protest" and later restated in his "Fort Hill Letter" of Aug. 28, 1832. On Jan. 26, 1830, Webster gave his "Second Reply to Hayne", a magnificent defense of the Union so stirring that James Madison stated, "It crushes nullification and must hasten an abandonment of secession."

> I profess, Sir, in my career hitherto, to have kept steadily in view
> the prosperity and honor of the whole country, and the preservation
> of our Federal Union. It is to that Union we owe our safety at home,
> and our consideration and dignity abroad. It is to that Union that we
> are chiefly indebted for whatever makes us most proud of our country.
> That Union we reached only by the discipline of our virtues in the
> severe school of adversity. It had its origin in the necessities of disordered
> finance, prostrate commerce, and ruined credit. Under its benign
> influences, these great interests immediately awoke, as from the dead, and
> sprang forth with newness of life. Every year of its duration has teemed
> with fresh proofs of its utility and its blessings; and although our territory
> has stretched out wider and wider, and our population spread farther and

farther, they have not outrun its protection or its benefits. It has been to us all a copious fountain of national, social, and personal happiness.

I have not allowed myself, Sir, to look beyond the Union, to see what might lie hidden in the dark recess behind. I have not coolly weighed the chances of preserving liberty when the bonds that unite us together shall be broken asunder. I have not accustomed myself to hang over the precipice of disunion, to see whether, with my short sight, I can fathom the depth of the abyss below; nor could I regard him as a safe counselor in the affairs of this Government, whose thoughts should be mainly bent on considering, not how the Union may best be preserved, but how tolerable the condition of the people when it should be broken up and destroyed.

While the Union lasts we have high, exciting, gratifying prospects spread out before us, for us and our children. Beyond that I seek not to penetrate the veil. God grant that in my day at least that curtain may not rise! God grant that on my vision never may be opened what lies behind! When my eyes shall be turned to behold for the last time the sun in the heavens, may I not see him shining on the broken and dishonored fragments of a once glorious Union; on states dissevered, discordant, belligerent; on a land rent with civil feuds, or drenched, it may be in fraternal blood!

Let their last feeble and lingering glance rather behold the gorgeous ensign of the Republic, now known and honored throughout the earth, still full high advanced, its arms and trophies streaming in their original luster, not a stripe erased or polluted, not a single star obscured, bearing for its motto, no such miserable interrogatory as "What is all this worth?" nor those other words of delusion and folly, "Liberty first and Union afterward;" but everywhere, spread all over in characters of living light, blazing on all its ample folds, as they float over the sea and over the land, and in every wind under the whole heavens, that other sentiment, dear to every true American heart – Liberty *and* Union, now and forever, one and inseparable!

Webster's peroration brought deafening cheers and applause from a packed Senate gallery. With its peerless eloquence, and intense emotional conviction to the Union, Webster's speech brought a captivated audience to tears; it also thundered of an indissoluble <u>national</u> Union of all Americans which no <u>state</u> had the right to destroy.*Abraham Lincoln thirty years later would claim the identical principle at Fort Sumter, but for the present, the question of states rights and nullification vs. federal authority had yet to be definitively answered. A critical showdown on this issue was approaching however, with <u>The Nullification Crisis of 1833</u>, but what exactly was this doctrine of nullification proposed by John C. Calhoun?

*Historian Gerald White Johnson summed up the effect of Webster's speech most aptly, "The celebrated *Reply To Hayne*...was not a reply to Hayne at all. It was the evocation of a mood, not the refutation of an argument – a histrionic, not a logical triumph. "Liberty and Union, now and forever, one and inseparable!" had nothing to do with the points Hayne had raised, but it stirred up a tremendous emotional reaction against the idea of disunion. Logic often eludes the grasp of the masses, but they understand feeling instantly and they understood Webster...."

Nullification – Intent, Theory, Process, and Reactions

John C. Calhoun formulated the doctrine of nullification to prevent numerical majorities from exercising unlimited legislative power over numerical minorities. He intended nullification to be utilized at the state and regional levels in order to protect the South's interests. However, variations of nullification would be imposed by Northern states against the Fugitive Slave Act in the 1850s, and a very similar procedure known as "interposition" would reappear in the South in the 1950s in an attempt to thwart the Second Civil Rights Movement. Calhoun based his doctrine on the Constitution's ratification procedure, the amendment process in the Constitution, the Tenth Amendment, and the VA and KY Resolutions of 1798, all documents which recognized in various degrees the rights of the individual states as opposed to the federal government. To nullify an offensive federal law:

1) A state legislature calls for a special convention to determine if the federal law is constitutional.

2) If the convention determines the law to be unconstitutional, it declares the law null and void and therefore unenforceable within that state.

Possible Reactions

1) The Federal Government does nothing, leaving the state free to nullify the law. (In effect, nullifying the law throughout the entire nation)
2) The Federal Government seeks to confirm the questionable law's constitutionality by proposing it as an amendment to the Constitution.
3) Other states may call conventions showing support or contempt for the original nullifying state, thus prompting a Congressional or presidential response.
*4) The Federal Government would use any means necessary to enforce the law in question.
5) State legislatures could call for the nullified law to be added as an amendment to the Constitution.
6) If the nullifying state received no support from the other states, or was seriously aggrieved by the law being added as to the Constitution, it had only two options available:
    A) - Accept defeat and repeal its ordinance of nullification
    *B) - Secede from the Union; ratification in reverse

The main reason nullification has such historical significance lay in its manifestation in 1832–33 by South Carolina, and in the secession of 11 Southern states in 1860–61.

---

* Both of these options were realized, nullification in 1833, and secession in 1860–61.

Federal Land Policy

Beginning in 1820, the federal government facilitated western settlement through a series of ever more accommodating land acts. The following list of acts demonstrates this trend.

Land Acts

1820 - 80 acres at $1.25 an acre, with installment payments abolished and full payment due upon purchase

1832 - 40 acres at $1.25 an acre

1841 - Preemption Act allows persons to settle on public lands for 5 years without payment. The settlers would subsequently gain legal title to the land for a nominal fee ($10)

Jackson was a strong supporter of easy terms for land purchases. Federal land sales between 1831 and 1836 totaled 46 million acres as opposed to only 10 million acres between 1821 and 1830! Unfortunately, 75% of the land purchases were made by land speculators who in many cases financed their purchases through loans from questionable banks. The "get rich quick" mentality of both the land speculators and the "wildcat" banks (named for the wildcats, bears, and other animals whose images were printed on bank checks and notes) would be major factors in the Panic of 1837. Jackson became alarmed at the land sales boom and pushed Congress into passing the Specie Circular Act in 1836. This act mandated that all federal land offices accept only gold or silver (specie) as payment for public lands. Although the act had the desired effect of sharply curtailing public land sales, investors now directed their attention to foreign markets which heightened an already serious foreign trade imbalance. This trade deficit also contributed to the Panic of 1837.

Indian Affairs and Removal

As during John Quincy Adam's administration, state governors in the South and West pushed hard for Indian removal to lands west of the Mississippi River. This was especially true in Georgia where the battle to extinguish Indian land titles had raged since 1802. Unlike Adam's however, Jackson agreed wholeheartedly with forced relocation schemes. In 1830 he signed into law the Indian Removal Act which allocated $500,000 for the removal of Southeastern tribes to present day Oklahoma. Jackson, the old Indian fighter sincerely believed Americans and Indians could not co-exist, and that the Indians as "savages" must make way for "civilized" cultures. He also felt that the Indians would be extinguished as a people if they remained, and as such, it was in **their** best interest to vacate their ancestral lands. Under Jackson, the United States negotiated 94 removal treaties with various eastern tribes! The treatment of the Cherokee in Georgia provides a particularly poignant example of Indian policy in the 1830s. Consider the following chronology:

<u>1791</u> - The United States and the Cherokee conclude a treaty which guarantees Cherokee land claims in Georgia and North Carolina.

<u>1802</u> - Georgia cedes her western land claims to the federal government. Georgia

agrees to this only because the U.S. promised to void all Indian land claims in Georgia. This new agreement abrogated the 1791 treaty. However, the U.S. did not immediately rescind the Cherokee land claims which paved the way for John Q. Adams confrontation with Georgia Gov. Troup in 1826.

1823 - In *Johnson and Graham's Lessee v. M'Intosh*, the Supreme Court held that no Indian or Indian tribe anywhere in the United States held legal title to their lands. They were merely "occupants"; any claims they may have had were first superseded by Great Britain, and subsequently devolving to the United States, through right of "discovery," or "exploration", one of the 4 rationales used by European nations and the U.S. in justifying and solidifying land claims; the others being "cession" (transfer of lands from one country to another, "contiguity" (claiming territory deemed necessary to protect adjacent undisputed territory, Spanish Florida to the U.S. for instance), and "settlement."

1824- The Cherokees vow not to sell any more lands to Americans, infuriating settlers in Georgia and North Carolina. The Cherokee by this time had become somewhat "Americanized", adopting settled farming techniques, and establishing a written alphabet (created by Sequoyah), formal schools, newspapers, and churches. These are obviously, impressive achievements for a culture considered by the president and a large number of Americans as "savage" and "backward!"

1827 - A "Cherokee" Nation within Georgia is proclaimed with a written constitution. It declares itself independent of any state or nation, and is recognized as such by the U.S. government. Georgia considers the Cherokee position unconstitutional under Article IV, Section 3, and declares the entire action invalid.

1828 - Georgia passes legislation which nullifies the Cherokee Constitution and subjects all Cherokees to Georgia law effective June 1, 1830.

1829 - Gold is discovered in western Georgia, initiating a miniature "gold rush."

1831 - *Cherokee Nation* v. *Georgia* reaches the Supreme Court. The case involved Corn Tassel, a Cherokee, who had been accused of murder and tried in Georgia state courts. The Cherokee claimed this action violated their jurisdictional rights and sued Georgia. Even though subpoenaed to appear in front of the Supreme Court, Georgia refused to send representatives and subsequently hanged Tassel. According to John Marshall, the Cherokee were a "domestic dependent nation" which had an unequivocal claim to its lands. The Court also held that the Cherokee were under federal not state jurisdiction. However, Marshall somewhat undercut his statements by claiming that the Cherokee were not a foreign nation according to the Constitution, and thus the Supreme Court lacked jurisdiction in the case. Marshall would clarify the Court's position the following year in the case of *Worcester* v. *Georgia*.

1832 - *Worcester* v. *Georgia*. This case involved two New England Christian missionaries, Samuel Worcester and Elizur Butler, who lived among the Cherokee in Georgia. They refused to obey a Georgia law which prohibited white settlers from residing on Cherokee lands without a state license. In addition, they would not swear an oath of allegiance to the state. They were tried, convicted, and sentenced to a harsh prison term (4 years hard labor). The Supreme Court would eventually adjudicate the case, and this time Marshall's opinion was unequivocal. Georgia's laws were unconstitutional, Worcester and Butler should be freed, and most significantly, the federal government had the sole authority to deal with the Indians.

In other words, Georgia did not have the constitutional right to impose any laws on the Cherokee Nation. This would <u>seem</u> to legally bind the federal government to the protection of the Indians from encroachments by individuals and state governments alike. Unfortunately for the Indians, Andrew Jackson did not consider himself constitutionally bound to uphold the decision. He is alleged to have stated rather bluntly, "John Marshall has made his decision, let him enforce it." As a result, the Cherokee were left defenseless. In 1835 they signed a removal treaty which paid them $5 million to evacuate their land and move to the Indian Territory (present day Oklahoma). Their migration, conducted under needlessly harsh circumstances, began in May 1838 and became known mournfully as the "Trail of Tears." About 4000 of the 15,000 Cherokee died en route of starvation, disease, and mistreatment. (Some North Carolina Cherokee resisted and eventually obtained a reservation in the western mountains from the state government.)

The Cherokee Nation was not alone in this process however. Approximately 100,000 Cherokee, Chickasaw, Choctaw, Creek, Fox, Sauk, and Seminole Indians were removed to the Indian Territory during the 1830s, of which at least 10,000 perished. Some of these groups attempted to resist relocation. As mentioned previously, a segment of the Cherokee managed to remain in North Carolina. Other resistance efforts were not as successful. The Sauk and Fox Indians of western Illinois were moved into the Iowa Territory in early 1832. Facing starvation and attacks from the Sioux, Chief Black Hawk attempted to return the tribes to their ancestral lands in the spring. The Illinois state militia, which included in its ranks Abraham Lincoln and Jefferson Davis, fought the returning Indians from April to August 1832 in what became known as the Black Hawk War. The Indians were slaughtered and once again removed west of the Mississippi.

The Seminoles resisted fiercely, waging a savage guerilla war in the Florida Everglades between 1835 and 1842. In 1832, the Seminoles were ordered to leave their ancestral lands in Florida and relocate to the Indian Territory. The Seminoles balked at the removal order. Under the effective leadership of Chief Osceola, they waged war against U.S. forces in the Florida swamps. In 1837, American forces flying a white flag of truce captured Osceola and imprisoned him at Ft. Moultrie, S.C. With Osceola's capture, Seminole resistance slowly abated, with the war finally grinding to a halt in 1842. The Seminole War cost the United States at least $25 million and 2000 lives, but most of the Seminoles were wiped out. Some managed to hide out in the Florida swamps, but most of the survivors were exiled to the Indian Territory. The fate of the Indians east of the Mississippi was settled. The author Ralph Waldo Emerson wrote about the removal of the Cherokee with poignant eloquence:

> Such a dereliction of all faith and virtue, such a denial of justice,
> and such deafness to screams of mercy were never heard in times
> of peace and in the dealing of a nation with its own allies and wards,
> since the earth was made.

Emerson's statement provides a fitting and sullen epitaph for this episode in American history.

Foreign Affairs

Jackson enjoyed considerable success in foreign affairs, especially with Britain and France. In 1830, the British finally reopened the lucrative West Indies trade with the U.S. In 1831, the French agreed to pay $1 million in damage claims to U.S. ship owners in six installments. The claims stemmed from France's harassment of the American merchant fleet during the Napoleonic Wars. The French had not complied by 1833 however, and Jackson threatened to seize French property within the United States. After brief and sometimes tense exchanges between the two governments, the French relented, making 4 of the 6 payments by 1836.

Jackson's Final Break With Calhoun

In 1830, two additional events occurred between Jackson and Calhoun which finalized the break between the two men. The first incident took place on April 13, 1830 at the Jefferson Day dinner held in Washington, D.C. Jackson, at Van Buren's request, proposed a toast which clarified his position on nullification. He announced, "Our Union – It must be preserved!", all the while glaring at Calhoun. Calhoun, trembling and spilling wine according to Van Buren, offered the next toast. "The Union, next to our liberty, most dear! May we all remember that it can only be preserved by respecting the rights of the States and by distributing equally the benefits and burdens of the Union." The next day Jackson was reported to have railed that he would "hang John C. Calhoun as high as Haman!"

The last straw for the two men broke a month later on May 12, 1830 when Jackson discovered the Crawford Letter. It revealed that as Secretary of War, Calhoun suggested Jackson be formally reprimanded for his actions in Florida in 1818. Subsequently, Jackson and Calhoun corresponded about the issue through a series of increasingly tense letters. Jackson's final reply to Calhoun was "et tu Brutus?!"("You too Brutus?!") This was the response Julius Caesar gave to his friend Senator Brutus after being stabbed in the back with a dagger in the waning years of the Roman Republic. It has been associated with treachery and betrayal ever since. Over the next two years, the political and personal animosity between Jackson and Calhoun continued to grow, culminating with Calhoun resigning as Jackson's vice presidential candidate in the election of 1832. His replacement, not surprisingly, was Martin Van Buren. Shortly afterwards, Calhoun was elected to the U.S. Senate representing South Carolina.

The Election of 1832

Jackson's forceful first term as president earned him both strong supporters and vehement enemies. Chief among the latter were Henry Clay, John C. Calhoun, and Daniel Webster. Despite their strong political differences, these men had one thing in common: an intense hatred of Andrew Jackson.* By the mid-1830s a new political party would emerge from this group and others opposed to Jackson known as the Whigs, the name of the opposition party in the British Parliament. Eventually the Whigs would revive the two-party system in American politics, and develop a political platform favoring a strong national banking system, federal funding for internal improvements, and a cautious approach to westward expansion. In 1832

*This personal enmity extended to a deranged unemployed painter Richard Lawrence, who in Jan. 1835 attempted to assassinate Jackson. At point blank range, his two pistols misfired however and an enraged Jackson beat him into submission with his cane! Lawrence was subsequently tried, adjudged insane, and committed to an asylum, the first of the so-called "lone nut" assassins or would be assassins in U.S. presidential history.

however, their primary goal was to defeat Jackson in the upcoming election. They chose Henry Clay as their candidate, but more importantly, they seized upon an issue designed to discredit and anger Jackson, the very powerful and profitable Bank of the United States (B.U.S.). It had long been known that Jackson disliked large banks due to both their financial power and their role in risky investment schemes which occasionally ruined their depositors. Because they knew Jackson would stridently oppose it, the Whigs made renewal of the B.U.S. the fundamental issue in the election.

To press the matter, Jackson's enemies sought passage of a re-charter bill prior to the election. On July 3, 1832 the bill easily passed in both houses of Congress only to be vetoed by Jackson one week later. Jackson considered the B.U.S. unconstitutional regardless of the Supreme Court's *McCulloch* v. *Maryland* ruling. (According to Jackson, "Each public officer who takes an oath to support the Constitution swears that he will support it as he understands it, and not as it is understood by others....") Congress failed to override the veto, and the stage was set for an election referendum supporting either the B.U.S. or Andrew Jackson. Despite the considerable influence of the Bank and the power of Jackson's opponents, the outcome was not particularly close.

Election of 1832	Party	Electoral Vote	Popular Vote
-Andrew Jackson	Democrats	219	687,502
-Henry Clay	National Republicans	49	530,189
-John Floyd	Independent Democrat	11	---------
-William Wirt	Anti-Mason	7	33,108

Thus armed with a considerable mandate from the public, Jackson set out to destroy the B.U.S. During the campaign, he declared to his future Vice President Van Buren, "The Bank is trying to kill me, but I will kill it!"

The Bank War
Despite his boast, Andrew Jackson faced a formidable foe in the Bank of the United States. Sen. Daniel Webster served as its' legal counsel, and the brilliant though arrogant Nicholas Biddle provided excellent leadership as bank president. The B.U.S. stood on shaky financial ground when Biddle became its' president in 1823. By 1832 however, it was the strongest financial institution in the nation. It held capital of $35 million, including $10 million in U.S. government deposits (a monopoly). The B.U.S. also conducted $75 million annually in business transactions, and its discount activities (buying, selling, and lending after the interest is deducted) stood at $40 million. In addition to its Philadelphia home office, the B.U.S. had 29 branches operating in cities throughout the U.S., and its paper notes (similar to today's checks or money orders) provided an effective paper currency for a nation chronically short of specie (gold or silver). Finally, under Biddle B.U.S. profits ran about $1.5 million annually. The B.U.S., through its sound financial policies, provided a vital component of the nation's financial structure.

However, the very success and power of the B.U.S. caused it to be regarded as a "monster" among several groups, including President Jackson. Small "wildcat" banks most prevalent in the West deeply resented both the B.U.S.' conservative fiscal policies in regards to credit, and its monopoly of government deposits. There were states-rights advocates who continued to challenge its constitutionality; others opposed it simply because they detested any use of paper money. Some felt the B.U.S. was an autocratic institution capable of destroying the nation's democratic institutions through bribery and corruption. New York banks and financial organizations were envious of Philadelphia's primacy in the nation's banking system, and finally there was Biddle's arrogance and conceit, as evidenced through numerous public and private statements. Biddle naively thought he could keep the B.U.S. insulated from political pressure, and even tried to accommodate Jackson prior to 1832, but once re-charter became an election issue, he contemptuously dismissed Jackson as a backwoods politician. According to Biddle, "As to mere power, I have been for years in the daily exercise of more personal authority than any President."

Regarding Jackson's Veto of the Re-Charter Bill on July 10,1832 : (To Henry Clay) "As to the veto message, I am delighted with it. It has all the fury of a chained panther biting the bars of its cage. It is really a manifesto of anarchy."
Concerning the Bank War: "This worthy President thinks that because he has scalped Indians and imprisoned judges, he is to have his own way with the Bank. He is mistaken."

As it turned out, he was mistaken. "Old Hickory" took dead aim at both "Ol' Nick"(also a name for the Devil!) Biddle and his Bank of the United States with dire consequences for the nation's economy in the near future. In 1833, Jackson decided to deprive the B.U.S of any new government deposits. Instead, all new government revenues, mostly derived from land sales and the tariff, were to be deposited in smaller banks throughout the nation. 23 of these so called "pet banks" received millions in deposits, and eagerly fueled a speculative boom by issuing reckless loans in many instances. (Consider the increase in federal land sales noted previously. Interestingly, some of these pet banks such as the Bank of America and the Manhattan Bank are among the most respected and profitable in the world today.)
This disbursement of federal receipts was not singularly negative for the U.S. economy, as it disseminated credit resources throughout the nation to a greater extent than when the B.U.S. enjoyed a monopoly of government revenues. However, in 1834 Jackson pushed through a bill removing all government deposits from the B.U.S., nearly 30% of its total assets. Biddle desperately tried to save the bank by calling in loans and contracting credit (interests rates tripled between 1833 and 1834) causing a sharp increase in both business failures and unemployment. When business leaders and congressmen appealed to Jackson to relax or rescind the removal order, he sardonically responded, "See Biddle." They did, and Biddle reluctantly eased credit putting an end to the so-called "Biddle's Panic", but also hurrying the B.U.S. to its demise. Ruined and prostrate, it failed to be renewed in 1836 and ceased to exist a few years later. Jackson's destruction of the B.U.S. deprived the nation of its most profitable and stable financial institution, and was

a major cause of the devastating economic Panic of 1837. His personal vendetta against the bank proved harmful for the nation as a whole. The Bank of the United States has never been reestablished.

The Nullification Crisis of 1833

Occurring simultaneously with the Bank War, a crisis erupted over tariff policy which threatened the Union. In his reelection bid, Jackson intimated that he would be amenable to a reduction of tariff rates. On July 14, 1832, a new somewhat lower tariff bill (overall tariff rates were reduced to about 25%) passed in Congress, stewarded through by Henry Clay and John Quincy Adams. The South did not receive significant relief from the new tariff however, as rates on items important to the region remained at about 50%. Virginia and especially South Carolina vilified the new tariff, with the latter state considering nullification as a possible remedy. In November 1832, South Carolina held its state legislature elections with the nullificationists' sweeping into power. The new state legislature immediately called for a special convention to consider nullifying the tariffs of 1828 and 1832 within South Carolina's borders. They also elected former Vice President John C. Calhoun, the father of nullification, to the Senate. On November 24, 1832, the convention nullified the tariffs, effective February 1, 1833. The stage was set for a showdown between Jackson and South Carolina. Jackson addressed the crisis with characteristic decisiveness. He immediately reinforced Ft. Sumter and Ft. Moultrie, and dispatched 8 naval vessels to Charleston Harbor to enforce tariff collection. He also issued a firm proclamation to the South Carolina nullifiers on December 10th 1832.

> I consider, then, the power to annul a law of the United States, assumed by one state, incompatible with the existence of the Union, contradicted expressly by the letter of the Constitution, unauthorized by its spirit, inconsistent with every principle on which it was founded, and destructive of the great object for which it was formed.

He followed this 4 days later with an ominous reference to secession.

> Can anyone of common sense believe the absurdity that a state has a right to secede or destroy the Union and the liberty of our country with it, or nullify the laws of the Union; then it is our Constitution, a rope of sand; under such I would not live.

In January, he also asked the Congress to pass the Force Bill which authorized him to call up 50,000 troops and the Navy to enforce tariff laws. South Carolina Governor Robert Hayne responded by calling up militia units to resist any federal coercion, supported by irregular bands of South Carolina "Minutemen." To make matters even worse, South Carolinians opposed to nullification began to form militia units of their own in preparation for an in-state conflict. South Carolina thus faced civil war within her borders, and possible federal invasion from without.

How did the rest of the South view South Carolina's Ordinance of Nullification? While largely of one mind concerning both state's rights and the tariff with South Carolina, the other Southern States condemned South Carolina's action. For example, the Georgia legislature referred to nullification as "abhorrent", Alabama proclaimed it "unsound in theory and dangerous in practice", and Mississippi "firmly resolved" to resist it. Even Virginia viewed nullification as a perversion of the 1798 Virginia and Kentucky Resolutions. Clearly, South Carolina stood alone and desperately needed a way out without losing face.

Sen. John C. Calhoun urged South Carolina to play for time. On January 21, 1833, South Carolina legislators moved to postpone enforcement of nullification until March 1st 1833, setting the stage for some sort of compromise. Enter the "Great Compromiser", Henry Clay. Clay pushed for a new tariff which would reduce rates over 10 years to about 20%, roughly those established by the Tariff of 1816. This proved acceptable to both Jackson and the nullifiers. On March 2, 1833, Jackson signed both the compromise tariff and the Force Bill into law, the latter to make certain the nullifiers knew that there would be no further concessions or compromises. Subsequently, a special South Carolina Convention repealed the Ordinances of Nullification in regards to the Tariffs of 1828 and 1832, but defiantly nullified the Force Act.

Who won the Nullification Crisis? That would depend on which side you asked. Jackson and his supporters claimed victory as federal authority had been upheld and the nullifiers forced to retreat. However, the South Carolina nullifiers successfully forced a national reduction of the tariff, their object to begin with. They also proclaimed that nullification as a political doctrine and as an exercise of state's rights had not been discredited. Regardless of which camp actually triumphed, the Nullification Crisis proved portentous for 3 reasons:

1)- John C. Calhoun became the undisputed philosophical and political champion of Southern interests.
2)- Calhoun and the South Carolina nullifiers knew that in future sectional disputes, the South would have to unite, to preserve the region's interests against the growing political power of the North. No single state could long hope to resist federal power.
3)- The tariff, while extraordinarily important to Southern interests, was only the first battleground of federal authority vs. state's rights, or as it would prove to be, North vs. South. Ominously, the next major area of dispute would be the "peculiar institution" of slavery.

Chapter 8

The Changing Debate Towards Slavery after 1830

The Quandary of Slavery

What of slavery? Since the Missouri Compromise of 1820, the issue had remained dormant politically, but gradually inserted itself to an ever expanding degree in the economic and social arenas. Economically, the profitability of cotton seemed to firmly rest with the maintenance of the slave system. Cotton production increased tenfold between 1800 and 1830 with both it and slavery expanding into the southwest. To a lesser, though significant extent, slavery's profitability continued in the cultivation of the South's other major staples - tobacco, rice, hemp, and sugar. Both slaveholders and non-slaveholders in the South might lament that slavery was "a necessary evil", but few people could conceive of abolishing the institution without destroying the region's, if not the nation's, economy. Throughout the ante-bellum period Southern apologists were quick to point out that the North's bourgeoning textile industry relied on cotton, and that the South, as the primary importing region supplied a the bulk of the nation's tariff revenues, fueling the internal improvement projects (canals, roads, etc…) linking the North and West physically and economically.

Slavery raised social concerns as well. Although the Quakers of Pennsylvania were the first group to formally condemn slavery, and all of the Northern states either prohibited slavery outright (The Northwest Ordinance) or provided for its gradual abolition. However, as described in Chapter 3, blacks in the North were far from treated as equals with whites. Concomitant with emancipation came disenfranchisement, exclusionary laws, and racial segregation. Indeed, as late as 1860 most white Northerners held the same views about black racial inferiority as their Southern white counterparts, and despite contemporary perceptions to the contrary, viewed abolitionists as dangerous troublemakers (see p.107–09).

In the 1820s there were actually more abolitionist groups operating in the South than in the North. The reasons for this were quite simple:

1) – Slavery in the North had been dealt with.
2) - In the South, the presence of millions of slaves was a cause for alarm. The great fear for the entire white South was race war. With slaves outnumbering whites in many areas of the South, this prospect proved especially terrifying.

Major slave revolts had already been uncovered in the past. In 1800, Gabriel Prosser planned an insurrection near Richmond with 1000 slaves. However, the plot was revealed, and Prosser and 24 co-conspirators were executed with an additional 10 deported. More recently in 1822, a literate free black carpenter named Denmark Vesey was <u>suspected</u> of organizing free blacks and slaves to wage war on Charleston's white community. As a result, Vesey and 35 slaves were executed and 34 others deported. In 1829, David Walker, a free black from North Carolina, published his *Appeal to the Colored Citizens of the World* in Boston. Walker exhorted slaves:

Now, I ask you, had you not rather be killed than to be a slave to a tyrant, who take the life of your mother, wife, and dear little children? Look upon your mother, wife, and children, and answer God Almighty; and believe this, that it is no more harm for you to kill a man, who is trying to kill you, than it is for you to take a drink of water when thirsty....

The threatening tone of the *Appeal* intensified white Southerners fears of Southern blacks and gave additional urgency to the question of what to do about slavery. One answer was individual <u>manumission</u> (freeing) of slaves. Some Southerners during this period manumitted their slaves in their wills; others freed individual slaves on the basis of a feat performed, such as saving the life of the owner's child. Still others callously freed old, sick, or crippled slaves to avoid caring for them. Interestingly, Southern state legislatures attempted to prevent such a practice by making emancipation contingent on the approval of local or county courts. However, individual manumission became increasingly difficult by the 1820s, as Southern state legislatures did not want the former slaves to remain in their states as free blacks. As a result, VA, TN, and most other slave states required that freed slaves leave the state promptly or face re-enslavement. As slaves had little or no means to repatriate, the considerable financial burden would fall on the owner or some benevolent sponsor.

In addition, very large numbers of whites in the free states were hostile to the idea of free blacks moving into their communities. Indeed, any black emigration into many Northern and Western states was prohibited. As a result of the serious obstacles to individual manumission, <u>emancipation and colonization</u> became the solution most seriously contemplated by Southern abolitionists for ending slavery prior to 1835. In 1817, advocates of this strategy founded the American Colonization Society in Washington, D.C. Supporters included a virtual "Who's Who" in American politics. John Marshall, Daniel Webster, Henry Clay, Andrew Jackson, and James Monroe ("Monrovia" is the name of Liberia's present capital) were all members, though their motives for colonization varied considerably. The immediate intent of the organization was to transport <u>freed</u> slaves to some portion of West Africa purchased from native African tribes. With the establishment of a free black republic in Africa, idealists within the Society anticipated that slave-owners would manumit their slaves for repatriation, thus eliminating both slavery and the presence of free blacks in the United States. In 1819, Society representatives purchased property along the west African coast and named the prospective colony "Liberia"("land of liberty") with colonization beginning in 1821.However, the emancipation-colonization effort proved a dismal failure. Why?

> 1)-Free blacks had little inclination to go to Africa, by then an unfamiliar foreign land inhabited by hostile native tribes, deadly animals and insects, and ridden with tropical diseases. In addition, most free blacks considered the United States their home, and wished to see their condition bettered on their native soil.

> 2)-The finances allocated for colonization were woefully inadequate to the task. In 1827, the Society sought a

government subsidy to bolster their efforts, but were angrily rebuffed by the state legislatures of the Deep South. As their economies depended on cotton cultivated by slaves, they had no interest in large scale colonization efforts. Such plans would both cripple production and drastically increase the price for slaves. The only scheme supported with any fervor in that region was the removal of the <u>free blacks</u> who were consistently viewed with suspicion.

3)-The population growth of American slaves was such that for every free black who emigrated to Liberia between 1821 and 1860 (approximately 15,000) there were <u>263</u> slaves by 1860! The slave population in the U.S. in 1860 was 3,950,511, while free blacks numbered 488,000. Any serious colonization plan would have required a truly Herculean effort, totally beyond the scale of any private enterprise.

The subsequent history of Liberia, though not the cornerstone of the emancipation movement in the U.S. as it was intended, nonetheless is interesting. In 1847, the Liberian Republic elected its first black president, emulating the political system of the United States. Unfortunately, the transplanted black Americans also brought with them their native country's proclivities towards slavery, enslaving the native Africans within their proximity. Liberia, the "land of freedom" for transplanted black Americans, did not officially abolish slavery <u>until 1935!</u>

<u>*The Liberator,* Northern Abolitionism, and Nat Turner's Insurrection</u>
   Although the colonization effort continued until 1860, events within the United States in 1831 radically altered both the debate concerning slavery and the actual nature of the institution. In January, William Lloyd Garrison a radical abolitionist, published the first issue of *The Liberator* newspaper in Boston, Mass. Fiery and unequivocal in his tone, Garrison <u>demanded</u> immediate emancipation with no monetary compensation for slave-owners. Garrison brooked no Constitutional arguments against his plan since he regarded the document as "a covenant with death and an agreement with Hell." To demonstrate his extreme contempt, he burned a copy of the Constitution in public. His personal experiences with slavery were minimal, but his conviction of its moral repugnance is evident in the very first copy of *The Liberator*. What is also evident in the first issue is Garrison's recognition of the violent prejudice against both abolitionists and blacks in the free North:

During my recent tour for the purpose of exciting the minds of the people by a series of discourses on the subject of slavery, every place that I visited gave fresh evidence of the fact, that a greater revolution in public sentiment was to be effected in the free states – and particularly in New England – than at the South. I found contempt more bitter, opposition more active, detraction more relentless, prejudice more stubborn, and apathy more frozen, than among slave-owners themselves.... *

He continued:

I am aware that many object to the severity of my language; but is there not cause for severity? I will be as harsh as truth, and as uncompromising as justice. On this subject, I do not wish to think or speak, or write with moderation. No! No! Tell a man whose house is on fire to give a moderate alarm; tell him to moderately rescue his wife from the hands of the ravisher (rapist); tell the mother to gradually extricate her babe from the fire into which it has fallen; but urge me not to use moderation in a cause like the present. I am in earnest – I will not equivocate – I will not excuse – I will not retreat a single inch – AND I WILL BE HEARD.

*Sections from French observer Alexis de Tocqueville's <u>Democracy In America</u> corroborate Garrison's observations. According to Tocqueville:

Turning my attention to the United States of our own day (1831), I plainly see that in some parts of the country the legal barrier between the two races is tending to come down, but not that of mores: I see that slavery is in retreat, but the prejudice from which it arose is immovable.... Race prejudice seems stronger in those states that have abolished slavery than in those where it still exists, and nowhere is it more intolerant than in those states where slavery was never known.... The Negro's son is excluded from the school to which the European's child goes. In the theaters he cannot for good money buy the right to sit by his former master's side; in the hospitals he lies apart. He is allowed to worship the same God as the white man but must not pray at the same altars. He has his own clergy and churches. The gates of Heaven are not closed against him, but his inequality stops only just short of the boundaries of the other world. When the Negro is no more, his bones are cast aside, and some difference in condition is found even in the equality of death. So the Negro is free, but he cannot share the rights, pleasures, labors, griefs, or even the tomb whose equal he has been declared; there is nowhere he can meet him, neither in life nor in death. In the South the master has no fear of lifting the slave up to his level, for he knows that when wants he can always throw him down into the dust. In the North the white man no longer clearly sees the barrier that separates him from the degraded race, and he keeps the Negro at a distance all the more carefully because he fears lest one day they be confounded together. Among the Americans of the South, Nature sometimes, reclaiming her rights, does for a moment establish equality between white and black. In the North, pride silences even the most imperious of human passions. Perhaps the northern American might have allowed some Negro woman to be the passing companion of his pleasures, had the legislators declared that she could not hope to share his nuptial bed; but she can become his wife, and he recoils in horror from her. Thus it is that in proportion in the United States the prejudice rejecting the Negroes seems to increase in proportion to their emancipation, and inequality cuts deep into mores as it is effaced from the laws. But if the relative position of the two races inhabiting the United States is as I have described it, why is it that the Americans have abolished slavery in the North of the Union, and why have they kept it in the South and aggravated its rigors? The answer is easy. In the United States people abolish slavery not for the sake of the Negroes but of the white men.

Garrison was heard, especially by Southerners who were understandably alarmed by his message, and deathly afraid of its possible influence on the slaves. Almost immediately, Southern politicians began demanding that such publications be barred from mail distribution, a practice which became nearly universal in the South by 1835. Despite intense hostility and threats to his life, Garrison remained one of the most outspoken of the radical abolitionists for the next 30 years, but he was not alone. Elijah P. Lovejoy, Theodore Weld, Lyman Beecher, the Grimke sisters, and Frederick Douglass were also prominent abolitionists active during the antebellum period. Abolitionists attacked slavery on both religious and secular grounds. The Christian arguments abolitionists leveled <u>against slavery</u> possessed the most widespread appeal in the North. They denounced slavery as contrary to Christian teachings. Did not Moses deliver the Israelites from bondage to the Promised Land (Exodus 13–17), and did not Christ proclaim the brotherhood of man, and "do unto others as you would have them do unto you" (Matthew 5–7)?! (An excellent collection of the Christian arguments against slavery is contained in Theodore Weld's _The Bible Against Slavery_.) On ethical grounds, they condemned the sale and ownership of men and women like animals or inanimate objects. The entire process dehumanized slave and slave-owner alike. One of the most compelling accounts of life as a slave came from former slave Frederick Douglass. His _Narrative of the Life of Frederick Douglass_ helped propel him to the front rank of international abolitionism. He also published an abolitionist newspaper aimed at free blacks entitled _The North Star_. Abolitionists also dismissed slavery as economically unsound. According to anti-slavery advocates, slaves, deprived of individual initiative and ambition, could never work as effectively as free laborers.

Additionally, the mere presence of slavery impoverished white non-slaveholders who could not compete against plantation slavery, and diminished their work ethic by associating manual labor with slave labor. _The Impending Crisis of the South_ published in 1857 was arguably the single most important work condemning the slave system on economic grounds. Interestingly, it was written by a Southerner, Hinton Helper of North Carolina, who moved to New York City due to death threats. Some of these economic assumptions and observations were erroneous, but they proved effective in convincing many Northerners that the South was a land stunted by laziness and unfulfilled potential. Finally, some abolitionists began (especially after 1845) excoriating slaveholders and the South in general as morally reprobate, a violent blight on freedom and democracy, barbaric, ignorant, and depraved. This theme is prevalent in many issues of Garrison's _Liberator_, and in Theodore Weld's immensely popular _American Slavery As It Is: Testimony of A Thousand Witnesses_ (1839). Their extreme, uncompromising approach to abolition undermined the position of those persons favoring a more gradual form of manumission. Their vitriolic denunciations of both slavery and Southern society in general helped create an anti-abolitionist reaction in the region. As such, the radical abolitionists were instrumental in derailing the entire emancipation movement in the South.

Another major event which took place in 1831 involved a charismatic Baptist slave preacher, Nat Turner. Turner lived with various owners (the last was Joseph Travis) in rural Southampton County, VA Turner's owners converted him to Christianity and taught him to read, a common practice within the South prior to 1831. He worked as a driver on the farm, a position of relative prestige within the slave community. In the late 1820s, Turner gained a loyal following among neighboring slaves preaching an apocalyptic vision of slaves winning their freedom by killing whites, a vision he claimed was divinely inspired:

> On the 12th of May, 1828, I heard a loud noise in the heavens,
> and the Spirit instantly appeared to me and said the Serpent was
> loosened, and Christ had laid down the yoke he had borne for the
> sins of men, and that I should take it on and fight against the
> Serpent, for the time was fast approaching when the first should
> be last and the last should be first…. And by signs in the heavens
> that it would make known to me when I should commence the
> great work….

The primary sign, a solar eclipse, occurred on February 11th 1831. Subsequently, Turner began planning his rebellion. The final sign came on Aug. 13th when the sun was partially obscured and appeared bluish-green. At approximately 2:00 A.M. Aug. 22, 1831, Turner and 8 followers began the insurrection by brutally murdering Turner's owner and his family. Over the next two days they proceeded to fan out in the countryside recruiting about 70 slaves and killing nearly 60 whites. Horrified, the white population of southeastern VA organized a volunteer defense force. In Addition, the state militia mobilized against Turner and the insurrectionists. At least 100 blacks were killed and Turner himself was eventually captured, tried, and executed.

As a result of the insurrection, a wave of hysteria swept through many Southern communities. Many Southerners blamed Garrison's *Liberator* as instigating Turner's uprising, but no evidence has ever surfaced indicating <u>any</u> connection between the two. As many as 200 slaves in Virginia were killed for alleged involvement in the plot. In Wilmington, N.C., 200 miles south of where the insurrection commenced, residents killed four "suspicious" blacks and put their heads atop poles to deter any slaves from emulating Turner's example.* Turner was caught on October 30th, and his trial began on Nov. 5th. After Turner's execution (he was hanged and skinned!) on Nov. 11, 1831 the violence subsided, but throughout the South new, more stringent slave codes were enacted to prevent any future uprisings. Laws were passed prohibiting slaves from interacting with free blacks, carrying firearms, owning horses, drums, or horns, leaving their homes without written passes, and assembling in groups without a white man present. Slave marriages were not legally recognized and strict guidelines were established in regards to interracial relations. Any black implicated in insurrection, either actual or planned, was punished with death. In most of the South, it even became a crime to teach a slave to read or write! However, this particular aspect of the slave codes proved nearly impossible to enforce, and authorities rarely prosecuted violators. The real terror for blacks was the slave patrols established in every community. They usually consisted of 4 or 5 armed white men appointed by the county who mustered about every two weeks. Any black they encountered on patrol was subject to beatings or worse. In addition, the white South increasingly viewed abolition as a dangerous doctrine which should be suppressed. By 1835, postmasters in the South routinely refused to distribute any abolitionist literature, and in 1836 a "gag rule"

*Their heads were displayed at various points around the city; one near the Smith Creek Bridge, one near Point Peter, to the north, one on Market Street near the Cape Fear River , and the last at the corner of 8th and Market Streets. Point Peter eventually became part of U.S.117, and a stretch of the highway was named "Negro Head Road" and listed on maps as such well into the 20th Century. Even today (2014), it is listed at Moore's Creek National Battlefield as "Negro Head Point Road", just south of Currie passed in Congress which automatically shelved any bills regarding slavery. This hearkened back to Congress' non-interference resolution of 1790. (see p. 33) The "gag rule" was eventually repealed in 1844, largely due to the efforts of Rep. John Quincy Adams.

The last serious attempt at manumission and colonization came in the Virginia State Constitutional Convention of 1831–32. Although its original intent was changing the state's voting requirements, in the wake of the Nat Turner revolt, intense discussions ensued concerning what to do about slavery within the state. The delegates subsequently considered a proposed amendment for gradual emancipation and colonization. The final vote was 73 opposed to the amendment, 58 in favor. If only 8 votes were switched in favor of the amendment, slavery would have been sent on the road to extinction not only in Virginia, but most likely throughout the Upper South (MD, VA, KY, MO, AR, TN, and NC) as well. This is not a spurious assumption as Virginia maintained both a leadership role in the region, and had the largest slave population in the United States. Gradual emancipation in VA would have posed enormous problems for her sister states regarding free blacks and runaways; problems which may have been rectified by similar schemes enacted within those states. However, the defeat of the amendment permanently silenced the entire colonization plan within the South.

From "A Necessary Evil" to "A Positive Good"
The Change In Southern Attitudes Towards Slavery 1830–61

The events of 1831 pushed the South towards a garrison mentality in regards to slavery. Some Southerners however were not content to simply react to abolitionist attacks on their "peculiar institution." Southerners such as South Carolina Governor Stephen D. Miller claimed that "slavery is not a national evil; on the contrary, it is a national benefit." More significantly, Thomas Roderick Dew, a young philosophy professor at William and Mary College in Virginia, published a compelling defense of slavery entitled *Review of the Debate of the Virginia Legislature of 1831 and 1832*. Dew claimed that slavery had been established in antiquity, with both religious and secular sanction. Slavery had been an accepted institution in both Ancient Greece and Rome, and passages throughout the Old and New Testaments' in the Bible countenanced it. In addition, Dew wrote of a natural inequality among the races which slavery profitably exploited. Indeed, according to Dew, economic calamity would befall any nation which immediately abolished the institution. Dew did not stand alone in his defense of slavery. Within a decade, Southern politicians, philosophers, scientists, writers, poets, and preachers developed an ever more insistent tone extolling the benefits of "the peculiar institution." John C. Calhoun and others contended that blacks were racially and mentally inferior, (this view was also nearly universally subscribed to by whites in the North) and incapable of high academic or professional development. However the South possessed significant numbers of free black barbers, preachers, skilled artisans, master craftsmen, managers, sailors, blacksmiths, metal workers, cooks, seamstresses, tailors, musicians, and shoemakers which seemingly belied these assumptions. For example, in 1860, there were nearly 8000 free black shoemakers and blacksmiths in Virginia alone! (see Addendum p. 253–55) Additionally, in 1860

262,000 free blacks lived in the South compared to 226,000 in the North. There were also a small number of black slave owners in the South, including John Carruthers Stanly of Craven County, NC, purportedly the South's largest black slave owner with 163 bondsmen. However, free blacks in the South were viewed with suspicion in many cases, and subject to discriminatory treatment, such as the wearing of "liberty" caps or badges, prohibitions on voting, travel restrictions, curfews, and in extreme cases, re-enslavement.

Despite this contradictory juxtaposition considering black racial inferiority, Southern apologists for slavery held firm. Blacks were lazy, superstitious, and irrational; if freed, the slaves would degenerate into barbarism and wreak death and destruction upon society. To prevent such a calamity, black slaves should perpetually be assigned to unskilled, compulsory labor under the benevolent supervision of whites. Whites, as the superior race, would naturally assume the leadership roles in law, politics, business, science, culture, mores, and the common defense. As such, a prosperous and harmonious multi-racial society depended on race based slavery. By the 1850s, some Southern writers went on the offensive against what they called the "wage slave" economy of the North. In William Grayson's poem "*The Hireling and the Slave*", and most notably, George Fitzhugh's books *Sociology for the South* and *Cannibal's All*, both writers railed at the wretched conditions suffered by free, white Northern workers. According to these and other Southern writers, Northern workers were paid near starvation wages for dangerous work subject to arbitrary dismissal with no provisions made for their future welfare. They were technically free, but were slaves to an uncaring system. While some of their allegations concerning working conditions in the North were undoubtedly true, Southern apologists pressed the issue further. They contended that in the South, slavery provided a truly altruistic socio-economic order akin to an extended family. Slaves were content, happy and cared for from cradle to grave by "kindly ol' Massa". For some Southerners, this argument "proved" the moral superiority of the slave system.

The issue of race and slavery also entered the scientific arena. In 1854, Dr. Josiah Nott and George Gliddon published *Types of Mankind*, a pseudoscientific analysis of different races. Nott and Gliddon contended that the black and white races were created separately and evolved at different rates. Their findings, especially in measuring the cranial cavity within skulls, led them to conclude that blacks had evolved slower than whites and thus were inferior human beings. However, this "separate evolution theory" provoked considerable criticism from other scientists and physicians. In *The Causes of the Variety of the Complexion and the Form of the Human Species*, Dr. John Wesley Monette argued that environmental conditions shaped racial traits and characteristics, not separate evolutions. Furthermore, when scientific arguments tended to diminish or contradict the Biblical explanation of mankind's creation, they were frequently viewed with suspicion and contempt by the vast majority of Southerners.

In the South as in the North, the Christian arguments regarding slavery proved the most effective. However, unlike the North, in the South the Bible was construed as supporting slavery. Ministers, preachers, priests, and rabbis cited passages in the

Old Testament countenancing slavery. The most widely used Biblical argument referred to the curse of Canaan, the son of Ham, found in Genesis 9:20–27 (King James Version). According to Scripture, Noah's youngest son Ham discovered Noah drunk and naked in a tent. Ham left Noah and told his two older brothers Japheth and Shem of their father's condition. To avoid witnessing their father in such a state, the two backed into the tent and flung a cloak over Noah. When he awoke and realized what had happened, Noah cursed Ham's youngest son Canaan to be "a slave of slaves." As Noah's sons were destined to populate the world, Canaan and his descendants were fated to be enslaved perpetually. (See Genesis 15:16, 19:5, Leviticus 18 to 20, and Deuteronomy 12:31) Another proslavery argument came from Leviticus 25:44–55, and 27:1–9. Here the Bible ascribes a monetary value to human beings, which presumes they could be bought and sold as commodities.

The New Testament also contains positive references towards slavery. In several sections (refer to Ephesians 6:5–9, Colossians 3:22–25, 4:1, Titus 2:9, Philemon 1:10–12, and Peter 2:8–9), slaves are encouraged to be loyal and obedient to their masters to obtain their just reward in Heaven. Southern clerics were also quick to point out Jesus' silence concerning slavery. The differences which emerged between Northern and Southern Christians over slavery ultimately split major denominations. Southern Methodists formed their own church in 1844, and the Southern Baptists followed suit in 1845. The Presbyterians formed a short lived Confederate Presbyterian Church in 1861.

Brief Chronology of Slavery in the United States 1793 – 1865

1793 - Eli Whitney invents the cotton gin which greatly increases the profitability of cotton and plantation slavery.

1800 - Gabriel Prosser's attempted slave revolt in Richmond, VA is uncovered. 25 slaves are executed, 10 others are deported.

1808 - The U.S. abolishes the overseas slave trade.

1822 - Denmark Vesey's attempted slave revolt in Charleston, S.C. is exposed. 35 slaves are executed, 34 others are deported.

   - The first freed slaves arrive in Liberia due to the efforts of the American Colonization Society, which formed in 1817 to repatriate freed slaves to Africa. By 1860, approximately 15,000 freed slaves had emigrated to Liberia.

1829 - David Walker's *Appeal….* Is published. It advocates violent slave uprisings in the South.

1831 - William Lloyd Garrison's *The Liberator* begins publication in Boston. Its tone is incendiary, and demands immediate emancipation of all slaves.

- Nat Turner's slave revolt in Southampton County, VA results in the deaths of nearly 60 whites and 200 blacks. It drastically increases racial tensions in the South and leads to the tightening of slave regulations.

1831–32 - The Virginia state constitutional convention debates over slavery. Delegates vote 73 to 58 against gradual emancipation and colonization.

1833 - The American Anti-Slavery Society forms.

1836 - The "Gag Rule" is instituted in Congress (House of Representatives), which mutes all discussion of slavery.

1837 - Prominent abolitionist Elijah P. Lovejoy is murdered by an anti-abolitionist mob in Alton, Ill. He is the first white abolitionist to be killed.

- Theodore Weld publishes *The Bible Against Slavery*.

1839 - Weld publishes *American Slavery As It Is: Testimony of A Thousand Witnesses* describing the accounts of abused slaves. 100,000 copies are sold the first year.

1844 - "Gag Rule" repealed.

1845 - *Narrative of the Life of Frederick Douglass* is published. Douglas, an escaped slave from Maryland, will become a celebrity and the most prominent black abolitionist in the world.

1847 - Douglass begins publication of an abolitionist newspaper for blacks *The North Star*, in New York.

1852 - Harriet Beecher Stowe's *Uncle Tom's Cabin* is released. It sells 300,000 copies its first year in print, is converted into a play, and becomes abolitions greatest influence on ordinary Americans in the North.

1854 - Mary Eastman publishes *Aunt Phyllis' Plantation* as a response to *Uncle Tom's Cabin*. Its pro-slavery tone is popular in the South.

- George Fitzhugh from Virginia writes *Sociology for the South:* or *The Failure of Free Society* which denounces the "wage slave" system in the North, and claims that Southern slavery is far more humane and benevolent.

1856 - William Grayson of South Carolina composes *"The Hireling and the Slave"*, a poem praising slavery and condemning free labor.

1857 - Hinton Helper of North Carolina publishes *The Impending Crisis* which condemns slavery because it impoverishes non-slaveholding whites.

   - George Fitzhugh writes *Cannibals All!* Or *Slaves Without Masters* which expounds that slavery "is the truest form of socialism as it provided security for the workers in sickness and old age…."

   - The Supreme Court issues the *Dred Scott* ruling which holds that slaves are not citizens of the United States, the Missouri Compromise of 1820 is unconstitutional, and slaves, being the legal property of their owners, can be taken into any U.S. territory.

1859 - John Brown is hanged after attempting to incite a slave insurrection at Harpers Ferry, VA. His raid terrifies the South, but some Northerners view his actions as justified. As a result, sectional tensions are greatly exacerbated.

1862 - Lincoln issues the Emancipation Proclamation freeing all slaves in areas still in rebellion. Although largely symbolic, it helps convince England and France to withhold formal diplomatic recognition of the Confederacy.

1865- The 13th Amendment is ratified abolishing slavery in the United States. It is enacted nearly 8 months (Dec. 6th 1865) after Lee's surrender at Appomattox.

Chapter 9

America to 1844: The Eve of "Manifest Destiny"

Jackson's Administration 1834-37

With the resolution of the nullification crisis in 1833, the Bank of the U.S. rendered impotent after 1834, and the relocation of southeastern Indian tribes well under way by 1835, Jackson's remaining tenure as president was relatively quiet. However, his tempestuous manner in dealing with political (and personal) foes galvanized the new Whig Party and permanently restored the two-party system to American politics. John C. Calhoun, Henry Clay, and Daniel Webster temporized their considerable philosophical differences as Whigs to carry on in Congress against their common foe, Jackson. In March 1834, a measure of formal censure condemned Jackson for illegally usurping legislative powers during the Bank War, the only instance of censuring a president in U.S. history. (It was removed from Congressional records in 1837 after intense lobbying on the part of Jackson's political supporters, most notably Thomas Hart Benton of Missouri.) By the mid-1830s, Jackson became more interested in international events. As mentioned previously, Jackson proved fairly successful in foreign affairs, especially with France and Great Britain. By 1835 however, developments in the American Southwest captured the attention of Jackson and a large number of his constituents; the area of interest was Texas.

Texas Chronology – 1800–1836

1803–1820 – American interest in Texas grew when the United States acquired the Louisiana Purchase in 1803. There was some dispute between the U.S. and Spain as to whether Texas was to be included in the Louisiana territory. Eventually, the U.S. attempted to purchase Texas. In the Adams-Onis Treaty of 1819, Sec. of State John Q. Adams accepted the Sabine River as the western boundary of Louisiana but still offered Spain $1 million for Texas. As president, he authorized $5 million to purchase Texas from the new Republic of Mexico. In both cases he proved unsuccessful.

1821 – Stephen F. Austin of Missouri began a colony consisting of 300 families on the lower Brazos River (near present day Houston). He had inherited a huge land claim from his father, Moses Austin, who had negotiated with the Spanish in the 1810s for a colonial land grant in Texas.

- Mexico gains independence from Spain with its borders extending north to the 42nd parallel and west to the Pacific Ocean. Mexico originally encompassed all of the present day states of Texas, New Mexico, Arizona, California, Nevada, and Utah, and contained portions of Wyoming, Colorado, Kansas, and Oklahoma.

1824 – Austin's colony consists of 1,790 residents including 1,347 whites and 443 slaves.
- Mexico adopts the Constitution of 1824, establishing a republican government consisting of several states, including the state of Coahuila -Texas with the Nueces River as its southern boundary.

1825 – The Mexican government passes the National Colonization Act which gave 66,774 acre land tracts free of charge to *empresarios* (colony land agents) who would sponsor colonization efforts. Each empresarios would receive these immense grants for every 200 hundred families brought into Mexico, and some subsequently sold plots of prime cotton land in east Texas for $.06 to $.10 an acre! In addition, the settlers were given tax exemptions for six years (a provision first proposed in 1823). Not surprisingly, immigrants poured in from the Southern States who brought their slaves with them despite Mexican laws prohibiting slavery.

1830 – Coastal Texas has about 20,000 white inhabitants, mostly Americans, along with 1000 slaves. This trend alarmed the Mexican government which passed laws restricting further American immigration, and positioned troops on the Texas-U.S. border to enforce the ban. In addition, the government tightened anti-slavery legislation, and reinstated customs duties (taxes and tariffs) between Texas and U.S. ports, such as New Orleans. However, these provisions did little to halt illegal American immigration into Texas, as it was very easy to slip across the border. By 1830, 25,000 Americans lived in Texas, 10 times the number of Mexicans! By 1835, that number approached 40,000.

1830–33 – Texans ponder 2 options for their future:

1) – Attempt to detach Texas from Coahuila and form a separate state, and work to reverse the restrictions imposed in 1830. This approach was favored by the older settlers such as Stephen Austin, who remembered the earlier benefits of Mexican citizenship.

2) - Seek independence from Mexico and become an independent republic, or seek admission into the U.S. as a new state. Independence was attractive to newer settlers who found Mexican laws and customs (such as no guaranteed trial by jury) both repressive and irksome.

1833 – Stephen Austin traveled to Mexico City to submit a petition requesting that Texas be granted statehood independent of Coahuila. He also presented a petition for the repeal of the restrictive laws of 1830. En route back to Texas, he is imprisoned for 18 months without formal charges or trial. He was released without any explanation and returned home broken in health, and justifiably bitter towards the Mexican government for his ordeal. As a result, Austin became a very powerful symbol of Texas' grievances against Mexico. He died in 1836.

1834 – General Antonio Lopez de Santa Anna seizes control in Mexico, determined to destroy federalism and establish a unified Mexico under a military dictatorship.

1835 – Texans adopt a "Declaration of Causes" and pledge to fight for the Constitution of 1824. Santa Anna, distracted by other trouble spots in Mexico, does not turn his attention to Texas until the winter of 1836. He subsequently dispatches 4000 troops into the region.

<u>1836</u> – Feb. 23 – Santa Anna's begins his siege and attack on the Alamo, a former
Spanish mission in San Antonio. Santa Anna has 4000 soldiers; the Alamo is
defended by 187 Texans, including Davy Crockett, Jim Bowie, and the commander
of the post, William Travis.

- March 2 – Texas declares independence from Mexico.

- March 6 – Santa Anna captures the Alamo but loses 1,544 casualties. All 187
    Texan defenders are annihilated. "Remember the Alamo!"
    becomes a fanatical rallying cry for Texas patriots.

- March 26 – 350 Texans are massacred at Goliad <u>after</u> they surrender to
    Mexican forces. A vengeful "Remember Goliad" is added to the
    cause of Texas' independence.

- April 21 – Texas forces led by Commander-In-Chief Sam Houston (formerly
    Governor of Tennessee and a friend of Andrew Jackson) attacked
    Santa Anna's forces just west of the San Jacinto River (near
    present day Houston). Although each army consisted of
    approximately 1200 men, the Texans won an overwhelming
    victory. In 18 minutes, the Texas Army (half of which was made
    up of American volunteers) killed or wounded about 600
    Mexicans and took the remaining soldiers, including Santa Anna,
    prisoner. Texan casualties were incredibly low, consisting of 16
    killed and 25 wounded, including Commander Houston. Santa
    Anna was compelled to surrender. Under duress, he negotiated a
    peace treaty with the Texans which granted Texas its
    independence, and established its southern and western borders
    at the Rio Grande River. The Texas Republic (a.k.a. "The Lone
    Star Republic") was born.

However, the new nation immediately faced grave difficulties. Texas had no money,
and at first, no real allies. Considering the number of Americans living in Texas, it is
hardly surprising that many Texans desired to join the United States. However, the
U.S. government voted down annexation twice, in 1837, and again in 1844. Why
would the United States reject Texas? There were two very important reasons:

1)– Mexico threatened war if the U.S. annexed Texas.
2)- Northern congressmen balked at the idea of admitting a gigantic new slave state,
    a considerable portion of which was located north of the 36 degree, 30 minute
    line which prohibited slavery.

However, Pres. Jackson formally recognized the new nation on March 3rd 1837.
The Mexican government never recognized Texas as independent, and actually
invaded Texas twice prior to 1843. The Mexicans also refused to accept the
Rio Grande as the Texas border. Texas' historical southern boundary lay farther to

the north at the Nueces River. If Texas' southern boundary stood at the Nueces River, it would lose roughly half its' territory. Nonetheless, Texas existed for 9 years as an independent republic served by three presidents, Sam Houston (1836–39, 1841–44), the expansionist minded Mirabeau Bonaparte Lamar (1839–41) who dreamed of a Texas Republic extending west to the Pacific Ocean, and finally, the pro-independence Anson Jones (1844–45).

The Election of 1836

Jackson's Vice President Martin Van Buren easily won the Democratic Party's nomination in 1836, promising to maintain Jackson's policies and to work for the creation of an independent treasury system to replace the B.U.S. The Whigs fielded 3 regional candidates in an effort to deprive Van Buren a majority in the Electoral College and force the election into the House of Representatives. The tactic failed.

Election of 1836	Party	Electoral Vote	Popular Vote
-Martin Van Buren	Democrat	150 (58%)	762,678 (51%)
-William Henry Harrison	Whig	73 (26%)	549,000 (36 ½%)
-Hugh Lawson White	Whig	26 (9%)	146,000 (10%)
-Daniel Webster	Whig	14 (4 ½%)	41,000 (2 ½%)
-Willie Mangum	Independent	11 (3 ½%)	---------

(Mangum was an anti-Jackson Independent from North Carolina)

Van Buren, the "Little Magician" who had maneuvered so skillfully throughout his career to reach the presidency, soon found the office a nightmare. Almost immediately after the election, the economy sank into a deep recession which lasted until 1844. The Panic of 1837 had begun.

The Panic of 1837 - Causes

1) Jackson's Bank War
2) Over-Speculation in Land
3) Trade Imbalance - After the passage of the Specie Circular Act in 1836 made land much more difficult to purchase, Americans spent lavishly on imported items creating trade deficits.
4) Economic depression in Europe, especially England, which subsequently resulted in the contraction of American overseas credit, and a drastic decline in European investments in the United States. Europeans also insisted that Americans pay their existing debts in gold or silver, which drained specie from U.S. banks.
5) Failure of the Wheat Crop and the Collapse of Cotton Prices (Cotton fell from $.17 a pound in 1835 to $.10 a pound by 1840)
6) State indebtedness amounting to $170 million, the result of over ambitious road, canal, and construction projects. As the economy slowed, states' were forced to slow or cancel these projects causing some businesses to collapse and unemployment to rise.

At this time in American history, the government did not provide <u>any</u> type of economic assistance, such as welfare or Social Security. Charity and relief efforts were private, usually provided by families, churches, and philanthropic organizations. Nevertheless, the government was at least expected to institute sound fiscal policies which would bolster economic growth. As the Panic wore on, Van Buren increasingly became the target of harsh public criticism. Ironically, his predecessor Andrew Jackson bore considerably more responsibility for the economic crisis, but Jackson had retired from public life to his beloved "Hermitage" plantation in Tennessee, safely removed from the political turmoil. The Panic of 1837 was not the only issue to vex Van Buren however. Troubles, foreign and domestic, bedeviled him throughout his presidency.

Van Buren's Administration 1837–41

In addition to the Panic of 1837, Martin Van Buren faced a daunting collection of problems. For example, he had to deal with the uncomfortable reality of a Democratic Party divided over fiscal policy. Conservative Democrats pushed for the re-creation of the B.U.S. and the curtailment of paper money. They reasoned correctly that the destruction of the B.U.S. had severely damaged the economy, and that creating a new Bank would prove beneficial to American business. However, the Radical Democrats (known as "Locofocos"*) contended that any <u>single</u> financial institution, such as the B.U.S., which could so drastically affect the nation's economy was dangerous and should not be restored. The "Locofocos" also railed against paper money which they contended devalued the dollar and caused inflation, which adversely affected working class wage earners. Van Buren disagreed with both wings of his party and worked tirelessly for a third option, the <u>independent treasury system.</u> In this scheme, the federal government would sever all its ties with private banks and instead keep all its revenue in independent treasuries located in cities throughout the U.S. In addition, the federal government would deal in specie only (hard currency), not paper money. After years of effort the "Locofocos" warmed to the independent treasury system and it became law on July 4, 1840. However, Whigs and Conservative Democrats successfully repealed the measure in 1841. The independent treasury system would be re-instituted by James K. Polk in 1846 and continues to the present day.

Van Buren also had to contend with scandal. Samuel Swartwout, an unethical schemer who had been involved with Aaron Burr in his 1805–06 misadventure, and a Tammany Hall Democrat, became the port collector of New York in 1838. Subsequently, Swartwout stole $1,225,705.69 and fled to Europe prompting a Congressional investigation which soon targeted the president. (After all, Swartwout had been appointed by Van Buren, and the president was a fellow member of the Tammany Hall political organization!) Eventually, Van Buren was exonerated of any wrongdoing, but the negative attention damaged him politically.

The slavery issue also reared its ugly head for Van Buren. Pro-slavery advocates claimed that Van Buren was an abolitionist as he did not push for the annexation of

*Conservative Democrats turned off the gas lights at their New York meeting place, Tammany Hall, to deny the Radical Democrats an opportunity to continue debate over financial issues. The Radicals struck their matches, known as "Locofocos", and lit candles, illuminating the hall and continuing the meeting. Hence, their nickname "Locofocos."

Texas. Opponents of slavery claimed that the protracted and bloody Seminole War in Florida was motivated by Van Buren's desire to see Florida added as a new slave state. In addition, thousands of anti-slavery petitions were submitted to Congress only to be immediately tabled according to the "Gag Rule." This measure was egregious to Northerners who worked without stint for its repeal.

Foreign Affairs

As if these domestic setbacks were not enough, Van Buren also had difficulties with the British over the U.S. - Canadian border, and the continuing conflict with the Seminoles in Florida. Unfortunately for Van Buren, these issues were not settled until after his term expired.

Canada

In 1837, a group of Canadians staged an insurrection against British rule. Many Americans along the U.S. – Canada border supported the rebels in the hopes that Canada might somehow be annexed to the United States. This prompted an angry response from Canadian officials. They seized the Caroline, an American vessel known to be a supply ship for the rebels, and burned it to the waterline of the Niagara River, killing one American in the process. Americans along the border were outraged and pledged to avenge the incident, but neither the U.S. or British governments wished to create a crisis over the Caroline. However, in 1840 a British citizen, Alexander McLeod, was arrested and indicted for murder in New York. A drunken McLeod idiotically had boasted of his role in the murder of the American on board the Caroline. If convicted, McLeod would be executed which may have led to war. However, he had a foolproof alibi and was subsequently acquitted.

Relations between the two nations continued to deteriorate due to a long simmering border dispute centered around the state of Maine and the Canadian province of New Brunswick. The controversy involved 12,000 square miles of territory and moved to the forefront of Anglo-American relations when the British announced they were constructing a road from Halifax to Quebec, right through the territory in question. The issue would not be settled until 1842 with the signing of the Webster-Ashburton Treaty. How was this dispute resolved? President Tyler asked Sec. of State Daniel Webster to negotiate with the British ambassador Lord Ashburton. The two men became friendly acquaintances based somewhat on their fondness for alcoholic beverages and fine food. (Bill of faire at their meetings might consist of diamond-back terrapin, salmon, oysters, casseroles, rich soups and stews accompanied by champagne, red wines, and an assortment of liquors and cordials, paid for by the British and American governments!) Webster and Ashburton eased tensions between their two nations through a combination of generalized apologies and promises, and skilled compromises. The final agreement stipulated that the U.S. would receive 7,000 of the 12,000 sq. miles of the disputed territory (the present day Maine-New Brunswick border), and a large portion of land situated between Lake Superior and the Lake-of-the-Woods (the present day Minnesota-Ontario border). The latter proved extraordinarily valuable in the future as it contained huge deposits of iron ore, known today as the Mesabi Range. It seemed once again the

U.S. had scored a great diplomatic success at the expense of a European nation, but appearances can be deceiving. In 1933, the "Red Line" map was discovered in Madrid, Spain which proved that the U.S. was entitled to <u>all</u> of the disputed territory!

The Election of 1840 – The "Log Cabin-Hard Cider" Campaign

Despite the considerable problems during his presidency, Martin Van Buren won re-nomination by maintaining control of the Democratic Party's machinery. In 1839, the Whigs bypassed frontrunners Daniel Webster and Henry Clay. Instead, they chose William Henry Harrison for president, and states rights advocate and former Democrat John Tyler of Virginia for vice president. Although "Ol' Tippecanoe" (Harrison's nickname) served in Congress in the 1820s, he gained the nomination because he was a hero of the War of 1812, and had few political enemies. The Whigs omitted any specific platform, and committed to electing to the presidency an image not a candidate, thus ushering in the wildest presidential campaign in American history. The Whigs instructed Harrison to say nothing and he dutifully complied, leaving the campaign solely in the hands of experienced politicians and publicists.

Predictably, the Whigs attacked Van Buren's political positions, but they devoted most of their energies to assailing his personal life. According to Whig campaign literature, Van Buren put cologne in his facial hair, drank French champagne out of fine crystal, and was so vain that he wore out patches of rug in front of giant mirrors in the "Blue Elliptical Saloon" in the White House. Pennsylvania Whig Congressman Charles Ogle claimed that the Executive Mansion featured "French bronze lamps… French comfortables… French bedsteads, gilt plateaus, gaudy artificial flowers, rich blue and gold bonbons…ice cream vases…olive boats…." while impoverished Americans wanted for food! The Whigs scornfully referred to Martin Van Buren as "Martin Van Ruin", and the Democrats themselves inadvertently aided the Whigs when a party newspaper, the *Baltimore Republican*, derisively and inaccurately implied that William Henry Harrison was poor, and would be satisfied by modest inducements. An editor at *The Baltimore Republican* stated, "Give him a barrel of Hard Cider, and settle a pension of $2000 a year on him, and my word for it, he will sit the remainder of his days in his Log Cabin." (In reality, Harrison had been born into the Virginia aristocracy, and "The Log Cabin" was his fine mansion on the Ohio River. This "simple man of the people" owned a pet South American parrot and enjoyed serving his houseguests expensive hams!) The Whigs had a carnival, creating an entire mythology contrasting their "man of the people" with the "elitist, effete snob" Van Buren. Mass meetings and parades complete with 40 foot long cabins on wagons, barrels of hard cider, and Harrison impersonators flooded cities and towns around the country. Gigantic balls were rolled through the streets by enthusiastic supporters signifying the growing momentum for Harrison.

What has caused this great commotion, motion, motion,
Our country through?
- It is the ball a-rolling on, for

TIPPECANOE and Tyler too: -

Tippecanoe and Tyler too.
And with them we'll beat little Van, Van, Van,
Oh! Van is a used up man.

There were dances (such as the "General Harrison Log Cabin March – A Quick Step"), newspapers, buttons, posters, stories, and songs all trumpeting the simple virtues of General Harrison. The most famous of these proclaimed:

Let Van from his coolers of silver drink wine,
And lounge on his cushioned settee.
Our man on his buckeye bench can recline,
Content with hard cider is he,
The iron-armed soldier, the true hearted soldier,
The gallant old soldier of Tippecanoe!

Some Democrats lamented these demonstrations as evidence of a moral decline in the country. The *Philadelphia Public Ledger* decried that the "Log Cabin" campaign was "a national drunken frolic". The editor of the *Ledger* was particularly incensed at the behavior of women at Whig rallies:

Was this the proper sphere of women?
Was this appropriate to her elevating, refining influence?
Did such things improve men?
No. They merely degraded women, and made men still
more degraded than they were before...."

The only interesting contribution from Van Buren's supporters during this election was the establishment of "OK" clubs which stood for "Old Kinderhook", Van Buren's home. This is the alleged origin of the common phrase "OK". The elderly Harrison won an electoral landslide, although the popular vote was considerably closer.

Election of 1840	Party	Electoral Vote	Popular Vote
- William Henry Harrison	Whigs	234	1,275,016
- Martin Van Buren	Democrat	60	1,129,102

Harrison would serve as President for only one month however, the shortest term in U.S. history. On March 4, 1841, in a raging snowstorm, the 68 year old Harrison delivered a 1 ¾ hour inaugural speech, the longest in U.S. history. He caught a cold, which developed into pleurisy and finally pneumonia. Harrison died on April 4th 1841. His last words were, "I cannot stand it…Don't trouble me…These applications, will they never cease…?", a pained reference to the incessant demands of office-seekers.

The Tyler Interim 1841–45

As a result, vice president John Tyler now became president. This was the first time a vice president assumed the presidency owing to death. As of 2010, the practice has been repeated 8 times.* The Whig leadership, especially Henry Clay, felt that Tyler should passively accede to their demands as he had not actually been elected president. They were in for a rude awakening, as Tyler proved to be a very stubborn and independent man. John Tyler became a Whig due to his dislike for the Jacksonian Democrats. His political philosophy rested firmly on states rights principles, and he resisted most of his own party's designs for expanding the federal government. Although Whigs were given federal patronage, he twice vetoed bills to reestablish the Bank of the U.S. and raise tariffs. He also vetoed legislation for improvements to harbors and roads, and distributing surplus funds to the states.** This infuriated Clay and the Whigs who scornfully referred to Tyler as "His Accidency", and subsequently expelled him from the party. He did not find a new home with the Democrats either, becoming the president without a party. (He also did not have a vice president, a distinction he shares with Andrew Johnson.) Nonetheless, he did manage a few significant achievements during his term. In 1841, Tyler signed into law the Preemption Act which encouraged westward settlement. In addition, the Webster-Ashburton Treaty was successfully negotiated during his tenure. However, there were more pressing matters facing the U.S. during Tyler's term, the most significant being the Texas Republic. Tyler would annex Texas at the very end of his presidency, largely due to issues raised in the raucous campaign of 1844.

The Temper of the Times

The German word *zeitgeist* can be defined as "the spirit of the age or time." Indeed in American history, different eras exude a different feel or mood. For example, in the 20th century, consider the emotional contrast in America separating the "Roaring Twenties" from "The Great Depression" of the 1930s, or more recently, the striking differences manifest between the "Me Decade" of the 1970s and the "Yuppie Years" of the 1980s. The 1840s have been referred to historically as the "Cheerful Forties", but the era's moniker may be somewhat misleading. Today, the pace and agents of change exhibited during that period appear both agonizingly slow and antiquated, but to 1840s Americans, they were both exhilarating and frightening. Consider the nascent "Industrial Revolution", which for all intents and purposes began with Scotchman James Watt's invention of the steam engine in 1765.

This heralded a revolutionary new age in the production of power and its applications to industry, transportation, and communications, but how? In all previous human history, power came from three sources: human beings, animals, and natural forces such as wind and water. For example, for humans living between 3500 B.C. and 1800 A.D., the ability to travel would depend on their own power (for example, their feet to walk or their arms to row a boat), that of an animal (such as a horse or camel), or a force of nature (such as wind to push a sailing vessel). Beginning in 1807 with Robert Fulton's application of the steam engine to a ship, the *Clermont*, human beings now could employ <u>artificial means</u> of power

*These presidents' died in office: Harrison, Taylor, Lincoln, Garfield, McKinley, Harding, Franklin Roosevelt, and Kennedy. Nixon resigned in 1974 and was succeeded by Gerald Ford.

** After Tyler vetoed these measures in 1841, an angry armed mob became so incensed that they descended on the White House smashing windows and leveling threats. Unintimidated, Tyler passed out guns to the White House servants and staff and personally backed them down!

for transportation. In an identical fashion, the development of the train (a.k.a. the locomotive) in the early 1820s, provided a radically new means of overland transportation. Concomitantly, new methods of communication transformed every possible human relationship and endeavor, from personal contact to business transactions to waging war. From the advent of recorded history to the 19th century, humans communicated primarily in two ways, the written word and the spoken word, with the obvious limitations such means entailed. In 1832, Samuel F.B. Morse invented the telegraph, the first instantaneous means of long distance communication. Using electromagnetic current, humans could transmit messages rapidly. It took time however to both perfect the telegraph and to convince the public of its usefulness and importance. In 1838, Morse developed a practical transmission code; by 1841, the first telegraphic message was sent between two cities, Washington, D.C. and Baltimore, MD, 40 miles apart. The first message was, "What hath God wrought?!", an obvious reference to the epochal impact the device and its technological descendants would have on humanity.

The steamboat, the train, and the telegraph all seem quaint, remote, and primitive inventions from a relatively distant past, but they evolved, as did the contrivances listed in the next section. Thus, consider this progression just for the telegraph:

Telegraph – Telephone – Wireless Telegraphy – Radio – Television – Satellite Communications – Future Developments?

Selected Inventions 1793–1844

1793 – Eli Whitney's cotton gin.

1807 – Robert Fulton's *Clermont*, first steam powered ship, makes its maiden voyage on the Hudson River in New York.

1809 – First ocean capable steamship, the *Phoenix*.

1819 – The *Savannah* becomes the first steamship to cross the Atlantic Ocean.

1828 – Construction of the first American commercial railroad to carry a steam-powered locomotive, the Baltimore and Ohio, begins in Baltimore.

1829 – Peter Cooper finishes work on the first American steam locomotive (train), the *To Thumb*. It makes its first run on the Baltimore and Ohio Railroad.

1832 – Samuel F.B. Morse invents the telegraph. He develops the Morse operating code by 1838. By 1860, there are approximately 50,000 miles of telegraph wire in the U.S.,

1834 – Cyrus McCormick patents the mechanical reaper.

1837 – L.J.M. Daguerre and J.N. Niépce invent the photograph, referred to initially as the "Daguerreotype."
  - John Deere invents the cast steel plow.

1839 – J.W. Draper and Samuel F.B. Morse produce the first photographs in the United States.

1843 – Elias Howe invents the sewing machine. Significantly improved in the 1850s by Allen Wilson and Isaac Singer.

1844 – Charles Goodyear develops the "vulcanization" process for rubber. Originally used to rainproof coats.

1861 - First transcontinental telegraph line completed; it renders the 10 day, 2000 mile "Pony Express" mail carriage system (1860–61) obsolete.

Ominously, developments in weapons technology and armaments paralleled the aforementioned inventions.

1811 - John Hall, the breech loading rifle.

1814 - First steam powered warship, the *Fulton I.*

1835 – Samuel Colt, the 6-shot revolver.

The changes effected by these and many other inventions were truly astounding. Exponential increases in production, quantity, quality, and diversity of goods, both of necessities and luxuries, improved the standard of living for Americans, and ushered in massive changes in manufacturing and management. Productivity and the value of manufactured goods exploded from the 1840s onward. The Davis Industrial Production Index registered 7.273 in 1800. In 1840, it reached 43.881; in 1850, 102.85, and in 1860, 157.94. The value of American industrial output in 1860 totaled approximately $1.8 <u>billion</u>, a tremendous leap from the less than $150 <u>million</u> in 1810. Finally, the burgeoning advances in technology and production spurred industrial growth and urbanization, especially in the Northeast and the Old Northwest (Ohio, Indiana, and Illinois). Rapidly expanding cities were also characterized by a likewise increase in manufacturing establishments, factories, banks, and financial institutions. Thus, it is hardly surprising that the nation's largest stock exchange, the New York Stock Exchange (established in 1817) would be located in its largest city. In 1840, the 5 largest cities in the U.S. were New York, Philadelphia, Baltimore, Boston, and New Orleans. In the North, the population of these cities grew enormously (in some cases, nearly tripling) between 1840 and 1860. For example, New York's population in 1840 stood at 390,288; in 1850, 696,490, and in 1860, 1,080,330. However, in the South the old Atlantic seaport cities of Savannah, Charleston, Wilmington, and Norfolk lagged far behind owing to an ever increasing reliance on agricultural exports, and a dearth of investment capital compared to their Northern counterparts. Even New Orleans, the South's most populous city and the largest cotton exporting port in the world, failed to keep pace numerically. While its population expanded 60.5% between 1840 and 1860, the actual numbers, 102,193 in 1840 to 168,675 in 1860, are far less substantial than in Northern cities. By comparison, Boston, the nation's fourth largest city, grew by 95%, from 93,383 to 177,840 inhabitants during the same time frame. Mechanization in industry changed the entire nature of work and production. For millennia, human beings almost exclusively produced items such as shoes, clothes, and cookware by the "putting out" process; that is, goods rendered and sold from the home or small shop. The proprietor frequently apprenticed or employed family members within the business. In addition, such small scale production mandated familiarity, if not friendship, between the employer and non-family employees. In short, the "putting out" workplace provided a vastly more intimate interpersonal environment than the large factory or plant. The origins of this factory system in America can be found in Waltham, Massachusetts in 1813 with the Boston Manufacturing Company, and later exemplified by the Merrimac Manufacturing Company's operation in Lowell, Mass. beginning in 1822. The "Lowell Factory System" served as the precursor for a new owner, manager, and laborer relationship inherently different from the "putting out" system. In a simplified illustration, owners and stockholders supplied the investment capital needed to finance and construct the factory, which was run by managers or foremen accountable to the owners for the factory's efficiency and profitability. In turn, the foreman controlled the workers and laborers. The factory workers, usually (defined as <u>not</u> having been extensively trained in a specific skill or trade, unlike a professional carpenter or plumber), typically worked 12 hour days, 6 days a week. In the case of the Merrimac Company's Lowell operation, most of the laborers were young women tending cotton spindles and other machines involved in producing cloth. By 1850, textile mills employ about 50,000 workers in the region.

As mentioned previously, productivity rose immensely, as did a growing physical, psychological, and economic disconnect between workers and owners which became larger as the 19th century progressed. Some of the results of this disconnect include a greater disparity in wages between workers and owners, and the early formation of unions and trade guilds. In political philosophy, socialism and communism arose condemning democratic capitalism. In the most important communist treatise, *The Communist Manifesto*, Karl Marx and Friedrich Engels railed at the class differences they perceived stemming from the Industrial Revolution and the factory system. In the following quote, Engels painted a helpless, desperate picture of the working class in Great Britain in the mid-nineteenth century:

> ….He possesses nothing in his two hands and he consumes today what he earned yesterday. His future is at the mercy of chance. He has not the slightest guarantee that his skill will in the future enable him to earn even the bare necessities of life. Every commercial crisis, every whim of his master (the manager or owner), can throw him out of work. He is placed in the most revolting and inhuman position imaginable.

> ….He may fight for survival in this whirlpool; he may try to maintain his dignity as a human being. This he can only do by fighting the middle classes, who exploit him so ruthlessly and them condemn him to a fate which drives him to live in a way unworthy of a human being.

The vast majority of Americans had little use for socialism, and even less for communism and its portents of class struggle and revolution. However, the rapid changes wrought by the Industrial Revolution, did produce concern, confusion, and trepidation among many Americans. For instance, how would the skilled artisan feel at being replaced by a machine, or the artist view the newly invented photograph? On a more commonplace level, would every American feel positively about their increasingly materialistic society, especially if they did not possess the wealth to accrue desirable items? In some instances, a gnawing discontent pushed groups of Americans to turn both inward and outward emotionally to cope with their changing society, manifest in 3 distinct ways; <u>reform</u>, <u>retreat</u>, and <u>religion</u>.

Reform

Without question, the greatest reform effort in the United States during the 19th century concerned the abolition of slavery (see Chapter 8), but it was by no means singular. Reform movements (then and now) usually employ two strategies One, reform the individual through personal suasion. Two, push for government action to address and ameliorate the problem. Frequently, both strategies are used concomitantly. Reformers also have a tendency to support a number of causes, resulting in overlapping. For example, an abolitionist might also be an advocate for temperance and women's suffrage. Both of these characteristics were widely evident among mid-nineteenth century reformers in the United

States, but who were some of these reform advocates, and what causes inspired them to action? An international peace or pacifist movement counted abolitionists Elihu Burritt and William Lloyd Garrison among its staunchest adherents, while Dorothea Dix spearheaded a drive for prison and mental hospital reform. A nascent women's rights movement emerged in the 1840s focusing on suffrage (voting) rights for women which were non-existent in America. Angelina Grimke, Sarah Grimke, Lucretia Coffin Mott, and most notably, Elizabeth Cady Stanton held a pro-suffrage conference at Seneca Falls, New York on July 19–20, 1848. Meeting in a Methodist church, 300 supporters approved the Seneca Falls Declaration. Patterned directly after the *Declaration of Independence*, it boldly asserted that "We hold these truths to be self-evident: That all men and women are created equal." The Declaration then goes on to list a series of grievances inflicted by men upon women. It concludes with a resolution to achieve female suffrage, "and for the securing to women an equal participation with men in the various trades, professions, and commerce." Though widely criticized and ridiculed at the time, the Seneca Falls Declaration served as the cornerstone of the women's rights movement. Women finally received the right to vote nationwide with the passage of the 19th Amendment in 1920.

In the 1840s and 1850s the temperance movement assumed a nationwide significance second only to abolitionism. In the first 30 years of the 19th century Americans consumed staggering amounts of alcoholic beverages, far surpassing contemporary drinking habits. Mean absolute alcohol intake per capita (age 15 and up) reached 7.1 gallons in 1830. In 2005, this figure was 2.24! Americans of every station drank virtually all day, from early morning ("Irish coffees') to 11:00 A.M. shots ("eleveners") to 4:00 P.M. pre-supper drams. Every business owner and shopkeeper was expected to allow time for their laborers to imbibe; farmer's frequently took whiskey breaks, ship captains provided daily rations of rum to the crew, and students of all ages were accustomed to periodic shots of whiskey during the school day. (Remember, the first organized rebellion in U.S. history (1794) under the Constitution of the United States was precipitated by a federal tax on whiskey.) Doctor's of the period possessed little understanding of the detrimental effects excessive drinking wrought on peoples' health. (The most notable exception was Dr. Benjamin Rush who lambasted alcohol abuse in *An Inquiry into the Effects of Ardent Spirits on the Mind and Body* published in 1784.) Indeed, alcohol was widely prescribed for virtually every ailment, from the common cold to rheumatism. It was also frequently the only form of analgesic or anesthesia available for relief from aches and pains, tooth extractions, bone settings, pregnancy and post-natal care, menstrual disorders, amputations, and operations. (Ether was not used as an anesthetic until the 1840s.) The deleterious effects of such Herculean tippling habits were quite obvious and predictable: accidents on the farm, in travel, and in the workplace, widespread drunken brawling and violence, absenteeism, joblessness, crime, child and spousal neglect, injury, and death.

Organizations critical of alcohol consumption had existed in the U.S since just after the Revolution. Some Protestant denominations, especially the Baptists and Methodists, had long denounced the effects of "Demon Rum", but it was not until the 1820s when temperance in America took on the appearance of a crusade. In 1826, Presbyterian minister (and abolitionist) Lyman Beecher published his *Six Sermons on Intemperance*, a series of blistering attacks on alcohol which found a wide public audience. That same year the American Temperance Society was established. Initially, there was some debate among temperance advocates concerning their goals. Should temperance organizations emphasize abstinence from hard liquor only, or all alcoholic beverages? By the end of the 1830s, the settled answer was total abstinence or "tee-totaling." Through countless sermons, lectures, forums, and publications, the temperance reformers were having a drastic effect. By 1840, alcohol consumption had dropped by 54% to 3.1. per gallons per capita, and they were far from finished. In 1840, 6 alcoholics were imbibing at Chase's Tavern in Baltimore when they decided to intrude upon a local temperance society meeting. They were so moved by what they heard that they quit drinking and formed their own abstinence society "The Washingtonians." The Washingtonians enjoyed immediate success, establishing local chapters throughout the country during the 1840s. Their goal was the individual salvation of alcoholics, not government restriction or prohibition of alcohol, which had become the aim of the American Temperance Society and the U.S. Temperance Union (formed in 1833). Publications such as the *Washingtonians' Teetotalers Minstrel*, and short stories and pamphlets including *Dear Father, Drink No More*, and *Mother, Dry That Flowing Tear*, had massive circulations. The two most famous anti-alcohol treatises of the period were popular illustrators' Currier and Ives 1846 lithograph *The Drunkard's Progress: From the First Glass to the Grave*, and Timothy Shay Arthur's *Ten Nights In A Barroom*, published in 1854. *The Drunkard's Progress* provides a devastatingly simple 9-step scenario of destruction for drinkers:

Step 1 – "A glass with a friend."
Step 2 – "A glass to keep the cold out."
Step 3 – "A glass too much."
Step 4 – "Drunk and riotous."
Step 5 – "The summit attained. Jolly companions. A confirmed drunkard."
Step 6 – "Poverty and disease."
Step 7 – "Forsaken by friends."
Step 8 – "Desperation and crime."
Step 9 – "Death by suicide."

Temperance forces scored their first major legal victory in the early 1850s. Championed by the tee-totaling mayor of Portland, Maine, Neal Dow, Maine passed the nation's first statewide prohibition law in 1851. The next year, the Minnesota Territory, Rhode Island, and Vermont went "dry." Michigan followed in 1853, Connecticut, New York, and Ohio in 1854, and Delaware, Illinois, Indiana, Iowa, New Hampshire, Tennessee, and Wisconsin in 1855. The effects of such laws were questionable, as violations were flagrant and widespread, and the statutes frequently ignored by law enforcement officials. The horrors of the War Between The States (a.k.a. The Civil War) completely derailed the temperance movement, but only temporarily. By the end of the century, spurred on by new organizations such as the Women's Christian Temperance Union and the Anti-Saloon League, prohibition marched anew, culminating with the ratification of the 18th Amendment, January 29, 1919. This amendment forbade "the manufacture, sale, transportation, importation, or exportation of intoxicating liquors" in the United States. The "Noble Experiment" (as it was called) of nationwide prohibition lasted only 13 years. The 18th Amendment was repealed with the ratification of the 21st Amendment on December 5th 1933. However, the 21st Amendment allows the individual states a great deal of latitude in legislating alcohol. For example, Mississippi remained legally "dry" until 1966. The American Prohibition Party, founded in 1869, continues to operate today. Its national platform in 2004, consisted of 26 items, not surprisingly one of which advocated the prohibition of alcohol production and consumption within the United States.

Note: It is significant to recognize that the various reform movements were comparatively weak, if not non-existent, in the Southern States. Abolitionists attacks on slavery and the South in general made Southerners much more reactionary towards any other reform impulses. In other words, there was a great deal of suspicion and resistance to any efforts, primarily Northern based, to reshape or remake society. The South was psychologically entrenching itself against revolutionary social and political change.

Retreat

From Antiquity to the present day, the tradition and practice has existed of removing oneself from the pressures and anxieties of day-to-day society, whether in the form of an individual choosing to live in virtual solitude, or among a like-minded group. This can be seen most readily and consistently in various religious orders and sects. Excellent examples include Buddhist Monks and the Catholic Franciscan monastic order. However, the tactic of retreating from the rigors of contemporary life has never been limited to religious groups alone. In the Hellenistic Era nearly 24 centuries ago, the philosopher Diogenes founded the *Cynic* school of thought in what today is northern Turkey. Diogenes believed that the pervasive materialism (obsession with material objects and possessions) of Hellenistic culture was obscuring or preventing his contemporaries from perceiving what was truly important in life. To correct this flaw, Diogenes urged cynics to reject both the material value system and vulgar politics, and pursue a simpler, "back to nature" lifestyle. 2300 years later, some Americans living in the 1830s and 1840s embraced a similar viewpoint and attempted to establish Utopian communities which would allow them greater opportunities for self-contemplation, fulfillment, and improvement. 120 years later in the 1960s and 1970s, small groups of committed "hippies" in the United States did much the same thing. Even (if not especially) today, there are Americans who feel overwhelmed and threatened by the revolutionary technological changes exponentially increasing the speed of life in the 21st Century, some of whom will certainly pursue a comparable strategy of retreat and reassessment.

Three (of about 100) of the more notable communal experiments of the mid-19th century are Robert Owen's New Harmony industrial cooperative in Indiana started in 1825, John Humphrey Noyes "perfectionist" communes in Putney, Vermont and Oneida, New York (which included free sex, multiple partner marriage and eugenics) beginning in 1836, and George Ripley's Brook Farm socialist inspired "phalanx" ("a compact or close-knit body of people") in West Roxbury, Mass. established in 1841.* All of these movements were defunct within a few decades, sadly the rather predictable outcome of human attempts to create functioning and enduring "paradises" on Earth. However, as a species we continue to feel compelled to try.

More durable were the developments in art, literature, and philosophy which maintain considerable influence in contemporary times. In the visual arts, the *Romantic Movement* ascended in the last third of the 1700s; in literature, romanticism flourished in the first half of the 1800s. The movement developed first in Europe but spread rapidly to the United States. Romanticism stressed that listening and reacting to one's emotions, instincts, and

*Noyes once remarked, "There is no reason why sex should not be done in public as much as music and dancing."

intuitions was at least as valuable as relying on intellect and logic. Romantics also believed that that the sensual observation of nature, with its endless cycles and patterns including life, death, and rebirth, could reveal timeless and sacred truths to receptive individuals. Some excellent American Romantic paintings include, "Lion Attacking a Horse" (1770) by George Stubbs, "The Death of General Wolfe" (1770) by Benjamin West, "Watson and the Shark" (1778) by John Singleton Copley, and "Fur Traders on the Missouri" (1845) by George Caleb Bingham.

In poetry and literature, American Romantics were also quite productive. Authors such as William Cullen Bryant, Walt Whitman, Herman Melville, Nathanial Hawthorne, and Edgar Allen Poe created literary classics in the genre (see below).

> Walt Whitman – *Leaves of Grass*
> *Song of Myself*
> *I Sing the Body Electric*
> *Drum Taps*
> William Cullen Bryant – *The Prairies*
> James Fennimore Cooper – *The Pilot*
> Herman Melville – *Moby Dick*

Hawthorne, and especially Poe, often visited the "dark night of the soul" in their works, creating macabre and terrifying characters and imagery that continue to transfix their readers. Hawthorne's *Young Goodman Brown* is a disturbing short story centered in New England concerning the dichotomous, and often overlapping, presence of good and evil. Poe's bibliography of macabre stories and poems is too extensive to list here. However, *The Gold Bug, The Pit and the Pendulum, The Cask of Amontillado, The Fall of the House of Usher, and The Raven* provide a superb segue into his talented though tortured psyche. The following excerpt from his 1840 work *Ligeia* is indicative of Poe's tone and style:

> Out – out are the lights-out all!
> And over each quivering form,
> The curtain, a funeral pall,
> Comes down with the rush of a storm,
> And the angels, all pallid and wan,
> Uprising, unveiling, affirm
> That the play is the tragedy, "Man",
> And its hero the Conqueror Worm.

In philosophy, a kindred school of thought, <u>Transcendentalism</u>, emerged simultaneously with romanticism, and shared important characteristics with it. For example, transcendentalism maintained that observing, appreciating, and indeed, attempting to commune with nature was indispensible for self-enlightenment. Nature also provided a primal gateway to a person's spiritual connection with God, the universe, and the "over-soul." (see below). The most important transcendentalist thinker and writer was Ralph Waldo Emerson. Emerson was virtually ubiquitous in the reform, retreat, and religious circles described in this section. An ardent abolitionist and supporter of women's rights, Emerson also practiced Unitarianism in the 1820s, spent time at Brook Farm, and virtually founded transcendentalism in Boston in 1836. He produced his greatest essays and novels expounding this philosophy during a 10 year period beginning the same year. Some of his most important writings include *Nature*, *The Over-soul*, and *Self-Reliance*, all published within a 5 year span. Consider the following selections from each of these works:

From *Nature*

> A third use which Nature sub-serves to man is that of language. Nature is the vehicle of thought, and in a simple, double, and three-fold degree.

> 1. Words are signs of natural facts.
> 2. Particular natural facts are symbols of particular spiritual facts.
> 3. Nature is the symbol of spirit.

From *The Over-soul*

> The Supreme Critic on the errors of the past and the present, and the only prophet of that which must be, is that great nature in which we rest, as the earth lies in the soft arms of the atmosphere; that Unity, that Over-soul, within which every man's particular being is contained and made one with all other; that common heart.

From *Self-Reliance*

> Trust thyself: every heart vibrates to that iron string. Accept the place divine providence has found for you, the society of your contemporaries, the connection of events. Great men have always done so, and confided themselves childlike to the genius of their age, betraying their perception that the absolutely trustworthy was seated at their heart, working through their hands, predominating in all their being. And now we are men, and we must accept in the highest mind that transcendent destiny; and not minors and invalids in a protected corner, not cowards fleeing before a revolution, but guides, redeemers, and benefactors, obeying the Almighty effort, and advancing on Chaos and Dark.

Emerson's close friend Henry David Thoreau also contributed mightily to transcendentalist literature, especially in his novel *Walden*, and his extraordinarily influential essay, *On Civil Disobedience*. In this section, Thoreau exhorts humans to obey the dictates of their own conscience, regardless of laws or statutes:

> Must the citizen ever for a moment, or in the least degree, resign his conscience to the legislator? Why has every man a conscience, then? I think that we should be men first and subjects afterward. It is not desirable to cultivate a respect for the law, so much as for the right. The only obligation which I have a right to assume is to do at any time what I think right.

It is apparent the import and impact Thoreau's words held for the most famous 20th century American advocate of non-violent civil disobedience, Martin Luther King, in the historic struggle against "Jim Crow" segregation and discrimination laws in the South.

Religion

Collectively, Americans have always been a deeply spiritual and religious people. Periodically, masses of Americans have been swept up by great waves of religious fervor and passion. These intense emotional and spiritual zeniths were known in the 18th and 19th centuries as "Awakenings;" one such "awakening" spiritually impacting the nation in the 1810s and 1820s spearheaded by northern Baptists and Methodists, moving into the South and West. In a similar fashion, most of New York State during the same period was characterized as a "burned-over" district, so named for the profusion of religious movements and sects sweeping through the state. In the 1830s and 1840s, Americans were still feeling the effects of these religious eruptions, as manifest by the emergence of several new sects and denominations. Religion, like reform and retreat, was (is) certainly not immune to the forces of change. To address and rectify the confusions and anxieties mentioned previously, many Americans sought solace, meaning, purpose, and salvation through religion, in both the established denominations, and in new, seemingly radical sects.

In the 1840s, the overwhelming majority of Americans belonged to one of these six churches: Baptist, Catholic, Congregationalist, Episcopal, Methodist, or Presbyterian. There were also a small number of Jews, living primarily in cities on the East Coast, most notably Charleston and New York. However, two small alternative Christian groups formed in Massachusetts, the Universalists and the Unitarians. The Universalists, founded by John Murray in the late 1700s, practiced a broad and optimistic form of Christianity. Generally defined, universalism contends that God is ultimately and perfectly benevolent and merciful towards his creations. Therefore, His true intention is to redeem everyone from sin and damnation. Unitarianism is similar in its hopeful outlook, but more focused on humanity's role in eternal salvation. Led by William Ellery Channing, the first Unitarians believed that people are by nature basically reasonable and good. As such, redemption from sin is available to all who seek it. Unitarians (not surprisingly, given their name) also rejected the idea of the Holy Trinity (God the Father, Jesus the Son, and the Holy Spirit). A guiding credo for the Unitarians has been "freedom, reason, and tolerance." In 1961, the Universalists and Unitarians merged into the Unitarian Universalist Association. It has 1041 chapters worldwide, the vast majority of which are located in the United States and Canada.

Other significant religious denominations which formed during this period include the Millerites and the Mormons. A charismatic Baptist minister in upstate New York, William Miller, founded the Millerites in the 1830s preaching that Christ's return was imminent, as was the concurrent Armageddon and Last Judgment. By 1843, Miller had interpreted a series of events and occurrences which convinced him the end was not only near, but set to ultimately transpire on a particular date, Oct. 22nd 1844. As the day passed without Jesus' return, Miller and his followers referred to the setback as "The Great Disappointment", but continued to believe that the end was imminent. After Miller's death in 1849, the Millerites and other millennial Christians formed the Seventh Day Adventist Church, and the Advent Christian Church. Miller is also credited with influencing the theological development of the <u>Jehovah's Witnesses</u>. All three denominations exist today with a core belief that the end of days is upon mankind.

By contrast, <u>Mormon</u> theology centered around new revelations and prophecies for Christians, especially Americans. The founder of the Mormon Church, Joseph Smith, was a young searcher of spiritual guidance in New York's "burned-over district. According to Mormon doctrine, in 1820 at age 14 Smith was visited by personages of Jesus and God the Father who told him that there were additional revelations to complete and clarify the true Christian faith. Smith was also told that he should await a messenger to receive these revelations. In 1823, Smith was visited by the angel Moroni who led him to two "Golden Plates" written in ancient script, which contained the Book of Mormon, the final revelations of Christianity. To translate them into English, Smith was also provided the Urim and Thummim. It took Smith 7 years to decipher the Book of Mormon, but by April 16th 1830, he completed the translation and the Mormon Church (a.k.a. The Church of Jesus Christ of Latter Day Saints) was established. To summarize, Mormon theology contends that Jesus visited America and the ancient Amerindians in the period between the Crucifixion and the Resurrection, and ascribed a special destiny to their spiritual descendants in America; in effect, another "Chosen People" in another "Promised Land."

Smith built his church on the cornerstones of collective endeavor, communal security, and the assignment of a God-given mission to Mormons. During the 1830s, Mormon converts numbered in the thousands. Counted heavily among their ranks were the destitute, the disillusioned, the dispossessed, and the disheartened. The Mormons settled en masse, and driven by a sense of purpose within the framework of this tightly knit community, began to gain both financial and political power in the areas where they settled. However, they were viewed everywhere with suspicion, fear, and contempt, and were forced to leave their original home in New York. They subsequently traveled to Ohio, then Missouri, and ultimately to the town of Nauvoo, Illinois in 1839. In Nauvoo, the Mormons prospered. They built a fabulous tabernacle and began to exercise considerable economic and political power. However, in 1844 the town exploded against the Mormons amidst charges that Joseph Smith condoned and practiced polygamy. Smith was arrested and incarcerated in the town jail, but an angry mob stormed the premises and killed Smith and his brother Hyrum on June 27th 1844. Leadership of the Mormons now devolved to Brigham Young who concluded that the Mormons should go west to avoid further persecution. In one of the best planned and organized mass migrations in U.S. history, approximately 15,000 Mormons trekked westward beginning in 1846. Their ultimate destination would be the "State of Deseret", better known as the Great Salt Lake region in Utah. Arriving in July 1847, the Mormons faced a daunting challenge in converting barren terrain into fertile farmland, but within a year they succeeded and prepared for their first harvest. There was one problem awaiting them however, a plague of grasshoppers known as "Mormon crickets." For three weeks, grasshoppers by the millions devastated their crops, despite the Mormons best efforts to eradicate them. They tried to drown the ravenous pests; they also tried to burn them out, as well as simply crush them, but nothing worked. In desperation, the Mormons turned to prayer for Divine deliverance. Miraculously, flocks of seagulls arrived and gorged themselves on the grasshoppers, saving the remainder of the harvest.

Today, the Mormon Church has approximately 13 million members worldwide, but its headquarters remains in Utah, as does its most sizable contingent of adherents.

Epilogue

Most Americans in the 1840s and 1850s did not become crusading reformers, join Utopian communes, or embrace new, purportedly extremist religious denominations. Instead, children played hide-and-seek, bucking horse, tug of war, and leap frog. They fished and camped and rode horses, just like children of every preceding generation. When they went to school, they were given moral instruction from *McGuffey's Eclectic Readers* and learned how to read and spell through Noah Webster's *Spellers*. They also worked, and worked hard, in farms, fields, and factories, as did their older brothers and sisters and parents. Young adults (and older adults still young at heart) flirted and courted and fell in love. They married and had children of their own. They worked and played, enjoyed the popular new sport baseball, attended county and state fairs, barn raisings, horse races, dances, cotillions, and soirees, afternoon band concerts in countless town and village squares, clapped and laughed at "Jim Crow" minstrel shows, and sang songs such as Stephen Foster's "Oh, Susannah!", "Open Thy Lattice, Love", "Camptown Races", and "Swanee River." Some adult males sought more bawdy enticements in taverns, saloons, gaming houses, and brothels. Finally, older Americans enjoyed many of the same amusements. If they sought more cerebral exercise, they read the Bible, newspapers, magazines, and periodicals such as *Godey's Ladies Book* and *De Bow's Commercial Review of the South and West*, and humorous books such as *Some Adventures of Captain Simon Suggs* by Johnson Jones Hooper (of Wilmington, NC) went to plays, comedies, lyceums, lectures, museums, exhibits, and marveled at performing acrobats and dance troupes. If they lived in New York, they might take one of the penny newspapers, such as the sensational and salacious *New York Sun* or *New York Herald*, or the more "serious" *New York Tribune*. They probably visited P.T. Barnum's American Museum, or anxiously awaited the arrival in 1850 of the famous European singer Jennie Lind, "the Swedish Nightingale", and they worked. In short, Americans did what we have always done, worked hard, played hard, worshipped hard, and made money. Most Americans also paid attention to politics in their town or city, and county and state. Some even followed political developments at the national level, especially as the map of the nation was being redrawn. As the 1840s became the 1850s, the United States expanded enormously, the outcome of victory in war and negotiated settlements and purchases. As a result, vigorous debates ensued over the nation's revised destiny, a destiny rain-bowed with promise and progress, but also clouded by an increasingly fractious and contentious sectional argument over the future of slavery. More specifically, this bitter internecine quarrel centered around the question of whether or not slavery would be allowed to expand into the newly acquired territories. By the 1850s, more and more Americans of every station would be drawn into a political, economic, and cultural maelstrom regarding the "Peculiar Institution", whether they chose to or not.

Chapter 10 Polk, Expansion, and The Crisis of 1850

Texas, Western Expansion and the Election of 1844

In the 1840s, the status of Texas became an increasingly worrisome topic for Americans, especially in the South. Having been rebuffed in their efforts to join the U.S., Texas' leaders had to look elsewhere for economic and military security. Their nation was nearly bankrupt, and they were faced by a hostile Mexico which seemed poised to invade the young republic at any time. Quite logically, the Texans turned to European nations, especially Britain and France, for loans, trade treaties and military alliances. These nations had compelling reasons to support Texas:

1) - Texas might provide an alternative source for cotton, thus depriving the U.S. a virtual monopoly on exports of that increasingly valuable staple.

2) - A strong, independent Texas would be a continental rival to the U.S., and provide a significant barrier to continued westward expansion by the Americans. This was especially important to the British considering their possessions in Canada and their territorial claims in the Oregon Country.

In addition, the British Foreign Secretary Lord Aberdeen was sympathetic to abolitionism, and insinuated that Britain would guarantee Texas' independence and provide economic aid if the fledgling republic abolished slavery. When word of these "suggestions" reached the U.S., many Southerners became alarmed. Why? Nervous Southerners reasoned that if Texas abolished slavery, any further western expansion of the institution would be blocked. Also, a "free" Texas would provide another possible haven for runaway slaves. As a result, in 1844 Southern politicians (especially the new Sec. of State John C. Calhoun) urgently pushed for the annexation of Texas as a new slave state to stave off these possibilities. However Northern politicians, especially in the Whig Party, defeated the proposal, fearing annexation would lead to war with Mexico. Also, as mentioned previously, anti-slavery politicians in both parties feared the addition of an enormous new slave state, especially considering that Texas' northern border extended well north of the Missouri Compromise line prohibiting slavery. The question of annexation festered and became a critical component of the Election of 1844.

By the spring of 1844, Henry Clay was assured of the Whig nomination, and it appeared that Martin Van Buren would again be the Democratic nominee, due to his considerable influence within the party. In regards to Texas, both men acted cautiously, fearing annexation would pose too many dangers for the U.S. In a series of personal letters*, they both agreed to reject annexation and downplay the Texas issue. This policy would prove disastrous for both men, as they failed to appreciate the latest wave of expansionism sweeping the nation. Americans in all sections became enthusiastic supporters of a United States extending to the Pacific Ocean, and indeed, encompassing all of North America! This was "Manifest Destiny" (a term coined in 1845 by editor John Louis O' Sullivan) – (it is) "our Manifest Destiny to overspread the continent allotted by Providence for the free development of our yearly multiplying millions." "Manifest Destiny" proved irresistible in the 1840s.

*Clay's "Raleigh Letter" of April 17, 1844 (published in the *National Intelligencer* on April 27th), and Van Buren's similar message printed in the *Washington Post* the same day.

Van Buren was pushed aside at the Democratic convention in favor of a compromise candidate, former Governor of Tennessee, James K. Polk. The Whigs attempted to deride Polk's <u>relatively</u> obscure public status (the first "Dark Horse" candidate) by printing flyers, circulars, and placards asking *"Who is James K. Polk?"** However, Polk, a tireless, humorless, hard-working man, ran on an ambitious and popular expansionist platform. He and the Democrats campaigned for the acquisition of the Oregon Territory, California, and Texas. In domestic matters, their platform included the restoration of the independent treasury system, and the passage of a new lower tariff. Henry Clay was caught off-guard by this aggressive stance on foreign affairs, but tried to recover in the summer by stating that he would not be opposed to the annexation of Texas, if it could be accomplished by peaceful and honorable means. The Democrats ran their campaign through a series of bombastic battle cries. Below are some of the most noteworthy:

"Fifty-four forty or Fight,
All of Oregon or none."
(Meaning all of Oregon or war with Great Britain)

<u>"The re-occupation of Oregon and the re-annexation of Texas</u> at the earliest practicable period are great American measures, which this convention recommends to the cordial support of the Democracy of the Union."

"Blow the trumpet, beat the drum,
Run Clay Koons, we come. We come."

There was also a "wild-card" in the election, the anti-slavery Liberty Party candidate, former Alabama and Kentucky slave owner James G. Birney. His presence on the ballot proved decisive. Birney received 15,182 votes in New York, most of which probably would have gone to Clay. If Birney had not run, Clay most likely would have carried the state, its 35 electoral votes, and the election. As it turned out, Polk carried N.Y. by a narrow margin (5,106 votes) and won the presidency.

Election of 1844	Party	Electoral Vote	Popular Vote
James K. Polk	Democrats	170	1,337,243
Henry Clay	Whig	105	1,299,062
James G. Birney	Liberty	-	62,300

Pres. Tyler interpreted Polk's victory as a mandate for the annexation of Texas, and he eagerly wished to accomplish that goal for himself before his term expired. As such, he asked Congress to annex Texas by joint resolution, a considerably easier process than ratification of a treaty in the Senate. The proposed resolution had 3 important conditions attached.

1)-Texas must pay its public debt. ($10 million)

*Polk actually had a significant political career, serving as a Representative from TN from 1825 to 1839, acting as Speaker of the House between 1835 and 1839, and Governor of Tennessee from 1839–41.

2)-Texas would retain its public lands.

3)-With Texas' permission, four additional states could be
   created within Texas' boundaries. Slavery would be
   permitted in the states created south of the Missouri
   Compromise line and prohibited in those states north of
   the line.

The vote on the resolution was very close, 120 to 98 in the House of Representatives
and 27 to 25 in the Senate. Tyler signed the resolution into law on March 1st 1845,
three days before leaving office. On July 4th 1845, a special Texas convention
accepted the resolution and joined the U.S. as the 28th state; the Lone Star Republic
became the Lone Star State.

The Polk Administration – 1845–49

In his four years in office, James K. Polk accomplished all his stated goals, a
unique feat in American history. By 1846, Polk signed into law bills which reduced
tariffs, and reestablished the Independent Treasury system. He proved no less
successful in foreign affairs, especially in obtaining territory for the U.S. In doing so
however, he opened up a "Pandora's Box" filled with sectional hostility which
helped precipitate The War Between the States (a.k.a. The Civil War).

Oregon

During his first full year in office, Polk was faced with the dreadful possibility
of simultaneous wars with Britain and Mexico over territorial disputes. He proved
quite adept at peacefully resolving the crisis with Great Britain over Oregon. The
United States and Great Britain had agreed in the Convention of 1818 to joint
settlement of Oregon, and renewed the agreement in 1827. By 1840, the British had
established a lucrative fur trade in an area north of the Columbia River to the town
of Vancouver. Conversely, Americans pursued the settlement of Oregon with little
enthusiasm. In 1843, this changed dramatically as reports reached the east of the
Oregon Country's fertile soil, unlimited timberlands, and moderate climate.
Thousands of Americans traveled west, settling primarily in the Willamette Valley
region just south of the Columbia River (near present day Portland). American
emigrants swiftly outnumbered the British in Oregon (by 1846, there were ten
Americans to one Briton), hence the boisterous demands for American annexation
during the 1844 campaign. Despite his militant public posturing, Polk had been
somewhat amenable to a division of Oregon, especially in lieu of imminent hostilities
with Mexico. After considerable initial difficulties in the negotiations, Sec. of State
James Buchanan and British Foreign Minister Richard Pakenham concluded a
treaty which divided the Oregon Territory on June 15, 1846. The U.S. Senate, by a
41 to 14 margin quickly ratified the treaty; only a small group of extreme northern
expansionists objected. Provisions included continuing the 49th Parallel to the
Pacific as the U.S. – Canada border (the present border), with Britain receiving
Vancouver Island. In the final analysis, the U.S. gained 286,000 square miles, or
about 55% of the Oregon Territory, certainly a favorable outcome for Polk.

The Acquisition of California and the Onset of the Mexican War

As Polk worked for a peaceful resolution with Britain over Oregon, conditions between the United States and the Republic of Mexico steadily deteriorated. During the campaign of 1844, Mexico threatened to sever diplomatic relations with the U.S. should it annex Texas. Mexico made good on its threat when Texas joined the U.S. in 1845, and the two nations moved closer to war. There were additional issues of contention between them, such as American citizens' damage claims against Mexico, the Texas-Mexico border dispute, and the growing U.S. interest in the Mexican states of California and New Mexico. Why the preoccupation with California and New Mexico? Even though there were only about 800 Americans in California at the time, American shippers and traders desired its Pacific ports and harbors. New Mexico, specifically the thriving outpost town of Santa Fe, had been economically attractive to Americans since at least 1821.

Polk attempted to solve these problems with money, and on Nov. 10, 1845 dispatched foreign minister John Slidell to Mexico to purchase a peaceful resolution. Slidell was authorized to dismiss American claims against Mexico, and offer up to $30 million if the Mexican government would accept the Rio Grande (as opposed to the Nueces River) as Texas' southern boundary, and perhaps sell New Mexico and California! These were palpable manifestations of Polk's ambitions for a trans-continental United States, which many Americans embraced as the logical and justifiable extension of "Manifest Destiny" precepts. To others, however (both then and now), Polk's plans and schemes seemed little more than naked aggressiveness which would inevitably and by design lead to a war of conquest over a weaker neighbor*. However, it must be noted that American claims against Mexico were considerable and ascribe a considerable degree of culpability to that nation for the conflict. From its founding in 1824, the Mexican Republic suffered from chronic instability and political chaos, which was mirrored in its dealings with foreign nationals, especially the United States. By the 1840s, dozens (if not hundreds) of American visitors and businessmen had been subject to abductions, ransoms, incarcerations, and servitude in abrogation of existing treaties of friendship and reciprocal rights. American ship captains found themselves the target of state sanctioned acts of piracy, impressment, and in rare instances, murder. According to noted Mexican War scholar Robert Merry, "In all there were some ninety-five instances of such abuses recorded by U.S. officials; they added up to millions of dollars in reparation claims;" claims which the Mexican government consistently ignored in negotiations. All of this stood in addition to the Rio Grande boundary dispute, in which both nations held legitimate claims which may have been peacefully resolved. However, the Mexican government severed diplomatic relations (the last step before war) with the U.S. upon annexation of Texas, claiming the action itself an act of war.

In any event, Slidell did not get the chance to formally submit his offer as the Mexicans angrily refused to receive him. Polk was notified of Slidell's rejection on Jan. 12, 1846, and responded the next day by ordering General Zachary Taylor to

*For example, a mere rumor of war with Mexico in 1842 prompted American Commodore Thomas Catesby Jones to enter Monterrey, Ca. and declare it American territory. When he discovered his error, he offered profuse apologies accepted by the Mexican governor who responded by hosting a banquet for the embarrassed Commodore! Although the incident appears almost comical today, it nonetheless did not amuse Mexicans already suspicious of the intentions of the Americans.

the banks of the Rio Grande. The crisis continued to escalate into the early spring. On March 12th the Mexican foreign minister suggested a new diplomatic arrangement in which Slidell would have to be replaced, and new negotiations were to be focused solely on the annexation of Texas. Polk scoffed at the proposal, and war appeared inevitable. Taylor's troops arrived at the Rio Grande on March 25th, with Mexican forces positioned nearby in the town of Matamoras.

On April 11th, the Mexican commander demanded the Americans withdraw to the Nueces River. On April 23rd, General Taylor attempted to force the Mexicans to withdraw by blockading Matamoras. Then on April 25th, Mexican troops moved across the Rio Grande and skirmished with a small contingent of Taylor's forces led by Captain Seth Thornton. American casualties included 11 killed, 5 wounded and 49 soldiers taken prisoner. Hostilities had commenced, but no one in Washington would become aware of it for weeks because of the difficulties in communications at that time. Nonetheless, Polk decided to present a war message to Congress on May 12 assailing Mexico with a variety of charges. On May 9 however, he received news of the battle and hastily rewrote his demand for war:

> The cup of forbearance has been exhausted.
> After reiterated menaces, Mexico has passed the
> boundary of the United States, has invaded our
> territory and shed American blood on American soil.

Congress quickly declared war on May 13, 1846 by the seemingly overwhelming margin of 174 to 14 in the House of Representatives, and 40 to 2 in the Senate. Ominously however, Sen. John C. Calhoun, a staunch supporter of the admission of Texas as a slave state, abstained from the vote. He desired Texas, but not war with Mexico. War would result in the U.S. gaining vast new territories. The consequence of conquest would reopen the portentous question of allowing or prohibiting slavery in the newly obtained lands, and lead to a drastic deterioration in relations between the North and South. Calhoun lamented presciently that "Mexico is the forbidden fruit, the penalty of eating it would be to subject our institutions to political death." Ironically, the Transcendentalist writer Ralph Waldo Emerson, who stood diametrically opposed to virtually everything Calhoun held dear, came to the identical conclusion:

> The United States will conquer Mexico, but it will be as the
> man who swallows the arsenic which brings him down.
> Mexico will poison us....

Both men were correct in their fatalistic predictions for the nation.

Onset of the War

Despite the predictions of American victory by Calhoun and Emerson, it appeared the U.S. faced a formidable task in waging war against Mexico. The U.S., despite forays into Canada in the Revolution and the War of 1812, had never truly engaged in a war of foreign conquest. Mexico was the second largest republic in the world, and its army at the outset of the conflict outnumbered the Americans 30,000 to 7,000. Nonetheless, American armed forces quickly proved more than a match for their Mexican counterparts due to superior equipment, organization, a professional officer corps, and the fighting spirit of the soldiers. Eventually, the American army grew to approximately 104,000 6 to 12 month volunteers, most of whom (about 70%) were Southerners. The "glory" of war frequently eluded these soldiers. They often found instead fleas, ticks, and lice, wretched food and drink, and a harsh environment. However, the war would be of relatively short duration, lasting about 18 months.

Plans and Politics

Pres. Polk desired a short war with specific territorial aims. He wished to gain California, the vast New Mexico Territory, and secure the Rio Grande as the southern boundary of Texas. He hoped for a brief conflict to minimize expenses and casualties, and to prevent the emergence of a great war hero, akin to Andrew Jackson in the War of 1812, given the tendency of successful generals to become presidents. Polk also realized the unpopularity of the war among many Northern Whigs who viewed the conflict as an unwarranted and aggressive land grab, and Northern abolitionists denounced the war as a southern scheme to expand slavery. The transcendentalist writer Henry David Thoreau served time in jail for tax evasion because he did not want to see his taxes go towards the war effort. In his *Bigelow Papers*, James Russell Lowell claimed Southerners:

> They may talk o' Freedom's airy
> Tell they're pupple in the face,-
> It's a grand gret cemetery
> For the birthrights of our race;
> They just want this Californy
> So's to lug new slave-states in
> To abuse ye, an' to scorn ye,
> An' to plunder ye like sin.

In the Senate, Thomas Corwin of Ohio shouted angrily:

> If I were a Mexican, I would tell
> you, "Have you not room in your
> country to bury your dead men? If
> you come into mine, we will greet you
> with bloody hands, and welcome you
> to hospitable graves!"

In the House of Representatives, the freshman Whig Congressman Abraham Lincoln challenged the president to show on a map exactly where American blood had been spilt, and if that "spot" was truly American or Mexican territory. (This is known historically as the "Spot Resolutions.")

However on August 8th 1846, freshman Democrat David Wilmot of Pennsylvania proposed the most divisive and controversial measure of the war. He attached an amendment to a $2 million war appropriations bill which would prohibit slavery from any territory acquired from Mexico. The Wilmot Proviso never became law, it passed repeatedly in the House of Representatives, but never cleared the Senate).

To counter the Wilmot Proviso, in 1847 John C. Calhoun drafted a series of resolutions which claimed that public territory belonged to all Americans, and to stop Southerners from bringing their slaves into these territories was a violation of the Due Process Clause of the

5th Amendment: ...nor shall any person... be deprived of
                        life, liberty, or property, without due
                        process of law;

The issue was further complicated by three additional propositions in 1847. Sen. John Clayton of Missouri suggested that the territories be organized without reference to slavery, leaving the matter to be resolved in territorial or federal courts. James Buchanan, with the tacit approval of Pres. Polk, advocated the extension of the Missouri Compromise line to the Pacific Ocean. Finally, Sen. Lewis Cass of Michigan introduced popular sovereignty as the common sense method to resolve the controversy. This doctrine would allow the settlers of a territory, acting through their legislatures, the choice of whether slavery would be permitted or excluded in that territory. However, many Southerners denounced the popular sovereignty solution, noting that Mexico had largely been opposed to slavery, and that Mexicans were racially unfit for republican government. Calhoun bluntly asserted that "Ours is a government of the white man. The greatest misfortunes of Spanish America are to be traced to the fatal error of placing these colored races on an equality with the white race." Thus, four distinct solutions were introduced for resolving the question of slavery in lands conquered from Mexico, consternating and polarizing the nation on a sectional basis. But in 1847, the war itself had not yet been brought to a favorable conclusion for the U.S. What about the generals, the strategies, and the battles?

The War – Primary Military Leaders

Theater	U.S.	Mexico
North Central Mexico	General Zachary Taylor	Generals Mariano Arista, Pedro de Ampudia, and after Sept. 1846, Antonio de Santa Anna
New Mexico to California	General Stephen Kearny	Irregular Resistance
Coastal California	Commodore Robert Stockton	Irregular Resistance
Coastal Mexico to Mexico City	General Winfield Scott	General Santa Anna

Strategies U.S.	Mexico
1) – Secure the Rio Grande Region, and proceed WSW into Mexico	1) – Repel the Americans north of the Rio Grande
2) – Take Santa Fe (in present-day New Mexico) and push to the southern California coast	2) - Passive resistance offered against the Americans. Encourage Indian uprisings against U.S. forces in California.
3) – Blockade Mexican ports	3) - Evade the blockade and encourage other countries to disregard it
4) – Amphibious invasion of Vera Cruz, with U.S. forces pushing west towards the Mexican capitol, Mexico City.	4) - City-by-city resistance to American incursions towards Mexico City

144

Campaigns - Northern Mexico

Zachary Taylor (nicknamed "Old Rough and Ready" due to his gritty character) scored 3 quick victories in succession at Palo Alto (May 8), Resaca de la Palma (May 9), and Matamoros (May 18), all within the Rio Grande region. He then began his move westward towards the Mexican city of Monterey. He took the city on Sept. 23, 1846. However, his successes and growing national popularity worried Pres. Polk who felt the general may become a viable political candidate for the Whig party in the future (he did). As a result, Polk began to explore other diplomatic and military options which might end the war quickly and limit Taylor's political appeal. In the first instance, Polk received an interesting proposal during the summer from General Santa Anna, the former dictator of Mexico living in exile in Havana, Cuba. Santa Anna suggested the U.S. allow him to travel to Mexico where he would quickly seize power and negotiate a peace treaty favorable to American interests. Polk, disregarding Santa Anna's prior record of duplicity with the Texans, readily agreed and ordered that he be permitted to land at Veracruz and proceed unmolested to Mexico City. The plan went smoothly. In Sept. 1846 Santa Anna entered the capital and proclaimed himself dictator with overwhelming public support. The problem was he had gained that public support by promising to expel the American invaders and win the war whatever the cost! Polk had not only been tricked, he had hand delivered Mexico's best general back to its army! So much for victory on the cheap!

California and the Southwest

American interest in California dated back to the 1790s, when New England ships would cruise the coast hunting sea otters. Eventually the shippers engaged in the "hide and tallow" trade with coastal California rancheros based in Monterey, about 80 miles south of present day San Francisco. Hides could be used for shoes or clothing, and tallow or animal fat could be processed into candles or lubricants.

After 1824, Monterey became the capital of California, a state in the newly independent Republic of Mexico. By the 1830s, Thomas Larkin and other American businessmen set up shipping companies in the small city. Simultaneously, American fur trappers entered the region. American commercial ties with California were slowly but definitely increasing. Some Americans began to entertain the idea of purchasing California and adding it as a state. American political efforts to acquire California were inept, blundering, and somewhat belligerent. For instance, in 1842 U.S. Navy Commodore Thomas Jones misconstrued his orders concerning California, and concluded that the U.S. and Mexico were at war. He invaded Monterey, and raised the American flag over the city! Jones eventually received official notice from the U.S. government that no war existed. He was ordered to promptly apologize and withdraw from Monterey. Jones sheepishly hauled down the U.S. flag and ordered an American military salute to the returned Mexican flag. The Mexican governor held a banquet for the "invaders" in an attempt to write off the whole incident as a laughable mistake. In Mexico City however, Mexican politicians were not so amused and became ever more wary of the intentions of their northern neighbor.

In 1843–44, Army officer John C. Fremont led a series of expeditions into the Oregon Territory and California. His written accounts of these expeditions, and the fertile lands he explored, were published in 1845, arousing American public interest in the Pacific Northwest. Fremont himself would return to the region in late 1845 with 60 armed frontiersmen apparently engaging in some ill-planned intrigue to secure California for the U.S. As mentioned previously, when the Mexican War commenced in 1846, there were only about 800 Americans in California. They were far outnumbered by the 10,000 "Californios" (descendants of the original Spanish settlers) who resided there. Like their American counterparts, many of the Californios resented the inadequacy, inefficiency, and intrusiveness of Mexican rule.

As such, both the Americans and a sizable number of Californios favored independence or American statehood for California. When word reached California that war between Mexico and the United States had broken out, opportunistic members of both groups took action and established the independent Republic of California (a.k.a. The "Bear Flag Republic") at Sonoma on June 14, 1846. Encouraged by John C. Fremont, the delegates proceeded to elect William B. Ide president. The "republic's" brief history proved chaotic, and within two weeks Commodore Sloat of the U.S. Navy arrived in Monterey and declared California American territory. Concomitantly, Commodore Stockton invaded southern California, occupied Santa Barbara and Los Angeles, and declared himself governor in July 1846. To the east, General Stephen Kearny, guided by pioneer Kit Carson, pacified Santa Fe, New Mexico and pushed towards the California coast. By the fall of 1846, California appeared to be firmly under American control. However, in October a surprise rebellion of poor Mexicans and Mexicanized Indians erupted, both groups fearful of American domination. It took U.S. armed forces 3 months to subdue the rebels. On Jan. 13, 1847, they were finally defeated and California officially became U.S. territory.

From Veracruz to Mexico City

After the debacle with Santa Anna, Polk devised a new strategy to win the war; an amphibious invasion of southeastern Mexico. Reluctantly, Polk (as he intensely disliked Scott), assigned command of the operation to the brilliant though irascible and vainglorious General Winfield Scott (a.k.a. "Ol' Fuss and Feathers"). Scott's forces would debark from New Orleans and land at Veracruz on the Gulf Coast of Mexico and proceed 200 miles west to Mexico City. Polk correctly reasoned this was the shortest and easiest route to the Mexican capital, and that American forces could be re-supplied from the sea. Scott concurred, and delighted in the fact that to accomplish the mission General Taylor would be required to divert half of his troops to Tampico (200 miles north of Veracruz) to rendezvous with his own forces. Presumably, this would prevent Taylor from embarking on additional offensive operations and dull his rising political star. Polk's hope of limiting General Taylor's fame would go unfulfilled however. In October, Taylor (under protest) ordered 5000 of his 10,000 troops to Tampico, and with Scott's simultaneous arrival, the city fell in November. In the meantime, Taylor and the remainder of his troops were situated in the middle of Mexico. They appeared vulnerable to the Mexican commander Santa Anna. In February 1847, Santa Anna moved to confront and hopefully annihilate the Americans. The biggest battle of the war was set to occur near the little town of Buena Vista.

On Feb. 22, 1847, Santa Anna with 20,000 troops attacked Taylor's army of 4700.

The battle, which featured some of the fiercest action of the war, raged for two days. Though technically a stalemate, on Feb. 23rd the Mexicans were forced to withdraw having failed to dislodge the Americans from their defensive positions. The superiority of American weaponry proved to be an important factor in the battle, as Americans utilized much more effective rifled cannon and Colt repeating pistols against the Mexicans. This advantage in armaments played itself out throughout the entire war. Back in the U.S., news of Taylor's stubborn resistance against a much larger foe confirmed his war hero status, which the Whigs would exploit in the Election of 1848. An interesting side-note to Buena Vista is the battlefield performance of Taylor's son-in-law, Colonel Jefferson Davis. Davis acquitted himself so admirably that he gained the attention of the Democratic Party. After the war, he was elected U.S. Senator from Mississippi. His political fortunes steadily rose, and he subsequently became Secretary of War under Pres. Franklin Pierce. By 1861, he would become President, not of the United States, but of the Confederate States of America!

Winfield Scott's Amphibious Campaign

Starting from Tampico in March 1847, General Winfield Scott and 14,000 troops sailed south to the port city of Veracruz. Scott's entire campaign was brilliant from the outset, alternately employing a variety of siege and flanking (attacking the enemy on either or both sides) tactics. Scott had at his disposal a cadre of able officers trained at West Point including Captain George B. McClellan, Lieutenant Ulysses S. Grant, Lieutenant P.G.T. Beauregard and Captain Robert E. Lee. These soldiers and many others would use their war experience in Mexico against each other within 15 years.*

Battle Chronology (American victories with the date of Mexican capitulation)
1) Veracruz – March 27, 1847
2) Cerro Gordo – April 17, 1847 - In a particularly bloody battle, Scott, with 9000 troops, defeats Santa Anna's army of 13,000 and forces them to retreat west.
3) Puebla – May 15, 1847 - After this battle, about 40% of Scott's troops leave the army and proceed back to the U.S., their enlistment terms expired! Scott would have to wait 3 months for additional troops and supplies before resuming the offensive.
4) Churubusco – August 20, 1847 – Santa Anna's army is decisively defeated.
5) Molino del Ray – September 8, 1847
6) Chapultepec – September 12, 1847 - Teenage students of the Mexican Military Academy ("Los Ninas") valiantly attempt to repel the Americans but are overwhelmed.
7) Mexico City – September 13, 1847 – American forces enter the capital. On September 17, the Mexicans surrender. The war is over and Santa Anna abdicates, leaving a temporary vacuum of power in the Mexican government.

*Other notable officers with Mexican War experience who served in either the Union or Confederate armies:
(Union) Winfield Scott Hancock, Joseph Hooker, George Meade, William Tecumseh Sherman, and George F. Thomas
(Confederate) Braxton Bragg, Albert Sidney Johnston, Joseph E. Johnston, James Longstreet, and John Pemberton.

The Costs

The Mexican War was neither a bloodless or inexpensive affair for the United States. In human terms, some 15,044 Americans died (the vast majority from disease) and more than 4100 were wounded, while approximately 25,000 Mexican soldiers perished. In addition, the war cost the U.S. $98 million, by far the most expensive war in terms of blood and treasure in which the nation had been engaged.

The Peace Treaty

In the Fall of 1847, Polk dispatched Nicholas Trist, the haughty chief clerk of the State Department, to Winfield Scott's army to head American peace negotiations with Mexico. In August, a brief armistice failed to produce results, so Trist was forced to wait until the final Mexican capitulation in September to initiate serious peace talks. Even then, given the chaotic state of the Mexican government, Trist was forced to wait an additional 2 months for the Mexicans to authorize an official commissioner to negotiate. By then, Polk had grown furious with Trist and dispatched orders for his recall. Trist received Polk's recall orders in mid-November but refused to obey them, feeling he was indispensable at this critical junction. He sent Polk a lengthy letter of explanation which only infuriated the president, but given the distance between Mexico City and Washington, there was little Polk could do. Peace talks began on January 2, 1848. Trist proved quite adept at negotiating the peace treaty (Treaty of Guadalupe-Hidalgo) which was completed and signed on February 2, 1848.

Treaty of Guadalupe-Hidalgo – Provisions

For the United States

1) – The Rio Grande is accepted as the southern boundary of Texas
2) - Received 529,000 square miles of Mexican territory in the southwest (All, or portions of the present states Arizona, California, Colorado, Kansas, Nevada, New Mexico, Oklahoma, Utah, and Wyoming)

For Mexico

1) - Received $18,250,000 from the U.S. ($15 million for the Mexican land cession, plus the U.S. assumed $3,250,000 in damage claims held by American citizens against Mexico)

Meanwhile in the U.S., public opinion began to favor the annexation of all of Mexico. Polk also seemed inclined to this proposal, but when he received the text of the Treaty of Guadalupe-Hidalgo, he prudently decided to submit it to the Senate. Why? The territorial acquisitions contained in the treaty were in accordance with his original aims. If he tried to obtain all of Mexico, a firestorm of objections would erupt in the North, which had been hostile to the war from the beginning. Polk realized the distinct possibility that all of the spoils of war might be lost in a bitter Senate battle over a revised peace settlement. The Senate eventually ratified the treaty, 38 to 14, on March 10, 1848. With the exception of the Gadsden Purchase in 1853, the United States had established the present day boundaries of the 48 contiguous states. In realizing the long held dream of a trans-continental nation, the intensely divisive question of slavery in the territories had ominously been reopened.

However, for most ordinary Americans at the beginning of 1848, settlement of the

Southwest appeared an intriguing but remote proposition, as most of the region consisted of harsh deserts and the daunting peaks of the Rocky Mountains. In addition, the area was inhabited by several Indian tribes suspicious if not hostile to American interests. As a result, American expansion into the Mexican Cession would likely take place at a relatively slow pace, which hopefully would lessen sectional passions concerning the expansion or restriction of slavery. If given enough time, the nation's political leaders might possibly reach a rational, long-term solution to the problem. Tragically, time was a luxury not afforded to the United States in the late 1840s. On January 24, 1848, a laborer named James Marshall discovered gold particles in a stream near Sutter's Fort (present day Sacramento), California touching off a tremendous gold rush. Within months, the news would reach the rest of the nation and the world, spurring tens of thousands of fortune seekers to California. The non-Indian population of California grew from 11,000 in 1846 to 100,000 in 1850 and over 220,000 in 1852! (Ironically, James Marshall would die penniless and insane.) The lawless conditions in California, especially in San Francisco, mandated the formation of a territorial government or perhaps immediate statehood given its large population. In addition, the New Mexico Territory, benefiting from the overland migration to California, contained 58,000 residents and was also nearing the population threshold for statehood. The vexing question of slavery in the territories was once again violently thrust onto the American political and social landscape. Ultimately, given the tense atmosphere of American politics from 1848 to 1861, only the territorial organization of Oregon remained relatively free of the inflamed sectional rancor. Oregon became a free territory on August 14, 1848, and a free state February 14, 1859, but the contentious and unresolved status of California initiated a crisis in 1849 which threatened to rend the Union asunder .

Chapter 11

The Tumult of the 1850s: Part 1 to 1856

Chronology of Disunion 1846 – 1861

1846 - Wilmot Proviso

1847 - Lewis Cass proposes popular sovereignty in regards to territorial settlement

1848 - Election of Zachary Taylor

1849 - Gold discovered in California

1850 - Nashville Convention
- Compromise of 1850

1850–1860 – Northern resistance to Fugitive Slave Law

1852 - *Uncle Tom's Cabin*

1854 - Ostende Manifesto
- Kansas-Nebraska Act
- Republican Party forms

1856 - "Bleeding Kansas"
- Brooks-Sumner Affair

1857 - Panic of 1857
- Lecompton Controversy in Kansas
- *Dred Scott* Decision

1858 – Lincoln-Douglas Debates

1859 - John Brown's Raid in Virginia

1860 - Election of Abraham Lincoln
- South Carolina secedes from the U.S. (Dec. 20)
- Crittenden Compromise proposed

1861 - (Jan. 9 - Feb. 7) Florida, Mississippi, Alabama, Georgia, Louisiana, and Texas secede from the U.S. and form the Confederate States of America.
- Virginia Peace Conference
- (April 12) Confederate bombardment of Ft. Sumter. The War Between The States (a.k.a. The Civil War) begins.
- (April 17 - May 20) Virginia, Arkansas, Tennessee, and North Carolina secede from the U.S. and join the Confederacy.

The Election of 1848

Pres. Polk insisted he would not seek reelection in 1848, due to physical exhaustion and the fact that he had accomplished all of his stated goals. His self-assessment proved correct. Polk's health had so diminished after his single term that he died on June 15, 1849, 3 months after leaving office. He was also accurate in fearing that a hero of the Mexican War would receive the presidential nomination of the Whig Party. Zachary Taylor, the hero of Buena Vista, a candidate who had never cast a vote in an election and whose prior connection to the Whig Party had been virtually non-existent, became the Whig candidate. Akin to the election of 1840, the Whigs omitted any platform and simply campaigned around Taylor's war record and personal popularity. The Democratic candidate was Senator Lewis Cass, the proponent of popular sovereignty. The Democratic Platform was purposely vague on important issues. It merely stressed the danger of abolitionism and the limits Congress had in regulating slavery. There was also another wild-card, the Free Soil Party, which consisted of an unwieldy coalition of Liberty Party abolitionists, Democrats unhappy with both administration policies and Lewis Cass, and anti-slavery Whigs. Significantly, many "Free-Soilers" disliked slavery not so much on moral grounds, but because they feared economic competition with slave labor. This group also viewed free blacks with considerable contempt, and advocated an exclusively white settlement of the western territories. The Free Soil Party nominated Martin Van Buren for president with a platform demanding the exclusion of slavery in the territories and a pledge to eliminate slavery in the future under constitutional means.

Election of 1848	Party	Electoral Vote	Popular Vote
Zachary Taylor	Whig	163	1,360,099
Lewis Cass	Democrat	127	1,220,544
Martin Van Buren	Free Soil	-	291,263

The Crisis of 1849–50

When Zachary Taylor took the oath of office for president on March 4, 1849, many Southerners felt a sense of relief. After all, Taylor had been born in Virginia, and owned land and slaves in Louisiana and Mississippi; they assumed his sentiments must surely lay with the South. However, Taylor had spent nearly 40 years in the U.S. Army with the requisite assignments throughout the country. His military service nationalized his political outlook, and his primary interests lay in national expansion, not the extension of slavery. Indeed, the Whig Senator from New York William H. Seward, a staunch anti-slavery activist, became one of Taylor's closest political confidants. When the grave sectional crisis of 1849–50 arose, Taylor would prove no friend of the South.

In 1849, the explosive population surge in California demanded some form of political organization. However, what kind of territory or state would California be, free or slave? The question was not merely hypothetical given the fertile soil and mild climate in large portions of California. However, many Californians were primarily interested in "get-rich-quick" financial schemes, not the slow development of a slave based plantation system. As such, Southern politicians realized California would try to organize as a free territory. It would eventually enter the Union as a free state and upset the free state (15) slave state (15) balance in the Senate. Unless the South received some sort of concession such as a new slave territory, Southern congressmen, led by John C. Calhoun, determined to stall the organizational process. Additionally, Southern politicians at all levels (again led by Calhoun) began calling for Southern conventions and meetings to discuss collective action if their demands were not addressed.* As sectional tensions increased in 1849, extreme Southern rights advocates such as Robert Barnwell Rhett of South Carolina, William Llowndes Yancey of Alabama, and Edmund Ruffin and Beverly Tucker of Virginia openly espoused secession from the Union as an option if California were admitted without concessions for the South. Concurrently, Californians were growing frustrated with Congress, as they urgently needed stable government to protect lives and property. By the fall of 1849, with President Taylor's approval, they decided to bypass territorial organization and proceeded to draw up a <u>state constitution</u> prohibiting slavery. Next, they petitioned Congress for immediate admission into the Union as a free state. Amidst this crisis atmosphere, Congress met on Dec. 3, 1849. Shortly thereafter, Pres. Taylor strongly proposed both the immediate admission of California as a free state, and the admission of New Mexico as a free state as soon as it reached 60,000 residents. Southerners were horrified and outraged, because if this occurred the free states would outnumber the slave states 17 to 15, with the definite possibility that the unfavorable imbalance would become permanent. Taylor also warned Southern secessionists forcefully, "Whatever dangers may threaten the Union, I shall stand by it and maintain its integrity."

In addition, the boundaries of the New Mexico Territory were hotly contested by its neighbor, the <u>slave state</u>, Texas. Beginning in 1835, Texas claimed the Rio Grande River as its southern and western boundary, which would extend Texas far west into land claimed by the New Mexicans. This was no small matter as the disputed area consisted of approximately 64,000 square miles of territory. Indeed, if the Texans prevailed, the New Mexico Territory would lose about 60% of its land to Texas! The possibility of a border war between Texas and New Mexico steadily increased through 1849 into 1850, further intensifying the crisis atmosphere already racking the nation.

As if all this were not enough, two more highly emotional issues forced their way onto the political stage in 1849–50. Not surprisingly, both concerned slavery. For years Northerners deplored the presence of slavery in Washington, D.C. This was the capital city of freedom, and yet manacled slaves were driven through the streets and bought and sold on the auction block! Many Northern politicians now demanded the abolition of slavery within the capital city's limits, but Southerners angrily countered that Washington, D.C. had been created from lands granted by the slave states of Virginia and Maryland. Again, they declared it would be illegal under the 5th Amendment to deprive slave-owners of their <u>property</u> within the District. For their part Southerners had their own grievance with the North

* A Southern Conference actually convened in Nashville, TN from June 3–12, 1850. 9 of the 15 Southern States sent 175 delegates to draw up a formal statement of Southern demands. The delegates resolved to extend the Missouri Compromise line to the Pacific, and pledged to convene again if their proposals were rejected. The Compromise of 1850 precluded the need for a future convention.

concerning runaway slaves. According to the Constitution, slaves did not become free when they escaped to free states or territories; they became fugitives. Also, the Fugitive Slave Law of 1793 gave slave-owners the legal right to recapture fugitives in free states and take them back to their former homes, but was extremely vague in establishing a specific process for doing so. After 1830, several northern states (Connecticut, Massachusetts, New York, Ohio, Pennsylvania, and Vermont) disgusted by the re-enslavement of fugitives passed "Personal Liberty Laws." Some of these statutes required extensive documentation from slave catchers, and provided habeas corpus and jury trial protections for suspected runaways, in effect crippling the Fugitive Slave Law of 1793. Southerners challenged the "Personal Liberty" laws in the Supreme Court case *Prigg* v. *Pennsylvania* (1842), and although the Court ruled the various Personal Liberty Laws unconstitutional, they were bitterly disappointed when the Court held that the Fugitive Slave Law of 1793 was a <u>federal law</u>, and as such, <u>individual states were not required</u> to provide any assistance in recapturing suspected runaway slaves. Immediately, several Northern states passed laws which effected this precisely, thus enraging Southerners who now vehemently insisted upon the passage of a new federal law to ensure the return of runaway slaves. In summary, the United States in 1849–50 faced the following:

1) - California was attempting to enter the Union as a free state which would upset the free state – slave state balance.
2) - The New Mexico Territory, a free territory, neared the population threshold for statehood which would further upset the sectional balance.
3) - The Texas – New Mexico boundary dispute was threatening to become violent.
4) - Northerners were disgusted by the presence of slavery in Washington, D.C.
5) - Southern anger at the Personal Liberty Laws in effect in several Northern states.

In 1850, an anxious nation faced daunting challenges, more so than at any previous time since the founding of the Republic, and two dire questions loomed ominously. Can a compromise be reached; will the United States remain united?!

<u>The Compromise of 1850</u>
   In the winter of 1850, the 31st Congress reconvened and attempted to resolve the serious problems confronting the nation. The debates during the session would be the last featuring the "Great Triumvirate" of Clay, Calhoun, and Webster. Younger congressmen such as Stephen Douglas of Illinois, William Seward of New York, and Jefferson Davis of Mississippi, would become prominent in the unfolding political drama of 1850, and for the rest of the decade as well. 72 year old Henry Clay addressed the Senate on February 5th 1850, delivering an eloquent description of the causes of the crisis, and more importantly, a complex solution to it. In short, Clay introduced a massive "Omnibus Bill" with the following propositions:

A. - California would be admitted to the Union as a free state.
B. - New Mexico would remain in the territorial stage.

C. - The New Mexico and Utah Territories would be organized without reference to slavery; in effect, popular sovereignty.

D. - Texas would relinquish its western land claims to New Mexico. In return, the U.S. government would assume Texas' $10 million public debt.

E. - The federal government would adopt a new, much stronger Fugitive Slave law, nullifying the various northern Personal Liberty statutes.

F. - The slave trade, but not slavery, would be abolished in Washington, D.C.

Clay appealed to his colleagues' patriotism, moderation, and desire for conciliation with considerable though not decisive effect. Defiant Southerners such as Jefferson Davis derided most of Clay's proposals as favoring the North. Indeed, they were waiting for their champion John C. Calhoun to deliver a response. On March 4th, Calhoun came into the Senate and sat at his chair. His throat was so clogged with mucous that he could not speak. He was near death and would expire on March 31st, but he had written a speech which James Mason of Virginia delivered for him. Mason began:

> I have, Senators, believed from the first that the agitation of the subject of slavery would, if not prevented by some timely and effective measure, end in disunion.... How can the Union be preserved...? The North has only to will it to accomplish it - to do justice by conceding to the South an equal right in the acquired territory, and to do her duty by causing the stipulations relative to fugitive slaves to be faithfully fulfilled – to cease the agitation of the slavery question, and to provide for the insertion of a provision in the Constitution, by an amendment, which will restore to the South, in substance, the power she possessed of protecting herself, before the equilibrium between the sections was destroyed by the action of this government.... But will she do this?... If you who represent the stronger portion, cannot agree to settle them on the broad principle of justice and duty, say so; and let the States we both represent agree to separate and part in peace. If you are unwilling we should part in peace, tell us so; and we shall know what to do, when you rescue the question to submission or resistance....*

Calhoun's speech reflected both the deepest fears of the South and the prescient warning of secession and disunion if an agreement could not be reached. It also completely disregarded Clay's proposals, and thus set the stage for Daniel Webster, who spoke to the Senate on March 7th. What would he say? Characteristically, he began with an eloquent and patriotic appeal for sectional calm and conciliation.

---

*Calhoun apparently believed the nation should have two presidents, one from the North and one from the South, with each president having full veto power over acts of Congress. Another possibility was the Concurrent Majority, in which a majority of Congressmen, from both North and South, would be required to enact legislation.

> Mr. President, - I wish to speak today, not as a Massachusetts man,
> nor as a northern man, but as an American, and a member of the
> Senate of the United States....
> I speak today for the preservation of the Union. "Hear me for
> my cause."

To Southerners he spoke of the impossibility of peaceful secession, and to Northerners he argued that slavery would never be possible in most of the Mexican Cession.

> I would not take pains to reaffirm an ordinance of nature nor
> to re-enact the will of God. And I would put in no Wilmot Proviso
> for the purpose of a taunt or a reproach. I would put into it no
> evidence of the votes of superior power to wound the pride, even
> whether a just pride, a rational pride, or an irrational pride – to
> wound the pride of the gentlemen who belong to the Southern States.

In addition, he counseled Northerners that the South had legitimate grievances which should be addressed to save the Union. Many statesmen, including Clay and Calhoun applauded his attempt to stir nationalist sentiment, but in the North Webster was vilified by editors, clergy, and antislavery writers. Typical of the attacks were these diatribes hurled by Ralph Waldo Emerson and John Greenleaf Whittier respectively:

> Liberty! Liberty! Pho! Let Mr. Webster for decency's
> sake shut his lips once and forever on this word. The
> word "liberty" in the mouth of Mr. Webster sounds
> like the word "love" in the mouth of a courtesan.

> from those great eyes
> The soul has fled:
> When faith is lost, when honor dies,
> The man is dead!

Nonetheless, Webster had done all in his power to move the nation towards compromise. But in the early spring of 1850, it was by no means certain that the sections could be reconciled. 4 days after Webster's speech, William Seward delivered his response to a largely vacant Senate chamber. He denounced any legislative compromise and declared that in regards to slavery "there is a higher law than the Constitution" further exacerbating the tense atmosphere.

By April, Clay's proposals had been sent to committee for consideration and attention shifted outside of Congress. In June several Southern states dispatched delegates to a conference in Nashville to formulate a united Southern response to the various problems. In the conference, the possibility of secession was raised on several occasions. During that same month, one aspect of the crisis threatened to explode into violence. In May, Pres. Taylor dispatched federal commissioners to the New Mexico Territory to facilitate the immediate organization of New Mexico as a state. These commissioners seemed to favor New Mexico gaining <u>all</u> the disputed territory with Texas. When the Texans found out about these developments, they went on the offensive, declaring that any unlawful seizure of Texas' territory would lead to an armed confrontation between Texas forces and the U.S. Army! Undaunted, at the end of June New Mexico sent a state constitution to Washington which Pres. Taylor pledged to approve whatever the hazards. By the beginning of July the country stood on the brink of disunion and war, but then fate intervened. In the hot summer sun in Washington, Taylor delivered several speeches for the 4th of July celebrations. Afterwards, he refreshed himself with some iced milk and cherries. Within hours, he became violently ill, and on July 9, 1850 he died of gastroenteritis (Cholera Morbus). Vice President Millard Fillmore assumed the presidency and strongly indicated he would support Clay's proposals. However, before he even gained the opportunity, Clay's "Omnibus Bill" was emasculated and the compromise defeated on July 31st. Exhausted by his efforts, Clay traveled to Newport, Rhode Island to rest, but Senator Stephen Douglas came forth to rescue the compromise. He quickly separated the major provisions of the "Omnibus Bill" into several individual bills. Douglas had worked for months behind the scenes to get influential politicians of both parties to vote for individual compromise measures. His tactic worked brilliantly, and one by one all 6 of Clay's proposals were enacted in August and September. By Sept. 17, the Compromise of 1850 was a reality.

With the passage of the final provision of the Compromise, a great sense of relief swept the United States. After all, the Union had been preserved and the great divisive issues which rent the nation appeared to have been laid to rest. In the immediate aftermath, Southern secessionists (a.k.a. "fire-eaters") and Northern abolitionists were viewed with suspicion, if not contempt, by many Americans. Americans went back to their favorite pursuit, making money, and the period from 1850 to 1857 proved quite prosperous. Yet, serious problems festered just below the surface regarding the Compromise. Concerned Southerners pointed out that the sectional balance between the states had been tilted, perhaps irrevocably, in the North's favor. In reality, the transplantation of slavery into the desert and mountainous terrain of the New Mexico and Utah territories was unlikely at best, meaning eventually they would come into the Union as free states further weakening the South. The only tangible benefit the South received in the Compromise was the Fugitive Slave Law, an ill-conceived, emotionally charged enactment. Southern politicians apprehensively watched and waited to see how and if their Northern colleagues would uphold it.

The Fugitive Slave Act of 1850

Rarely in American history has a law proved so contentious as this statute. Stringent and abrasive, the Fugitive Slave Law contained 5 basic provisions:

1. Alleged fugitive slaves were denied a trial by jury. They were instead adjudicated by a single magistrate.
2. A slave catcher received $10 for each captured fugitive ruled to to be a slave.
3. A slave catcher could receive $5 for each captured black ruled

a freeperson. In other words, if you delivered a free black to the judge alleging that he or she was a slave and they were proven to be free, you may still earn $5 for your efforts!

4. Federal marshals could deputize citizens and force them to help capture suspected fugitives. Citizens who refused could be fined $1000.
5. Any citizen attempting to rescue a fugitive or suspected fugitive could be fined $1000 and jailed for 6 months.

Many Northern politicians either voted against or abstained from voting on the Fugitive Slave Law. When it passed, Northern abolitionists such as Frederick Douglass, William Lloyd Garrison, and Ralph Waldo Emerson roundly excoriated the act. One of the most thoughtful attacks came in 1852 from Martin Delaney. An unsung black American leader, Delaney was a doctor, explorer, philosopher, poet, author, and the first black field officer in the U.S. Army. Concerning the Fugitive Slave Law, he wrote:

> By the provisions of this bill, the colored people of the United States are positively degraded beneath the level of the whites, are made liable at any time, at any place, and under all circumstances to be arrested, and upon the claim of any white privilege, even of making a defense, sent into endless bondage. Let no visionary nonsense about *habeas corpus*, or a *fair trial*, deceive us; there are no such rights granted in this bill, and except where the commissioner is too ignorant to understand, when reading it, or too stupid to enforce it when he does understand, there is no earthly chance, no hope under heaven for the colored person who is brought before one of these officers of the law. Any leniency that may be expected must proceed from the whims or caprices of the magistrate. In fact, it is optional with them, and *our* rights and liberty entirely at their disposal. We are slaves in the midst of freedom, waiting patiently and unconcernedly, indifferently, and stupidly, for masters to come and lay claim to us, trusting to their generosity, whether or not they will own us and carry us into endless bondage.

Beginning with Vermont in 1850, 9 Northern states eventually passed new forms of Personal Liberty laws to make recovery of fugitives difficult, if not impossible. For example, some Northern states made it illegal for state officials to incarcerate suspected fugitives, and the Supreme Court of Wisconsin in 1854 ruled that the Fugitive Slave Act of 1850 violated the Constitution and was therefore invalid. The net effect of these new laws and rulings was again the <u>nullification of a federal law</u>, something South Carolina had attempted in 1833! (The United States Supreme Court overturned the Wisconsin decision in <u>Ableman</u> vs. <u>Booth</u> in 1859, but the Wisconsin state legislature declared that the Supreme Court lacked jurisdiction in the case and thus its ruling was null and void!) Southerners were exasperated by the enactment of these measures, and by the highly publicized rescue of fugitives in Boston, Mass., Christiana, Penn., and Syracuse, N.Y. in 1851. They also claimed that the illegal activities of an informal "Underground Railroad" run by Harriet Tubman, Levi Coffin, Josiah Henson and others had spirited tens of thousands of slaves out of the South over the past few decades. In reality, it is difficult to ascertain the exact number of slaves who successfully escaped. Consider however that in the first half of the 19th century, the population of free blacks in the North grew at a much slower rate than the white population. If free blacks were flooding into the North in numbers as great as both Southerners and abolitionists claimed, the discrepancy would have been much less. Modern estimates of escapees between 1810 and 1860 range from 40,000 to 100,000, a small number considering 3,198,324 slaves lived in the U.S. in 1850. That number reached 3,950,511 in 1860, so it is difficult to countenance any wholesale exodus of slaves from the South.

Nevertheless, irate Northerners and Southerners continued to vituperate over the enforcement of the Fugitive Slave Act, which leads to some interesting questions. For instance, "How many fugitives were rescued from kidnappers?", and, "How many slaves were returned to their owners?"
In the first case, only 22 slaves were forcibly rescued between 1850 and 1860! In response to the second question, refer to the statistics below.

Fugitive Slave Cases 1850–60

Total Number - 191
Number Returned to Custody - 157 (82%)!
Rescued from Federal Custody - 22 (12%)
Released from Federal Custody - 11 (5.5 %)
Escaped from Federal Custody - 1 (.5%)

It appears that contrary to public opinion, North and South, in the early 1850s fugitives by an overwhelming percentage were being returned to their owners. Apparently, the emotional furor raised during the Crisis of 1849–50 had not completely subsided.

The Election of 1852

Despite the furor over the Fugitive Slave Law, the vast majority of Americans in 1852 were neither abolitionists or "fire-eaters"; most simply wanted to enjoy the benefits a prosperous America offered and to avoid a renewal of sectional tensions. Not surprisingly, the Election of 1852 did not feature any politicians associated with the crisis. In the political arena, northern Whigs prevented Pres. Millard Fillmore from receiving their party's nomination due to his support of the Fugitive Slave Law. Instead, after 53 ballots they chose Mexican War hero General Winfield Scott. The Whig Platform consisted of support for the Compromise of 1850, and little else. Scott proved to be a rather awkward candidate who possessed limited popular appeal. (His campaign statements were so unclear, hardly anyone knew whether he favored or opposed the Compromise!) The Democrats also bypassed their most likely candidates. It took them 48 ballots to nominate another "dark horse" candidate, former Congressman Franklin Pierce of New Hampshire. Even more than the Whigs, the Democrats pledged unswerving support for the Compromise. The Free Soil Party nominated abolitionist John P. Hale. Their platform denounced the Fugitive Slave Law, and again called for "Free Soil, Free Speech, Free Labor, and Free Men."

Election of 1852	Party	Electoral Vote	Popular Vote
Franklin Pierce	Democrat	254	1,601,274
Winfield Scott	Whig	42	1,385,580
John P. Hale	Free Soil	-	155,825

Pierce carried 27 states, while Scott won only 4, and Hale won 135,000 less popular votes than Van Buren in 1848. At least superficially, the election results seemed to confirm widespread popular support for the Compromise. However, throughout the 1850s a series of volatile issues suddenly and continuously emerged, disrupting and ultimately demolishing national unity.

Uncle Tom's Cabin

A strong case can be made that next to the Bible, Harriet Beecher Stowe's *Uncle Tom's Cabin, or Life Among the Lowly* has exerted the most significant cultural and historical impact on the United States. Consider that within a year of its publication in March 1852, *Uncle Tom's Cabin* sold 300,000 copies, an astounding number considering the U.S. population at the time was approximately 24 million. It became the first American novel to reach the million seller mark. By 1859, sales figures reached 3 million in the U.S. and 3.5 million worldwide making it the world's second best seller after the Bible. In addition, *Uncle Tom's Cabin* was made into a play that appeared in more than a 1000 towns and cities throughout the U.S. and around the globe. In the South, both Stowe and her novel were vilified, and 30 anti-*Uncle Tom's Cabin* novels quickly appeared, the most notable, Mary Eastman's *Aunt Phyllis' Plantation, or Southern Life As It Is.* Unlike newspaper accounts of fugitives being returned to slavery, or inflammatory abolitionist publications, *Uncle Tom's Cabin* reached the Northern masses on an intensely personal and emotional level. In December 1862, Pres. Lincoln invited Mrs. Stowe to the White House for tea and a light lunch. He is rumored to have said, "So you're the lady who wrote the book that caused the great war!" Whether or not the statement is accurate, *Uncle Tom's Cabin* undoubtedly proved pivotal in shaping and hardening Northern public opinion about slavery.

Harriet Beecher Stowe developed an interest in abolitionist causes in her twenties while living with her father (Lyman Beecher) in Cincinnati, Ohio. (She was also the sister of prominent temperance advocate and abolitionist Henry Ward Beecher.) Living in close proximity to the slave state Kentucky gave her some opportunity to observe slaves and slavery, though interestingly she apparently only visited a plantation on one occasion. Stowe intensified her abolitionist activities after the passage of the Fugitive Slave Act in 1850. In June 1851, she began writing *The Man Who Was A Thing*, the original title of *Uncle Tom's Cabin*, as a weekly serial for a Washington, D.C abolitionist newspaper, the *National Ledger*. Although originally set to run for only 10 weeks, Stowe continued her story in the *Ledger* for an additional 26. By 1852, *Uncle Tom's Cabin* was published in book form. The characters are shallow and stereotypical, but not completely slanted either for the

North or against the South, as Stowe tried to display the detrimental effects slavery exerted on the entire nation. The Southern slaveholders Augustine St. Claire and Colonel Shelby are depicted as decent and humane towards their slaves, but misguided in their support of slavery. Little Eva, the young white girl who befriends Uncle Tom, is almost a Christ-like figure. Eliza is a daring slave heroine. Her flight across an ice choked river to freedom in the North is one of the book's most dramatic scenes. Old Uncle Tom can best be characterized as a white victim imprisoned under black skin. *Uncle Tom's Cabin* primary villain and most memorable character is the sadistic, drunken, <u>Northern</u> transplant to the South, Simon Legree. With his black cape and hat and leather whips, Legree became the prototype for infamous stage and movie characters for at least the next century. With *Uncle Tom's Cabin*, Harriet Beecher Stowe personalized slavery to an astounding degree for millions of Northerners. The novel also heightened negative perceptions many Northerners held towards the South and Southerners. It also created a reactionary backlash among Southerners defending their "peculiar institution", and their region. (Refer to the section "From a Necessary Evil to a Positive Good") In short, *Uncle Tom's Cabin* greatly intensified the emotional stakes in regards to slavery.

The Pierce Administration 1853–57

Franklin Pierce of New Hampshire was a virtual unknown with limited political experience when he entered the White House in 1853. He had been a state legislator in New Hampshire in the late 1820s, and served in Congress during the 1830s, which seemingly concluded his political career. He served in the Mexican War and returned to New Hampshire to practice law. However, influential friends proposed Pierce as the Democratic nominee for President in 1852. He was handsome and charming and most importantly, completely untouched by the recent crisis, and won election rather easily. However, 2 months prior to his inauguration, his 11 year old son died in a train accident, leaving him emotionally vulnerable. Subsequently, during his presidency Pierce relied heavily on his cabinet members, most of whom were Southerners. Perhaps the most influential of these was Secretary of War Jefferson Davis. Davis was born in Kentucky, but eventually moved to Mississippi, establishing a prosperous plantation *Beauvoir* near Biloxi. Davis was an ardent expansionist and encouraged Pierce to pursue territorial acquisitions. Like both his predecessor Fillmore and his successor Buchanan, Pierce became known as a "Doughface" president; that is, a Northern man with Southern sympathies.

"Filibusters" and the Ostend Manifesto

In his inaugural speech, Pierce suggested that he would not be "timid" in regards to national expansion, a position which immediately alarmed many Northerners who objected to any <u>possible</u> addition of slave territory. However, with the question of slavery in the Utah and New Mexico territories ostensibly settled by the Compromise of 1850, where could new slave territories and states possibly be obtained? The answer was south into Mexico, central America, Cuba and other Caribbean islands, and possibly into the slaveholding empire of Brazil! Some Southern expansionists were quite enthusiastic about possible additions in areas south of the border. Still seething over the admission of California, they contended that the annexation of Latin American countries would merely restore the free-state/slave-state balance destroyed in 1850. Throughout the 1850s, private adventurers (a.k.a. "filibusters") attempted to bring this dream to fruition. The most notable (and notorious) of the filibusters was William Walker of Tennessee. Walker led private expeditions into Mexico (Baja California and Sonora) and most infamously, Nicaragua, to add these regions to the U.S. as slave states. In 1856, Walker established a short-lived dictatorship in Nicaragua and tried to re-impose slavery which had been abolished in 1824. He ultimately lost control in May 1857 and fled to the U.S., where most Southerners (and some Northerners) considered him a daring, heroic figure. However in 1859, Walker once again ventured to Central America chasing his dreams of conquest and empire. Instead, he would die at the hands of a Honduran firing squad on Sept. 12, 1860.

In an official capacity, the Pierce Administration moved rapidly to obtain foreign territory for economic and political reasons. Southern expansionists had long viewed the island of Cuba as a natural area for American annexation. Cuba, just 95 miles south of Florida, had a thriving tobacco and sugar industry and 550,000 slaves. During the 1800's, the United States and Cuba developed an extensive economic relationship; in fact, the U.S. was Cuba's most profitable trading partner. In addition, Cuban nationalists became increasingly restive with their colonial master Spain, and some were advocating independence with possible annexation to the U.S. Spain's power had declined precipitously over the past 50 years, and the Spanish government increasingly had difficulty maintaining control over her profitable island. The expansion-minded President Polk attempted to purchase Cuba from Spain for $100,000,000 in 1848, but was angrily rebuffed by the Spanish authorities. (Remember, the U.S. obtained the Louisiana Purchase for $15 million by comparison!) Why? Perhaps the Spanish government interpreted the offer from an upstart and aggressive young republic as insulting to a once great nation. In 1854, President Pierce at the urging of Sec. of War Jefferson Davis dispatched three foreign ministers to Europe to again try to persuade the Spanish to sell Cuba, and also to discern the reactions of France and Great Britain if the U.S. should acquire the island. The ministers, James Buchanan of Pennsylvania, James Mason of Virginia, and Pierre Soule of Louisiana, were authorized to offer Spain $130,000,000 for Cuba!

The entire episode proved comical, ridiculous, and counterproductive for the United States. (For instance, Ambassador Soule fought a duel with a Spanish nobleman during his stay in Madrid!) In October 1854, the three ministers convened in Ostend, Belgium to commiserate and draft a policy document in regards to Cuba; the result was the Ostend Manifesto, a bombastic expostulation of American "Manifest Destiny" which basically proclaimed that if Spain would not sell Cuba for an "honorable" price, the U.S. would be justified in taking the island by force. Consider the conclusion of the document:

> After we shall have offered to Spain a price for Cuba,
> far beyond its present value, and this shall have been
> refused, it will then be time to consider the question,
> does Cuba in the possession of Spain seriously endanger
> our internal peace and the existence of our cherished

Union? Should this question be answered in the affirmative,
then, by every law human and Divine, we shall be justified
in wresting it from Spain, if we possess the power;
and this, upon the very same principle that would justify
an individual in tearing down the burning house of
his neighbor, if there is no other means of preventing
the flames from destroying his own house.

Although the Ostend Manifesto was a confidential diplomatic communiqué, its
contents were published in Nov. 1854 by the *New York Herald*. The timing could not
have been worse considering the recent intense furor over the Kansas-Nebraska Act
(See Kansas-Nebraska Act section). The Ostend Manifesto utterly failed in its call
for the acquisition of Cuba by the U.S., and the publication of the document acutely
embarrassed the Pierce Administration. Many outraged Northerners considered it
another plot by an aggressive "slaveocracy" intent on gaining new slave territory by
any means necessary.

The Gadsden Purchase

   American expansionists had long sought the construction of a trans-continental
railroad linking the east and west coasts of the U.S. Such a railroad would connect
consumer markets to natural resources, and stimulate both settlement and
commerce. Leaders in the North, South, and West vied for routes which would be
most advantageous to their respective regions. Secretary of War Jefferson Davis
pushed for a deep southern route, with New Orleans the most likely eastern
terminus. In 1853, he appointed South Carolina railroad magnate James Gadsden
as Ambassador to Mexico, and dispatched him to Mexico City to negotiate the
purchase of land south of the Gila River in present day Arizona and New Mexico.
After successful talks with the Mexican President Santa Anna, the U.S. purchased
29,640 square miles of barren desert on Dec. 30, 1853 for the considerable sum of
$10,000,000. The Gadsden Purchase would finalize the southern boundary of the
United States and place the South in a favorable position for a southern route for
the first trans-continental railroad. An interesting side note concerns Santa Anna.
The Mexican Congress was so disgusted by his sale of the territory that they
removed him from office and again banished him from the country. Nonetheless,
Mexico needed the money and the treaty was mutually ratified on June 30, 1854.

The Kansas-Nebraska Act

   In terms of political and social impact, both the Ostend Manifesto and the
Gadsden Purchase paled in comparison to the controversy raised by the
Kansas-Nebraska Act. In 1854, vast stretches of the Louisiana Purchase west of
Missouri and Iowa and extending north to the Canadian border were still
unorganized and primarily inhabited by Sioux (Lakota) Indians. The area however
possessed considerable commercial potential, especially if a trans-continental
railroad could be constructed through it. Proposals to organize this territory had
been raised in Congress since the mid-1840s, but none had come to fruition. With
the Gadsden Purchase concluded in 1853, supporters of a northern route for the

first trans-continental railroad realized that time was running out. A southern route possessed extant advantages. After all, New Orleans was a thriving Southern port, the state of Louisiana's neighbor to the west was the state of Texas (not an unorganized territory), and the extreme southern route would bypass both the highest peaks of the Rocky Mountains and the areas most heavily populated by Indian tribes.

On Jan. 4, 1854 Senator Stephen Douglas of Illinois, the powerful chairman of the Senate Committee on Territories, introduced the first of several bills to organize the section of the Louisiana Purchase west of Wisconsin, Iowa, and Missouri. Douglas had both personal and political reasons for promoting organization. He owned land in the west which would certainly appreciate in value with American settlement, and he fervently desired Chicago as the terminus for the trans-continental railroad as it would prove an economic boon to his home state of Illinois. His bill called for the region to be organized into two separate territories, Kansas (west of Missouri) and Nebraska (west of Iowa). Both territories would be north of the Missouri Compromise Line of 1820, therefore prohibiting the introduction of slavery. Realizing that Southerners would balk at the prospect of new free territories, Douglas proposed that the Missouri Compromise be repealed in regards to the Kansas and Nebraska territories, thus raising the possibility that slavery might be introduced into the region. He also stipulated that popular sovereignty should be the basis for the organization of these territories. In principle, this arrangement appears equitable as the Kansas Territory bordering slave state Missouri would likely allow slavery, and the Nebraska Territory bordering free state Iowa would prohibit it. If Douglas' bill worked as planned the region would be settled and organized, Northern and Southern interests balanced, and the railroad would be built in the North. However, the political volcano which erupted after the introduction of the Kansas-Nebraska bill once again demonstrated the volatility of the issue of slavery in the territories.

Immediately, "Free-Soilers", anti-slavery "Conscience" Whigs and anti-slavery "Barnburner"* Democrats in the North attacked the Kansas-Nebraska bill as it would repudiate the 34 year old Missouri Compromise and potentially open free territory to slavery. Southern politicians in both the Whig and Democratic parties largely supported the measure as it seemed to promote southern interests in the territories. (Democrat Sam Houston of Texas brought up an interesting point during the debates when he reminded his uninterested colleagues that extensive lands in both territories were promised to the Indians!) The furor over the bill was bitter and rancorous both in and out of Congress. Nonetheless, through Douglas' exhaustive efforts the Kansas-Nebraska Act became law on May 25, 1854 by the vote of 113 to 100 in the House and 37 to 14 in the Senate. Douglas, who never fathomed the intense depth of emotions surrounding slavery, had won the battle, but the nation would pay a heavy price as sectional tensions were greatly exacerbated. The Whig Party at the national level would disintegrate over the Kansas-Nebraska Act, and the Democrats would begin to split into northern and

*"Barnburner" was a contemporary expression suggesting that burning down a barn may be the only way to get rid of the rats infesting it, in this case, pro-slavery Democrats within the Democratic Party.

southern wings. Also, the act resulted in the formation of the <u>Republican Party</u>, a Northern based political party which pursued a purely sectional agenda. Northerners, incensed at the emasculation of the Missouri Compromise, scoffed at any future enforcement of the Fugitive Slave Act. Southerners became increasingly embittered both by Northern reactions to the new law, and Northern resistance to the organization of Kansas as a slave-holding territory. The dangers to the Union had heightened portentously. (By the way, the first trans-continental railroad was not completed until May 10, 1869. It ran from Sacramento, Ca. to Omaha, Neb. and <u>then</u> to Chicago.)

The "Know-Nothing" Party and the Republican Party 1854–56

In 1854, two new political parties emerged in the United States. One, the <u>"Know Nothing"</u> (a.k.a. American) Party originally formed as a secret society, the "Order of the Star Spangled Banner" in 1849. Its' members were <u>nativists</u>, hostile towards both immigrants and Catholicism. Why? During the 1840s, large numbers of German and Irish immigrants came to the United States, settling primarily in the large cities of the northeast, especially Boston and New York. Many Americans viewed these newcomers as dangerous political radicals imbued with radical socialist and communist ideas. According to the "Know Nothings", the ever increasing numbers of immigrants (1.7 million came to the U.S. in the 1840s; 2.6 million in the 1850s.) made them capable of corrupting the political process. They were also stigmatized as intemperate hellions intent on consuming "lager bier" or "Irish whiskey." Also, German and Irish immigrants were accused of stealing American jobs by accepting low wages for their labor. Religious differences also added to American resentment of the new arrivals. As many of these immigrants were Catholic, Protestant leaders felt that the Pope would gain undue and unwanted influence in the U.S., especially in education and schools. This was exacerbated in 1853 by the visit of a special emissary of Pope Pius IX to the U.S. His behavior helped spark anti-Catholic riots in several cities. In the summer of 1854, the Order of the Star Spangled Banner coalesced into the American Party. Members became popularly known as the "Know-Nothings" because when questioned about their party, they were instructed to respond "I know nothing." This secrecy served the party well as members covertly renounced their old party affiliations without reprisal. On June 17, 1854, delegates from 13 states convened in New York City and drafted the Know-Nothing platform which included:

> 1.-Restricting immigration
> 2.-Restricting the sale of alcohol
> 3.-Extending citizenship requirements from 5 to 21 years
> 4.-Allowing only native born Americans the right to vote or hold political office
> 5.-Prohibiting any non-Protestant from teaching in public schools
> 6.-A pledge from its members never to vote for any Catholic or immigrant candidate for any political office.

The Know-Nothings enjoyed meteoric though short-lived success. They were most popular in New England due to their staunch objection to the Kansas-Nebraska Act, and also because large numbers of immigrants had moved into the region. Ironically, they also showed considerable strength in the Upper South, playing on fears that immigrants were against slavery. Between 1854 and 1856, Know-Nothing governors were elected in 7 states and took control of the Massachusetts legislature. Former president Millard Fillmore ran as a Know-Nothing in the presidential election of 1856 and received nearly 900,000 popular votes. But almost as quickly as it had arrived, the Know-Nothing movement splintered due to the sectional divide over slavery. After 1856, anti-slavery Know-Nothings gravitated towards the Republicans, while the rest returned to the Democrats, or to the dying remnants of the Whig Party.

As mentioned previously, the modern <u>Republican Party</u> formed amid the turmoil over the Kansas-Nebraska Act and remains one of the two major political parties to the present, although many of its tenets have changed over time. Disgust over the passage of that act prompted large numbers of "Free-Soilers", "Conscience" Whigs, "Barnburner" Democrats, anti-slavery Know-Nothings, and Liberty Party abolitionists to seek a new umbrella organization or political party to further their economic and political aims. In February 1854, Wisconsin lawyer Alvan Bovay called for representatives of these groups to meet in Ripon, Wisconsin to launch a new party. It would be labeled "Republican", a reference to Thomas Jefferson's party, the Democratic-Republicans. The movement caught on rapidly. By May, thirty Congressmen became Republicans; in July, delegates in Ripon drafted a formal platform:

1.- No slavery in the territories. (More specifically, in their election platform of \ 1856, Republicans demanded the admission of Kansas as a free state.
2.- Cheap or free public land grants in the West to encourage <u>white</u> settlement
3.- Federal government support (subsidies, land grants, loans, etc...) for internal improvements, and most importantly, a trans-continental railroad with a northern terminus (origin point).
4.- High tariffs to protect Northern industries, especially after 1856.

This platform reflected the aspirations of a large number of Northerners, as election results would soon attest. However, there was virtually nothing of benefit in the Republican Party for Southerners who almost uniformly condemned restrictions on slavery in the territories, high tariffs, and large public expenditures for internal improvements. (Louisiana sugar planters were an exception to this rule as they favored protective tariffs because of competition from Cuba and Hawaii.) It was clear from the beginning, that the Republican positions reflected Northern interests exclusively.

<u>Tensions in Kansas</u>
American settlers quickly emigrated to the Kansas region after the passage of the Kansas-Nebraska Act in 1854. While many of the settlers were primarily motivated by the opportunity for a fresh start on newly obtained lands, ideologues from the North and South came to Kansas determined to either prohibit or extend slavery

into the territory. Some Northern settlers were sponsored by new organizations such as Eli Thayer's "New England Emigrant Aid Society." Southerners, primarily from neighboring state Missouri, also moved into Kansas. By early 1855, the Kansas territory held enough settlers to hold elections for a territorial legislature, with the actual election being scheduled for March 30. However, on election day 5,000 Missourians (eventually referred to as "Border Ruffians" by Northerners) crossed into Kansas and voted illegally to ensure that the Kansas legislature would be dominated by pro-slavery representatives. (Ironically, there was no need for the Missourians to skew the election because at the time pro-slavery settlers outnumbered anti-slavery settlers in Kansas.) As a result, there were thousands more votes cast in the election than there were eligible voters in Kansas! Predictably, the fraudulent vote elected a vast majority of pro-slavery men to the legislature. The territorial governor Andrew Reeder promptly disavowed the election, but did nothing to prevent the legislature from passing laws allowing slavery into Kansas. Free state advocates angrily met in Topeka in 1855 and began petitioning for Kansas' direct admission into the Union as a free state, therefore bypassing the pro-slavery territorial legislature. Their proposed state constitution prohibited both slavery and the emigration of free blacks into Kansas. By late 1855, Kansas was bitterly divided between pro-slavery settlers who established themselves in Leavenworth, and anti-slavery settlers who concentrated around Lawrence, less than 100 miles apart. Both sides began to arm heavily, and violent confrontations between the two groups proved imminent.

"Bleeding Kansas"

By the Spring of 1856, tensions in Kansas boiled over into violence. On May 21st "Border Ruffians" and pro-slavery Kansans went on a drunken rampage in Lawrence, attacking the offices of the free-state newspapers, *Kansas Free State* and the *Herald of Freedom*, and setting fire to the Free State Motel and other buildings. In what came to be known as "the sack of Lawrence", only one person died, a pro-slavery settler hit by falling debris. However, John Brown, a violent abolitionist from Connecticut who emigrated to Kansas in 1855, determined to avenge the attack. On May 24th Brown, along with a small band of followers including 4 of his sons, descended on a small community of pro-slavery settlers clustered around Pottawatomie Creek. Brown and his men brutally murdered 5 men, splitting their heads with broadswords, and hacking their corpses to pieces. The "sack of Lawrence" and the "Pottawatomie Massacre" ushered in a period of violence and disorder which Northern newspapers referred to as "Bleeding Kansas." By the end of the year, about 200 people had been killed in the fighting with nearly $2 million in property damaged or destroyed. However, the violence began to subside with the appointment of a strong new territorial governor, John Geary. For the next year, Kansans concentrated more on making money in land speculation than waging civil war on each other. Eventually, a new dispute over a proposed state constitution would bring the Kansas Territory back into the national political spotlight in 1857–58.

The Brooks-Sumner Affair

At precisely the same time Kansas was racked by disorder, a disgraceful and divisive episode took place in the U.S. Congress. On May 19th and 20th, Republican Senator Charles Sumner gave an insulting and vitriolic speech entitled "The Crime Against Kansas." Sumner had been elected in 1851 as an outspoken abolitionist and advocate for equal rights for black Americans. (He served in the Senate until his death in 1874.) He was alternately eloquent, intelligent, abrasive, passionate, and extremely self-righteous during his 23 year career in the Senate. The title of his speech suggested a critique of government policies in Kansas; however, its' content centered on personal attacks and execration of 3 colleagues, Sen. Stephen Douglas of Illinois, Sen. James Mason of Virginia, and especially, Sen. Andrew P. Butler of South Carolina, who was not even present in Congress during the speech! Permeated with references to ancient Greece and Rome, as well as sexual allusions, the 7 page peroration certainly is not sparing in its language:

> ...But the wickedness which I now begin to expose is immeasurably aggravated by the motive which prompted it. Not in any common lust for power did this uncommon tragedy have its origin. It is the rape of a virgin Territory, compelling it to the hateful embrace of Slavery; and it may be clearly traced to a depraved longing for a new slave State, the hideous offspring of such a crime, in the hope of adding to the power of slavery in the National Government....

> ...But, before entering upon the argument, I must say something of a general character, particularly to what has fallen from Senators who have raised themselves to eminence on this floor in championship of human wrongs. I mean the Senator from South Carolina (Mr. Butler), and the Senator from Illinois (Mr. Douglas), who, though unlike as Don Quixote and Sancho Panza, yet like this couple, sally forth together in the same adventure. I regret very much to miss the elder Senator (Mr. Butler) from his seat; but the cause against which he has run such a tilt, with such activity of animosity, demands that the opportunity of exposing him should not be lost; and it is for this cause that I speak. The Senator from South Carolina has read many books of chivalry, and believes himself a chivalrous knight, with sentiments of honor and courage. Of course he has chosen a mistress to whom he has made his vows, and who, though ugly to others, is always lovely to him; though polluted in the sight of the world, is chaste in his sight, I mean the harlot, Slavery. For her, his tongue is always profuse in words. Let her be impeached in character, or any proposition be made to shut her out from the extension of her wantonness, and no extravagance of manner or hardihood of assertion is then too great for this Senator. The frenzy of Don Quixote, on behalf of his wench, Dulcinea del Toboso, is all surpassed....

With regret, I come again upon the Senator from South Carolina, who, omnipresent in this debate, overflowed with rage at the simple suggestion that Kansas had applied for admission as a State, and with incoherent phrases, discharged the loose expectoration of his speech, now upon her representative, and then upon her people. There was no extravagance of the ancient parliamentary debate, which he did not repeat; nor was there any possible deviation from truth which he did not make, with so much passion, I am glad to add, as to save him from the suspicion of internal aberration. But the Senator touches nothing which he does not disfigure with error, sometimes of principle, sometimes of fact. He shows an incapacity of accuracy, whether in stating the Constitution, or in stating the law, whether in the details of statistics or the diversions of scholarship. He cannot open his mouth, but out there flies a blunder....

Sumner's intensely derisive language and tone elicited nearly universal condemnation from his peers. Indeed, the entire event quite possibly could have discredited Sumner and embarrassed the abolitionist movement had it not been for the retaliatory actions of Sen. Butler's nephew, South Carolina Congressman Preston Brooks. Brooks brooded over Sumner's speech, and contemplated how to redress the insults to his uncle. He considered challenging Sumner to a duel, or horsewhipping him in the streets of Washington, D.C., before finally settling on a "suitable" response. On May 22, Brooks approached Sumner sitting at his Senate desk, verbally assailed him, and then began beating him over the head with a gutta-percha cane! After several blows, the cane broke. Sumner, attempting to escape, wrenched his desk from its moorings and collapsed bleeding onto the floor. Sumner sustained physical and psychological injuries which prevented his return to the Senate until 1859. Brooks was fined $300 by a Washington judge for simple assault and battery. He was also censured by his peers, and subsequently resigned from the House of Representatives on July 14th.

Northern and Southern reactions to the Brooks-Sumner affair reveal how culturally divided the nation had become by 1856. In the North, Sumner was regarded as a fallen martyr, a victim of the savagery engendered by the barbarous slave system in the South. The Massachusetts legislature solemnly kept Sumner's Senate seat vacant until he could resume his duties. Brooks was depicted in Northern editorials and cartoons as an uncivilized, violent brute, a perfectly loathsome example of "Southern Chivalry." In the South, Brooks was lauded as a hero, an avenging and dutiful son to his family and state, who had justifiably punished a libelous coward for delivering a vulgar invective. Supporters sent him dozens of canes (one even sent a gold-handled bullwhip) to similarly discipline "impudent Yankees." In addition, South Carolinians immediately reelected Brooks to Congress. Brooks and Sumner, with their reckless and disturbing actions, highlighted the rising sectional hostilities.

Chapter 12

The Tumult of the 1850s: Part 2 to First Manassas (First Bull Run)

The Election of 1856

Just as in 1852, the Election of 1856 was a 3 party contest, but with a very different lineup. Instead of Democrats, Whigs, and Free-Soilers, this election featured Democrats, Republicans, and Know-Nothings. The Democrats quickly jettisoned Pres. Franklin Pierce due to his troublesome association with the Ostend Manifesto and the Kansas-Nebraska Act. Instead, they opted for a career politician, James Buchanan, who had been out of the country during the fray over Kansas. The Democratic platform supported the Kansas-Nebraska Act, popular sovereignty in the territories, and enforcement of the Fugitive Slave Law. The Republicans nominated an explorer and soldier of somewhat dubious qualifications, John C. Fremont. Nicknamed "the Pathfinder", Fremont's greatest political asset was his beautiful and intelligent wife, Jesse Benton Fremont, the daughter of prominent Missouri Congressman Thomas Hart Benton. The Republican platform echoed their stated positions in 1854, and was encapsulated in a catchy slogan, "Free Speech, Free Press, Free Soil, Free Men, Fremont and Victory!" The Know-Nothings nominated Millard Fillmore. They advocated immigration restriction, but were coming apart over the slavery issue. This would be their first and last appearance as a major party in a presidential election.

Election of 1856	Party	Electoral Vote	Popular Vote
James Buchanan	Democrat	174	1,838,169
John C. Fremont	Republican	114	1,341,264
Millard Fillmore	Know-Nothing	8	874,534

What is striking about this election is not that Buchanan won, but the immediate strength exhibited by the Republicans, a party catering solely to the North. Fremont carried 11 states, all in that region. If he had won in Pennsylvania and Indiana, (or Illinois), he would have won the presidency. This fact was not lost on nervous Southerners who were increasingly aware of their minority status within the Union. If a future Republican candidate carried all of the Northern states, he would become president by virtue of winning a majority in the Electoral College. This would occur regardless of the election results in the South.

Crisis in 1857

After enduring the traumatic events of 1856, most Americans probably hoped for a respite in 1857. Instead, a fresh series of judicial, territorial, and economic crises' confronted the nation. A court case involving slavery reached the Supreme Court in 1856, and its imminent ruling would send shockwaves throughout the country. The controversial issue of statehood for Kansas arose once again in 1857. Finally, an economic slowdown, particularly hard felt in the North, wracked the nation. All of these occurrences exacerbated sectional ill-will, and continued pushing the U.S. towards possible disunion and war.

The *Dred Scott* Decision

On March 4, 1857, James Buchanan became President and delivered his inaugural speech. During his address, he stated that the Supreme Court would in the immediate future hand down its ruling on an important case concerning slavery in the territories. He pledged to dutifully and unconditionally accept the Court's ruling, whatever the outcome, and urged all Americans to do the same. (In reality, Buchanan's statement was quite disingenuous as he already knew of the Court's decision and supported it!) Two days later, the Supreme Court issued its infamous _Dred Scott_ Decision, one of the most ill-reasoned and destructive rulings in U.S. history.

Dred Scott was born a slave on the Blow family plantation in Virginia in 1795. In 1827, his owner Peter Blow took him to St. Louis. He eventually sold Scott to an army physician, Dr. John Emerson, in 1834. Shortly thereafter, Emerson took Dred Scott (Scott worked as a hand servant) to Fort Armstrong, Illinois, and then to Fort Snelling in the Wisconsin Territory (present-day Minnesota). Scott was held as a slave in a <u>free state</u> and a <u>free territory</u> for four years, before returning to St. Louis in 1838. Dr. Emerson died in 1843 and Scott became the property of his widow.

Mrs. Emerson subsequently remarried and moved to Massachusetts, leaving Scott under the control of her brother John Sanford. Sanford himself moved to New York, leaving Scott under the supervision of a property agent. However, in 1846 Scott, encouraged by his former owner's son Henry Blow, decided to seek his freedom in court on the grounds that living in a free state and territory had made him a free man. A Missouri Circuit Court quickly concurred and ordered him released. Mrs. Emerson appealed the decision to the Missouri Supreme Court. In 1852, the justices ruled that Scott was a slave, not a citizen, and thus not entitled to sue in court. Because the case involved persons in several states, it was then sent to Federal Circuit Court in 1853, where the ruling once again went against Dred Scott. Upon appeal, the case of _Scott v. Sanford_ eventually reached the U.S. Supreme Court in 1856. It was adjudicated for several months before the ruling was announced on March 6, 1857. The vote was 7 to 2 against Scott. Seven judges, 5 of whom were Southerners, ruled against Scott on a variety of grounds. Indeed, each justice in the majority wrote a separate opinion to clarify their particular position. As a result, Chief Justice Roger B. Taney's opinion received the most attention and scrutiny. Taney contended that:

A. Dred Scott was not a citizen and therefore could not sue in federal court. (This had been the ruling issued by the lower court, and could have concluded the case at that point.)

B. Blacks, whether free or slave, were not citizens of the United States. "The descendants of Africans who were imported into this country and sold as slaves, when they shall become emancipated, or who are born of parents who had become free before their birth, are not citizens of a state in the sense in which the word _citizen_ is used in the Constitution of the United States."

C. The Missouri Compromise was unconstitutional.

D. Slavery was permissible in <u>all</u> the territories. "Neither Dred Scott himself, nor any of his family were made free by being carried into such territory, even if they had been carried there by their owner with the intention of becoming permanent residents."

The *Dred Scott* decision in many aspects defied historical realities in the United States. For example, there is no mention in either the Declaration of Independence or the U.S. Constitution, sources cited prominently in Taney's opinion, that black Americans could never be citizens. Indeed, in some states free black males were allowed to vote, a right reserved to citizens. The Supreme Court's decision in one dramatic action legitimized the extreme Southern position that slaves as property could be transported into <u>any</u> territory, regardless of <u>any</u> action taken by Congress. Understandably, Southerners were elated, while Northerners were vehemently outraged by the decision. Many Northerners considered the decision a perversion of constitutional guarantees of freedom and further evidence that a Southern "slaveocracy" was usurping control over the federal government. Dozens of attacks were hurled at the decision by angry Northern politicians, preachers, and pundits. Consider this blistering editorial published on March 9, 1857, in the Albany, New York *Evening Journal*:

> The three hundred and forty-seven thousand five hundred and twenty- five slaveholders in the Republic, accomplished the day before yesterday a great success – as shallow men estimate success. They converted the Supreme Court of Law and Equity of the United States of America into a propagandist of human Slavery. Fatal day for a judiciary made reputable throughout the world, and reliable to all in this nation, by the learning and the virtues of Jay, Rutledge, Ellsworth, Marshall, and Story!
>
> The conspiracy is nearly completed. The Legislation of the republic is in the hands of this handful of Slaveholders. The United States Senate assures it to them. The Executive power of the Government is theirs. Buchanan took the oath of fealty to them on the steps of the Capitol last Wednesday. The body which gives the supreme law of the land, has just acceded to their demands, and dared to declare that under the charter of the Nation, men of African descent are not citizens of the United States and can not be – that the Ordinance of 1787 was void – that human Slavery is not a local thing, but pursues its victims to free soil, clings to them wherever they go, and returns with them – that the American Congress has no power to prevent the enslavement of men in the National Territories – that the inhabitants themselves of the Territories have no power to exclude human bondage from their midst – and that men of color cannot be suitors for justice in the Courts of the United States!
>
> The *Lemmon* Case* is on its way to this corrupt fountain of law.

* *Lemmon v. The People* originated on November 6, 1852. A free black citizen of New York, Louis Napoleon, filed suit in New York Superior Court against Jonathan Lemmon who brought 8 slaves from Virginia to New York City. He held them in a boarding house while awaiting steam ship passage to Texas. Southerners had been accorded for decades the privilege of bringing slaves to free states for short periods of time while in transit to other countries or slave states. The Superior Court ruled against Lemmon, but with the aid of the State of Virginia, he appealed the decision to the New York Court of Appeals. The Court of Appeals also ruled against Lemmon (with 3 justices dissenting) in March 1860. If secession and war had not interrupted the process, the case would have "arrived" at the Supreme Court, and may indeed resulted in a decision legalizing slavery everywhere!

Arrived there, a new shackle for the North will be handed to the servile Supreme Court, to rivet upon us. A decision of that case is expected which shall complete the disgraceful labors of the Federal Judiciary in behalf of Slavery – a decision that slaves can be lawfully held in free States, and Slavery be fully maintained here in New York through the sanctions of "property" contained in the Constitution. That decision will be rendered....

The ramifications of the Dred Scott Decision were momentous. Northerners were intransigent in their opposition to the ruling, and the Republican Party's membership enlarged substantially because of it, its members determined to stop any further expansion of slavery. Southerners were equally enraged at Northern unwillingness to adhere to the Supreme Court's decision. They also resented continuing Northern resistance to the Fugitive Slave Law, free-soil competition in Kansas, and the ever more venomous attacks hurled at their region and their culture by outspoken abolitionists. Encouraged by the radical secessionists known as "fire-eaters", more and more Southerners became increasingly convinced that their position in the Union was unsafe, if not untenable. The Dred Scott Decision proved a watershed in the cataclysmic events to come in 1861.

What became of Dred Scott? In the spring of 1857, John Sanford died, and Dred Scott became the property of Taylor Blow, a son of Dred Scott's original owner Peter Blow. Mr. Blow freed Scott on May 26, 1857. Scott subsequently found work as an attendant at a St. Louis hotel. He died of tuberculosis on Sept. 17, 1858.

The Lecompton Controversy in Kansas

The controversy over slavery's status in Kansas again became a prominent political issue in 1857. In March 1857, the pro-slavery territorial legislature of Kansas called for a special convention to meet in Lecompton to draft a state constitution. Anti-slavery forces, convinced that the whole process was corrupt and would result in a pro-slavery constitution, boycotted and refused to participate. As a result, supporters of slavery dominated the convention. In May, a new territorial governor Robert J. Walker arrived in Kansas and tried to convince the anti-slavery forces to involve themselves in the ongoing deliberations, but to no avail, and the pro-slavery delegates maintained control of the convention. He did convince them to vote in the elections for a new territorial legislature scheduled for October. As a result, opponents of slavery won the elections handily resulting in an anti-slavery legislature and a pro-slavery constitutional convention. The convention's finished document, the Lecompton Constitution, was designed to permit slavery in Kansas under any circumstances. The convention scheduled a referendum on the constitution for Dec. 21, 1857, with voters given the choice of approving it "with slavery" or approving it "without slavery". If a resident voted for the constitution "with slavery", slaves could be brought into Kansas legally. If a resident voted for the constitution "without slavery", no additional importation of slaves into Kansas would be allowed. However, in 1857 there were about 200 slaves already in Kansas. They and their children would remain as slaves in Kansas indefinitely!

The anti-slavery forces recognized this trap. As such, they again boycotted and refused to vote. Proponents of slavery easily passed the referendum and pushed for Kansas' statehood under the Lecompton Constitution, as it became known. Gov. Walker, who had promised fair elections in Kansas, now went to Washington to convince Pres. Buchanan and Congress to disavow both the referendum and the constitution as unrepresentative and fraudulent. Pres. Buchanan, heavily influenced by his Southern supporters, refused and declared that Kansas should be admitted to the Union under the Lecompton Constitution. Northern Democrats, especially Sen. Stephen Douglas, railed against Lecompton, essentially declaring the entire process a perversion of popular sovereignty. Southern Democrats loudly supported it for the obvious reason of gaining a new slave state. The rancor continued into 1858, when Kansas voters overwhelmingly rejected the Lecompton Constitution twice, once on Jan. 4th and finally on Aug. 2, 1858. The issue of slavery in Kansas was settled. It entered the Union on Jan. 29, 1861 as a free state. The Lecompton Controversy however split the Democratic Party into Northern and Southern wings, and earned Stephen Douglas animosity and execration in the South. The results would be keenly felt in the presidential race of 1860.

The Panic of 1857

Concomitant with the Dred Scott Decision and the Lecompton Controversy, in 1857 the nation entered into another of its periodic economic depressions; this one however was more regional in its effects than the previous Panic of 1837. The causes of this economic downturn are similar in some respects to those which precipitated the Panic of 1819.

Causes
A. The Crimean War (1854–56) created an artificially high demand for American agricultural products. When the war ended, European imports of American goods lessened substantially. Customs receipts dropped from $348 million to $263 million between 1857 and 1858, the biggest one year decline in history to that point.
B. Land over-speculation, especially in the West. In many instances, reckless investments focused on new railroad lines in sparsely settled territories.
C. Business failures; the bankruptcy of the Ohio Life Insurance and Trust Company in August 1857 created a ripple effect of business closures throughout the nation. This also adversely affected the stock market.
D. Problems manifest in the irregular bank note system. (Too many different types of paper money in unregulated circulation)
E. Inflation caused by the massive influx of gold from California after 1849. A related cause involved the passenger-cargo vessel the S.S. *Central America.* Between 1852 and 1857, the *Central America* carried approximately 1/3 of the gold mined in California (valued at $150 million) from ports in Panama to the East Coast, most importantly New York City. On Sept. 3rd 1857, she departed from Colon, Panama en route to New York City carrying 578 passengers and crew and 6000 pounds of gold, much of it already minted into coins. On Sept. 11th, the ship encountered a hurricane off the North Carolina coast, 160 miles east of Cape Hatteras, and sank the next day with the loss of

426 persons and the entire gold cargo. The loss of this tremendous fortune had a devastating effect on New York's financial institutions, which found themselves unable to repay creditors or meet payroll obligations. Consequently, many went out of business causing a ripple effect throughout the nation's economy, <u>especially in the North</u>. (By the way, in 1986 salvage operators located the *Central America* and retrieved some of the gold, valued at between $100 and $150 million.

The Panic of 1857, though lasting only until 1859, caused unprecedented unemployment and business failures, most keenly experienced in the Northern States. Northern politicians and pundits, especially within the Republican Party quickly blamed their economic woes on the new Tariff of 1857 which significantly reduced import duties. In the Oct. 22, 1857 edition of the *New York Tribune*, editor Horace Greeley complained that, "No truth of mathematics is more clearly demonstrable than that the ruin about us is fundamentally attributable to the destruction of the Protective Tariff." The tariff enjoyed wide support among Southerners and Southern Democrats in particular (infuriating Northerners), but was not a major cause for the Panic. It did however contribute to the existing sectional antagonism, because the South enjoyed continued economic good fortune in the face of Northern hard times. Why was the South largely insulated from the economic collapse? Cotton demand and prices worldwide remained high during the Panic. Many Southerners viewed this prosperity as a clear vindication of their slave based economic system and the Southern way of life in general. A rising number of Southerners began to consider secession and the creation of an independent Southern nation as a viable prospect for the future. In popular periodicals such as the *Southern Literary Messenger* which began publication in Richmond in 1834, and the New Orleans based *De Bow's Review of the Southern and Western States* launched in 1846, editorials consistently appeared supporting the theme of a safe and prosperous South based on agriculture, slavery, free trade, and general economic development. Southern commercial conventions met regularly in the 1850s discussing such wide ranging topics as the reopening of the African slave trade, establishing tariff free trade with other nations, industrial development, economic self-sufficiency, secession, and Southern unity. On March 4, 1858 during the debates over Lecompton, James Henry Hammond of South Carolina delivered a defiant speech to the Senate expostulating several of these themes:

> …If we never acquire another foot of territory for the South,
> look at her. Eight hundred and fifty thousand square miles.
> As large as Great Britain, France, Austria, Prussia, and Spain.
> Is not that territory enough to make an empire that shall
> rule the world? With the finest soil, the most delightful
> climate, whose staple productions none of these great
> countries can grow, we have three thousand miles of sea-shore
> line so indented with bays and crowded with islands, that
> when their shore lines are added, we have twelve thousand
> miles. Through the heart of <u>our country</u> runs the great

Mississippi, the father of waters, into whose bosom are poured thirty-six thousand miles of tributary rivers; and beyond we have the desert prairie wastes to protect us in our rear. Can you hem in such a territory as that? You talk of putting up a wall of fire around eight hundred and fifty thousand square miles so situated! How absurd.

Later in this speech, Hammond vocalized on both the perceived power of Southern cotton, and the social affinity enjoyed in the South :

What would happen if no cotton was furnished for three years? I will not depict what everyone can imagine, but this is certain: England would topple headlong and carry the whole civilized world with her, save the South. No, you dare not make war on cotton. No power on earth dares to make war upon it. Cotton is king…. Who can doubt, that has looked at recent events, that cotton is supreme…?

But, sir, the greatest strength of the South arises from the harmony of her political and social institutions. This harmony gives her a frame of society, the best in the world, and an extent of political freedom , combined with entire security, such as no other people ever enjoyed upon the face of the earth…. The South, so far as that is concerned, is satisfied, harmonious, and prosperous, but demands to be let alone.

At the time, Hammond had reason to feel sanguine about the prospects of an independent South. Cotton had reached the pinnacle of its economic power in the late 1850s, and the South produced 90% of the world's supply. In 1860, cotton accounted for nearly 61% of the value of all products exported from the U.S.! Thus, even though the Panic of 1857 stemmed from forces largely unrelated to the extant sectional issues, it nevertheless contributed to the growing divisions within the nation.

The Lincoln-Douglas Debates of 1858

In 1858, elections at all levels were held throughout the United Sates, yet no contest captured the nation's attention as did the Illinois senatorial race, pitting the veteran Democrat Stephen Douglas against Republican Abraham Lincoln. Douglas, a powerful and well known Congressman since 1843, seemed to have several advantages over Lincoln. Lincoln possessed little national political experience and exposure, though he did serve in the Illinois state legislature in the 1830s, and was elected to a term in the U.S. House of Representatives in 1846 as a Whig. Shrewd, folksy, and intelligent, Lincoln did however have a solid reputation in Illinois based on his successful law practice. He also never strayed too far from the political arena. In regards to slavery, Lincoln believed the institution a moral wrong which should be kept out of the territories in the hope that it would gradually wither and die. However, he was an extraordinarily patient and pragmatic politician, who at this stage in his career condemned the violent pronouncements of extreme abolitionists as dangerous to the Union. Lincoln began his rise to prominence with a speech delivered in Peoria, Illinois on Oct. 16, 1854. In a remarkable response to Sen. Stephen Douglas' public defense of the Kansas–Nebraska Act, Lincoln stated:

> I surely will not blame them (slaveholders) for not doing what
> I should not know how to do myself. If all earthly power were
> given to me, I should not know what to do as to the existing
> institution….When they remind us of their constitutional rights,
> I acknowledge them – not grudgingly, but fully and fairly, and I
> would give them any legislation for the reclaiming of their fugitives
> which should not in its stringency be more likely to carry a free
> man into slavery than our ordinary criminal laws are to hang an
> innocent one….But all this furnishes no more excuse for permitting
> slavery to go into our free territory than it would for reviving the
> African slave-trade by law.

Subsequently, he joined the Republican Party in 1856 and actively campaigned for presidential candidate John C. Fremont. Lincoln was a rising star in the Republican Party and a formidable political force within his region, the Old Northwest, but national attention eluded him until he was nominated to challenge Douglas in 1858.

<u>Interesting Election Note</u>:
Before the passage of the 17th Amendment in 1913, senators were elected by each state's legislature, not statewide popular vote. Why would there be such public interest in an election system which did not allow direct voter participation in U.S. Senate races? Rival candidates for the Senate had to make their positions clear to the public, so state legislators and candidates for state office could accurately gauge which candidate and party had the most popular appeal. This was extremely important in a process where virtually all state legislators, as well as the members of the U.S. House of Representatives, <u>were</u> elected by direct popular vote. When elections for state legislatures were held, voters would be selecting not only their actual state officials, they would also be indicating their preference for U.S. Senator. In other words, voters elected the state legislators which in turn would elect their favorite candidate to the U.S. Senate.

<u>The Debates</u>
Lincoln fired the opening shots of the contest with a famous speech delivered in Springfield, Illinois on June 16, 1858. In his oration, he commented that:

> We are now far into the fifth year since a policy
> (the Kansas-Nebraska Act) was initiated with the
> avowed object and confident promise of putting an end
> to slavery agitation. Under the operation of that policy,
> that agitation has not only not ceased, but has constantly

augmented. In my opinion it will not cease until a crisis shall have been reached and passed. *"A house divided against itself cannot stand."* I believe this government cannot endure permanently half slave and half free. I do not expect the Union to be dissolved – I do not expect the house to fall – but I do expect it will cease to be divided. It will become all one thing, or all the other. Either the opponents of slavery will arrest the further spread of it, and place it where the public mind shall rest in the belief that it is in the course of ultimate extinction; or its advocates will push it forward till it shall become alike lawful in all the states, old as well as new, North as well as South.

Lincoln also challenged Douglas on the viability of popular sovereignty in the territories. Douglas responded on July 9 in Chicago, asserting that Lincoln was an extremist who "advocates boldly and clearly a war of the sections, a war of the North against the South, of the Free States against the Slave States." In addition, Douglas attempted to portray Lincoln as supporting racial equality, a radical and extremely unpopular position at that time in all sections of the country. "He (Lincoln) objects to the Dred Scott decision because it does not put the Negro in the possession of citizenship on an equality with the white man." Lincoln's next step in the campaign was to challenge Douglas to a series of debates. Douglas agreed, and seven debates with Lincoln were held at various locations throughout Illinois between August 21 and October 15, 1858. Arguably the most important of the debates took place at Freeport on Aug. 27th . Lincoln opened by restating his positions on various issues. He then asked Douglas an apparently vexing question in light of the Dred Scott decision:

"Can the people of a United States Territory, in any lawful way, against the wish of any citizen of the United States, exclude slavery from its limits prior to the formation of a state constitution?"

Douglas was more than ready for this trap, and responded with what became known as the Freeport Doctrine:

I answer emphatically, as Mr. Lincoln has heard me answer a hundred times from every stump in Illinois, that in my opinion the people of a Territory can, by lawful means, exclude slavery from their limits prior to their formation of a State constitution.... It matters not what way the Supreme Court may hereafter decide as to the abstract question of whether slavery may or may not go into a Territory under the Constitution, the people have the lawful means to introduce it or exclude it as they please, for the reason that slavery cannot exist a day or an hour anywhere unless it is supported by the local police regulations. Those police regulations can only be established by the local legislature, and if the people are opposed to slavery they will elect representatives to that body who will by unfriendly legislation effectively prevent the introduction of it into their midst. If, on the contrary, they are for it, their legislation will favor its extension. Hence, no matter what the decision of the Supreme Court may be on that abstract question, still the right of the people to make a slave Territory or a free Territory is perfect and complete under the Nebraska bill.

The Results

In the November elections, Douglas supporters won a majority in the Illinois state legislature, and they subsequently reelected him to the Senate. However, Douglas' Freeport Doctrine, along with his objections to the Lecompton Constitution, destroyed him in the South, increasingly the power base of the Democratic Party. Lincoln, although defeated, gained a national reputation. His moderate stance on slavery (compared to radical abolitionists) appealed to many Northern Republicans. This new found stature would prove decisive in the presidential campaign of 1860.

John Brown's Raid

1858 passed into 1859 with no lessening of antagonisms between the North and South. Major churches had already divided over the slavery issue, and the Republican Party was gaining strength in the North. The Democrats, the last remaining national party, seemed to be splintering into Northern and Southern wings. The Union could ill afford any new crisis. However, in October 1859, John Brown, architect of the Pottawatomie Massacre, precipitated perhaps the greatest crisis of all at Harpers Ferry, Virginia (now West Virginia). From 1856 to 1859, Brown traveled back and forth between Kansas and New England. In Kansas, he continued his violent efforts to liberate slaves, while in New England, he attempted to solicit funds from prominent abolitionists for a far more ambitious scheme. Brown, still a wanted man for his actions in Kansas, was warmly received in Boston by such influential men as William Lloyd Garrison, Ralph Waldo Emerson, Henry David Thoreau, and Theodore Parker, a widely respected Unitarian minister. In 1858, Parker, along with five other men known as the "Secret Six", supplied Brown with financial support, which he used to purchase supplies, guns, and a thousand pikes (pointed spikes for use on spears). Brown's plan was to seize the federal arsenal at Harper's Ferry, arm the slaves, and set up a base in the mountains of Virginia. From there, he would initiate a massive slave insurrection throughout the South! Brown's plan was doomed before it started. His ill-equipped forces totaled just 22 men, Harper's Ferry could be easily cut off and surrounded, and the neighboring slaves who were supposed to be liberated had not even been informed! Even if they had, it is highly doubtful they would have joined Brown only to face certain death in such a poorly planned misadventure.

Brown began his "revolution" on the night of Oct. 16, 1859. He easily captured the arsenal, as most of its employees were at home. The next day everything went wrong. No slaves joined the insurrection, and that evening Virginia and Maryland militia along with U.S. Marines under the command of Colonel Robert E. Lee, completely surrounded Brown and his men. On Oct. 18, Lieutenant J.E.B. Stuart ordered Brown to surrender. When he refused, the marines stormed the armory injuring Brown and killing 10 of his men. Brown was immediately charged with incitement to slave insurrection and treason against Virginia. (A compelling alternative to Brown's indictment and trial was available to Virginia. Although there was no doubt of Brown's guilt, his sanity was in question, and it would have been quite possible to have Brown committed to an asylum. Such a course could have prevented his subsequent martyrdom.) His trial began on Oct. 25th, he was convicted on the 31st, and sentenced to hang in Charleston, VA (now WV) on Dec. 2nd. It was during his trial however that Brown reversed the utter failure of Harper's Ferry. In a letter to his wife, Brown wrote, "I have been whipped but am sure I can recover all the lost capital occasioned by that disaster, by only hanging a few moments by the neck." Few statements have ever been so prescient, as Brown conducted himself during the trial with such dignity, eloquence, and strength of purpose, that he even earned the respect of his enemies. Prior to his sentencing , Brown made this statement to the court:

> I believe that to have interfered as I have done, as I have
> always freely admitted that I have done, in behalf of His
> despised poor, is no wrong, but a right. Now, if it is deemed
> necessary that I should forfeit my life for the furtherance
> of the ends of justice, and mingle my blood further with the
> blood of my children and with the blood of millions in this
> slave country whose rights are disregarded by wicked, cruel
> and unjust enactments, I say, let it be done.

On the day of his execution, Brown kissed a little black girl on his way to the gallows and delivered this final statement:

> I, John Brown, am now quite certain that the crimes of this
> guilty land will never be purged away, but with Blood. I had
> as I now think, vainly flattered myself that without very much
> bloodshed, it might be done.

In the North, politicians in both parties viewed Brown's raid as the misguided actions of a fanatic. Initially, public opinion in the region also denounced Brown, but his demeanor during the trial and execution caused many Northerners to regard him as a martyr on the altar of slavery. Prominent clergymen such as Fales Newhall, Theodore Parker (actually, one of the "Secret Six"), and Edwin M. Wheelock declared that Brown had sanctified treason . Authors Bronson and Louisa Mae Alcott, Henry Wordsworth Longfellow, William Dean Howells, William Cullen Bryant, Henry David Thoreau, and Ralph Waldo Emerson praised Brown as a hero, a saint, or even a Christ-like figure! During the trial, Emerson wrote of Brown:

> "That new saint, than whom nothing purer or more brave was

ever led by love of men into conflict and death – the new saint
awaiting his martyrdom…. will make the gallows glorious
like the Cross.”

The public outpouring of support and sympathy visible in some quarters was
astonishing. There were memorial services in towns and cities across the North,
including New York, Philadelphia, and Boston. Black bunting streamed from
buildings, flags lowered to half-mast, prayer vigils held, hymns sung, eulogies
delivered, and women skulked through the streets in widows black. Brown’s
gravesite in North Elba, N.Y. even became a focal point for anti-slavery pilgrims!

While many Northerners thought John Brown was a lunatic, a sentiment
continually expounded by several Northern politicians (including Lincoln) and
newspaper editors, Southerners were shocked, horrified, and outraged by the
martyrdom of Brown. For many, this was the clearest sign yet that they were unsafe
within the Union. Southern newspapers printed foreboding editorials on what the
South could expect from their Northern countrymen in the future. Consider the
following excerpt from the Dec. 5, 1859 issue of the Wilmington, N.C. *Daily Herald*:

It is useless to disguise the fact, that the entire North and Northwest
have been hopelessly abolitionized. We want no better evidence than
that presented to us by their course in this Harper’s affair. With the
exception of a few papers (among them we are proud to notice that
sterling Whig journal, the New York *Express*) that have had the manliness
to denounce the act as it deserved, the great majority have either
sympathized with the offenders, or maintained an ominous silence….
The *“irrepressible conflict”* between the North and South then, has
already commenced; to this complexion it must come at last. It is
useless to talk of the conservativism of the North. Where has there
been any evidence of it? Meetings upon meetings have been held for
the purpose of expressing sympathy for murderers and traitors; but
none, no not one solitary expression of horror, or disapprobation even,
for the crime committed, have we seen yet from any state north of
Mason and Dixon’s line. And yet they claim to be our brethren, speak
the same language, worship the same God….
We confess that we look forward with gloomy apprehension towards
the future. If Congress fails to apply the remedy, then it behooves the
South to act together as one man – ship our produce direct to Europe,
-- import our own goods, -- let the hum of the spinning-wheel be heard
in our homes, as in the days of the Revolution, -- manufacture our own
items of necessity or luxury, and be dependent on the North for -- nothing.

Southern responses to John Brown’s raid were by no means limited to newspaper
editorials. Throughout the region, Northerners increasingly came under suspicion.
In some cases, they were forced from their jobs or driven out entirely. Local and
state militia units in the South intensified their drills and training activities in
preparation for another Brown-style attack. Brown may have failed in his

attempted slave insurrection, but he succeeded completely in creating an atmosphere of reactionary terror and anger in all the Southern states. His actions pushed the nation to the brink of disunion.

The Last Straw – The Election of 1860

The emotional climate of the United States in 1860 provided arguably the worst possible backdrop for a presidential election in the nation's history. The cultural fabric of the nation had been tattered due to the traumas of the past decade, and there were precious few social and political institutions that remained truly national in character. During the campaign of 1860, one of these, the Democratic Party, would finally split under the sectional strain. After the election in November, the nation itself would similarly divide.

In April, the Democrats met in Charleston, S.C. to draft a platform and nominate a candidate for president. From the outset, it became clear that the Democratic Party was divided in everything but name. The frontrunner was Stephen Douglas but he faced intense opposition from the supporters of Pres. Buchanan and Southern Democrats incensed by his positions. Douglas repeatedly won a majority of votes for nomination, but not the prerequisite 2/3 majority. The focus now shifted to the party platform which needed only a simple majority for passage. Southern delegates, especially from the Deep South, demanded a federal slave code protecting slavery in the territories, while their Northern counterparts supported a weak form of popular sovereignty. They adopted the position that all territorial matters, including questions of jurisdiction, should be decided by the Supreme Court. The Northern platform passed, and angry Southern delegates, primarily from the Deep South, bolted the convention. Having reached an impasse, the convention adjourned. The reconvened in June in Baltimore, but sectional divisions quickly resurfaced. A controversy arose over which delegates from the Deep South would be recognized within the convention; when the Douglas forces prevailed, many Southern delegates again walked out. The remaining delegates nominated Douglas, and adopted a weak platform based on popular sovereignty. The renegade Southern delegates reassembled at another meeting hall in Baltimore and drew up their own platform and nominated sitting Vice President John C. Breckinridge of Kentucky for president. The division of the Democratic Party into Northern and Southern wings was complete.

Dismayed by the rift within the Democrats and distrustful of the Republicans, a new party briefly appeared in 1860. Consisting primarily of conservative former Whigs and Know-Nothings, the Constitutional Union Party met on May 9th in Baltimore. They avoided any particular platform; their aged leaders simply pledged to obey the Constitution and support the Union. They nominated Sen. John Bell of Tennessee.

Concomitantly, the Republican Party's convention in Chicago displayed much more enthusiasm than the Constitutional Unionists and little of the rancor which split the Democrats. The main question at their convention was who would receive the nomination. William Seward of N.Y.(a.k.a. "Mr. Republican") was the early favorite, but his abolitionist sympathies made him appear too radical to win the general election. Abraham Lincoln, backed by an excellent and somewhat unscrupulous organization, quickly outmaneuvered Seward and won the nomination on the third ballot. The Republican platform, although relatively moderate on slavery, catered solely to Northern interests. A united and jubilant Republican Party adjourned their convention on May 18.

The Platforms

Party	Platform
Northern Democrats	Popular sovereignty in the territories, with the Supreme Court possessing discretionary power
Southern Democrats	Federal Slave Code protecting slavery in the territories
Constitutional Union	The Constitution upheld, the Union preserved, and the laws enforced
Republicans	No slavery in the territories Federal funds for internal improvements Protective tariffs for industries Free public land for settlers

The Campaign

The Election of 1860 was actually two contests, one in the North between Lincoln and Douglas, and the other in the South pitting Breckinridge against Bell. (Lincoln was not even on the ballot in 10 Southern States!) In the North, the Republicans ran a spirited campaign reminiscent of the Whig's "Log Cabin- Hard Cider" tactics in 1840. They also dismissed Southern threats of secession as meaningless bluffs. The Northern Democrats continually ridiculed Lincoln's meager qualifications, and stressed that the Republicans were the party of abolition and racial equality. In the South, the Breckinridge forces carried the banner of Southern Rights against Lincoln and the "Black Republicans", Douglas and his treacherous followers, and the submissive Constitutional Unionists. For their part, the Constitutional Unionists warned that only their cautious and prudent leadership could prevent the disaster of disunion. The only candidate who seemed to truly understand the imminent danger to the nation was Douglas. He campaigned in the North, trying to impress upon the populace that the South was deadly serious about secession if Lincoln should win. He also went South, warning that Northerners would never allow secession. In the end, he was correct on both counts.

On Nov. 6, 1860, 4,680,193 Americans (over 81% of all registered voters) cast their ballots in the most momentous election in U.S. history. (see following page)

The Election of 1860 – Specific Results

Candidate	Party	Electoral Vote	Popular Vote	States Carried
A. Lincoln	Rep.	180	1,866,452 (39.9%)	All 18 Free States
S. Douglas	N. Dem.	12	1,375,157 (29%)	Missouri

(Douglas also won 3 of New Jersey's 7 electoral votes. Lincoln won the other 4)

Candidate	Party	Electoral Vote	Popular Vote	States Carried
J. Breckinridge*	S. Dem.	72	857,953 (18.1%)	DEL, MD, NC, SC, GA, FLA, ALA, MISS, LA, AR, TEXAS
J. Bell	Const. Union	39	590,631 (13%)	VA, KY, TN

Lincoln won the popular vote with only a plurality (about 40%) of the total. His victory in the Electoral College however was decisive, 180 to 123, with all of his votes coming from the Northern states. It is important to note that he did not win a single electoral vote in any of the 15 slave states. With Lincoln's election, a portentous question loomed threateningly over the nation; what would the Southern States do, now that a Republican was President-Elect of the United States?.

The First Wave of Secession

The question did not go unanswered for long. On Nov. 10, the South Carolina legislature called for a special convention to consider secession. Delegates were elected on Dec. 6, and the convention commenced in Charleston on Dec. 17. The delegates spent three days drawing up a 30 page ordinance which contained both grievances against the North and pronunciations of state sovereignty.* On Dec. 20th 1860, a unanimous convention declared:

> We, therefore, the people of South Carolina, by our delegates
> in Convention assembled, appealing to the Supreme Judge of the
> world for the rectitude of our intentions, have solemnly declared
> that the Union heretofore existing between this State and the
> other States of North America is dissolved, and that the State of
> South Carolina has resumed her position among the nations of
> the world, as a separate and independent State, with full power
> to make war, conclude peace, contract alliances, establish commerce,
> and to do all other acts and things which independent States
> may of right do.

South Carolina had acted quickly and apparently unilaterally, but in reality the South Carolina secessionists were working in close concert with their compatriots throughout the South. In the weeks that followed, one after another of the Deep South states followed her lead.

*Strangely enough, Vice President Breckinridge confirmed Lincoln's Electoral College victory to the Senate, Feb. 13th 1861!
**James L. Petigru, a South Carolina politician and jurist opposed to secession sarcastically remarked that "South Carolina is too small for a republic and too large for an insane asylum."

First Wave of Secession – Chronology

State	Date of Secession
South Carolina	December 20, 1860
Mississippi	January 9, 1861
Florida	January 10, 1861
Alabama	January 11, 1861
Georgia	January 19, 1861
Louisiana	January 26, 1861
Texas*	February 1, 1861

*Texas was the only one of the original seven Confederate States to submit its Ordinance of Secession to a popular vote.

On Feb. 4, 1861, representatives of six seceded states met in the small city of Montgomery, Ala. to form a new nation, the Confederate States of America. On Feb. 7, they ratified the Constitution of the Confederate States of America, and two days later they elected Jefferson Davis as the provisional President of the C.S.A. The Confederate Constitution, although patterned after the U.S. Constitution, contained important changes which distinguished the Confederacy from the Union.

Confederate States Constitution – Significant Provisions

1. The Bill of Rights guarantees enumerated in the first 10 Amendments to the U.S. Constitution were incorporated into the main text.
2. The Preamble affirmed the principle of states rights:

> We, the people of the Confederate States,
> each State acting in its sovereign and
> independent character, in order to form a
> permanent government, establish justice,
> insure domestic tranquility, and secure the
> blessings of liberty for ourselves and our
> posterity – invoking the favor and guidance
> of Almighty God – do ordain and establish
> this Constitution of the Confederate States
> of America.

3. The President possessed a line-item veto over bills submitted by Congress. This allowed the President to strike out objectionable portions of a bill without vetoing the entire measure.
4. Tariffs could be imposed, but only for revenue. Protective tariffs for individual industries were prohibited.
5. Funds for internal improvements were prohibited, except for coastal or river navigation.
6. Established a self-sufficient Post Office, funded by its own revenues.

7. The President was elected for a single six year term.
8. New states could enter the Confederacy with a 2/3 majority vote of Congress.
9. The Constitution could be amended by a 2/3 majority of the states.
10. The Constitution expressly protected the right to own slaves.
11. Slaves could not be purchased from any foreign country or territory <u>except</u> the United States.

The seceding states had created a new government with lightning speed, but what, if anything, was the United States doing during this winter of secession? Also, what position would the 8 slaveholding states which remained in the Union adopt towards the fledgling Confederacy?

<u>Efforts at Compromise</u>
   Almost immediately after Lincoln's election in November 1860 and continuing into February 1861, moderate leaders from the Upper South attempted to negotiate a compromise which would stave off further secession and bring the recalcitrant states back into the Union. It is no coincidence that politicians from this region worked so diligently to maintain the Union. If war ensued between the North and South, the Upper South would be the primary battleground. Also, these states had extensive commercial ties with the North; disunion would obviously disrupt their market connections. Finally, in the Upper South states of Missouri, Kentucky, Maryland, and Delaware, the percentage of slaves in the population had decreased steadily since 1830, a sure sign of the waning importance of the institution. Not surprisingly, the most significant compromise effort came from a 73 year old Kentucky senator, John C. Crittenden. On Dec. 18, 1860, he submitted a six-part compromise bill to the Senate. The <u>Crittenden Compromise</u> consisted of:

A. Restoring and extending the Missouri Compromise Line to California.
B. Guarantees that slavery would be preserved in the 15 slave states and Washington, D.C.
C. The repeal of the personal liberty laws enacted by Northern states, although Northerners would no longer be required to assist in the capture of a runaway slave.
D. Tighter restrictions on the illegal African slave trade.
E. Compensation for slave owners in cases where runaways could not be apprehended due to riotous conditions or mob interference.
F. A constitutional guarantee that these amendments could never be repealed.

   Crittenden's proposals were sent to a special Committee of Thirteen for consideration. They were defeated however on Dec. 31, 7 to 6. In early January, Crittenden and his supporters steered the compromise directly into the House and Senate. Deliberations would continue until March. Concurrently, on Jan. 19th the legislature of VA called for a national "Peace Conference" to save the Union. Chaired by former president John Tyler of Virginia, the conference assembled on

Feb. 4. Only 21 of the 34 states attended the conference which reflected the growing unwillingness between the regions to compromise. The proposals adopted by the conference mirrored those of Crittenden. One notable exception involved the admission of new territories. The delegates suggested that new territory could be added to the United States only with the approval of a concurrent majority of both free state and slave state senators. The last chances for compromise and restoration of the Union came and went in late Feb. and early March 1861. On Feb. 27, the House voted down the Crittenden Compromise 113 to 80. The VA Peace Conference adjourned the same day. Its resolutions were never considered by the Congress. On March 3, the Senate voted against the Crittenden Compromise 20 to 19. (Ironically, the only measure which passed both the House and Senate guaranteed slavery forever in the states where it existed. If the war had not ensued, this legislation probably would have been added to the Constitution as the Thirteenth Amendment.) With these legislative defeats, there would be no compromise akin to those fashioned in 1820, 1833, or 1850, to save the Union in 1861.

Fort Sumter

During the secession winter of 1860–61, the Northern public and their political leaders watched the events transpiring in the Deep South with dismayed astonishment; they could see what was occurring but refused to accept it. Pres. Buchanan's reactions to secession reflect this confused sentiment. On Dec. 3, he gave a speech calling for a constitutional convention to resolve the sectional disputes. At the same time, he declared that secession was illegal, but that he had no constitutional authority to stop it! In all fairness to Buchanan, no president had ever been confronted with a crisis of this magnitude. His dilemma was daunting. If he acted decisively against the Confederacy, it would mean war, and the other slave states would most likely leave the Union in support of their sisters in the South. If he allowed secession to continue, it might mean the end of the republic. Some Northerners seemed content to let the Southern States leave. Horace Greeley, editor of the *New York Tribune,* stated in 1860 that, "If the Cotton States shall become satisfied that they can do better out of the Union than in it, we insist on letting them go." Many more however did not wish to see the Union sundered for a variety of social, economic and political reasons. These persons were disgusted by the perceived impotence of the government. As wealthy New York lawyer George Templeton Strong lamented in his diary, "the bird of our country is a debilitated chicken, disguised in eagle feathers."

In the first months of 1861, supporters of the new Confederacy were not afflicted by the same inaction. In Washington, Southern Congressmen and Cabinet members resigned their posts and went home, usually to serve in the new Confederate government. As they exited, they absconded with United States funds, guns, and supplies, all destined to find new homes in Confederate treasuries, arsenals, and warehouses. Also, between Dec. and March, federal installations, mints, and forts in the seceded states were peacefully handed over to the various state governments or the Confederacy. By March, only Ft. Pickens in Pensacola, Fla., and Ft. Sumter in Charleston, S.C. remained in U.S. possession. Concurrently, Confederate commissioners traveled overseas attempting to gain foreign recognition for their government. Closer to home, they actively attempted to recruit the other slave states, especially Virginia, into the new nation. Virginia, the "mother of Presidents", possessed power, prestige, and resources the Confederacy desperately sought. In both instances however, they were unsuccessful. Britain and France adopted a passive wait-and-see posture towards the Confederacy, and the Upper South states overwhelmingly defeated secession initiatives. In general, they condemned secession and continued to hope for compromise and reunion. William G. "Parson" Brownlow of the *Knoxville Whig*, railed, "The man who calculates upon a peaceable dissolution of the Union is either a madman or a fool. I am among those who believe the Union is not going to be dissolved, because the disunionists have no right to do the thing; they have no power if the right existed, and there is no cause for dissolution." Northerners, especially President-elect Lincoln, misconstrued this reluctance to leave the Union as evidence that the entire secession movement was an elaborate bluff; in their view, the Deep South was merely threatening the North to obtain unacceptable demands, such as allowing slavery into the territories. This proved a grave miscalculation, as the Upper South's ties to the Union were directly related to compromise. As prospects for reconciliation waned, so did attachment to the Union. When conflict ensued, half of the Upper South states would follow their sympathies and join the Confederacy. Also, the Confederacy was in earnest. Leaders of the new nation were not interested in reintegration into the Union, as evidenced by their refusal to participate in the Virginia Peace Conference. Instead, their energies were focused on making their new nation viable.

The most important action taken by the Union during the winter of 1860–61 came not from the President or Congress but from a U.S. Army officer, Major Robert Anderson. Anderson was the commander of Ft. Moultrie in Charleston . In late Dec. South Carolina officials pressured Pres. Buchanan to order the evacuation of the fort. Buchanan stalled for time paying lip service to the South Carolinians. In the meantime, Anderson, after consultation with superior officers, decided to leave Ft. Moultrie due to its vulnerability to attack. At sundown on Dec. 26, Anderson and his forces dismantled the weapons at Ft. Moultrie and surreptitiously slipped off to the much more formidable Ft. Sumter, right in the center of Charleston Harbor. His actions were discovered the next day by angry South Carolinians. South Carolina officials felt the move betrayed the "agreement" reached with Buchanan. For Buchanan's part, he never explicitly promised the South Carolinians anything, and in January he demonstrated uncharacteristic resolve by dispatching the ship *Star of the West* to re-supply Ft. Sumter. The ship arrived in Charleston Harbor on Jan. 9th 1861. South Carolinians (Citadel cadets) manning shore installations immediately fired on the ship. It withdrew undamaged from the harbor, and Anderson did not order a counterattack from Ft. Sumter. Buchanan chose to ignore that a U.S. vessel had been fired upon, much to the chagrin of the Northern public. Still, Anderson occupied Ft. Sumter. As secession spread and the Confederacy coalesced, this lonely outpost became an extraordinarily potent symbol of U.S. resolve.

On March 4, 1861, Lincoln took the oath of office as 16th President of the United States. In his inaugural speech, he made a heartfelt plea for peace and reunification:

> In *your* hands, my dissatisfied fellow countrymen, and
> not in *mine*, is the momentous issue of civil war. This
> government will not assail *you*. You can have no conflict
> without being yourselves the aggressors. *You* have no
> oath registered in Heaven to destroy the government,
> while *I* shall have the most solemn one to "preserve,
> protect, and defend it."
> I am loath to close. We are not enemies, but friends.
> We must not be enemies. Though passion may have
> strained, it must not break our bonds of affection. The
> mystic chords of memory, stretching from every battlefield,
> and patriot grave, to every living heart and hearth-stone, all
> over this broad land, will yet swell the chorus of the Union,
> when again touched, as they surely will be, by the better angels
> of our nature.

The section of his speech which most interested the Confederacy however, forcefully condemned secession as "the essence of anarchy", and pledged Lincoln "to hold, occupy, and possess the property and places belonging to the government, and to collect the duties and imposts;" to Confederate officials, this was tantamount to a declaration of war. It was also obvious to Northerners and Southerners alike that Ft. Sumter, in the heart of South Carolina, the first state to secede, was the "property and place" Lincoln most wished to "possess."

In March 1861, the most pressing issue concerning Ft. Sumter centered on how long Major Anderson could hold out. His supplies were dwindling, and he informed both the U.S. and Confederate governments that unless he received additional supplies, he would be forced to withdraw by mid-April. From mid-March onward, Confederate officials negotiated with officials of the U.S. State Department for the evacuation and transfer of Ft. Sumter. Sec. of State William Seward, apparently with the tacit approval of Lincoln, communicated to the Confederates that Ft. Sumter would be abandoned shortly. However, on March 29 Lincoln authorized the re-supply of Ft. Sumter and Ft. Pickens; he also sent word to the governor of South Carolina that provisions, but not weapons or additional soldiers, were being dispatched to Ft. Sumter. The relief vessels were to set sail on April 6.

Attention now shifted to Montgomery, Ala., the capitol of the Confederacy. The Confederates viewed this apparent change in policy as treachery. Lincoln simply could not be trusted. After intense debate, Pres. Jefferson Davis decided that Ft. Sumter must be taken before the supply ships reached Charleston. Orders were sent to Confederate General P.G.T. Beauregard in Charleston to prepare the assault. Subsequently, Beauregard demanded that Major Anderson surrender the fort. Anderson politely refused. At precisely 4:30 A.M. April 12, 1861, the Confederates opened fire. Major Anderson surrendered 36 hours later. Ironically, the opening battle of the bloodiest war in U.S. history had been bloodless. The first death occurred during Anderson's evacuation. He had ordered a fifty gun salute to the retiring U.S. flag, and one of the cannon had been overstuffed with gunpowder and exploded, killing one soldier and wounding 5 others!

The Second Wave of Secession

The attack on Ft. Sumter set off a dramatic chain of events. Lincoln requested 75,000 volunteers from every state to suppress the insurrection. Davis called for 300,000 volunteers to repel the "Yankee invaders." In the Upper South, the time for decision had arrived. There was no doubt about Delaware's loyalty to the Union, but the question was much more agonizing in Missouri, Kentucky, and Maryland. Ultimately, all three would remain in the Union, though provisional Confederate governments were established in Missouri and Kentucky, and only occupation by federal troops in the Spring of 1861 secured Maryland for the Union. The slave states which stayed in the Union were subsequently referred to as the "Border States"; all of them supplied troops to both the Union and the Confederacy during the War Between the States (a.k.a. the Civil War).*

This was not the case in Virginia, Arkansas, Tennessee, and North Carolina. On April 17th 1861, Virginia seceded from the Union and joined the Confederacy. As a reward, the Confederate capitol was moved to Richmond where it remained until April 1865. Virginia however would be literally torn apart by its secession from the Union. On June 11th 1861, delegates representing 48 counties in western Virginia met in Wheeling to secede from the rest of Virginia and remain within the Union. This mountainous section of Virginia contained few slaves and had a long history of political and social estrangement from the Tidewater. West Virginia formally entered the United States as the thirty-fifth state in 1863. Arkansas seceded on May 6th, Tennessee on May 7th, and finally, North Carolina on May 20th. The Confederate States of America were complete.

The firing on Ft. Sumter signaled the end of the old Republic. The time for sectional conciliation had passed. The last attempts at compromise had failed. What lay ahead for the American people was the crucible and consequence of total, fratricidal war. No American alive in 1861 could possibly conceive of the transformation of the nation caused by the war and the reconstruction which followed.

*White Southerners from the Confederacy also served in the Union Army during the War. For example, Tennessee supplied about 42,000 soldiers to the Union, Virginia - 22,000, Arkansas - 10,000, Louisiana - 7,000, North Carolina - 5,000, Alabama - 3,000, Texas - 2,200, Florida - 1,500, Georgia - 700, and Mississippi - 545 (no reliable figures exist for South Carolina, though the number is almost certainly the smallest of any Confederate state). By comparison, very few Northerners sided with the South, though some officers and West Point graduates, such as General John Pemberton from Ohio, did fight for the Confederacy.

Chapter 13 – The War Between The States (a.k.a. The Civil War) 1861 - 1862

Under Two Flags

Despite the ironic catharsis many Southerners felt after secession and war had finally commenced, independence for the Confederacy seemed unlikely at best. In virtually every material asset, the North far outpaced the South. Consider the following statistics:

	North	South
Population	22 million	9.1 million (including 3.5 million slaves)
Wealth Produced	75% (of national total)	25% (of national total)
Railroad Mileage	22,000 miles	9,283 miles
Farms	67%	33%
Bank Deposits	81%	19%
Manufacturing (value)	$1.7 billion	$156 million
Firearms production	97%	3%
Factories	110,000	18,000

The North also possessed enormous advantages in pig iron production, textiles, railroad equipment, and shoes, all of which were vital wartime items. In agricultural products and livestock, the North was superior in the production in corn, wheat, oats, horses, sheep, and dairy cows. (The South by contrast led in tobacco, cotton, rice, pigs, mules, jackasses, and raised more beef cattle.) With all of this and more in the North's favor, the question presents itself of how was the South able to fight for four years and nearly win independence on more than one occasion?

Southern Advantages

Despite the overwhelming disparity with the Union in material resources, the Confederacy possessed important advantages which manifested themselves in military strategies and the overall will to fight. For one, Southerners were primarily fighting a defensive war against the Union with the stated goal of winning Confederate independence. The North would have to conquer a nation which consisted of 757,853 square miles, not including West Virginia, Oklahoma, Missouri, and Kentucky, all of which were claimed by the Confederacy. This meant that Southern military leaders could position themselves in strong defensive postures and make Northern armies pay heavy prices for their offensives. Such an objective also implied that the Confederacy could afford to lose territory, at least temporarily, as the Union suffered immense losses and wearied in their war effort. In other words, the South might be able to wear down the Union and negotiate a peace based on the recognition of the Confederate States as a separate nation. In fact, during the summer of 1864, it appeared that the Confederates were on the verge of achieving this goal.

Secondly, most Southerners had a stronger incentive to fight than their Northern opponents. Although this seems a subjective statement, it nonetheless is accurate, but why?* The war is often simplified as a struggle over slavery, with the North

*For example, 70% of white military-age male Virginians served in the Confederate armed forces during the war; the Northern mobilization rate was 35%.

seeking its eradication while Southerners fought doggedly to preserve the institution. This contention is somewhat misleading in a variety of aspects. The initial war aim of the North until 1863 was simply to preserve the Union, without regard to slavery. Consider this letter from Lincoln to newspaper editor Horace Greeley dated August 22, 1862:

> I would save the Union. I would save it the shortest way under the Constitution. The sooner the national authority can be restored, the nearer the Union will be "*the Union as it was*." If there be those who would not save the Union, unless they could at the same time save slavery, I do not agree with them. If there be those who would not save the Union unless they could at the same time destroy slavery, I do not agree with them. My paramount object in this struggle is to save the Union, and is not either to save or to destroy slavery. If I could save the Union without freeing any slave I would do it, and if I could save it by freeing all the slaves I would do it; and if I could save it by freeing some and leaving others alone I would also do that. What I do about slavery, and the colored race, I do because I believe it helps to save the Union; and what I forbear, I forbear because I do not believe it would help to save the Union.

After the Emancipation Proclamation (which <u>technically freed only some of the slaves</u>) was issued in 1863, Northern war aims were adjusted to include the abolition of slavery, but this alteration was widely criticized in the North and might have led to Lincoln's defeat in his bid for reelection in 1864. In an 1863 editorial printed in the *Chicago Times*, Lincoln was assailed for having "…at last weakly yielded to the 'pressure' put upon him about which he has so bitterly complained, and issued his proclamation of negro emancipation…he has no constitutional power to issue this proclamation – none whatsoever….The government, then, by the act of the president is in rebellion and the war is reduced to a contest for subjugation…." Many Northerners chafed at the idea of fighting to "free the slaves", and subsequent developments reflected their displeasure. The New York City Draft Riot of 1863 was <u>at least</u> indirectly caused by the negative reaction to the inclusion of emancipation as a war aim, as was the rise of the "Copperheads", the peace at any price faction within the Democratic Party.

To summarize, Northern support for the war was never as strong as that in the South, because deep reservations existed within the Union as to why the war was being waged. In the South however, where 75% of Southern families owned no slaves, the question of cause was immediately evident, the defense of your home from an outside invader. Most Southerners were motivated by the primal instinct of self-preservation, not the abstract political theory of states rights, or the desire to fight and die and court ruination to preserve slavery. It was the reality of hundreds of thousands of "Yankees" marching into their homes that gave Southerners the stamina to fight desperately until all hope was lost.

Finally, the South had the benefit of better generals, at least for the first two years of the war. The Confederate president Jefferson Davis, as a West Point graduate and former Secretary of War, had considerable military experience and determined quite quickly to organize his new army around a corps of trained professional officers. Southerners, at least among the upper classes, viewed military service as an honorable vocation and career, as evidenced by the region's establishment of military schools and colleges in the antebellum period. In 1860, only one of the eight state supported military colleges in the entire United States was located in the North. Institutions such as the Louisiana Military Academy (of which William Tecumseh Sherman was commandant until 1861), and especially the still extant Citadel in Charleston, S.C. and the Virginia Military Institute (V.M.I.) in Lexington, VA produced a fine cadre of officers which served the Confederacy admirably. When secession and war came, 313 officers in the U.S. Army resigned their commissions to serve in the Confederate Army, including about 33% of West Point graduates. (The addition of Virginia to the Confederacy in 1861 was invaluable to the Confederate Army as more West Point graduates hailed from Virginia than any other Southern State.) A large number of the West Pointers were experienced and talented soldiers, including P.G.T. Beauregard, Albert Sydney Johnston, Joseph Johnston, Thomas J. Jackson, Braxton Bragg, John Bell Hood, James Longstreet, John Pemberton, John Magruder, Josiah Gorgas, Bernard Bee, George Pickett, J.E.B. Stuart, and the incomparable, Robert E. Lee.[*]

Robert E. Lee, who graduated second in the West Point Class of 1829 and never received a single demerit in his college career, was considered by General Winfield Scott the best soldier in the U.S. Army. Not surprisingly, he was offered field command of all Union forces in April 1861 by President Lincoln. Lee, who held a profound aversion to slavery and viewed secession and disunion as a dreadful calamity, nonetheless could not accept the offer. On April 20th, he wrote his sister:

> With all my devotion to the Union and the feeling of loyalty and duty
> of an American citizen, I have not been able to make up my mind to
> raise my hand against my relatives, my children, my home. I have
> therefore resigned my commission in the Army, and save in defense of
> my native State, with the sincere hope that my poor services may never
> be needed, I hope I may never be called upon to draw my sword....

Such was not to be his fate however, as in 1862 he would assume command of the Army of Northern Virginia. The course of the war would have been drastically altered had Lee accepted Lincoln's offer.

"Forward to Richmond" and "On to Washington"

After the Confederate bombardment and capture of Fort Sumter, Northerners and Southerners eagerly flocked to recruiting stations to defend their respective flags and nations. On both sides, so many volunteers attempted to enlist that thousands had to be turned away. Again, on both sides the initial call was for 90 days military service, a hopelessly optimistic testament to the widespread belief that the war would be mercifully brief. After all, in Northern conventional wisdom it would only take one major battle for Union troops to whip the rebels and march

[*]Also, "between 1849 and 1861, all of the secretaries of war were Southerners, as were the generals-in-chief of the army , and two of the three brigadier generals...."(James J. McPherson)

triumphantly into the Confederate capital, now located in Richmond, VA Southerners were just as certain that they would thrash the impotent Yankees and perhaps seize Washington, D.C. They would subsequently dispose of Lincoln and the "Black Republicans", and celebrate the independence of the Confederacy in the summer of 1861. Professional military men on both sides were not nearly as sanguine in their assessment of the war's duration. The Union's senior military commander General Winfield Scott, 75 years old, overweight, and in poor health, could not lead the Union troops in the field, but he instantly grasped the enormous magnitude of the upcoming struggle and fashioned the overall Union strategy accordingly. Scott was contemptuous of the three-month recruits, correctly discerning that such a brief tenure would be completely inadequate for the task ahead. He believed an entire year should be devoted to creating a real army centered around the 16,000 troops constituting the U.S. Army in 1861. What exactly was Scott's plan? Immense in scope and lengthy in its implementation and timetable for success, the Northern press derided Scott and his "Great Snake" or "Anaconda Plan."

The "Anaconda Plan"

Scott called for a simultaneous and sustained three-pronged assault on the Confederacy which consisted of:

        A. the establishment and maintenance of a naval blockade of the entire Confederate coastline from Texas to Virginia to halt supplies coming into the Confederacy and weaken it into submission.

        B. constantly pressuring the Confederate capitol Richmond to tie up Southern armies and hinder the fledgling government's operations.

        C. capturing the Mississippi River to bisect the Confederacy and subsequently use adjoining rivers, especially the Tennessee, to further divide and incapacitate the C.S.A.

Considering that the U.S. Navy at the time consisted of only 42 ships, it would take a great deal of time to shut down the 189 ports, harbors, and river-mouths located along the over 3500 miles of Confederate coastline. To make matters worse, most of the small fleet was scattered around the world. Also, most Northerners scoffed at both the prospect of a long war and Scott's strategy. However, they would come to the painful realization that Scott's predictions of a lengthy conflict would be accurate, and grudgingly recognize the efficacy of his ideas after the battle of First Manassas (First Bull Run). (Many battles in the war bore two names because Southerners tended to name the battle after the nearest town, in this case Manassas. Northerners referred to the nearest significant natural feature, in this instance, the small Bull Run creek.)

Southern Strategy

Confederate military strategy was predicated on one simple goal: winning independence. To accomplish that end, the Confederates were at first committed to fighting a defensive war in the hopes of wearing down the North, resulting in a negotiated peace settlement. The problem with this approach however lay in the fact that the Confederate armies were scattered throughout the Confederate States, which usually led to a numerical disadvantage when facing the advancing Union troops. Eventually the Confederacy adopted an "offense-defense" strategy where Southern armies, when powerful enough, would invade the North to draw Northern armies out of Confederate territory. In addition, Confederate leaders felt a Southern victory on Northern soil would both demoralize Northerners and bolster the chances of official foreign recognition of the Confederacy as an independent nation. Foreign recognition, especially by Great Britain and/or France, was deemed crucial by Southern leaders as it would greatly facilitate loans and the shipment of vital supplies and weapons to the fledgling nation, and perhaps lead to military alliances with the Confederacy. If the Confederacy could enlist the British and/or French in their war for independence, the chances for success would improve dramatically. To secure foreign intervention, the Confederacy engaged in a self-imposed cotton embargo hoping that the British and French textile industries, a vital component of their economies, would collapse thus forcing those nations to aid the South to restore the cotton supply. On the surface this does not seem a bad idea considering that the South supplied 90% of the world's cotton, but the so-called "cotton famine" was partially ameliorated until 1863 by existing British and French stockpiles of cotton, purchased in the record harvest year of 1860. The United States for its part was just as determined to keep the conflict a solely American affair and worked mightily to prevent foreign intervention, especially between 1861 and 1863.

First Manassas (First Bull Run)

Throughout the remainder of the spring and into the summer of 1861, both Union and Confederate troops assembled in and around Virginia preparing for what they thought would be the great battle that would decide the war. General Irwin McDowell (West Point, Class of 1838) was the Union commander of the Army of the Potomac garrisoned outside Washington, D.C. McDowell was a competent officer, but was deeply (and understandably) concerned about the fighting capabilities of his largely untrained raw recruits. The Union volunteers were eager for battle but totally unprepared for it. The complex maneuvers and military discipline essential to any army's success were sorely lacking. Extensive training and drill was required in order to fashion a professional fighting force from the farm boys, merchants, lawyers, doctors, businessmen, artisans, and street urchins who mustered to advance the "Stars and Stripes" (the U.S. Flag) into rebel territory. McDowell however did not have the luxury of time on his side. Political exigencies mandated that he lead the Army of the Potomac into Virginia at the earliest possible moment to crush the rebellion. The "earliest possible moment" did not correspond very well with the actual abilities of his men, but when McDowell complained to President Lincoln that the army simply was not ready to commence offensive operations, Lincoln replied, "You are green, it is true; but they are green also; you are green alike." Lincoln was correct in his assessment. The Confederates, most of whom had either no military service or just a cursory amount of militia training, were just as ill-prepared as their Union foes, but nonetheless the inertia of war carried them along in a similar manner. With the news of McDowell's impending invasion, Confederate political and military leaders determined that "the sacred soil of Virginia" must not be desecrated by the Yankee hordes. The Confederate commander of the Army of Northern Virginia was the highly experienced General Joseph Johnston (West Point, Class of 1829), the highest ranked regular officer in the U.S. Army to resign and serve the Confederacy. However, actual field command at First Manassas (First Bull Run) fell to General P.G.T. Beauregard, the victor at Fort Sumter, due to his greater familiarity with the terrain around Manassas. Overall Confederate troop strength amounted to approximately 32,000 men, while McDowell commanded about 35,000 troops when he crossed the Potomac River into Virginia on July 17th 1861. The stage was set for the first real land battle of the war. Stage is a peculiarly macabre and appropriate description of the forthcoming engagement as dozens of Washington notables, politicians, business leaders, lawyers, professionals, and their families, followed McDowell's army to Manassas as if attending the opening night of a long anticipated play or production. They got more than they bargained for.

On July 21st 1861 the two armies finally met in battle. Considering the degree of training they had received, both the Yankees and the Confederates acquitted themselves quite well in their first "trial by fire." In the initial phase of the battle, the Union forces gained the advantage, slowly pushing back the Confederate lines, but at about 12:00 P.M. events took a sudden and dramatic turn. Colonel Thomas J. Jackson (West Point, Class of 1846), a former natural science instructor at the Virginia Military Institute, led a brigade of Virginians in stubborn resistance to repeated Yankee attacks. A nearby Confederate General, Bernard Bee of South Carolina, yelled to his dispirited troops, "There stands Jackson like a stone wall. Rally behind the Virginians!" From that moment onward, Thomas J. Jackson would be immortalized as "Stonewall" Jackson, one of the greatest Confederate commanders of the war. His stand at Henry House Hill was one of the two turning points of the battle. The other occurred later in the afternoon. General Beauregard's troops were tenaciously holding Henry House Hill, but fatigue was setting in and there was again the danger of a Union breakthrough. At about 4:00 P.M., both the Confederate and Union forces saw a dust cloud indicating troops approaching from the southwest. The question was who were they, Yankee or Confederate? The flags and standards carried by the approaching army gave no certain indication as the Confederate "Stars and Bars" and the Union "Stars and Stripes" bore a marked resemblance, especially at a distance or hanging limply in the breezeless conditions. (After the battle, Beauregard designed a new, square battle flag based on the Episcopal Cross of St. Andrew to prevent future confusion in identifying Confederate and Union forces.) When this new army came within approximately 100 yards of Beauregard's men, it was discovered that they were indeed Confederates, led by Generals Edward Kirby Smith and Jubal Early. Beauregard immediately ordered a counterattack, and an officer (most likely Jackson) exhorted the Confederate soldiers to "scream like Furies", the first time the famous "Rebel Yell" was heard in the war. The Yankees broke under the strain, and degenerated in their retreat to a panic stricken rout, made all the more difficult and terrifying by a sudden thunderstorm which turned the escape routes into muddy paths. Making matters even worse were the fleeing Washington spectators who obstructed the roads and bridges leading back to the U.S. capital. The battle of First Manassas (First Bull Run) was a resounding Confederate victory, although it could very easily have turned out the other way. Even so, if the Confederates had not been so disorganized by their victory, they may have been able to pursue the Union army into Washington and seize the city itself which would have profoundly affected the prosecution of the war. For their part, the Yankees were sullen and demoralized by their defeat and the subsequent "Great Skedaddle" and were abruptly persuaded that this would be no easy 90 days war. Indeed, the casualties on both sides were substantial (and horrific to Americans on both sides expecting a relatively bloodless war), though they paled in comparison to the forthcoming horrors of 1862 at Shiloh (Pittsburgh Landing), the Seven Days Battles, and Sharpsburg (Antietam).

First Manassas (Bull Run) Casualties

	Killed	Wounded	Missing / Captured
Union	460	1124	1312
Confederate	387	1582	13

The war had now begun in bloody earnest.

Fortunes of War 1861–62
   Despite their victory at Manassas (Bull Run), the Confederacy suffered serious setbacks over the next several months. For the better part of the next year, the Confederates would lose battle after battle stretching from New Mexico to North Carolina (see the list below).

Confederate Defeats 1861–62
Fort Hatteras and Fort Clark, NC–8/29–30/61
Mill Springs, KY – 1/17/62
Ft. Henry, TN – 2/6/62
Roanoke Island, NC – 2/8/62
Ft. Donelson, TN – 2/16/62
Pea Ridge, AR – 3/6–7/62
Glorieta Pass, NM – 3/28/62
Ft. Pulaski, GA – 4/11/62
Nashville, TN – 4/ 15/62 – first Confederate state capitol taken by Union troops
New Orleans, LA – 4/25/62 – captured by Union troops
Norfolk, VA – 5/10/62 – captured by Union troops
Memphis, TN – 6/6/62 – captured by Union troops

The cumulative effect of these defeats was much more profound than just demoralization. For instance, the loss of Ft. Henry and Fort Donelson, both captured by General Ulysses S. Grant* forced the Confederate commander General Albert Sydney Johnston to abandon Kentucky and Nashville, TN in order to regroup farther south in Corinth, Mississippi, which set the stage for the bloody battle of Shiloh (Pittsburgh Landing) in April. In addition, the loss of New Orleans deprived the Confederacy of its largest city and the outlet of the Mississippi River to the Gulf of Mexico.

To make matters even worse, the initial terms of enlistment for Confederate soldiers were expiring, even though they had been expanded from 90 days to one year. As Northern armies seemed to be everywhere (Confederate Congressman Louis T. Wigfall of Texas lamented that…. "The enemy are in some portions of almost every state of the Confederacy…."), there was the imminent prospect of Confederate defeat unless soldiers could be compelled or coerced to remain in the ranks. Conversely, on the Union side, the mood was so optimistic that on April 3rd the new Secretary of War Edwin Stanton closed all the Northern recruiting offices, believing that the existing armies were probably large enough to win the war! However, just when it seemed as if the Confederacy would collapse in defeat, critical changes were effected in both the organization of the armies and the mobilization of and utilization of vital war materials and supplies. As a result, the fortunes of war in the late spring of 1862 took a surprising and almost decisive turn in a positive direction for the Confederacy.

---

* Grant's policy towards the defeated Confederates at the stage of the war was "no terms but unconditional surrender." These victories gave him a nickname ("Unconditional Surrender" Grant) and short lived heroic status, which would be temporarily derailed by the Battle of Pittsburgh Landing (Shiloh).

Chapter 14 – The War Between The States (a.k.a. The Civil War 1862–1863

Spring of 1862 – The Draft

As mentioned in the last chapter, circumstances appeared grim for the Confederate States of America in the first few months of 1862. Important Southern cities were now in Union hands, and the maintenance of Southern armies in the field had become a concern with desperate ramifications. To rectify the problem, the Confederate government on April 16th 1862 enacted the first draft in American history which required all able-bodied white men (with several exceptions, both legitimate and spurious) between the ages of 18 and 35 to serve for three years. In addition, substantial incentives were offered to potential draftees to enlist prior to getting drafted. The draft and the incentives resulted in the substantial enlargement of the Confederate Army during the rest of the year, totaling about 125,000 additional soldiers. During the entire 4 years of the war, the Union mustered about 2.2 million men in arms, the Confederacy, about 900,000. The policy of hiring substitutes however, proved decidedly unpopular in the Confederacy, as it would subsequently for the Union when it instituted the draft on March 3, 1863. The idea of "a rich man's war and a poor man's fight" as stated by a Confederate soldier was so offensive, that hundreds (if not thousands) of draftees or even potential draftees fled to mountains, swamps, forests, and other remote areas to avoid compulsory service, and indeed armed bands of draft resistors would sometimes fight conscription agents rather than submit to the draft. Conscription was the most unpopular measure adopted by the Confederacy , as it also would become for the Union. For example, from July 13 -16, 1863, an anti-draft riot erupted in New York City which degenerated into a bloody racial conflagration with 102 persons killed and 1000 persons injured, the worst race riot in U.S. history. It was finally crushed by army units called in from Gettysburg, Pennsylvania after the great battle.

Confederate Finances and Industrialization

From the outset of the war, the Confederacy suffered from both a severe lack of specie (gold and silver) and an underdeveloped banking and finance system which was largely the result of its export based economy. Ironically, northern and foreign bankers and brokers dominated many of the financial aspects (credit arrangements, loans, advances, interests rates, prices, etc...) related to the trade in cotton, rice, tobacco, and other Southern staples. The end result is that the Confederacy would have to basically start from scratch in financing its expenses, a daunting task during peacetime, a desperately difficult one during war. As such, how did the Confederate States attempt to pay for the war? There were different measures applied:

1. A flat tariff on imported items (15%) which proved of little value due to the Union blockade and the irregular arrangements between the Confederate government and blockade runners.
2. Loans and bonds.
3. Internal Taxes.
4. The printing of massive amounts of paper money ($1.5 billion) which proved disastrous. The Confederacy was flooded, especially after 1862, with ever increasing amounts of paper dollars of every denomination. These notes were

never classified as "legal tender" (redeemable "for all debts, public and private." Refer to the top left of a dollar bill today.), and relied on the public's faith in the Confederacy to accept them at face value. As the war wore on, the value of Confederate paper dollars plummeted and cataclysmic inflation set in. (Generally defined, inflation means the increase in consumer prices in a given year or period.) By 1864, inflation rates in the Confederacy stood at 600%, and a Confederate dollar was worth just $.05! By the end of the war, the inflation rate hit 9000%! Consider the prices of the following items in Richmond in 1864:

- Bacon $10 a pound*
- Turkey $100
- A Bushel of Corn Meal $72
- A Barrel of Flour $425
- A Doctor's Visit $30

In industrial mobilization, the South performed much more admirably, especially considering that the pre-War South accounted for only 10.3% of the entire value of U.S. manufacturing. Under the inspired leadership of the head of the Ordnance Bureau Josiah Gorgas (as well as the directors of the Army and Navy's supply bureaus), the Confederacy achieved remarkable success in producing war materials. Largely under direct government control or ownership, arsenals were established in Atlanta and Augusta, GA, Charleston, SC, Fayetteville, NC, Richmond, VA And several other Southern cities. Foundries for producing cannon, rifles, small arms, and ammunition could be found in Columbus and Macon, GA, Petersburg, VA, and Salisbury, NC The Confederacy's largest iron manufacturer, the privately owned Tredegar Iron Works in Richmond, VA, employed over 2500 workers by 1863. The Confederate government also ran and operated salt processing facilities (Wilmington, NC), coal mines, leather factories (Clarksville, VA), and after 1863, began the construction of a 150 ship navy, of which nearly 50 vessels were completed by 1865. On an individual basis, citizens donated piano wire and liquor stills for copper, sash weights were made into bullets, church bells were smelted into cannon balls, and a Confederate reconnaissance balloon was constructed out of silk dresses! (Women in Selma, Ala. even received an official request to save their human waste for use in making nitre, a vital component in gunpowder!) Thus, the Confederacy created and nationalized (government ownership) vital industries for the war effort, and indeed their armies did not suffer from a lack of weapons or ammunition, even at the end of the war.

However, the government did not display the same proficiency in directing rail traffic along the Confederacy's sub-standard and irregular gauged (width) rail network. This glaring deficiency led to costly delays in the transport of both goods and soldiers. Finally, a major and eventually insurmountable problem existed in providing consumer needs, most notably food, which led to desperate shortages for the army and civilians alike, especially after 1863 (see p. 222) Ultimately, it was not

*In Wilmington, NC, in 1861 bacon cost $.17 a lb., beef at $.05 a pound, and $.85 for a bushel of corn. In 1864, bacon cost $6 a lb., $2.50 a lb. of beef, $19 for a bushel of corn, $500 for a barrel of flour, coffee at $100 a lb. and $600 for a suit of clothes!

the lack of guns which doomed the C.S.A. to defeat at the hands of the Union soldiers and sailors; it was brought down by a lack of shoes, clothes, and food.

Union Finances and Industrialization

In stark contrast to the Confederacy's desperately innovated financial strategies, the Union benefited from a well balanced agricultural – industrial economy, and also from a cogent and feasible scheme for financing the war . On August 5th 1861, Lincoln signed into law the first income tax in U.S. history, which attached a 3% rate to annual incomes of $800 and up. It was revised upwards by the Internal Revenue Act of 1862, and again in 1864, to rates of 5% on incomes from $600 to $5000, 7 ½ % from $5000 to $10,000, and 10% on incomes in excess of $10,000. The Internal Revenue Act also implemented taxes on virtually every item purchased and every profession engaged in by the Northern public, and to collect and enforce the new taxes, the Internal Revenue Service was created. In addition, the Legal Tender Act of 1862 created a new national paper currency, the "Greenback" which was given legal tender status (see p. 203). About $450 million in "greenbacks" were circulated during the war. To rectify the problems caused by a largely unregulated banking structure, the Union's banking system was modernized and streamlined by the National Banking Act of 1863. Also, new excise taxes and a highly protective tariff act, the Morrill Tariff of 1861, almost doubled existing rates. Finally and most importantly, the Union paid for nearly 2/3 of its war effort through the sale of $2 billion in war bonds, expertly marketed by Philadelphia banker Jay Cooke. These remarkable innovations helped maintain a strong Northern economy with only a fraction of the inflation (an average of 80% for the entire war) so ruinous to the Confederacy.

Western Settlement and Early Emancipation Efforts

Lincoln and the Republican dominated Congress also pushed through large portions of the Republican Party program. To encourage western settlement and development, the Homestead Act and the Morrill Land Grant Act were passed in 1862. The Homestead Act stipulated that settlers (aged 21 and up) could claim a 160 acre plot of public land, live on it for 5 years and/or develop it, and the land would be theirs for a processing fee of only $10 (actually, the final total was $18 after commissions and closing costs). The Morrill Land Grant Act offered federal grants to new colleges providing agricultural and mechanical instruction. (The reason that many Midwestern and Western schools bear the suffix "A and M" today.)

Beginning the process that would ultimately lead to the legal destruction of slavery in 1865, the U.S. abolished slavery in Washington, D.C. on April 16th 1862. However, the government compensated the owners, owing to the sensibilities of slave owners in the Border States. To ensure that the territories would never countenance slavery, on June 19th 1862 slavery was prohibited in all U.S. territories.

The Battlefront – 1862

As mentioned previously (p. 199), the Confederacy lost battle after battle from the Fall of 1861 to the Spring of 1862, giving up both important cities and coastal regions to Union control. To a significant extent, Confederate failures on the battlefield can be attributed to ineffective organization and bureaucratic incompetence, but that began to change especially after April 1862. Another aspect of the war had also changed, the degree of death and bloodshed on both sides. After the capture of Ft. Henry and Ft. Donelson in February 1862, the Union forces under General U.S. Grant continued pushing farther south into Tennessee encountering little resistance. The Confederates, commanded by General Albert Sydney Johnson gave ground before encamping themselves near Shiloh (Pittsburg Landing) on the banks of the Tennessee River. Reinforced by General P.G.T. Beauregard, the Confederates mustered about 42,000 troops against roughly the same number of Union soldiers. Grant and General William Tecumseh Sherman rather lackadaisically positioned their forces on the west bank on the river awaiting reinforcements when the Confederates launched a pre-dawn surprise attack on April 6, 1862 which threatened to destroy the Union forces or compel them to surrender. The battle raged all day, and the Confederates ("Rebels") planned to renew the assault in the morning to finish off the Union army ("Yankees"). During the night the anticipated Union reinforcements under General Don Carlos Buell arrived just in time, and when the next Rebel attack came on April 7, the Yankees held and responded with a furious counterattack. By the end of the day, Union and Confederate forces were approximately back in the same positions they held before the battle, technically a stalemate. However, of much more significance was the nearly 25,000 killed and wounded soldiers on both sides, the bloodiest battle in U.S. history to that point. Shiloh (Pittsburg Landing) cost almost twice the total losses incurred during the entire Mexican War, and in a shocking manner forced both sides to the traumatic realization that this war would be longer and more devastating than anything Americans had ever previously encountered. Why? What had changed about warfare which incurred such horrific casualties?

The Weapons of the War

The tactics of war were still very much influenced by the Napoleonic Wars 50 years earlier which stressed the concentration of force, coordinated movements, and devastating offensive attacks. However, the weaponry developed over the subsequent half-century forced a dramatic reappraisal of these tactics, especially by 1864. In personal firearms, the 6-shot revolver pistol (most notably, the Colt) had been effective during the Mexican War and continued in widespread use between 1861–65. There were several rifles used by both sides in the War such as the single-shot Springfield .58 Caliber rifled musket, the breech loading, single-shot Sharps Carbine, the British-made Enfield rifle, the breech loading, 7-shot Spencer Carbine, the Whitworth .45 Caliber sharpshooter, and the 13-shot Henry Repeater, proved particularly devastating. They hurled bullets and "minie-balls" far greater distances (500 to 1400 yards) and at different muzzle velocities than previous guns, inflicting far more serious and mortal injuries. In artillery, the most common weapon was the 12 pound smoothbore cannon firing spherical shot, but the more accurate and longer ranged 10 pound rifled cannon firing conoidal (cone-shaped) shot came increasingly into effective use as the war went on. These rifled cannon had an effective range of up to 2 miles. Also, Richard J. Gatlin patented an early version of the machine gun, the Gatlin Gun on Nov. 4, 1862, but thankfully that weapon would not come into widespread use during the War.

However, the most innovative and far-reaching advancements in weapons development could be found in naval technology, specifically in the creation of ironclad ships and submarines. Naval engineers and designers around the world had been fulminating on the possibility of iron made ships which would be nearly impervious to damage from existing naval cannon, but daunting questions remained, especially concerning flotation and propulsion. In early 1862, the British had two experimental "ironclads" under construction, but the Confederacy and the Union had two afloat and prepared for battle by March, the C.S.S. *Virginia* and the U.S.S. *Monitor*. The Confederates began construction of their ironclad first, in 1861, as a result of the Union evacuation of Norfolk and Portsmouth, VA. As the U.S. forces left the cities, they attempted to destroy all the ships and armaments they could not transport, but with only partial success. The U.S.S. *Merrimac*, a steam frigate, was only damaged and Confederate designers led by John Brook and encouraged by the Confederate Sec. of the Navy Stephen Mallory, worked quickly to not only repair the vessel but radically alter its structure at the Norfolk Naval Shipyard. Shipyard workers fastened iron plates (produced by the Tredegar Iron Works in Richmond) to the superstructure and rechristened the vessel the C.S.S. *Virginia*. In the Union, naval experts and Sec. of the Navy Gideon Welles initially balked at the ironclad idea as impractical and brushed off pleas by Swedish naval designer John Ericsson for the United States to construct the radical new warships. However, as reports reached the North about the South's new "super-ship", the U.S. government, almost in a panic, commissioned Ericsson to build his ironclad, eventually christened as the U.S.S. *Monitor*. Upon completion, the *Monitor* was to be towed south to Hampton Roads (the waters adjacent to Norfolk, Portsmouth, and Hampton, Virginia). It arrived on March 9th, but the previous day, the *Virginia* had devastated the Union fleet blockading Hampton Roads, sinking the U.S.S. *Cumberland* and *Congress*, and running the U.S.S. *Minnesota* aground. For a brief moment in time, the *Virginia* was the most powerful warship in the world, the terror of the seas. However, as it steamed back out on March 9th to finish off the *Minnesota*, the *Virginia* encountered the *Monitor* which had arrived in Hampton Roads just hours earlier. Subsequently, the two ironclads engaged in a ferocious battle, at times firing shells at point blank range, but the battle concluded in a stalemate with the *Virginia* retiring to the shipyard. Expectations of a rematch were high, but it never occurred. After General George McClellan's massive invasion force landed at Fortress Monroe in Hampton, VA, the decision was made to abandon Norfolk to the advancing Yankee forces, and to destroy the *Virginia* rather than let it fall into enemy hands. As such, the *Virginia* met its doom on May 10th 1862. The *Monitor* succumbed to a similar fate, though under different circumstances. As it was being towed south, it sank in a storm off Cape Hatteras, NC on Dec. 31, 1862. Regardless of their brief careers, the *Virginia* and the *Monitor* revolutionized naval warfare from that time forward. During the war the Confederacy produced a total of 22 "ironclads", the Union, 58.

The Confederacy also developed a metal submarine the C.S.S. *H.L. Hunley* in 1863. After several mistrials, sinking's with the loss of crewmembers, and salvage operations to resurface the vessel, the *Hunley* was dispatched in Charleston Harbor on the evening of Feb. 17, 1864 taking aim at the U.S.S. *Housatonic*. Armed with a torpedo connected to a spar, it rammed the *Housatonic* and detonated the torpedo, sinking the Union ship in just 5 minutes. However, the *Hunley* also sank in the attack carrying her 8 man crew to their deaths. Nonetheless, this was the first time in the history of warfare that a ship had been sunk by a submarine.

The Peninsular Campaign

As mentioned previously, Union General George McClellan had moved a massive force to Hampton Roads, VA in the early spring of 1862. McClellan became the commander of the Army of the Potomac on July 22, 1861. McClellan proved to be a brilliant trainer and organizer, beloved by his troops, but real success in battle would always elude him. He lacked the will, the "killer instinct", for taking the daring risks or challenging the long odds so unmistakably a trait in the great military leaders of history. Nonetheless, after the debacle at Manassas (Bull Run), Union strategy in the east settled on a plan to move the army south to the mouth of the Chesapeake Bay and then northwest up the peninsula between the James and York Rivers to Richmond. The plan had many commendable aspects, not the least of which was the ability to re-supply at will using the captured Chesapeake Bay as a conduit. By May 1862, the Army of the Potomac numbering over 100,000 men was positioned 8 miles outside Richmond, close enough to hear the chiming of the church bells within the city. With victory seemingly within their grasp, things suddenly began to go wrong for McClellan and his formidable army. On May 4th, General "Stonewall" Jackson with 17,000 troops was ordered to march north to the Potomac River (near Harpers Ferry) ostensibly to threaten Washington, D.C., but in reality to prevent General McClellan from receiving the reinforcements he felt necessary to capture Richmond. (He reported to Lincoln that rebel forces amounted to about 200,000. However, only about 72,000 Confederate troops actually stood between McClellan and Richmond, not including Jackson's men near the Potomac.) In a brilliant campaign in which his soldiers marched up to 45 miles in a day, Jackson scored 5 victories against much larger Union armies (averaging over 33,000 troops) and kept the Union reinforcements in Washington from joining McClellan. With Jackson still in the field, General Joseph Johnston launched an attack against McClellan near Richmond, the battle of Fair Oaks (Seven Pines), on May 31st. The attack was a partial Confederate success as the Union forces were driven back slightly from Richmond, but the real significance of the battle came when Johnston's suffered a severe shoulder wound during the action. As a result, President Davis named General Robert E. Lee as commander of the Army of Northern Virginia on June 1st. One of the greatest military leaders America has ever produced, Lee performed brilliantly and heroically, becoming a source of unparalleled inspiration for the Confederacy between 1862 and 1865. As Johnston himself remarked, "The shot that struck me down is the very best that has been fired for the Southern cause yet. For I possess in no degree the confidence of our government, and now they have in my place one who does possess it." However, Lee's reputation as a general was less than remarkable when he assumed command. He was derided as "Granny Lee" (for alleged caution in battle), and "the King of

Spades" (a reference to his practice of constructing defensive fortifications) among Confederate critics, and "cautious and weak under grave responsibility…" by his foe General McClellan. That perception changed dramatically by the end of the month. Lee quickly surmised that McClellan would have to be driven away from Richmond by a Confederate offensive, a formidable task considering McClellan's superior numbers even without the reinforcements from Washington. He recalled Jackson which gave him a total of about 87,000 troops and then dispatched the daring and flamboyant (he wore a feather plumed cap and a red-lined cape, and hoped to die in battle, a wish that was granted at Yellow Tavern near Richmond on May 11, 1864) cavalry commander 29-year old Colonel James Ewell Brown (J.E.B.) Stuart to direct a reconnaissance mission to ascertain Union strength and positions. With 1200 men, he set out on June 12th. When he returned on June 16th, he had not only fulfilled his mission, he had ridden 100 miles completely encircling the Union forces and successfully eluding his pursuers, captured wagonloads of supplies and dozens of prisoners and horses, and established himself as one of the greatest cavalrymen of the war. Lee now possessed all the information necessary to launch a series of attacks known as the <u>Seven Days Battles</u>. Beginning on June 26th and concluding on July 1st, Lee's forces attacked McClellan's army east of Richmond at Mechanicsville, Gaines's Mill, Savage's Station, White Oak Swamp and Frayser's Farm, and Malvern Hill. In every encounter except Gaines's Mill, Lee's forces were tactically defeated. However, by the end of the fighting, it was McClellan who retired from the field, strategically beaten. Convinced he was fighting against an army twice the size of his own, McClellan abandoned his offensive against Richmond and retreated back to the James River, effectively clearing Virginia of Union forces, at least temporarily. In addition, after the battle Lee reorganized the Army of Northern Virginia into a much more effective combat unit. Southern morale, which had withered due to Northern victories over the past 9 months, soared as a result and new heroes for the "Cause" were created, but it all came at a dreadful cost, 36,000 men killed or wounded (20,000 Confederate - 16,000 Union) in less than a week.

<u>Second Manassas (Second Bull Run)</u>

The Union setbacks in the <u>Seven Days Battles</u> led to a shake up in the actual command of the Army of the Potomac. Although General McClellan was not technically replaced, General Henry "Old Brains" Halleck, who had been linked with the impressive Union successes in the West, now assumed actual control as general-in-chief of the Union forces. Arrogant and vainglorious General John Pope also came east to Virginia eager for "success and glory." (Military leaders on both sides despised him, referring to him as an "ass" and a "villain.") On August 29–30, Pope with a total force of about 65,000, was attacked concurrently by 55,000 Confederates under "Stonewall" Jackson and General James Longstreet in a brilliant offensive masterminded by Robert E. Lee. Once again a Union army was routed at Manassas, and by September 1st, Pope and his defeated forces were back in Washington, while Lee's troops were positioned only 20 miles outside the city. Nearly all of Virginia had been cleared of Yankee troops, morale in the South swelled, and the British and French governments were giving serious consideration to formally recognizing the Confederacy as an independent nation. As mentioned on page 196, official recognition by European nations, a critical goal of Confederate foreign policy, might lead to forcible mediation (that is, the U.S. would be forced to accept Confederate independence or face economic and/or military reprisals from the British and/or the French) and perhaps military alliances with the Confederacy against the United States, At this point, Confederate armies in both the east and west began offensives aimed at the Northern states.

In the west, Confederate forces led by General Braxton Bragg were preparing to invade Kentucky to rally support for the Southern cause and bring the state formally into the Confederacy. In the east, General Lee and his lieutenants were planning to accomplish virtually the same goals in Maryland, with the additional incentives of demoralizing Northerners and gaining foreign recognition by capturing a Northern city, perhaps even Washington, D.C. In the first few weeks of September 1862, the Confederate cause seemed tantalizingly close to realization.

Foreign Affairs - Union and Confederacy (Britain and France)

There were several appealing reasons for Britain and France to support an independent Confederacy, or conversely to see a weakened and divided United States. What were they? (Some of the following contentions are generalized, but not without merit.)

A. There were many in France and especially Britain who viewed the United States as a ruthless commercial rival, not an economic partner.

B. Britain and the Northern section of the United States had a long history of territorial disputes in Maine and New Brunswick, Canada, and more recently the Oregon Territory in 1845–46. Although the disputes were resolved peaceably, there were lingering suspicions on both sides concerning the U.S. – Canada border.

C. The British and French aristocratic classes in many instances felt the United States (especially the North) socially and politically boorish and unsophisticated, if not downright vulgar. The Southern aristocracy however, with its emphasis on kinship, class distinctions, manners, and privilege (without question largely influenced by the maintenance of slavery) appeared similar to a degree and thus more acceptable as "kindred spirits."

D. In 1860, the South produced 90% of the world's cotton, and the British and French textile industries depended on it. Consider that Britain purchased 4 times the amount of cotton than Northern textile manufacturers, and that 93% of French processed cotton came from Southern planters. However, cotton alone could never secure foreign recognition for the Confederacy (see p. 196), although it was vital as collateral in Confederate efforts to obtain substantial loans from Britain and France (see p. 210) However, its position as the sole invaluable American commodity was now challenged by Northern exports of corn, grains, and wheat, especially to Great Britain.

E. Lincoln's *Emancipation Proclamation* issued Sept. 22nd 1862 and "effective" beginning January 1, 1863, proved significant in dissuading

European recognition of the C.S.A., as Britain and France were largely supportive of abolition by 1861. However, as long as Union war aims centered on reunification and not the elimination of slavery, the moral quandary of supporting a slave-based Confederacy against an emancipationist United States simply did not exist. (Remember, <u>5</u> Northern or "Border States" (Missouri, Kentucky, West Virginia, Maryland, and Delaware) maintained slavery and their status as states in the Union. Also, refer to Lincoln's war aims letter to Horace Greeley on p. 194.) The *Emancipation Proclamation* technically, though not actually, freed 3,063,392 slaves in 10 <u>Confederate States</u>, while leaving slavery relatively intact in the 5 "Border States" and the areas of the Confederacy under Union control. The number of slaves in those areas? 441,702. Nonetheless, Lincoln's brilliant and pragmatic action gave the Union the moral component it previously lacked, at least in the eyes of much of the population of Britain and France.*

These and other variables however did not exist in a vacuum. Critical events could and almost did succeed in garnering formal recognition of the Confederacy. Although the ultimate key to recognition was success on the battlefield, incidents at sea brought the United States and Great Britain close to war on two occasions:

1. The *Trent* <u>Affair</u> – On Nov. 8, 1861, the U.S.S *San Jacinto* fired upon and stopped a British mail ship the R.M.S. *Trent* in the Bahama Channel north of Cuba. Why? The *Trent* carried two Confederate emissaries, James Mason and John Slidell, who were on their way to Britain seeking an official audience with the foreign ministry. Capt. Charles Wilkes of the *San Jacinto* seized the two men and imprisoned them at Fortress Monroe in Virginia, after which they were taken to Boston. Wilkes' actions violated international law and constituted an act of <u>impressment</u> (see p. 46, 63–65), which prompted a furious response from the British Prime Minister Lord Palmerston, Foreign Secretary Lord Earl Russell, and the British press. The British were also supported by the French government. They demanded a formal apology and the release of the Confederate emissaries. In addition, 11,000 British troops were sent to Canada, purportedly singing "Dixie" (the unofficial anthem of the South) as they departed! In the North, Wilkes was considered a hero and for a few weeks war seemed likely between the U.S. and Britain, but tensions quickly abated for three very important reasons. One, Lincoln realized that war with Britain would be disastrous, and without apologizing, instructed U.S. Sec. of State William Seward on Dec. 25th, to announce that Mason and Slidell would be "cheerfully surrendered" and allowed to resume their mission. Two, the United States at this juncture depended on Britain for a vital component of gunpowder, saltpeter. If the U.S. and Britain went to war, obviously the supply would be cut off. Finally, the British government despite its protestations did not want war and accepted the gesture. Akin to the United States and saltpeter, the British were becoming increasingly dependent on foodstuffs produced by the Union and

*It must be noted however that due to its obvious inconsistencies regarding slavery, some Europeans viewed the *Emancipation Proclamation* quite cynically.

did not wish to see the trade interrupted. <u>The *Trent* Affair</u> however proved the most dramatic <u>single</u> incident between Britain and the United States during the entire war.

2. <u>The Laird Rams</u> – Throughout the war, the Confederacy purchased (and attempted to purchase) ships of advanced design from Britain for two purposes, blockade running and revenue raiding. The former were sleek vessels designed to slip through the Union blockade and deliver desperately needed war materials (and also luxury items) to the Confederacy. By the end of the war, 1650 blockade runners (for example, the *Flamingo*, the *Flora*, the *Iona*, and the *Lizzie*) made approximately 8000 round trips between the Confederacy and foreign ports. About 600,000 weapons, mostly small arms, and a wealth of other goods were smuggled into Confederate ports, most notably, Wilmington, NC. The revenue raiders however were designed primarily to attack Union merchant vessels and disrupt trade, which they accomplished quite successfully. The two most notorious raiders, the *Florida* (commanded by Capt. John Maffitt) and the *Alabama* (commanded by Capt. Ralph Semmes) sank or captured 55 and 58 ships respectively. A third, the *Shenandoah* (commanded by Capt. James Waddell) took 38 and did not cease fighting until August 2, 1865! These and other raiders were constructed in British ports by British firms, including the Laird Shipyard in Birkenhead. In 1862, the shipyard had been contracted to build two state-of-the-art ironclad rams for the Confederate Navy. When completed in the summer of 1863, they were capable of wreaking havoc on both the Union fleet and Northern coastal cities, <u>if</u> they could be turned over to the Confederacy. To avoid breaking international neutrality laws, the rams were registered to foreign owners. When they had reached international waters, they were to be transferred to Confederate control. The U.S. ambassador to Britain, Charles Francis Adams (the son and grandson of two former presidents) knew all about the rams, and warned his British counterpart Lord Russell on Sept. 5, 1863 that "It would superfluous in me to point out this (if the rams get into Confederate hands) is war...." They never did, and thus another threatening crisis between Britain and the United States was averted. Indeed, Charles Francis Adams' performance as ambassador throughout the war was exemplary. In short, he proved superior to his Confederate counterparts.

The French government (especially Emperor Napoleon III) was perhaps even more enthusiastic towards the Confederate cause than the British. At various times between 1861 and 1863, the French foreign ministers, Édouard-Antoine de Thouvenel and his successor Édouard Drouyn de Lhuys, proposed mediation talks aimed at ending the war and securing Confederate independence. However, in nearly every case they proceeded cautiously, preferring to act in concert with the British. After the disastrous Union defeat at Fredericksburg on December 13, 1862, Napoleon III proposed peace talks (for a variety of reasons) but was rebuffed by the U.S. Despite the setback, in 1863 the Confederacy negotiated a $14.5 million loan with the Erlanger financial firm in France (based on cotton) which temporarily shored up Confederate finances and credit. Napoleon III continued to contemplate recognition of the C.S.A. well into 1863. However, the twin Confederate military disasters of Gettysburg and

Vicksburg convinced the French emperor that the Confederacy was in too precarious a situation to officially welcome it into the community of independent nations. If the Confederate States of America were to achieve that status, it must occur on the battlefield, or due to the war weariness of their Union adversaries.

The Amerindians

The Confederate government also tried to cull alliances with the various Amerindian nations located in present day Oklahoma. Confederate commissioner Albert Pike secured agreements with the "Five Civilized Tribes" of the region promising protection against the United States and autonomy for the tribes, in exchange for military alliances with the Confederacy. Why would some Amerindians side with the Confederacy against the Union? For one, some of the Amerindian nations countenanced slavery. Another plausible explanation would be the historical mistreatment meted out by the United States to the Amerindians. Beginning with colonization, and continuing through removal policies of the 1830s and 1840s, as well as the harsh measures applied to Amerindians in California and the Southwest, the record of the United States towards Native Americans was virtually uniformly destructive. If the Confederacy promised a better political and financial disposition for allied tribes, and protection against U.S. incursions into Amerindian territory, it certainly appeared positive compared to previous U.S. actions and policies. In other words, could Confederate treatment of the Amerindians possibly be any worse than that pursued by the U.S. government? As such, many (but not all) Amerindians reasoned that their lot would be more favorable with the Confederacy, and fought alongside Confederate soldiers in battles from Chustenahlah, Indian Territory in Dec. 1861 to skirmishes in the West fought after Appomattox in 1865. Probably the most important single reason for Amerindians to fight for either side were ancient feuds (the "blood law") which transcended political grievances. (This proved especially true of the Cherokees which split into bitter eastern and western factions in the 1830s.The western group tended to ally with the Confederacy, the eastern Cherokee with the Union.) Most notably, Confederate Brigadier General Stand Watie was of Cherokee ancestry, and eventual Creek Nation Chief George Washington Grayson served as a captain for the C.S.A. Watie fought in 18 engagements and was the last Confederate general to surrender to U.S. forces (June 23, 1865). However, it must be noted that the Confederates were unable after 1862 to provide real security for their Amerindian allies against U.S. forces in the West, so their overall military significance in the war was limited. In a bitter irony, after the war, the various Native American groups which sided with either the Union or Confederacy received harsh terms from the U.S. government. For example, the Creeks were forced to give up half of their tribal lands, and made subjects to U.S. judicial control. Finally, a strange aspect of the relationship between the Confederates and the Amerindians is the fact that Southerners prior to the war had been at least as culpable in their misdeeds against the Native Americans as their Northern counterparts.

Sharpsburg (Antietam)

As mentioned previously, in the aftermath of the Union debacle at <u>Second Manassas (Second Bull Run)</u>, the Confederate armies began offensives in both the east and the west, aimed at securing Maryland and Kentucky for the Confederacy. President Lincoln also responded to the defeat by recalling George McClellan to command the Army of the Potomac. McClellan was not particularly surprised by his reinstatement; he "modestly" informed his wife in a letter that, "Again I have been called upon to save the country." However, for all his faults, McClellan was beloved by his men and by early September he had lifted their spirits and put them again in fighting trim.

At the end of August 1862, about 50,000 Confederates under Generals Braxton Bragg and Edmund Kirby Smith were in south central Kentucky, and on Sept. 4th, Lee's 55,000 troops entered Maryland. Bragg and Lee hoped for enthusiastic volunteers to flock to their ranks, but were sorely disappointed by the response of the men of Kentucky and Maryland. They did however strike terror in Ohio and Washington, D.C. and forced Northern commanders to pursue them. In addition, on Sept. 14th, British Prime Minister Lord Palmerston wrote to Foreign Secretary Russell that the time may be ripe to forcefully propose joint Anglo-French mediation of the war on the basis of Confederate independence. Russell agreed and commiserated with his French counterpart Édouard-Antoine de Thouvenel. The key would be the Confederate campaigns in the North.

Lee's military strategy was to cut off Washington, D.C. from its rail connections to the north and east and perhaps seize Harrisburg, Pennsylvania. To accomplish this, he divided his army, although he knew McClellan had twice the number of troops under his command. Lee was certain that McClellan would be too slow to stop him, and he may have been right, except for an incredible discovery by two Union soldiers on Sept. 13th. First Sergeant John Bloss and Corporal Barton Mitchell found a copy of Lee's battle plans (Special Order # 191) lying on a road wrapped around three cigars. They had been accidentally dropped by a Confederate courier, and were immediately brought to General McClellan who enthusiastically proclaimed,
"Here is a paper with which if I cannot whip "Bobbie Lee,' I will be willing to go home." McClellan's histrionics notwithstanding, he responded to the critical information too slowly which allowed Lee the time to reunite most of his divided army. Lee had been informed that McClellan knew his battle plans on Sept. 13th and acted immediately. McClellan however moved more slowly and nearly an entire day passed before he began moving his troops to confront Lee. On Sept. 17th, the two armies clashed outside the town of <u>Sharpsburg</u>, MD along the Antietam Creek, in what became the bloodiest day in American history. In a battle best characterized by savage fighting and missed and unexploited Union opportunities, 6000 soldiers, Northern and Southern, were killed and 17,000 more wounded. Soldiers present at <u>Sharpsburg</u> (<u>Antietam</u>) most poignantly described the carnage:*

> Every stalk of corn in the northern and greater part of the field
> was cut as closely as could have been done with a knife, and the
> slain lay in rows precisely as they stood in their ranks a few minutes
> before. (Union officer)

> The sun seemed to go backwards, and it appeared as if night would
> never come. (Confederate soldier)

*For example, "of 250 men in the 6th Georgia Regiment at Antietam, only 24 remained unhurt."

Lee's army had barely escaped destruction, having been bailed out at the end of the day by General A.P. Hill and his reinforcements. On the 18th, both armies merely looked at each other, and that night Lee retreated unmolested south into Virginia. McClellan, who had received additional troops overnight, would not attack Lee's depleted forces, owing to the carnage of the battle and the persistent belief that Lee outnumbered him! Upon hearing the news, Lincoln was furious and relieved McClellan once and for all from command, but because Lee's invasion had been blunted, he used the "victory" as a springboard for the *Emancipation Proclamation*, delivered on Sept. 22nd. (See p. 209–10). The reversal of Confederate fortunes in Maryland and in Kentucky, (the inconclusive battle of Perryville on Oct. 8th resulted in the Confederate evacuation of the state) gave Britain and France pause towards forced mediation as did the *Emancipation Proclamation*.

From Fredericksburg To Gettysburg

Despite staggering losses, Lee was able to gradually rebuild his Army of Northern Virginia and await yet another Union thrust into Virginia. It did not take long. General Ambrose Burnside was now the latest commander of the Union Army of the Republic. Instead of moving towards Manassas as McDowell and Pope had done, he and his 110,000 marched to Fredericksburg, VA on the Rappahannock River north of Richmond. Lee positioned his 75,000 troops atop Marye's Heights west of the town and waited. On the foggy morning of Dec. 13th, Burnside ordered the attack, which initially had a chance of success at breaking through sectors of the Confederate lines, but miscommunication and mismanagement squandered Union opportunities. Later in the battle, Burnside ordered a series of suicidal frontal assaults across a 400 yard field rimmed by Marye's Heights which would prove a ghastly killing zone. Even before they began, Confederate General James Longstreet promised General Lee, "General, if you put every Union soldier now on the other side of the Potomac on that field to approach me over the same line, I will kill them all before they reach my line." His words proved prophetic. Wave after wave of courageous Union soldiers attempted to storm the heights and were mowed down by the thousands. By the end of the day 12,600 Union soldiers were dead or wounded compared to 5,300 Confederates. Lee himself commented of the battle, "It is well that war is so terrible—we should grow too fond of it." The defeat served as another demoralizing set back for the United States. Predictably, Burnside was relieved of command, and he and Lincoln bore the brunt of public condemnation for Fredericksburg. Lincoln lamented after the battle, "If there is a worse place than Hell, I am in it."

Next on the list of Union commanders of the Army of the Potomac came General Joseph "Fightin' Joe" Hooker. In the spring of 1863, with 120,000 reorganized and well supplied troops, the audacious and determined Hooker marched south near Fredericksburg planning to split his army and surround Lee, one of the Southern commander's most oft used tactics. In April, he asserted, "My plans are perfect, and when I start to carry them out, may God have mercy on Bobby Lee, for I shall have none." Confident indeed, but in early May at <u>Chancellorsville</u> (VA), Lee made him eat his words. In the four day battle between May 2–4, Lee divided and re-divided, his 60,000 man army, consistently anticipating Hooker's actions. Lee also constantly seized the initiative, attacking Hooker, and then redeploying troops where necessary to prevent Hooker's army from responding in kind. In short, Hooker was out-thought and out-maneuvered. Although his officer corps on May 4th urged him to attack Lee and not yield the field, that is precisely what Hooker did, withdrawing his army to the Potomac River on May 5th. Chancellorsville was Lee's most brilliant victory of the war, but also one of his costliest. Lee lost 12,821 casualties, Hooker 17,278, but while the Union could easily replenish the ranks, the Confederacy could not. Additionally, upon returning from an evening reconnaissance of the enemy position on May 2nd (for the purpose of launching a nighttime assault), General "Stonewall" Jackson was shot and seriously wounded by Confederate sentries unaware of his identity. Although his left arm was amputated, Jackson appeared to be recovering nicely, but then pneumonia set in and he died on May 10, 1863. The loss to Lee was incalculable as he had lost his best field commander, a loss that would haunt the Confederacy in the fateful days to come.

Action In The West

The Western Theater, which seemed to have taken a backseat in importance, nonetheless witnessed significant action in late 1862 – early 1863. A major battle took place at <u>Murfreesboro (Stones River)</u> in central Tennessee between Dec. 31, 1862 and Jan. 2, 1863. Despite success at the outset, General Braxton Bragg hesitated (fast becoming an unfortunate trademark of the Confederate general) and ultimately Union forces under General William Rosecrans and his talented subordinate General William Tecumseh Sherman forced Bragg and his Army of the Tennessee to retreat southward. It had been a bloody encounter with 12,906 Union and 11,739 Confederate casualties. It was becoming clear that the war was becoming more and more deadly as the years wore on. Despite this defeat, the Confederacy still had cause for optimism. Galveston, Texas had been recaptured in January and the Confederates still controlled Vicksburg, Mississippi and 250 miles of the Mississippi River despite concerted Union attempts to capture both the city and control of the waterway. The hopes for foreign intervention again rose (See p. 208–12) and the Confederate nation "appeared" a permanent reality, but the exigencies of war in the late spring and early summer of 1863 once again thwarted the Southern dream of independence.

Vicksburg

At about the same time as the battle of Chancellorsville, General U.S. Grant devised a new strategy to conquer Vicksburg. Previously, Union forces had attempted to surround the city by digging bypass canals from the Mississippi River in order to circumvent the Confederate defenses. The task proved impossible as the endless swamps, bayous, and streams were virtually impenetrable, and Union troops were ravaged by malaria, yellow fever and other diseases indigenous to the sub-tropical South. In late April, Grant decided to transport his army south of Vicksburg and then advance northeast to Jackson, Mississippi. From there, the army would follow the Southern Mississippi Railroad west to the outskirts of Vicksburg, and with the aid of Union gunboats in control of the river, besiege the city. With his field commanders Generals Sherman, James McPherson, and John McClernand, Grant was able to position the Union forces just east of Vicksburg and the Confederate trenches by May 18, 1863. The siege now began in earnest. Inside the city were 3000 civilians and Confederate General John Pemberton in command of approximately

30,000 troops. Initially both Confederate citizens and soldiers alike were in good spirits as they had enough supplies to withstand a siege for several weeks and believed Confederate forces under the now recovered General Joseph Johnston would break through the Union lines and save the city. As time passed however, their circumstances grew increasingly grim. By mid-June, they were eating horses, then dogs and cats, and finally rats to avoid starvation. The ceaseless pounding of Union siege guns made the strain more and more unbearable, and by the end of the month, the city was on the verge of capitulation despite the desperate orders of Confederate President Jefferson Davis to hold out at all cost. Why had Johnston not attacked Union forces from the east; why had Pemberton not attempted a breakout from the city? The answer is relatively simple. Johnston felt he did not have the number of troops necessary for any reasonable chance at success against Grant's overwhelming forces (Johnston had 31,000, Grant, 70,000). For Pemberton, the situation was more or less the same. From the minute the siege commenced, his forces grew weaker while those of the U.S. grew stronger. Perhaps if Johnston and Pemberton could have coordinated a joint attack early in the campaign, they may have achieved the breakthrough so desperately needed for both Vicksburg and the Confederacy as a whole, but such an operation never materialized due to logistical problems and poor communications. Ironically, the Confederate government came to the decision that the only hope for saving Vicksburg lay far to the east, in Virginia and points north.

Gettysburg

On May 15th, a Confederate council of war met in Richmond to discuss the military situation in both the east and at Vicksburg. Robert E. Lee dominated the meeting with a grandiose and optimistic plan for invading the North again. Lee fervently believed such a move would end in fabulous success; the Army of the Potomac would be routed (again), Northern support for the war diminished, and the chance for foreign intervention reinvigorated. Lee beamed with pride regarding his once again reorganized Army of Northern Virginia, "There were never such men in an army before. They will go anywhere and do anything if properly led." President Davis agreed and in early June, Lee and his army of 75,000 set out for enemy territory. For his part, General Hooker seemed to be reluctant to "have mercy on Bobbie Lee" a second time and shied away from confronting him. An exasperated Lincoln replaced Hooker with General George Meade, a capable if unheralded commander. His 90,000 battle-hardened veterans were to test their mettle this time on Northern soil...home. The first Confederate units under General James Longstreet arrived in the North on June 28th, and the bulk of the Confederate Army of Northern Virginia would make it to Pennsylvania by the end of the month. Their ultimate destination may have been the state capital of Harrisburg, however, as fate would have it the largest battle in the history of the Western Hemisphere was destined to take place in an anonymous little town to the south, Gettysburg. The Confederates were interested in the town as it was rumored to have a large stockpile of shoes. Awaiting them however was a contingent of Northern soldiers led by John Buford who accurately surmised the strategic value of Gettysburg. The battle commenced in earnest on July 1st, with Lee's forces gaining the early initiative. The extant problem for the Confederates proved to be the absence of Lee's "eyes and ears" General J.E.B. Stuart's cavalry which was off foraging in Maryland. As such, Lee was left with a critical lack of intelligence concerning the location and deployment of units of Meade's Army of the Potomac. To make matters worse for the Confederates, the Union army was securing the hills to the south of Gettysburg, putting themselves in a fortuitous defensive position. Lee had previously ordered General Richard Ewell to seize the hills, but Ewell hesitated until it was too late. Lee also ordered Longstreet to attack the Union positions promptly on July 1st, but Longstreet, who believed Lee's strategy of attack incorrect, did not begin his offensive until late in the afternoon. Despite an immense effusion of blood and heroics on both sides, the climax of the battle would not take place until July 3rd. Lee still believed that the Union army could be destroyed by a coordinated frontal assault. As such, beginning at 1:07 in the afternoon, the Confederate artillery unleashed a 150 gun cannonade designed to blast the Yankees off aptly named Cemetery Ridge. The barrage lasted two hours, and upon its conclusion Confederate General George Pickett and 14,000 men advanced across a mile-wide field towards the Union forces waiting atop the ridge. When the Confederates came within 200 yards of the line, the Yankees opened up on them with blistering effect. It was a replay of the disaster at Fredericksburg, but this time the victims of the onslaught were the Southerners. In half an hour, Pickett and his 7000 survivors retreated back to the Confederate line. Lee immediately blamed himself. "It is all my fault. It is I who have lost this fight, and you must help me out the best way you can," he lamented, and the Confederates began their long march back to Virginia. General Meade, having won a great victory but at great cost, did not pursue Lee, much to the consternation of Lincoln. The battle resulted in 23,000 Union and 28,000 Confederate casualties, the bloodiest 3 days in American history. Concomitantly, on July 4th 1863, the Confederates yielded at Vicksburg. An exultant Lincoln proclaimed that "the Father of the Waters again goes unvexed to the sea." Lincoln commemorated the battle of Gettysburg with a magnificent speech on November 19th 1863 delivered to a surprisingly unreceptive and critical audience.

> Four score and seven years ago our fathers brought forth, upon this continent, a new nation, conceived in Liberty, and dedicated to the proposition that all men are created equal. Now we are engaged in a great civil war, testing whether that nation, or any nation, so conceived, and so dedicated, can long endure. We are met here on a great battlefield of that war. We have come to dedicate a portion of it as a final resting place for those who here gave their lives that that nation might live. It is altogether fitting and proper that we should do this. But in a larger sense we can not dedicate---we can not consecrate--- we can not hallow this ground. The brave men, living and dead, who struggled here, have consecrated it far above our poor power to add or detract. The world will little note, nor long remember, what we say here, but can never forget what they did here. It is for us, the living, rather to be dedicated here to the unfinished work which they have, thus far, so nobly carried on. It is rather for us to be here

dedicated to the great task remaining before us---that from these honored dead we take increased devotion to that cause for which they here gave the last full measure of devotion---that we here highly resolve that these dead shall have not died in vain, that this nation shall have a new birth of freedom; and that this government of the people, by the people, for the people, shall not perish from the face of the earth.

The twin losses of Gettysburg and Vicksburg were the greatest disasters yet to befall the young Confederacy, and they all but eliminated any hope of foreign recognition. However, the belief held by Lincoln and many in the North that the Confederacy was one step away from defeat and collapse was premature. Although, the Confederates were never again to launch a major offensive in the North, they were determined to now fight a brutal defensive war and literally bleed the Union to the peace table.

Chapter 15 – The War Between the States (a.k.a. The Civil War) 1863–65

Black Americans During The War – North and South

When the war began, free black Americans on both sides of the Mason-Dixon line sought to enlist in the opposing armies. An interesting question however is why? For the first two years of the war, the abolition of slavery was not a stated goal for the Union, and the maintenance of slavery in the Confederacy was a cardinal principal for the new nation, and yet black men came to Union recruiting stations in New York, Boston, and Washington, D.C., and to their Confederate counterparts in Charleston, S.C. and Richmond, VA. In all cases, their service was refused. While it is impossible to know precisely each man's motivation to serve under one flag or the other, one reason seems especially plausible. Wartime service might earn freedom from slavery for all black Americans. In the North, this is essentially what occurred by 1865. The 200,000+ black soldiers and sailors sacrifices made it virtually unthinkable that slavery would survive the war, especially when the majority (119,000) of black Union volunteers had once been slaves.* Their actions in 41 major battles and 449 lesser skirmishes and engagements from 1863 onward, and the valor displayed by units such as the Massachusetts 54th at Fort Wagner, S.C. (July 18, 1863) and the 39th U.S. Colored 9th Corps at Petersburg, VA (July 30, 1864) could not be denied. Just as the Vietnam War led to the passage of the 26th Amendment giving 18 year old citizens the right to vote (the average age of the Vietnam War soldier was 19), black service in the Union Army was partly responsible for the passage of the 13th, 14th, and 15th Amendments after the war which ended slavery, extended full citizenship to former slaves, and gave adult black males the right to vote respectively. After 1863, it was becoming clear that slavery, one way or the other, was to be extinguished. Despite these historical changes, black servicemen were overtly discriminated against in the Union ranks. There were no black officers, blacks were routinely assigned labor duties such as latrine digging and trash cleanup, subject to slavery-style disciplinary action such as public whipping, and were paid less than their white counterparts, $10 a month for blacks, $13 a month for whites.

In the South, the situation was far more complex. Whites were constantly alarmed by the prospect of a massive slave uprising while a large proportion of Southern white men were away from their homes with the various Confederate armies. One of the manifestations of this fear was the extraordinarily unpopular exemption for slave-owners who owned 20 or more slaves. However, there were no major slave rebellions in the South during the war, but slavery as an institution began to unravel. Quite simply, slavery is based on physical force or the threat of it. Remove the adult white male population from this dynamic, and slaves begin to act less like slaves, and those left in charge of them, in many cases women, old men, and teenagers, find themselves compelled to ask for service, not command. Consider this hypothetical example. A young wife with two small children finds herself alone on the family farm with 3 male slaves. Her husband and brothers have gone off to war. When assigning the slaves to perform a chore, how can she force them to do it? Indeed, if Union troops are in the vicinity, how can she prevent them from fleeing to their lines? The answer again is she must <u>ask</u>, and extend privileges and liberties previously unheard of in the slave system. The slaves, for their part did not rise up

*37,723 black recruits in the U.S.C.T. came from the Northern free states, while 41,719 came from the Border States, and 93,542 came from the Confederate States.

in rebellion. Instead, they watched and waited for several reasons. For one, until the issuance of the *Emancipation Proclamation*, standard Union policy in regards to runaway slaves in the Confederacy was to return them to their owners. Second, a slave insurrection in the wartime South most certainly would have been a suicidal proposition, considering the military mobilization of the white male population. Third, the farm or plantation offered some protection against both the privations caused by the war and the physical danger created by it, whether posed in the form of soldiers, thieves, or bandits. Fourth, in individual cases, slaves and their owners had formed bonds of affection, especially now that the dynamics of the institution were so radically evolving. (A related example of this change is illustrated by a quote from a black Union soldier to his former owner, a captured prisoner-of-war. "Hello, Massa; bottom rail on top dis time.") Fifth, and most significant, beginning in 1863, slaves could bide their time and wait until Union forces were in close proximity, and then flee to freedom, which approximately 500,000 did. This created a dual problem for the Confederacy, the loss of valuable workers who would in countless instances return as enemy soldiers.

Recognizing the value of the slaves, the Confederate armies utilized thousands of black Southerners in a wide variety of endeavors. Slaves as well as free blacks worked in factories and mines, and as stevedores, teamsters, hospital attendants, unskilled laborers, fortifications builders, cooks, spies, body servants, grave diggers and in some cases combatants, the latter only a fraction of the number of former slaves who fought for the Union. By 1864, as the Confederate cause grew more desperate and the inability to replenish the soldiers ranks became critical, some Confederate leaders considered what would have unthinkable in 1861, freeing and arming the slaves to fight for the South. A celebrated commander in the western theater General Patrick Cleburne proposed the measure at a military conference on January 2nd 1864, claiming it was a simple question of whether it was more important to maintain slavery than for the Confederate States of America to win its independence. Initially, the scheme met with profound skepticism. A leading Confederate politician and sometimes general Howell Cobb lamented with more prescience than he knew, "The day you make soldiers of them is the beginning of the end of the revolution. If slaves make good soldiers our whole theory of slavery is wrong." However, by the fall of 1864, influential newspapers from Virginia to Alabama endorsed the measure and the governors of Alabama, Georgia, Mississippi, North Carolina, South Carolina, and Virginia urged that slaves be inducted into some form of military service. On March 23, 1865, the Confederate War Department issued General Order Number 14 which called for the freeing, arming, and training of 200,000 slaves. Two companies in Virginia actually began to drill but the Confederacy itself was near death by March 1865. If the proposal had been passed years earlier, perhaps the Confederacy would have won a permanent existence in the community of nations, but again the cost would be the destruction of slavery, ironically at the hands of Southerners themselves.

Women At War

During the war women fulfilled traditional, though absolutely vital, roles for both the Union and the Confederacy. The scope, scale, and bloodshed incurred by the conflict meant that hundreds of thousands of women would serve as nurses, nurses aides, and medical technicians, some of the most notable included Florence Nightingale (of Crimean War fame), Alabamian Kate Cummings, Elizabeth Blackwell, "Mother" Mary Ann Bickerdyke, and Clara Barton. Women also labored as seamstresses, factory and arsenal workers, government employees, (especially in the Confederacy) clerks, accountants, and secretaries, all pre-cursors of women's roles in 20th century conflicts. Northern and Southern women also worked the fields as farmers and both sides utilized women as spies. One of the most successful Northern spies was the alluring Kentucky actress Pauline Cushman. Two of the most colorful and intrepid female Confederate spies were Maria Isabella "Belle" Boyd ("La Belle Rebelle"), and Rose O'Neal Greenhow who drowned off Wilmington, NC in 1864 while trying to smuggle gold through the Union blockade. In the South, women had the additional burden of overseeing plantations. Some women even disguised themselves as men and served in the armies. These roles stood in stark contrast to the idealized view of Southern women, that is the refined "southern belle", revered and untouched by the crudity and vulgarity of the "real world" (see page 203). Always more myth than reality, this ideal melted away quickly due to the exigencies of war. Nowhere can this be seen more clearly than in the food riots in the South during 1863. Mobs of starving women, some armed with knives and pistols, stormed shops, storehouses, food depots, and even army convoys demanding food and supplies for themselves and their children on at least a dozen separate occasions. Predictably, these rampages were aimed at merchants widely believed to be hoarding goods or gouging prices, but rioters also targeted Confederate officials viewed as criminally negligent in their attention to the welfare of the general populace. The riots took place in the streets of Atlanta, Ga., High Point, and Salisbury, NC, Mobile, ALA, and the largest of all in the capital of the Confederacy itself, Richmond, VA, where incensed women threatened "Bread or Blood!" in April 1863. Eventually, the unrest died down after both promises of relief and threats of severe punishment were issued by both the Confederate government and various Confederate state governors and legislators.

Unfortunately for most women, North and South, the war was a grueling, emotionally devastating experience that tested their endurance and strength somewhat akin to the traumas faced by their husbands, brothers, and sons in the field.

Politics – The North

No war ever operates in a complete vacuum from politics and the War Between The States exemplifies this contention. In the North, Lincoln was hounded by both Republicans and Democrats almost from the outset of his presidency. Leading Republicans such as Salmon Chase and Lincoln's own Secretary of State William Seward initially viewed the new president with contempt. Seward ("Mr. Republican" during the formative years of the party) even assumed he would act as something of an American Prime Minister, the person in actual control of the government while Lincoln would serve as a bemused figurehead president. Lincoln's second Secretary of War Edwin Stanton referred to him as the "original gorilla", and his Secretary of Treasury Salmon Chase actively worked against his re-nomination in 1864. The editorial attacks on Lincoln continued almost to his death, criticizing his character, his appearance, his intelligence, and his conduct of the war. Consider the following:

> Filthy Story-Teller, Despot, Liar, Thief, Braggart, Buffoon,
> Usurper, Monster, Ignoramus Abe, Old Scoundrel, Perjurer,
> Robber, Swindler, Tyrant, Fiend, Field-Butcher, Land Pirate.
> *Harper's Weekly*, 1864

> Mr. Lincoln evidently knows nothing of the philosophy of history,
> or of the higher elements of human nature.... His soul seems
> made of leather, and incapable of any grand or noble emotion....
> He lowers, never elevates you. You leave his presence with your
> enthusiasm damped, your better feelings crushed, and your hopes
> cast to the winds.... When he hits upon a policy, substantially good
> in itself, he contrives to belittle it, besmear it in some way to render
> it mean, contemptible, and useless. Even wisdom from him seems
> but folly.
> *Brownson's Quarterly Review*, 1864

Lincoln's efforts to prosecute the war were under constant attack by the "Radical Republicans" within his own party. The "Radicals" (who came to dominate Reconstruction after the war) included Stanton and Chase, as well as Congressmen Thaddeus Stevens, Benjamin Wade, Charles Sumner, Zachariah Chandler, Jonathan Andrew, and Indiana Governor Oliver Morton vilified Lincoln for his war strategies, choice of generals, home-front security, and emancipation, to name but a few points of contention. The main forum for their criticisms was the ever-present Joint Committee on the Conduct of the War which convened until the war ended.

On the other side for Lincoln lay the Democrats, divided into two groups, War Democrats and Peace Democrats. The latter was to give the president the most difficulty, especially in 1863–64. The War Democrats agreed with Lincoln to continue the war until the Confederacy surrendered and rejoined the Union, but they disagreed with him on the same issues as the Radical Republicans, and most importantly, on emancipation. They (as did the Peace Democrats) also bitterly criticized his suspension of certain civil liberties, most notably, the right of *habeas corpus*. By doing this, Lincoln could order the arrest and imprisonment of any citizen <u>without</u> a warrant, <u>without</u> charge, <u>without</u> bail, and <u>without</u> trial. During the war (which was undeclared), over 14,000 Northerners were incarcerated usually for "disloyalty", which was broadly interpreted. (Lincoln even considered arresting the Chief Justice of the Supreme Court Roger B. Taney due to his ruling in *ex parte Merriman* in 1861 which held that Lincoln had violated that Constitution when he suspended *habeas corpus*.)

The Peace Democrats, also known as <u>"Copperheads"</u>, desired peace at any price, and their actions sometimes bordered on treason. The most notable of the "Copperheads" were Ohio Congressman Clement Vallandigham and New York City Mayor Fernando Wood. Vallandigham continuously railed against Lincoln, the war, and emancipation. "Defeat, debt, taxation, sepulchers, these are your trophies" (of war), he proclaimed in Congress on July 14, 1863. His actions were so disagreeable to Lincoln that he had him arrested and exiled to the Confederacy in May 1863, but Vallandigham returned to the United States the next year and worked to defeat Lincoln in the critical presidential election of 1864. Fernando Wood wanted New York City to secede from the Union in 1861 and become a "free city" in order to continue its lucrative financial dealings with the South. It was estimated that the Southern states poured $200 million a year into the city's economy. Although, the attack on Ft. Sumter forced many influential businessmen to reappraise their sympathy for the South, New York City remained a hotbed of anti-war sentiment. As mentioned on pages 192–93, the worst race riot in U.S. history occurred in New York from July 13–16, 1863.

In addition to organized political criticism of the war, Lincoln also had to contend with pro-Confederate collaborators operating in secret societies such as the "Knights of the Golden Circle", and the "Order of American Knights". These groups engaged in a wide variety of anti-war actions, from resisting the draft and espionage, to robbery and sabotage. They even plotted to burn down New York City (which was actually attempted on Nov. 25, 1864) and gave Lincoln some justification for the suspension of *habeas corpus*. Considering the depth and breadth of opposition to the war, it seems hardly surprising that Lincoln felt his chances for reelection were slim in the summer of 1864.

Politics – The South

The Confederate President Jefferson Davis also had his own set of problems to contend with during the war. Davis, unlike Lincoln, was not particularly personable. He was rigid and irritable, and not very skillful in the most essential tool in politics, compromise. As Texas Governor Sam Houston said of him, "He is as ambitious as Lucifer, cold as a snake, and what he touches will not prosper." In the Confederacy, there were no political parties, and criticism of the war effort and strategy was focused squarely on Davis. His Vice President Alexander Stephens referred to him as "my poor old blind and deaf dog," and Confederate congressmen and political leaders such as Henry Foote, Robert Toombs, and especially Louis T. Wigfall excoriated Davis continuously, characterizing him as "false, hypocritical, pernicious, perverse, pigheaded, and ruinous" to name but a few examples. As they were never part of an opposition party, opponents to Davis failed in many instances to put forward constructive alternatives for waging the war, and they also attacked Davis' wartime measures such as the draft, taxes, and his suspension of *habeas corpus* in February 1864 (Davis obtained approval from the Confederate Congress for its suspension. Lincoln bypassed the U.S. Congress.) as unconstitutional and a violation of the states rights principles under which the Confederacy had been founded. In addition to his congressional and administration critics, Davis faced staunch opposition from the governors of Georgia and North Carolina, Joseph Brown and Zebulon Vance, respectively. These men deferred thousands of their states residents from the draft, withheld supplies from Confederate armies <u>outside</u> their states, and consistently asserted that states rights were more important than the Confederacy itself. Both

Brown and Vance entertained notions of a negotiated peace on the basis of Confederate independence, and actively suggested such a course in 1864.

The South also had Confederate counterparts to the anti-war groups operating in the North. The "Red Strings", the "Peace and Constitution Society", and the "Heroes of America" all plotted for peace at any price and reunion with such ardor that their actions could be viewed as treasonable. The "Heroes of America" were especially powerful in western North Carolina and eastern Tennessee where they actively aided deserters and sometimes fought Confederate draft agents. In addition, they backed the editor of the *North Carolina Standard* and extreme peace advocate William Holden in North Carolina's 1864 gubernatorial race against Zebulon Vance. Holden was overwhelmingly defeated, as Vance was able to cast him in a treasonable light.

The Battlefront – Late 1863 – Chickamauga and Chattanooga

After Gettysburg, the main actions of the war shifted to Tennessee and Georgia. The carnage endured by both Lee and Meade's forces seemed to give the commanders pause in resuming major offensive operations, and after Vicksburg Union strategy revolved around the subjugation of the Deep South, especially the city of Atlanta. To accomplish this, Union armies moved towards Chattanooga in extreme southeast Tennessee. Chattanooga was an important railroad terminus, being served by spurs of the E. Tennessee and Georgia Railroad, and the Western and Atlantic Railroad, the latter a direct link to Atlanta. Union General William S. Rosecrans (Ol' Rosy) and his Army of the Cumberland skillfully moved towards the city in mid-August, forcing Confederate General Bragg to evacuate the city and move south into northwest Georgia. Bragg then awaited Rosecrans pursuit, receiving reinforcements from Virginia. As Rosecrans crossed the mountains, his troops became separated and skirmishes broke out near Chickamauga Creek on Sept. 19th. Bragg launched an attack on Sept. 20th at Chickamauga, and aided by a stroke of luck (Union forces had left a gap in their lines that Confederate forces under General Longstreet were able to breakthrough) scored a ghastly victory as the battle was the second bloodiest of the war, behind only Gettysburg, with 18,454 Confederate and 16,170 Union casualties. However, Bragg and the Confederates who enjoyed a numerical majority in battle for one of the few times during the entire war (70,000 to 56,000), failed to heed the demands for an all-out assault by his subordinates Generals Longstreet and Forrest, and the battered Union forces limped back into Chattanooga. Their entire army may have been destroyed or forced to surrender had Bragg listened to their pleas. Forrest was so incensed at Bragg, he refused to serve under the general again and threatened him directly:

> You have played the part of a damned scoundrel, and are a
> coward, and if you were any part a man I would slap your
> jaws and force you to resent it…I say to you that if you ever
> again try to interfere with me or cross my path it will be at
> the peril of your life.

In addition, Union troops under the courageous command of General George H. Thomas (the "Rock of Chickamauga") fought heroically, holding off the advancing

Confederates and allowing the bulk of their army to safely escape. Nonetheless, Rosecrans and his army were now trapped in Chattanooga, and Bragg settled down for a siege. The Confederates cut off the rail lines and took the high ground surrounding Chattanooga, Missionary Ridge and Lookout Mountain. Although the Union army was reaching desperate straits in terms of food and supplies, the response of Lincoln and Generals Grant, Sherman, and Thomas proved decisive. With amazing speed, massive Union reinforcements arrived in November to attempt to lift the siege while Bragg looked on passively, believing his position "impregnable." On November 24th, the battle of <u>Chattanooga</u> commenced with the Union forces initially facing stiff opposition. However, on the next day, General Thomas' troops screaming "Chickamauga!" broke through the center of the Confederate line on Missionary Ridge, and without orders, proceeded to drive the now panicky Confederates right off the ridge! The Confederates retreated all the way into Georgia. Chattanooga was now firmly in Union hands and the Confederacy had suffered yet another disastrous defeat. The North lost 5,475 casualties, the South, 2,521. Bragg was relieved of active command and transferred to Richmond and then to Wilmington, N.C. to oversee the city's defenses in 1864–65. He was replaced as commander of the Army of the Tennessee by General Joseph Johnston. Of his failure at Chattanooga, he typically laid blame on his subordinates and his soldiers themselves, something he had been wont to do after previous battles. "A panic I had never before witnessed seemed to have seized upon officers and men, and each seemed struggling for his personal safety..." It is an unanswered question if he included himself in that assessment.

1864 - Bloodbath

The new year dawned with the Confederacy in a most precarious position. The summer and fall of 1863 had been disastrous on the battlefield, losses had been staggering and the Confederate home front was racked by shortages, inflation, and increasing disillusionment. By contrast, the Union cause had been bolstered by successes, and Lincoln finally had the overall commander Ulysses S. Grant he believed could win the war quickly. In general, Lincoln, Grant, and Sherman all believed the best way to secure victory was by annihilating the two main Confederate armies, Lee's Army of Northern Virginia and Johnston's Army of Tennessee. To accomplish this, the Union armies would have to be almost constantly on the offensive, continually wearing down the Confederates, but such tactics can be quite costly. As such, this plan ran the risk of alienating the Northern populace. As described on pages 194 and 222–24, there existed simmering discontent in the North with the war for a variety of reasons which could erupt at any time. If victory were not forthcoming and the human and financial toll of the war continued its dreadful rise, the Northern public might express their discontent, frustration, and fatigue with the war in the presidential election of 1864, and vote for the candidate and the party most likely to negotiate peace. By the spring of 1864, there were ominous signs that this was precisely what was developing.

The Wilderness, Spotsylvania Court House, Cold Harbor, and Kennesaw Mountain

When the spring campaign of 1864 began, the Army of the Potomac was firmly in

Grant's hands, and he swiftly initiated his plans against Lee. His army crossed the Rapidan River located north of Richmond and proceeded south into a jungle-like morass of woods, thickets, briars, and bushes known as The Wilderness. He had hoped to draw Lee's 64,000 troops out into the open where his 115,000 men would overwhelm them, but Lee had other plans. Lee realized that the conditions in The Wilderness would minimize Grant's mobility, as well as his ability to utilize his numerical superiority. The dense forest would also render artillery useless, and when Grant moved his men into it on May 5th, Lee's forces were waiting. The battle was savage, with visibility minimized by both the woods and overgrowth and the smoke emanating from the firing guns. In some areas of the battle, the bushes and scrub actually caught fire, suffocating and burning to death wounded soldiers who could not escape the smoke and flames. The battle resumed the following day with Grant's forces temporarily gaining the upper hand, but the Confederates rallied and won the day, or did they? They had inflicted 17,666 casualties on their Union foes while suffering 7,750 themselves, and had the Army of the Potomac been commanded by McClellan, Pope, Burnside, or Hooker, it almost certainly would have retreated towards Washington. Grant, however was determined to keep up the pressure on Lee regardless of the cost. In other words, he was waging a gruesome war of attrition against the Confederates. Rather than withdrawing, Grant moved his army southeast towards Fredericksburg forcing Lee to pursue. Grant took up a position near the Spotsylvania Court House on May 8th and launched a ferocious attack against the well entrenched Confederates. In a battle that raged for nearly 12 days, Grant lost 18,000 casualties, Lee 12,000, in arguably the most brutal combat of the entire war. At one particular gruesome portion of the battlefield, known as the "Bloody Angle", the opposing armies fought hand-to-hand for over 18 hours! On May 20th, Grant once again moved south before settling in at a little town named Cold Harbor on June 1st. Both sides dug in, but Grant determined to break through the Confederate lines at all costs. The incessant fighting over the past month was more than some soldiers and officers could take, leading to both physical and mental breakdowns, and the idea of a frontal assault against a well fortified enemy moved some Union soldiers towards the grim recognition that they were about to die. For example, just before the main assault on June 3rd, several Union soldiers had their comrades pin sheets of paper on their backs listing their names so they could be identified after they were killed. It proved tragically prescient, as 7000 Union soldiers were killed or wounded in 10 minutes; the Confederates by contrast lost 1500. Grant withdrew his decimated forces on June 12th and began to move towards Petersburg on the south bank of the James River. Petersburg was a vital rail and supply link to Richmond, and Grant had an early opportunity to take the lightly defended city. However, his subordinates (specifically General William F. "Baldy" Smith) hesitated and Lee was able to bring his army to bear at the nick of time. Thus a lengthy siege commenced on June 20th with Grant commanding forces that eventually reached 125,000 men. Lee by contrast fielded no more than 60,000.

In one month, Grant's losses totaled about 55,000 men, Lee's nearly 30,000, but Grant had failed to achieve his objective of totally destroying Lee's army*, and the

*Between May 5th and June 3rd 1864, Lee lost 46% of his fighting effectives, while Grant lost 41%!

Confederate capital in Richmond was still safe. There were other setbacks as well; the Confederate cavalry still controlled the Shenandoah Valley, the "breadbasket of the Confederacy", despite the efforts of Union General Franz Siegel. The Union likewise had not secured the port of Mobile, Alabama on the Gulf of Mexico, another strategic goal. Finally, the city of Atlanta still eluded the grasp of General Sherman, as he and his Confederate opponent maneuvered and entrenched outside the city. Indeed, when Sherman attempted to break through Johnston's lines at <u>Kennesaw Mountain</u> on June 27th, the results were morbidly similar to Cold Harbor. Sherman lost 3000 men, Johnston, 540. The losses on the battlefield in the summer of 1864 were appalling, and had a devastating effect on Northern morale, but they were only the most visible of the horrors of this war. Behind the scenes, another tragedy was unfolding in prisoner-of-war (POW) camps in both the Union and the Confederacy.

The POWs

During the first two years of the war, the practice of prisoner exchange was more or less standard operating procedure, but that arrangement disintegrated rapidly beginning in 1863 for two reasons. One, the utilization of black troops after the issuance of the *Emancipation Proclamation* infuriated Southerners. As a result the Confederate government threatened the summary execution or re-enslavement of any black soldier captured in battle. In response, the U.S. government threatened that captured Confederates would be shot. This forced a reappraisal of policy by the Confederate government, which began to make distinctions between captured free blacks and captured ex-slaves. The former were treated harshly, though not as a general rule executed. It is difficult to know precisely the disposition towards the captured ex-slaves, although undoubtedly some were put to work as forced laborers on Confederate fortifications, itself a violation of the accepted Articles of War for the treatment of POWs. Unfortunately, there were slaughters of black soldiers by Confederates even if they were attempting to surrender, the most notorious examples at Fort Pillow, TN, Plymouth, NC, and at the Battle of the Crater (at Petersburg) all occurring in the spring and summer of 1864.

The second reason for the cessation (until the very end of the war) of prisoner exchanges was more calculating and brutal. As Grant began his war of attrition, he stated with cold logic, "Every man we hold, when released on parole or otherwise, becomes an active soldier against us...." In other words, Grant does not want the Confederate armies to be replenished with former POWs. As the war grinds out greater and greater casualties, he realized that he can make up his losses in manpower while the Confederacy cannot, thus prisoner-of-war camps on both sides begin to swell in numbers from 1863 onwards. Over 400,000 Yankees and Rebels found themselves in camps, some of which were so horrendous and pitiless as to strain the imagination. In the South, the worst were Libby and Belle Island in Virginia, Salisbury, NC, Florence Stockade, SC/ and the most infamous of all American POW camps, Andersonville, GA. Andersonville had originally been intended to hold a maximum of 10,000 prisoners, but after prisoner exchange broke down, its population swelled to 33,000. The conditions were deplorable, no shelter, common latrine ditches, and starvation rations. Men succumbed by the hundreds weekly to exposure, disease, dehydration, hunger, and brutal treatment. Some of the survivors of Andersonville upon liberation appeared to be living skeletons, and the photographs of these victims mirror the images of the survivors of the Nazi death camps of World War II. Of a total of 45,000 men imprisoned at Andersonville, 13,000 (about 28%) perished. After the war, Northern outrage over the camp resulted in the trial and conviction of the camp commander Colonel Henry Wirz under the charge of war crimes. He was executed on Nov. 10, 1865, but was he truly the monster responsible for the deaths of so many men? The answer is, partially. The disruption and destruction of food supplies within the Confederacy by 1864 led to the civilian food riots mentioned on page 202, and every available scrap of food was allocated for the troops. Under such desperate circumstances, the captured POWs unfortunately were a low priority. Wirz was without question incompetent, but the lack of food was a problem primarily out of his control. In addition, Grant knew about the suffering in Andersonville and could have re-initiated exchanges, but this ran counter to his overall strategy for victory.

What about the North? The Union also operated hellish POW camps, most notoriously at Fort Delaware, Del., Elmira, NY, where 3000 prisoners (24%) died out of 12,000 incarcerated, and worst of all, Camp Douglas, outside of Chicago, Illinois. Under the command of a succession of officers culminating with the sadistic Colonels Charles De Land and Benjamin Sweet, Camp Douglas became known as "Eighty Acres of Hell" and the "Andersonville of the North." There were no food shortages in the North during the war, and yet the prisoners there were given starvation rations and were even denied fruits and vegetables. In countless cases, the inmates resorted to eating rats, the so-called "Rat Pies." Additionally, shelter, sanitation, and medical treatment were nearly non-existent resulting in thousands of deaths. The camp overseers also devised a cruel punishment device known as "Morgan's Mule", named after the notorious Confederate raider John Morgan. The "Mule" was a wooden sawhorse of two by four's with a sharp rail. Prisoners would be forced to straddle it for long periods of time with their feet dangling in the air, with weights attached to their ankles to make the pain even more excruciating and crippling. Of a total of perhaps 18,000 POWs sent there*, at least 6,000 died.

During the war, an estimated 30,218 Yankees and 26,976 Confederates perished in the prisoner of war camps, a total nearly equaling the total American fatalities lost in Vietnam. Sherman once commented of war, "War is cruelty. There is no use trying to reform it. The crueler it is, the sooner it will be over." Unfortunately, this too easily applies to treatment of the POWs' during this conflict.

The End Game – Summer 1864 – Spring 1865

As mentioned previously, by the summer of 1864 the dreadful casualties suffered by the various Union armies and the failure to breakthrough at Petersburg and Atlanta were causing many in the North to question continuing the war. From every quarter Lincoln was being assailed. The "Radical Republicans" wanted to replace him as their nominee for in the upcoming election, and moderates seriously

---

* It is impossible to know exactly how many prisoners were sent to Camp Douglas during the war as many of the records were destroyed after the conflict ended.

suggested that he rescind the *Emancipation Proclamation* due to its unpopularity in many areas of the North. War Democrats criticized that Grant's strategy had failed and was suicidal, while Peace Democrats and the "Copperheads" urged a negotiated peace. Lincoln believed his re-election "exceedingly unlikely", and an event at Petersburg on July 30th only provided his critics with more ammunition. Pennsylvania miners and their regimental commander convinced General Burnside that they could dig a shaft underneath the Confederate lines, pack it with explosives, detonate them, and charge through the broken Confederate lines and seize Petersburg. The plan commenced on July 25th and it was ready to be implemented 5 days later. The fuse was lit, and at 4:45 A.M. on the 30th, 8000 pounds of gunpowder exploded ripping a massive hole (170 feet long, 70 feet wide, and 30 feet deep) in the Confederate entrenchments. 278 Confederates were killed instantly and there appeared a real chance for a Union breakthrough. Instead, Union forces charged down into the hole as opposed to both sides of it, the original plan, and found themselves confused and unable to scale the steep sides of "the Crater", as the battle would be known hereafter. The Confederates under Major General William Mahone regrouped and successfully counterattacked, shooting Union soldiers as they attempted to crawl out of the Crater. Black units of the U.S. 9th Corps commanded by General Edward Ferraro were especially targeted by the Confederates and suffered grievous losses. Shortly after 1:00 P.M., the battle was over with Union casualties exceeding 4,000, Confederate, 1,500. Burnside was relieved of command, and Grant lamented that "It was the saddest affair I have witnessed in the war." For Lincoln, it was yet another black eye, and the Democrats ramped up the pressure by nominating General George McClellan for president in August. McClellan was a popular choice as he symbolized both discontent with Lincoln, and possessed the great affection of many soldiers he trained and commanded earlier in the war. The Democratic Platform, written by Clement Vallandigham, was decidedly for peace:

> *Resolved*, That this convention does explicitly declare, as the sense of the American people, that after four years of failure to restore the Union by the experiment of war, during which, under the pretense of a military necessity of war-power higher than the Constitution, the Constitution itself has been disregarded in every part, and public liberty and private right alike trodden down, and the material prosperity of the country essentially impaired, justice, humanity, liberty, and the public welfare demand that immediate efforts for cessation of hostilities, with a view of an ultimate convention of the States, or other peaceable means, to the end that, at the earliest practicable moment, peace may be restored on the basis of the Federal Union of the States.

McClellan himself favored reunion through victory, but he at least gave tacit approval to the idea of a negotiated armistice. As the campaign heated up, the Republicans labeled the Democrats as defeatists, Confederate collaborators, and even traitors. For their part, Lincoln and the Republicans were savaged as heartless war-mongers and advocates for racial-mixing (miscegenation). Consider the following Democratic campaign song:

> Little Mac, little Mac, you're the very man,
> Go down to Washington as soon as you can…
> Democrats, Democrats, do it up brown,
> Lincoln and his Niggerheads won't go down.

In August 1864, the only thing which might stave off defeat for Lincoln would be dramatic military success, and as fate would have it, such victories were looming in the near future. Actually the Union had scored a victory on August 5th when Admiral David Farragut broke through the defenses at Mobile Bay proclaiming, "Damn the torpedoes! Full speed ahead, Drayton!", and sealed off the port from Confederate blockade runners. Heroic and significant though it was, Farragut's victory was still not enough to swing the election to Lincoln. That would occur on Sept. 2nd at Atlanta.

The Fall of Atlanta

Sherman's campaign outside of Atlanta had by midsummer produced no more results than Grant's efforts to subdue Petersburg. The main difference lay in the relative lack of casualties suffered by both Sherman's and Johnston's armies. With the exception of the battle of Kennesaw Mountain (see p. 228) both commanders had sought to outmaneuver their opponent and conserve their strength until the proper moment for attack came. The end result was that by July, Sherman was closer to Atlanta but still outside its defenses and Johnston's waiting army. Also, the railroads serving and supplying the city from the south and east were still controlled by the Confederates. However, on July 17th, Jefferson Davis made a fateful decision that quite possibly lost the war for the Confederacy. Believing both that Johnston might surrender Atlanta without a fight, and that Lincoln's re-election bid would be crushed by a successful Confederate attack on Sherman, he replaced Johnston with General John Bell Hood. Hood had suffered grievous wounds during the war, losing the effective use of a leg and an arm, but the Texan held a profound penchant for aggressive action. The problem with Hood was his judgment; to attack Sherman's superior forces ran the real risk of wrecking the fine Army of Tennessee. Yet, this was what Davis desired and this is what "Ol' Woodenhead" (Hood's nickname) would deliver. To contemporary historians of the war, both amateur and professional, Davis' actions seem incomprehensible, if not inexplicable. If Atlanta had held out, Lincoln most likely would have lost the election and the mandate for continuing the war. If Johnston had remained in command and preserved his army for just a few more months, this may well have happened. By choosing military action over political strategy, Davis probably sabotaged his primary goal of an independent Confederacy.

Hood wasted no time in launching an attack against Sherman, the first occurring on July 20th at Peachtree Creek north of Atlanta. The fighting was fierce though not decisive, a harbinger of things to come. Hood attacked again on the outskirts of Atlanta on July 22nd, but again to no decisive effect save the casualties incurred.

Finally, on the 28th another terrific battle took place at the Ezra Church west of Atlanta but again, the results were inconclusive, except in the fact that Hood had lost 15,000 casualties in just over a week, while Sherman suffered just 6,000. Hood was attacking, the Yankees were counterattacking, Atlanta was still a Confederate city, but the Confederate army was hemorrhaging men in the process. In August, Sherman decided to lay siege to the city which lasted almost a month. Then on August 28th, he dispatched units to the south of Atlanta to seize the Macon and Western Railroad, prompting a furious pursuit by Hood. On August 31st the Confederates were defeated at Jonesboro, and Atlanta lay open to U.S. forces. Hood withdrew the army and Sherman marched into the city on Sept. 2nd. The impact of the loss of Atlanta for the Confederacy cannot be overstated. The major urban hub of the Deep South was now in enemy hands, and Lincoln finally had something to show for the efforts expended after such a long and bloody summer. The capture of Atlanta practically guaranteed Lincoln's reelection, and with it the continued prosecution if the war. Another boost for Lincoln came with General Philip Sheridan's decisive defeat of Confederate General Jubal Early's cavalry at the Battle of Cedar Creek in the Shenandoah Valley of Virginia on Oct. 19th. Sheridan had been instructed to destroy the productive capabilities of the valley, the "breadbasket of the Confederacy", and like Sherman (see the following section), he performed his task thoroughly. In the election, Lincoln won 55% of the popular vote, and an overwhelming percentage in the Electoral College:

Election of 1864	Party	Electoral Vote	Popular Vote
Abraham Lincoln	Republican (Union)	212	2,213,665
George B. McClellan	Democratic	21	1,805,237

McClellan carried only three states, Delaware, Kentucky, and New Jersey. It was clear from the result that the Northern people intended to see the war through to a victorious outcome. (Nevada, which entered the Union just days before the election, also went for Lincoln.)

Before fleeing Atlanta, Hood's army destroyed everything of military value it could not transport, and then headed west to Tennessee hoping to sever Sherman's supply lines and forcing him into pursuit. This is not what happened. Sherman, after consulting with a less than sanguine Grant and Lincoln, proposed a total war on the Confederate heartland. He would dispatch a portion of his army to destroy Hood which occurred on Nov. 30th at the Battle of Franklin in Tennessee,* but utilize the bulk of it in a devastating "March to the Sea." Every barn, corncrib, railroad, warehouse, storehouse, everything of use to either Confederate citizen or soldier alike was to be confiscated or destroyed, and along a 60 mile swath from Atlanta (which Sherman put to the torch) to Savannah, Sherman's army accomplished the mission. When Georgia civilians pleaded for mercy, Sherman responded, "If the people of Georgia raise a howl against my barbarity and cruelty, I will answer that war is war, and not popularity seeking." The goals of Sherman's pillage and plunder included breaking the fighting spirit of the civilians of the Southern home-front to the point where they would entreat the Confederate soldiers to abandon the fight and return home. He also wished to discredit the Confederate

*This occurred, as in 5 hours the Confederates lost more men than U.S. forces did in 19 hours on D-Day in 1944!"

232

government as impotent and powerless to protect its own people, and in these efforts Sherman was at least partially successful. However, it must be noted that his actions also had the reverse effect, as some survivors of Sherman's "March To the Sea", redoubled their commitment to the Confederacy, a testament to their hatred of the Yankees who had rendered such destruction, and a seething bitterness at the prospect of a defeat driven reunion with them.

One example of Sherman's strategy of total war was the "Sherman necktie." Railroads were torn up and the wooden ties were gathered into piles and set aflame. Then the steel rails were thrown upon the fire until they became red hot. Finally, soldiers with tongs would pick up the rails and twist them around the trunks of trees, not only destroying the railroad but killing the trees as well! Sherman's men were aided in their spree of destruction by deserters and criminals, collectively referred to as "bummers", who eagerly joined in the robbery, destruction, and rape. By the time Sherman reached Savannah, after destroying by his own estimate $100 million worth of property and livestock*, the Confederate army stationed there withdrew in the hopes that he might spare the lovely coastal city. He did, and presented it to Lincoln as a Christmas gift. Then he and his army cast a vengeful eye on South Carolina, the first state to secede. His men and the "bummers" put 18 cities and towns, including the capital Columbia, to the torch and their rampage of wanton destruction did not abate until they reached North Carolina. North Carolina, the last state to join the Confederacy, seemed to inspire mercy in the Union army. (Ironically, only Virginia supplied more soldiers to the Confederacy.)

However, Wilmington in the southeastern corner of the state was the last supply line open for the Confederacy to the outside world and the Union was determined to seize it. Located on the Cape Fear River, Wilmington possessed both an excellent port, and railroad connections to Weldon in the northern portion of North Carolina. As the war dragged on, the "Port City" became increasingly invaluable strategically, and served as a prime location for blockade runners, ship captains, and large contingents of soldiers. It also attracted Confederate political leaders, as well as spies, counterspies, entrepreneurs, grifters, gamblers, and prostitutes, becoming comparable in attitude and action to San Francisco during the wide-open days of the Gold Rush.

On December 24–25, 1864, 55 Union ships with 8,000 troops attempted to blast their way past the sand and earthen Fort Fisher at the mouth of the Cape Fear River. Fort Fisher with its 47 big guns and 1900 Carolinian defenders was a daunting challenge and this first Union attempt to subdue it ended in failure, largely due to a critical loss of nerve by the Union commander, General Benjamin Butler, one of the most notorious Northern "political generals." A second attempt occurred on January 13th 1865, with Union forces totaling 10,000 men and 58 ships. Under the able command of Admiral Alfred Terry, the fort was subjected to the heaviest

---

*While no definitive total of the property seized or destroyed has ever been compiled , one of Sherman's commanders Major General O.O. Howard kept detailed accounts of his army's actions. Here is a tally of selected confiscated items:

Food Captured (in lbs.)	Ordinance Seized
Corn - 4,867,326	Small Arms Ammo - 1,230,000 (rounds)
Salt Meats - 797,500	Powder - 70,350 (lbs.)
Fresh Beef - 670,000	Rifles and Muskets - 13,929
Breadstuffs - 927,000	Artillery Pieces - 67

artillery bombardment in the history of warfare up to that point. (In the two battles for Ft. Fisher, 40,000 shells were fired by Union ships.) The actual attack took place two days later, and after several hours of fierce fighting, the Union forces prevailed, with nearly 4000 total casualties in both battles (1,341-Union, 2,583-Confederate). The fort commanders General W. H. C. Whiting and Colonel William Lamb had pleaded with district commander General Braxton Bragg to rush up reinforcements from Wilmington but Bragg refused, believing they would be better utilized in defending the actual city. As a result Whiting lamented to Lamb, "Lamb my boy, I have come to share your fate. You and your garrison are to be sacrificed." Indeed they were (Lamb was mortally wounded and Whiting suffered a serious leg injury), and Wilmington itself would be captured on February 22nd.

The next major action in North Carolina took place at <u>Bentonville</u> about 90 miles north of Wilmington. General Joseph Johnston had once again been returned to command a Confederate army of about 20,000 men. Facing him was Sherman and 60,000 Union veterans. On March 19th, Sherman's forces were surprised by the Confederates, but eventually regained the initiative in the battle. The battle, the largest ever fought in North Carolina, ended with Union victory, but at a cost of over 4000 casualties (1,517 - Union, 2,606 - Confederate). Johnston withdrew to the center of the state while Sherman seized the rail hub at Goldsboro. The end of the Confederacy was now in sight.

Appomattox

The severing of Confederate supply lines from both the Shenandoah Valley and Wilmington was taking a severe toll on Lee's army. As supplies dwindled, so did morale, and more and more Confederate soldiers deserted. By late March, Lee had concluded that the best chance for saving his army was to abandon Petersburg and march west to Danville, VA. From there, he would transport his troops via railroad south into North Carolina where they could link up with Johnston and continue the fight. This was a desperate measure and would involve the sacrifice of the capital at Richmond, but Lee had little choice. President Davis concurred and prepared to move the Confederate capital also to Danville, its final destination. To break out of Petersburg, Lee launched a series of attacks beginning on March 24th which ultimately proved disastrous. By April 1st, Lee had lost nearly 11,000 men. He subsequently abandoned Petersburg and headed west. Richmond fell to Union forces on April 3rd, but not before a large portion of it had been engulfed in flames set by fleeing Confederates. On April 5th, Lee's exhausted army, now numbering only about 35,000 stopped at the Amelia Courthouse crossroads expecting to find a wagon train of food. Instead, it was loaded with ammunition, the one thing they did not need. Additionally, their goal of reaching the Danville railroad had been rendered untenable as the railroad had been severed by Union cavalry units commanded by General Philip Sheridan. The Army of Northern Virginia was in real danger of being surrounded and annihilated by Grant's forces. At Sayler's Creek on April 6th, Union forces inflicted a devastating defeat on a large portion of Lee's forces, with Confederate casualties and captured totaling nearly 7000. On April 7th, Grant asked for Lee to surrender, but the Confederate general still believed he could break free and make it to the Blue Ridge. On April 9th, the rebels charged at

Appomattox Court House in a final futile attempt against the Union forces now outnumbering them at least 5 to 1. After the battle, Lee came to the painful realization that all was lost and offered to surrender to Grant. The two men and their staffs met in Wilmer McLean's home. Grant was compassionate and generous in his terms. The Confederates were to be paroled, given three days rations and sent home without Union harassment. Officers could keep their side arms and men who owned horses were allowed to retain them. Grant's and Lee's actions were profound for the future. Other Union officer's were compelled to follow Grant's example when setting terms for the various surrendering Confederate armies, and there would be no mass post-war treason trials for Confederate soldiers. Lee, the most potent symbol of the Southern cause, had sent the unmistakable message that the war was lost. Any more bloodshed at this point was useless. In addition, Lee had resisted this ominous call to arms by Jefferson Davis on April 4th:

> We have now entered upon a new phase of a struggle the memory of which is to endure for all ages....Relieved from the necessity of guarding cities and particular points, important but not vital to our defense, with an army free to move from point to point and strike in detail detachments and garrisons of the enemy, operating on the interior of our own country, where supplies are more accessible, and where the foe will be far removed from his own base and cut off from all succor in case of reverse, nothing is now needed to render our triumph certain but the exhibition of our own unquenchable resolve. Let us but will it, and we are free.

What exactly would this mean? A guerilla war replete with ceaseless violence, destruction, and terror that could go on for decades, destroying any sense of an American union. If Davis' plan had been adopted, the modern bloody history of the Middle East probably would have been be realized in the _former_ United States with devastating results.

On April 12th, the Army of Northern Virginia mustered for the last time in the face of a saluting and respectful enemy, and began the long journey home. The scene would be repeated on April 26th when Johnston surrendered to Sherman near Durham, NC under terms very similar to those Grant offered Lee, and Johnston like Lee refused Jefferson Davis' orders to initiate guerilla warfare. For all intents and purposes, this bloodiest conflict in American history had finally concluded, but one last tragedy awaited the newly reunited country.

The Death Of Lincoln

John Wilkes Booth, a prominent actor and pro-Confederate had been scheming with a motley group of collaborators for months to do something to derail the Northern war effort. One of their ideas focused on kidnapping Lincoln, but after Appomattox, their plans turned to murder. On April 11th, Lincoln delivered the last public speech of his life from the White House, with John Wilkes Booth in attendance. In a very brief segment of his address, Lincoln intimated support for limited black suffrage:

> It is also unsatisfactory to some that the elective franchise is not given to the colored man. I would myself prefer that it were now conferred on the very intelligent, and to those who would serve our cause as soldiers.

With that statement, Booth flew into a homicidal rage, proclaiming to a confidant, "That means nigger citizenship. Now, by God I'll put him through!" They would kill Lincoln, Vice President Johnson, and Sec. of State Seward in order to disrupt the United States government, which they believed would somehow breathe new life into the withering Confederacy. Booth was the most determined of the would-be assassins and set out on April 14th to shoot the president. On that night Lincoln and his wife Mary were attending a comedic play "Our American Cousin" at Ford's Theater in Washington. Outside of Lincoln's booth, only <u>one</u> guard stood watch and he left his post to either get a drink or to get a better view of the play himself. The end result was that Booth was able walk into Lincoln's compartment unmolested. He did so and shot the president in the back of the head with a small pistol. He then leapt from the booth onto the stage breaking his leg in the process and then shouting to the audience "Sic Semper Tyrannis ("Thus ever to tyrants", on Virginia's state seal and flag), Virginia is avenged!" The crowd was confused and astonished and this allowed Booth to safely flee the theater. Lincoln was mortally wounded and would expire the next day, but as has happened before and since in our history, the death of a president did not destroy the government, and it continued. Booth, after having his leg set by Dr. Samuel Mudd, temporarily escaped into Virginia. He was subsequently surrounded in a barn by U.S. troops who forced him out by setting the structure aflame. Booth was shot through a large crack in the barn door by Sergeant Boston Corbett and mortally wounded, the bullet shattering his spine in his neck. As he lay dying, he asked a soldier to lift his limp hands above his face. When the soldier did so, he muttered "useless, useless" and died. What had he done? For one, he had taken away a president who had promised a compassionate reconstruction for the defeated South, "with malice toward none; with charity for all…," were Lincoln's own words given during his Second Inaugural Address just 5 weeks before. For example, Lincoln had even considered partial monetary compensation for former slave owners, and his <u>10% Plan</u> would allow for a swift reintegration of the former Confederate States back into the United States. All of that changed with the bitter partisan rancor to come.

   The "Radical Republicans" who desired harsh punishment for the former Confederate States clashed with the tactless new president Andrew Johnson, who possessed neither Lincoln's pragmatism nor his prestige with the American people, the latter the result of winning the war. The Reconstruction Era dragged on until 1877 and left lingering scars between the North and South which may have been avoided had Lincoln not been murdered. We shall never know for certain, but we do know the costs of this fateful conflict. 1 million men were missing or wounded and as many as 675,000 to 750,000 men were killed, 2% of the entire American population. The South's infrastructure was destroyed and would take decades to rebuild and recover. However, the heinous institution of slavery in America was also demolished, without question the most positive outcome of this brutal war. In a larger sense however, the old United States too was destroyed. The collection of semi-autonomous states held loosely together by a remote federal government in 1787 had been replaced by a tightly knit nation with a strong central government which continued to grow in size and power from 1865 to the present, to a degree which would have been incomprehensible to the 55 "Founding Fathers." This third United States would ultimately and dramatically expand in size, wealth, and power, ascending in the 20th and 21st centuries to a position of world dominance not realized since Ancient Rome.

Chapter 16 – The Reconstruction of the Union – The Third United States

The End of the War and the Emergence of the "Third United States"

Epilogue and Prologue

On April 9, 1865 at the Appomattox Court House in central Virginia, Confederate General Robert E. Lee surrendered to Union General Ulysses S. Grant effectively ending the most costly conflict in American history, The War Between the States (a.k.a. The Civil War). However, the North's victory over the South signified much more than just the triumph of the United States over the Confederate States; it brought forth an entirely new nation which can accurately be referred to as the Third United States of America. Indeed, the Third United States bears scant resemblance to its predecessors, the First United States which existed between 1781–87 under the Articles of Confederation, and the Second United States of 1787–61 under the Constitution of the United States and twelve subsequent Amendments. The American Revolution established the United States as an independent nation from Great Britain, but the new nation revealed itself as very conservative in nature. Under the Articles of Confederation, the individual states retained virtually all of the important powers and functions of government, in many aspects appearing as small independent nations loosely tied together under a distant national government, a situation not dissimilar to the relationship between the Thirteen Colonies and Great Britain up to 1763. After the Constitution became the fundamental law of the American nation in 1788, the federal government gained substantially in power, bolstered by significant Supreme Court decisions in the first quarter of the 19th Century. However, the federal government remained remote. Individual town, county, city, and state governments' had the greatest impact on the everyday lives of most Americans. (It is surprising to contemporary Americans that their ancestors prior to The War Between the States (a.k.a. The Civil War) referred to the United States as a plural nation, not a singular one. For example, today Americans often say, "the United States is a great nation". Until 1865, Americans said, "the United States are a great country".) Indeed, the Bill of Rights acted as a restraining force over the federal government in relationship to American citizens, and the 9th and 10th Amendments specifically reserved powers to citizens and the states. Additionally, if a state or states felt aggrieved within the United States, there was no provision in the Constitution that specifically proscribed secession. Indeed the right of revolution was inherent to Americans, a legacy of the Revolution. All of that changed after the guns ceased firing in 1865. First, the verdict of the war obliterated secession and dramatically weakened states' rights. Second, the war transformed the Union government. As a result, we live in a United States with an extraordinarily powerful federal government which affects the daily lives of all Americans. Finally, the centralization of power necessitated by the war propelled the United States to the zenith of world power in the 20th and 21st centuries. However, these fundamental changes which define the Third United States have come with both positive and negative manifestations, for the past and the present.

The Cost of the War

The physical and psychological toll of the war was horrendous. Death totals amounted to between 620,000 and 700,000 (World War II resulted in 405,399 deaths), while at least 1 million men were wounded or missing. These totals do not just include white Americans. 40,000 black Union soldiers and sailors perished during the war, as did an unknown number of American Indians of several different tribes. A particularly grotesque statistic involves Union and Confederate POWs (prisoners of war). 56,194 Americans died in <u>American</u> POW. camps during the war. By contrast, the decade long Vietnam War cost the lives of approximately 58,000 American soldiers. All told, about 2% of the American population did not survive the conflict. In the North, at least 360,000 soldiers died with additional hundreds of thousands wounded or missing. But the economic, social, and political infrastructure remained intact. In other words, the North was largely spared the physical destruction of the war, similar to the United States as a whole during World War II. In the South, the scenario was quite different. At least 260,000 Southerners were killed during the war. This amounts to <u>25%</u> of the Southern white male population between the ages of 20 and 40. As a result, the demographics of the South as a region were fundamentally altered. Even today, women outnumber men by a considerable margin in the former Confederacy, a lingering aspect of the war. Physically, the South was ruined and destroyed. Even before the war ended, the Confederate economy had collapsed. Inflation rates in 1865 (increase in consumer prices) stood at <u>9000%</u>! (By contrast, inflation rates in the United States in 2005 stood at <u>3.19%</u>!) For example, in 1864 turkeys sold for $100 in Richmond, VA and a pound of bacon cost $10. Before the War, Southern per capita income (the average amount of money made by individuals) was about 2/3 of the North's; in 1870, it was 40%. By 1865, Southern agricultural and industrial wealth declined by just under 50%, and half of the farm machinery and nearly 40% of all livestock in the South was lost due to the war. Nearly all of the region's railroads, trains, bridges, warehouses, port facilities, and canals, were damaged or destroyed. It took two decades for cotton and tobacco to reach pre war production levels, three for sugar. In regards to slavery, the economic losses associated with emancipation were staggering. Between <u>3 and 4 billion dollars</u> (in 1860 money) disappeared with the elimination of slavery. In short, the South was devastated and became a virtual economic colony of the North for decades to come. On top of that, the humiliation of having lost a war and a way of life weighed heavily on the collective psyche of Southerners, an aspect of the Southern persona that persists to the present day.

Two Paths Towards Reconstruction

On Dec. 8, 1863, President Lincoln proposed his plan for reconstructing the Union, known historically as the <u>10% Plan</u>. It is notable for both its conciliatory nature towards the Confederate States, and its pragmatism. Basically, all Confederate citizens (except Confederate officials, officers, and other prominent individuals who would have to apply personally for amnesty) would be pardoned, granted amnesty, and returned all property, except slaves, seized during the war upon formally pledging allegiance to the United States. Rebel states could begin the process of reentering the Union when a number of voters equal to 10% of those voting in the 1860 presidential election had taken this oath. Elections would then be held and the state would rejoin the Union. This actually occurred in Tennessee, Arkansas, and Louisiana in 1864, but Congress refused to recognize these "reconstructed" states, (The Constitution in Article I, Sec. 5, Clause 1 gives Congress this power.) because many Congressmen felt that the Congress should have exclusive jurisdiction over reconstruction, and that Lincoln's plan was too lenient. Why was Lincoln prepared to allow the seceded states to return so easily? Most likely because:

1. Considering both Confederate fatalities and the support of the Southern population for the Confederacy, it might prove difficult to muster up a high percentage of male citizens to take the oath.
2. The mere fact that the policy was so accommodating might convince a substantial number of war weary Southerners to give up the fight.
3. Lincoln never believed that secession had actually taken occurred; the Southern States were merely out of their "proper" place within the Union.

Had Lincoln lived, his personal popularity, embellished by having seen the war through to a successful conclusion, might have allowed him to force his reconstruction program through Congress. But John Wilkes Booth assassinated him at Ford's Theater in Washington on April 14, 1865, thus making certain that he would never see the Union restored along these lines.

The "Radical Republicans" and the Wade-Davis Bill

There were many important Northern leaders however who did not share Lincoln's compassion for the defeated South. These persons wanted to punish the South and its leaders and dramatically restructure the region. Chief among these vengeful groups stood the "Radical Republicans", including Benjamin Wade of Ohio, Charles Sumner of Massachusetts, and most notably, Thaddeus Stevens of Pennsylvania. Stevens referred to the Southern States as "conquered provinces", and seemed to relish a harsh reconstruction:

> I have never desired bloody punishments to any great
> extent, but there are punishments quite as appalling and
> longer remembered than death. They are more advisable,
> because they would reach a greater number. Strip a proud
> nobility of their bloated estates; reduce them to a level with
> plain Republicans; send them forth to labor and teach their
> children to enter the workshops or handle a plow, and you
> will thus humble the proud traitors.

Why did the Radical Republicans despise the South? For one, they considered the secession movement treason and those who supported it traitors. In the case of Stevens, there seemed to be a personal animus towards the South and Southerners, perhaps because Robert E. Lee's Army of Northern Virginia destroyed his family's Conestoga Iron Works during the Confederate invasion of Pennsylvania.

Additionally, they wished to obliterate the existing power structure in the South and supplant it with a Southern Republican Party.* Finally, there was a genuine desire to extend civil rights to former slaves. Some of the Radicals sought to empower the freedmen to bolster Republican Party membership in the South. After all, the party of Lincoln and emancipation would be the logical and emotional choice for newly empowered blacks. Less cynically, other Radicals, especially Charles Sumner, were deeply committed to improving the welfare of black Americans. Regardless of the motivations, tremendous changes in the status of the former slaves could not be accomplished without a fundamental alteration of Southern society.

A perfect encapsulation of the wrathful sentiments of the Radicals came in July 1864 in the <u>Wade-Davis Bill</u>. Although vetoed by Lincoln, the provisions of the bill provide a striking contrast with Lincoln's 10% Plan. Aspects of the bill included:

1. A majority of the voters (not 10%) must take the oath of allegiance before the readmission process could begin.
2. Political participation limited to Southerners who had remained loyal to the Union.
3. Denied citizenship and suffrage rights to all Confederate officials.
4. Abolished slavery. (Lincoln's Emancipation Proclamation had <u>technically</u> freed the slaves in most of the Confederate States.)
5. Repudiate (disallow) the Confederate debt. In other words, if you had Confederate money, had purchased Confederate bonds, or had loaned money to the Confederate government, it could never be redeemed and you would never be paid back!

Lincoln's veto of the bill eventually prompted the passage of the <u>13th Amendment</u> on Dec. 18, 1865 which abolished slavery and involuntary servitude "except as a punishment for crime...." (Mississippi was the only former Confederate state which did <u>not</u> ratify the 14th Amendment.)

Presidential Reconstruction Under Andrew Johnson

Lincoln's death propelled Vice President Andrew Johnson from Tennessee to the presidency. Johnson was the only Southern congressman who did not resign his seat when his state seceded. Johnson, a Democrat, felt secession was treason and the Southern leaders who precipitated it must be punished accordingly. For his Unionist fervor, he was rewarded with the Republican (referred to as the Unionist Party during the campaign) Vice Presidential nomination in the election of 1864. At first, he was enthusiastically supported by the Radical Republicans. Benjamin Wade said to Johnson approvingly, "Johnson, we have faith in you. By the gods, there will be

*In the pre-War years, Republicans bitterly resented Southern dominance of the federal government. Indeed, between 1789 and 1861 Southerners held the presidency for 49 years, numbered 23 of the 36 Speakers of the House, 24 of the 36 presidents pro tem of the Senate, and 20 of the 35 Supreme Court justices! (James J. McPherson)

no trouble now in running the government." Wade's faith was premature, as Johnson's motivations fundamentally differed from those of the Radicals, due in large part to his personal history. Johnson was born in North Carolina, but moved with his family to Greeneville, TN at a young age. His upbringing was working class, far removed from the aristocratic leaders of Tennessee society. Johnson was self-educated with the help of his wife, and in his early adult years ran a fairly successful tailoring business. He developed an interest in politics, emerging as an excellent "stump speaker" (informal orator) advocating the interests of the small, non-slave-owning farmer. Johnson despised the planter class, because he felt they and their slave based plantations impoverished ordinary white farmers. However, he was certainly not an abolitionist (he once prayed that every family in the United States had one slave to relieve the "drudgery" of life!), or an advocate of black Americans. His antipathy towards the slave system was based on class not race. In addition, although violently opposed to secession, he was a staunch advocate of "strict construction" (strict interpretation) of the Constitution. As such, after the war he gravitated towards a quick reconstruction, with a minimum of social, political, or economic restructuring or experimentation applied to the South. Finally, Johnson was a stubborn, combative individual who did not have Lincoln's talents for persuasion or compromise. By 1866, President Johnson and the Congress were heading for a dramatic showdown over reconstruction policy.

<u>Proclamations, Pardons, and the State of the South to 1867</u>

On May 29th 1865, President Johnson issued his "Proclamation of Amnesty and Pardon" which in most respects echoed Lincoln's 10% Plan. However, one interesting addition involved personal pardons. All Confederate officials, officers, and citizens whose <u>personal fortunes amounted to $20,000 and up</u> were required to apply for a personal presidential pardon. This was precisely the group whom Johnson had born such animus to prior to the war. (Perhaps he relished the chance to see them grovel!) In any event, prominent Confederates flocked to Washington, D.C. to seek clemency, and acted obsequiously towards Johnson. Showering compliments and pronouncements of "respect, regard, and confidence" in Johnson's abilities, these former leading citizens of the Confederacy were able to regain their citizenship with lightning speed. Everyday, <u>half</u> of Johnson's official duties centered around hearing requests for amnesty. He responded by issuing <u>13,500 personal pardons by the end of 1865</u>! The results of the pardons were four-fold:

1. The former Confederate states were quickly preparing to re-enter the Union.
2. The former Confederate leaders were once again resuming their positions of power.
3. The "Radical Republicans" felt betrayed by Johnson.
4. Moderate Northerners were becoming increasingly anxious with the direction of reconstruction, and subsequently began to side with the "Radicals" favoring harsher terms for the South. Other events occurring in the South strengthened these sentiments.

The Black Codes

After the war, the Southern state legislatures devised laws defining the status of the former slaves. Known collectively as the "Black Codes", they conferred upon the freed blacks certain rights and privileges, but also attempted to assign them to a permanent subservient status, a second-class labor source. On the positive side, slave marriages were now recognized as legal unions, blacks could own and purchase property (a right slaves did not enjoy in the pre-War period), could sue and be sued in court, and could testify in court in cases involving blacks in all the Southern states, and whites in 6 of them. However, the "Black Codes" prohibited inter-racial marriage, and prevented many blacks from owning firearms. In all cases, blacks were denied voting rights, the ability to serve on juries, or hold public office. Also, blacks were severely limited in their employment opportunities, usually consigned to agricultural work, and held to strict accountability in labor contracts. Worst of all, blacks (and some whites) were subject to strict vagrancy laws. Consider Florida's <u>partial</u> definition of a vagrant:

1. Rogues and vagabonds.
2. Idle or dissolute persons who go about begging.
3. Persons who use juggling, or unlawful games or plays.
4. Common pipers and fiddlers.
5. Lewd, wanton, and lascivious persons.
6. Persons who neglect their calling or employment, or who are without continuous employment or regular income and who have not sufficient means to sustain them and misspend what they earn without providing for themselves and the support of their families.
7. Persons wandering or strolling about from place to place without lawful purpose or object.
8. Persons neglecting all lawful business and habitually spending their earnings by frequenting houses of ill fame, gaming houses, or tippling shops.
9. Persons able to work but habitually living upon the earnings of their wives or minor children.
10. All able-bodied, male persons over the age of 18 years who are without means of support and remain in idleness.

A fairly all-encompassing list, and there were ten other categories! Fines for vagrancy ranged from $10 to $100, a considerable sum for the period. If a convicted vagrant could not pay, he could be put to work or leased to a farm or plantation owner, usually for a dollar a day, until the fine was paid! Repeated convictions for vagrancy could result in a prolonged involuntary work term, not too dissimilar from slavery.

The Special Elections

Due to the substantial number of presidential pardons, former Confederate leaders regained their citizenship, and became eligible for political office. Thus in the summer and fall of 1865, the former Confederate states more or less complied with the conditions of Johnson's Proclamation, drew up new state constitutions, held elections, and prepared for re-entry into the Union. Imagine the consternation and outrage of many Northern congressmen when 4 Confederate generals, 8 Confederate colonels, 6 Confederate cabinet members, and the former Vice President of the Confederacy, Alexander Stephens, presented themselves as new Southern congressmen! Not surprisingly, the Northern congressmen refused to seat these Southerners (permissible under Article I, Section 5, Clause 1 of the Constitution). Clearly, aspects of Johnson's reconstruction process were proving unacceptable to the "Radicals" and a growing number of moderate Republicans. Subsequent events in 1866 would intensify and finalize the split between Johnson and most Republicans.

Race Riots, the Ku Klux Klan, and the "Swing Around the Circle"

Deadly race riots occurred in the summer of 1866, most notably in Memphis and New Orleans, underscoring an increasingly violent white reaction to the newly emancipated blacks, and in Pulaski, TN General Nathan Bedford Forrest and other Confederate veterans established the Ku Klux Klan. Originally intended as an American Legion style organization for former Confederate officers, it quickly degenerated into a terrorist group targeting freed persons (former slaves), "Carpetbaggers" (Northerners who emigrated South to exploit the region's calamity), and "Scalawags" (native Southerners who cooperated with them). It must be added that many Northerners and Southerners who had these negative labels applied to them were simply interested in making new and better lives for themselves, not in fleecing the crippled South. The K.K.K. utilized intimidation, ostracism, violence, and murder against their enemies, and inspired imitators such as the Knights of the White Camellia, the South Carolina Red Shirts, the White Leagues, and the Rifle Clubs who spread mayhem throughout the South.

Finally, Johnson increasingly resisted the "Radicals" legislative initiatives. He successfully vetoed their attempt to extend the Freedmen's Bureau (a federal agency designed to aid the former slaves in their transition to freedom), but failed to stop the passage of a civil rights bill giving the former slaves citizenship. As a result, he aggressively campaigned against the Radicals in the 1866 congressional elections. In his "Swing Around the Circle" tour of the Old Northwest, especially in Ohio, Indiana, and Illinois, Johnson excoriated the "Radicals", referring to Stevens, Sumner, and Wendell Philips as traitors. He also engaged in tasteless verbal confrontations with his audiences. The results were disastrous for Johnson. In the subsequent elections, Northern voters, infuriated with the pardons, the "Black Codes" and the overall recalcitrance of the South, voted overwhelmingly for the Radicals and other candidates favoring harsher treatment for the South. The Radicals were now in complete control of Congress*, and soon they would drastically change the direction of reconstruction.

The 14th Amendment

On June 16, 1866 Congress passed the 14th Amendment and sent it to the states for ratification. If ratified, the amendment would vastly expand the power of the federal government. It would also fundamentally transform the relationship between the federal government, the states, and the citizens. How?

*Republicans held majorities of 143 to 49 in the House and 42 to 11 in the Senate!

The 14th Amendment consists of four major sections. Section 1 is the most important and far reaching:

1. Established a national definition of citizenship. ("All persons born or naturalized in the United States, and subject to the jurisdiction thereof, are citizens of the United States and of the state wherein they reside.") Previously, citizenship was primarily conveyed by each state (Article IV, Sec. 2). Also, the 5th Amendment guarantees of due process of law were extended to the states, and a new equal protection under the law requirement was included . In effect, this section of the amendment nationalized most of the provisions of the Bill of Rights. (Note: Prior to this, the Bill of Rights only applied to actions of the <u>federal</u> government. For example, (1st Amendment) "<u>Congress</u> shall make no law respecting an establishment of religion, or prohibiting the free exercise thereof;") On the surface, this appears a tremendous extension of the rights of citizens, but it also greatly expands the power of the federal government, especially the judiciary. In questions where the rights of individuals and local and state laws seem to conflict, the federal courts now could exercise jurisdiction, or the power to adjudicate cases. Over time, this has meant that virtually <u>every</u> issue (for example, school prayer and public religious displays, abortion, gay marriage, the Pledge of Allegiance, drug statutes, search and seizure laws) at <u>any</u> level of government is subject to a federal court decision. Keep in mind, if a case reaches the Supreme Court and a verdict is rendered, that verdict can <u>only</u> be overturned by a subsequent Supreme Court ruling or a Constitutional amendment, very rare occurrences. As such, local, state, and even federal laws cannot reverse an unpopular Supreme Court decision. Finally, consider that federal judges are unelected officials appointed for life; they can only be removed by impeachment and conviction. Between 1787 and 2009, a total of 16 federal officials have been impeached. 7 were convicted and removed, 1 resigned, and 8 were acquitted.
2. The amendment proportionally reduced a state's representation in the House of Representatives, if any male citizens aged 21 and over were denied the right to vote. This was designed to force the Southern states to extend suffrage to black male citizens. However, Section 3 applied a very different formula to white Southern males.
3. Any Confederate official who had previously held a federal or state office is disqualified from holding "any office, civil or military, under the United States, or under any state....." Congress, with a 2/3 vote of each house, could pardon any such person. This would seem to be an <u>ex post facto law</u>, a law operating retroactively, creating a law to punish individuals for past actions. For example, in 2009 the drinking age in the United States is 21, whereas in 1981 in many states it was 18. If enacted today, an ex post facto law might read that anyone aged 18 to

20 who drank in 1981 is subject to prosecution even though it was not against the law at the time! By the way, Ex post facto laws are prohibited in Article I, Sec. 9, Clause 3 in the Constitution. Additionally, this section appears to also establish a <u>Bill of Attainder</u>, a "legislative act pronouncing a person guilty of a crime, usually treason, without trial…." This too is prohibited in Article I, Sec. 9, Clause 3.

    4. This section repudiated the Confederate debt.

After the 14th Amendment's passage in Congress, it was sent to the individual states for ratification. However, considering the aforementioned provisions of the amendment, it seemed highly unlikely that the Southern states would vote to approve it, depriving it of the ¾ majority of the states necessary for addition to the Constitution. Indeed, the original count in 1867 to ratify the 14th Amendment proved insufficient for adoption.

States in the United States	- 37
States Needed to Ratify	- 28
States Voting "Yes"	- 22
States Voting "No"	- 12
States not Voting	- 3

Thus, the 14th Amendment appeared defeated, but the amendment process typically lasts 7 years and the Radicals, emboldened by their success in the mid-term elections, were determined to continue the fight for passage. Their means for doing so was extraordinary.

<u>Military Reconstruction</u>

    Undaunted by their initial failure in ratifying the 14th Amendment and committed to a far different vision of reconstruction than that of President Johnson, on March 2, 1867 Congress passed (over Johnson's vetoes) the Military Reconstruction Act, the Command of the Army Act, and the Tenure of Office Act. The Military Reconstruction Act in effect expelled 10 Southern states from the Union (Tennessee was exempted because it ratified the 14th Amendment), and divided them into 5 military districts, each under a military governor supported by Union soldiers. The military governor had the authority to maintain "peace and order", suspend civil courts and establish military tribunals, and to register "qualified" adult males to vote and hold office. The Southern states could rejoin the Union only after new state constitutions providing for black male suffrage had been drawn up and approved by both the states' voters and the U.S. Congress. Additionally, the state legislatures must ratify the 14th Amendment. After the 14th Amendment had been formally added to the Constitution, the new Southern delegations to Congress would be allowed to take their seats, the troops would be removed and reconstruction would be completed.

    Thus, nearly two years after Lee's surrender at Appomattox ended a war fought to a large degree to preserve the Union, 10 Southern states found themselves outside of it. Also, from a constitutional standpoint, there are some troubling aspects to this entire process:

A. How can states denied their representation in Congress participate in the amendment process? Article 5 of the Constitution, which also defines the amendment process, states "that no State, without its consent, shall be deprived of its equal Suffrage in the Senate."

B. From 1865 to March 2, 1867, the Southern states were in the Union, participating in Congress and in the ratification process of both the 13th (which abolished slavery) and 14th Amendments. However, after March 2, the functioning governments of 10 Southern states were disqualified and replaced by military rule. According to Article IV, Section 4 of the Constitution, "The United States shall <u>guarantee to every State in this Union a Republican Form of Government</u>, and shall protect each of them against Invasion;" This section continues with, "and on Application of the Legislature, or of the Executive (when the Legislature cannot be convened) against domestic violence."
This aspect of Article IV may justify the dispatching of troops to quell violence in the South perpetrated by the K.K.K. and similar groups, but it seems somewhat far-fetched that it would allow civil government to be suspended indefinitely. This was seemingly confirmed in an 1866 Supreme Court ruling. In *Ex parte Milligan*, the court contended that military rule in areas where civil governments were operational was unconstitutional.

C. Finally, the actual ratification of the 14th Amendment is highly questionable. Three Northern states, New Jersey, Ohio, and Oregon rescinded their initial approval on constitutional grounds, but their retractions were ignored.

Despite the constitutional contradictions and inconsistencies, as well as the irregularities in the ratification process, the 14th Amendment became part of the Constitution on July 28, 1868. The impact on the nation has been enormous.

With little choice but to comply with the conditions or remain under martial law, most of the Southern states submitted to these new terms for readmission. By 1868, North Carolina, South Carolina, Florida, Alabama, Louisiana, and Arkansas were once again part of the Union. In 1870, Virginia, Georgia, Mississippi, and Texas reentered the Union, but with an additional condition; these states also had to ratify the 15th Amendment which in effect gave black males the right to vote. (This amendment was ratified March 30, 1870.) So, in 1870, five years after the war was over, a transformed United States was again a single nation.

<u>The Reconstruction Governments in the South</u>
The new governments in the South shared several general characteristics, and all encapsulated modest reform measures such as:

A. More equitable reapportionment (re-drawing of electoral districts).

B. Universal adult male suffrage, except for those Confederates disenfranchised by the 14th Amendment. There were however provisions made for re-enfranchisement.

C. Black male participation in politics at the federal, state, and local level until about 1900. About 2000 blacks served in offices ranging from county commissioners to U.S. Congressmen. (20 black citizens served in the House of Representatives, and 2, Blanch Bruce and Hiram Revels, were U.S. Senators from Mississippi.)

D. Many formerly appointive offices were made elective, meaning citizens could choose more officials (judges, for example) through popular elections.

E. Creation or expansion of the public education system.

F. More progressive taxation (increasing in rate as the taxable amount increases), and substantial increases in taxes in general.

G. Improved public facilities for the poor and the handicapped.

H. Greater property rights for women.

In effect, the new Southern governments mirrored their Northern counterparts, and were not particularly revolutionary. In fact, after Reconstruction ended in 1877, many of the reforms were left untouched. However, most Southerners bitterly denounced even the positive aspects of these governments and demanded "conservative redemption" from them and a return to "home rule." Why?

1. The belief that the newly enfranchised blacks were wholly unsuited for participation in government, a belief shared by many white Northerners.

2. Resentment at the "Carpetbaggers" and "Scalawags" included in these governments. ("The Yankees and traitors are destroying our beloved South" may have been how a contemporary Southerner expressed these sentiments.)

3. Anger aimed at the rampant corruption, embezzlement, and fraud (which was also prevalent in Northern states and the federal government). The increased tax burdens mandated by the costs of new programs and services were also targets for Southern ire.

Conservative rule was actually restored in most of the Southern states by 1875; by 1877 conservative governments were also in place in South Carolina, Louisiana, and Florida.

The Impeachment of President Johnson

As mentioned previously, on the same day Congress passed the Military Reconstruction Act, it also approved the Tenure of Office Act. In effect, this act prevented a president from firing and/or replacing a Cabinet member whom he appointed, without Senate approval. The real intention of the act however was to goad Johnson into violating it and thus subject to prosecution. Johnson's vetoes, and his appointment of conservative generals to oversee the reconstruction of the South drew the ire of the Radicals. The question is, how could the Tenure of Office Act be used to get rid of Johnson? The Radicals in Congress knew Johnson wanted to fire Secretary of War Edwin Stanton, a supporter of their policies.

The ever combative Johnson believed the law was ridiculous and unconstitutional, and obliged the Radicals by dismissing Stanton on Aug. 12, 1867 while Congress was out of session. Stanton refused to obey the president's order and barricaded himself in his office, finally having to be carried out by soldiers while still hanging onto his chair! When Congress reconvened in 1868, the House quickly voted to impeach Johnson on 11 counts, 8 of which centered around the Tenure of Office Act. (# 9 accused him of violating an army appropriations act, # 10 accused him of insulting the Congress and attempting to disgrace it, and # 11 was basically a summary of the 10 previous accusations, and a charge of obstruction of Congress' reconstruction laws.) On March 5, 1868 the impeachment proceedings began in the Senate. Johnson himself did not appear, but he was ably defended by a group of lawyers who dismantled the case on two primary grounds:

1. Johnson was not technically guilty of violating the Tenure of Office Act, because Lincoln had appointed Stanton as Sec. of War, not Johnson.
2. Although Johnson's behavior had been boorish and undignified, this was not sufficient cause to convict and remove a president. To do so would set a dangerous constitutional precedent.

On May 16, the Senate voted 35 to 19 to convict, just 1 vote shy of the 2/3 majority necessary for conviction. In the end 7 Republican Senators agreed with Johnson's lawyers and voted to acquit. Subsequent American history might have been far different if they had achieved his conviction and removal.

"Grantism" and The End of Reconstruction

Although Johnson was acquitted, his political power disappeared after impeachment, and he was never considered a candidate for president in the upcoming 1868 elections. Indeed, Johnson's presidency is almost universally regarded as a failure by historians. However, during his time in office, Johnson did achieve a significant foreign policy success, though it was ridiculed at the time. In 1867, Sec. of State William Seward purchased Alaska from Russia for the paltry sum of $7,200,000 (or a little over $.08 per square mile!). The Russian Foreign Minister offered to sell the territory on the evening of March 28th and Seward concluded the deal before midnight. Though initially ridiculed as a colossal waste of money, (it was called "Seward's Folly" and "Seward's Icebox" by contemporary critics), the purchase of Alaska turned out fairly well for the United States! Also in that year, Nebraska entered the Union.

The Republicans chose war hero Ulysses S. Grant while the Democrats nominated the war governor of New York, Horatio Seymour. The election was not particularly close:

Election of 1868	Popular Vote	Electoral Vote
Rep. - Ulysses S. Grant	3,012,833	214
Dem. - Horatio Seymour	2,703,249	80

Grant had been a brilliant war commander, but he lacked political experience. Once in office, he deferred in many instances to his advisors and congressional leaders, whose judgment varied widely in talent and effectiveness.

   In addition, Grant, though personally scrupulous, appointed a significant number of corrupt individuals to important political offices. Not surprisingly, most scholars consider Grant's two-terms in office as the most corrupt in U.S. history. Between 1869 and 1876, Grant was surrounded by corruption and scandal. His brother-in-law, vice president, personal secretary, Sec. of War, Sec. of the Treasury, Sec. of the Navy, and several congressmen (including future president James Garfield) were all implicated or indicted in various major scandals, "Black Friday," "Credit Mobilier," the Bureau of Indian Affairs swindle, and the St. Louis "Whiskey Ring" to name just a few. The multitude of scandals earned the negative nickname "Grantism." Despite the ubiquitous corruption (which continued in his second term), Grant was reelected in 1872, defeating newspaper editor Horace Greeley, and several other minor challengers (see below).

Election of 1872	Popular Vote	Electoral Vote
Rep. - Ulysses S. Grant	3,597,132	286
Dem. - Horace Greeley	2,834,125	*66
------------	------------	------------
Ind. Dem. - Hendricks	Total	42
Ind. Dem. - Brown	for	18
Ind. Dem. – Davis	these candidates	2
Ind. Dem. - Jenkins	35,097	1

*Greeley actually won only 3 electoral votes; the other 63 went to the 4 independent candidates.

Grant and Reconstruction

   During Grant's two terms in office, a few significant Reconstruction laws were enacted.

1.   The Ku Klux Klan Act (Feb. 28, 1871) and
2.   The Force Act (May 31, 1871)

Collectively, these acts imposed stiff fines and /or imprisonment for anyone attempting to intimidate voters, either openly or in disguises, and authorized the military to enforce the 15th Amendment. To enforce these acts, more federal troops were deployed to the South. By 1872, Grant's aggressive enforcement virtually destroyed the Klan and similar groups.

3.   The Civil Rights Act of 1875 – the project of Charles Sumner, this act passed after his death (1874) and in reality was the death rattle of Radical Reconstruction. It prohibited discrimination in public accommodations ("inns, public conveyances on land and water, theatres, and other places of public amusement") except schools. Citizens who felt subject to discriminatory practices could file suit in federal court. It would seem that this sweeping law, in addition to

previous anti-discriminatory statutes and amendments, would permanently restructure race relations in American society, but this would not be the case. Foreshadowing things to come, the Supreme Court virtually overturned the act in 7 *Civil Rights Cases* in 1883. The Court ruled that Congress had no jurisdiction over discrimination by private individuals and groups, and that the 14th Amendment only prohibited <u>states</u> from enacting discriminatory laws against citizens. By 1896, even this emasculated protection would disappear.

By the end of his second term, Americans had grown weary of the seemingly endless scandals associated with Grant and "Grantism." Also, the North quite simply had lost interest in reconstruction, or as one New York editor put it in 1873, the region "was tired of the Negro." Other important factors such as Western settlement, industrialization, the economic Panic of 1873, and the deaths, electoral defeat, and/or retirement of many of the Radical Republicans contributed to Northern fatigue with reconstruction. By the election of 1876, it was clear that it was time for a change.

The Election of 1876 and the Compromise of 1877

In the campaign season of 1876, there was actually a significant number of Republicans who wanted Grant to be nominated for a third-term. However, reform elements in the Republican Party carried the day and nominated former Union general and reform governor of Ohio Rutherford B. Hayes for president. The Democrats likewise chose a candidate who promised to eliminate the corruption in Washington, Governor Samuel J. Tilden of New York, a humorless man who successfully toppled "Boss" Tweed's swindling operations in New York City. The platforms of both parties bore little differences. Both were pledged to restore integrity and honesty in government, maintain protective tariffs (taxes on imports), and end military reconstruction. When the votes were counted, it <u>appeared</u> Tilden had won. He had 4.3 million popular votes to Hayes 4.03 million, and an electoral advantage of 184 to 165. However, to win the election, Tilden would have to gain <u>1</u> more electoral vote, which was a problem because of disputed returns in 4 states, Oregon, South Carolina, Louisiana, and Florida. Combined, these states accounted for 20 electoral votes. Despite pleas to concede the election to Tilden, the Republican Party's National Chairman Zachariah Chandler refused to budge, and an electoral crisis resulted. The aforementioned states continued to dispute the election returns and Congress remained divided by a partisan impasse. On Jan. 28, 1877, Congress established a special electoral commission to determine a valid count of the votes and decide the election. (Interestingly, in the disputed election of 2000, the Supreme Court fulfilled that duty.) The commission was composed of 15 members – 5 Representatives, 5 Senators, and 5 Supreme Court Justices. The all important party alignment consisted of 7 Republicans, 7 Democrats, and <u>1</u> Independent, Justice David Davis of Illinois. However, before the commission had completed its work, Illinois offered Davis a U.S. Senate seat which had just become vacant. He eagerly accepted, and was replaced by Republican Justice Joseph P. Bradley. Politicians in both parties realized that the disputed returns were almost certainly to be counted in favor of the Republicans, and decided to make a deal to prevent a further national crisis or even bloodshed. Spearheaded by Northern Republicans James

Garfield and John Sherman and Southern Democrats John Gordon and L.Q.C. Lamar, an agreement was reached on Feb. 26, 1877, which stipulated that in exchange for not contesting the commission's findings, the South would receive certain benefits. This agreement became the core of the <u>Compromise of 1877</u>. Not surprisingly, on March 2, 1877 the commission voted 8 to 7 in favor of Hayes in all 4 disputed states (highly suspect), and he won the election 185 to 184 in the Electoral College.

Election of 1876	Popular Vote	Electoral Vote
Rep. - Rutherford B. Hayes	4,036,298	185
Dem. - Samuel J. Tilden	4,300,590	184

<u>The Compromise of 1877 – Provisions:</u>

1. The last federal troops (25,000) would be removed from the South.
2. Southerners would receive federal patronage (government positions). Ex-Confederate David M. Key became Postmaster General.
3. Federal subsidies were to be provided for a southern railroad to the Pacific Ocean.
4. Southerners would respect the political rights of black Southerners.
5. Southern Democrats would allow Republican James Garfield to become Speaker of the House of Representatives.

Provisions #1 and #2 were honored, and #4 was (for the most part) adhered to until the 1890s. However, Southern Democrats prevented Garfield from becoming Speaker, and President Hayes did not sanction railroad subsidies. Nonetheless, with the Compromise of 1877, reconstruction was over.

Phil McCaskey
August 13th , 2014

There are few subjects in American history that are more discussed and yet less understood than the tragic institution of slavery. Ironically, there is extensive documentation and research information available concerning slavery. The following statistics gleaned from contemporary newspapers, auction records, and U.S. census documents may illuminate certain aspects of "the peculiar institution."

1)-Cotton

Year	Amount of Cotton per million pounds	Price per pound
1800	37	$.44
1805	73	.23
1810	89	.16
1815	105	.29
1820	177	.16
1825	265	.12
1830	365	.09
1835	530	.17
1840	673	.10
1845	902	.08
1850	1,066	.12
1855	1,608	.10
1860	1,918	.11

*In 1860, the leading cotton producing state was Mississippi with 1,202,507 bales produced, Virginia the least with 12,727 bales. North Carolina processed 125,514 bales. Bales of cotton averaged about 500 pounds.

2)-Slave Prices

Year	Virginia	Charleston	New Orleans
1800	$375	$500	$500
1805	$425	$550	$600
1810	$500	$550	$900
1815	$475	$500	$650
1820	$700	$800	$1100
1825	$400	$500	$800
1830	$425	$500	$850
1835	$650	$750	$1150
1840	$750	$800	$1000
1845	$550	$575	$700
1850	$700	$650	$1100
1855	$1000	$950	$1350
1860	$1250	$1200	$1800

3)-Free Black Population

1840	1850	1860
386,345	428,637	488,000

In 1860 261,878 free black Americans lived in the South, while 226,122 lived in the North.

4)-Free Black Population In The Slaveholding States And Washington, D.C. – 1860

Alabama	– 2,690
Arkansas	– 144
Delaware	– 19,829
Florida	– 932
Georgia	– 3,500
Kentucky	– 10,684
Louisiana	– 18,647
Maryland	– 83,942
Mississippi	– 733
Missouri	– 3,572
North Carolina	– 30,463
South Carolina	– 9,914
Tennessee	– 7,300
Texas	– 355
Virginia	– 58,042
Washington, D.C.	– 11,131

What did free blacks (and slaves) do? Almost anything. Many blacks worked as domestic servants, barbers, preachers, artisans, seamen, managers, cobblers, shoemakers, cooks, and blacksmiths. In VA in 1860 4,224 free blacks were registered blacksmiths, and 3,728 were listed as shoemakers according to census data. Did any free blacks own slaves? Yes.

For instance, in 1860:

3000 free blacks in New Orleans owned slaves! In Charleston, SC 125, free blacks owned slaves, and 69 free blacks owned slaves in North Carolina. William Tiler Johnson of Natchez of Mississippi owned 3 barber shops, 1500 acres, and 8 slaves. In one year he issued 16 loans to whites totaling $2000. He was killed in 1851 after winning a court case over land boundaries against his murderer! Cyprien Richard purchased a Louisiana estate with 91 slaves for $250,000, and John Walker of New Hanover County, NC owned 44 slaves in 1830, while John Carruthers Stanley of Craven County owned 163 bondsmen, the largest black slave holder in the South. Also in North Carolina, the free black population (2/3 mulatto) numbered 30,463, behind only VA and MD, totaling 10% of the state's black population. In Wilmington, the state's largest city, 45.5% of the 9552 inhabitants were black, including 573 free blacks, about 6% of the total population.*

An additional anomaly involving the Southern free black population involved voluntary re-enslavement. This unusual practice evolved out of an 1854 case in which two former Virginia slaves (brothers) actually petitioned the state for re-enslavement to a trusted white friend. From this incident grew a general law in Virginia in 1856 for voluntary re-enslavement by former slaves, actually initiated by the state's free black population! (Similar laws will be passed in 6 other Southern states between 1856 1nd 1864.) During that period 110 former Virginia slaves filed suit to that purpose, including the noteworthy cases of William Williamson, a respectable farmer, and Wyatt Love, a shrewd and prosperous entrepreneur.

*Other NC cities with large free black populations included New Bern, Fayetteville, Elizabeth City and Raleigh.

Important questions beg however – What could possibly be a rational motivation for re-enslavement? Who could be re-enslaved?

In the first case, Virginia (akin to many other Southern states) enacted a law in 1806 which required freed slaves to emigrate from the state within one year of manumission or face possible involuntary re-enslavement. Although sporadically enforced, the possibility of a return to bondage remained real for thousands of freed blacks in the state. Many of these former slaves had carved out a pleasant existence in the land of their birth and had little practical reason nor emotional impetus to leave their homes, farms, businesses, families, friends, and even former owners. To prevent this, a former slave might solicit the assistance of a <u>trusted</u> white friend or even former owner for re-enslavement. The former slave would transfer title to all property to his/her new owner in order to prevent confiscation by the state in the event of involuntary re-enslavement for failure to leave the state. Also, the newly re-enslaved person and the new owner would personally negotiate the terms of bondage. In general, the new owner would provide assurances that the property would be maintained and that life and labor would go on as usual for the re-enslaved individual. Also, the new owner must testify in court regarding the upright character of his new bondsperson, as well as accept personal responsibility for their actions, and pay a monetary deposit to the state; a very formal and involved process, but what actual guarantees might the re-enslaved person receive from their new owner protecting against negative "unintended consequences", such as reneging on previous agreements or even resale? Obviously, trust is the absolute prerequisite and paramount consideration in such a peculiar arrangement, but as evidence of that bond, the new owner might draft a new will bequeathing <u>back</u> all of the property deeded to him by the re-enslaved person, in the event of their death.

Who could be re-enslaved? The entire process was resisted by the state of Virginia whose legislators felt very uneasy about sanctioning the forfeiture of freedom by an individual, thus there were significant limitations. Predictably, whites could not be enslaved, but nor could the children of re-enslaved blacks, both born and unborn. Also, the wives of those seeking re-enslavement could not be remanded to enslavement. A very strange side-note to the "Peculiar Institution" indeed!

5)-<u>Slave Population</u>	<u>1790</u>	<u>1850</u>	<u>1860</u>
	698,000	3,198,324	3,950,511

6a)-<u>Slave Ownership -1850</u>

<u>Slaves Held Per Owner</u>	<u>Number Of Owners Holding This Number Of Slaves</u>
1(slave)	69,000(owners)
2-4	106,000
5-9	81,000
10–19	55,000
20-49	30,000
50-99	6,000
100-200	1,500
200-300	189

6b)-Slave Ownership –1860

Slaves Held Per Owner	Number Of Owners Holding This Number Of Slaves
1(slave)	77,000(owners)
2-4	110,000
5-9	89,000
10-19	62,000
20-49	36,000
50-99	8,000
100-200	2,000
200-300	224
500–1000	12

7)-Slaveholding States-1860

State	Total Slaveholders	Holding 50+ Slaves	Slave Population
Alabama	33,730	1,687	435,080
Arkansas	1,144	10	111,115
Delaware	587	0	1,798*
Florida	5,152	205	61,745
Georgia	41,084	1,314	462,198
Kentucky	38,648	70	225,483
Louisiana	22,033	1,576	331,726
Maryland	13,783	115	87,189
Mississippi	30,143	1,675	436,631
Missouri	24,320	38	114,931
North Carolina	34,658	744	331,059
South Carolina	26,701	1,646	402,406
Tennessee	36,844	382	275,719
Texas	21,870	336	182,566
Virginia	52,128	860	490,865
Washington, D.C.	930 (Approximately)		3,185

*In 1790, Delaware's enslaved population stood at 8868; the dramatic drop by 1860 was unique among the slaveholding states.

8)-Slaves And Slaveholding In The South-1860

State	Slaves As % Of Total Population	Slaveholding Families As % Of White Families
South Carolina	57%	46%
Mississippi	55%	49%
Louisiana	47%	30%
Alabama	45%	35%
Georgia	44%	37%
Florida	44%	34%
Texas	30%	29%
The Lower South As A Region		
	47%	37%
North Carolina	33%	28%
Virginia	31%	26%
Arkansas	26%	20%
Tennessee	25%	25%
The Upper South As A Region		
	32%	25%
Kentucky	20%	23%
Maryland	13%	12%
Missouri	10%	13%
Delaware	2%	3%
The Border States As A Region		
	14%	16%

The Evolution and Erosion of Slavery During The War Between The States

1. **Introduction: The Five Great Turning Points In American Slavery**

    a. <u>1619</u> – the beginnings at Jamestown (although the Trans-Atlantic Slave Trade began in 1503 in South America).

    b. <u>1697</u> – end of the British Royal African Company's monopoly of the slave trade after 25 years led to the rapid expansion and domination of the Trans-Atlantic slave trade by Britain. The number of slaves transported to the West on British ships increased 9-fold, from 5000 to 45,000 persons annually, although all told, only about 5% (400,000 to 500,000 persons) were brought to what would be the United States.

    c. <u>1793</u> – Connecticut native Eli Whitney's invention of the cotton gin after a visit to Mulberry Hill Plantation in Georgia slows the tide of emancipation in the South.

    d. <u>1831–32</u> – the actions of 3 men, William Lloyd Garrison (white Northern abolitionist publisher of *The Liberator*, Nat Turner, a Virginia slave, and Prof. Thomas Dew, a philosophy instructor at William and Mary College, electrify the South, crush general emancipation and colonization efforts, silence abolition and abolitionists, and greatly amplify the process of justifying slavery in the South as "a positive good", as opposed to apologizing for it as "a necessary evil."

    e. <u>1860–61</u> – secession and the formation of the Confederate States of America with explicit protections for slavery (Article I, Sec. 9, Cl. 4) and the subsequent War Between the States will determine the ultimate fate of human bondage in a reunited United States of America in 1865.

2. <u>**The Status of Slavery, North and South, during the he War 1861–62**</u>

    a. "a white man's war", despite attempts by blacks to enlist on both sides.

    b. Union - Return of slaves to their owners ordered by Lincoln in response to General John C. Fremont's emancipation orders in 1861. However, a change begins to occur with General Benjamin Butler's "contraband" definition of slaves who have either run away from their Confederate owners, or have been taken from them by Union forces; simply put, they are enemy "goods useful in war."

    c. Gradual changes on the periphery – Union.

    1. April 10, 1862 – paid compensation to those states which would agree to gradual emancipation and colonization to Haiti and Panama. (never implemented)

    2. April 16, Washington, D.C. – slavery abolished, with paid compensation to owners.

    3. June 19, slavery prohibited in the territories

4. July 17, 2nd Confiscation Act "liberated all slaves of all persons aiding the rebellion", and a subsequent act "forbade the army from returning runaways."
5. Lincoln's contradictory and calculated statements indicated a cautious approach to emancipation
   a. to a deputation of black men at the White House, Aug. 15, 1862 – Lincoln suggests colonization of all black Americans to some location in Central America (very coolly received).
   b. response to Horace Greeley, editor of the *New York Tribune*, Aug. 22, 1862 – The war is to save the Union. "My paramount object in this struggle is to save the Union, and is not either to save or to destroy slavery…."
   c. Emancipation Proclamation – Sept. 22nd 1862 issued after the Union victory at Sharpsburg (Antietam) on Sept. 17th, and effective as of
   Jan. 1st 1863. The Proclamation only frees slaves in areas still in rebellion"; in other words, areas that the Union armed forces do not control. It also does not apply to the 5 slave states (Border States) which never seceded.

3. <u>The Changes – 1863–64</u>
   a. Northern enlistment of black soldiers and sailors (215,000+)
   b. Confederate authorization of both free blacks and slaves in noncombatant military support roles, such as body servants, hospital attendants, teamsters, stevedores, fortifications builders, laborers, and cooks (who were paid $15 a month and clothed).
   c. The unraveling of slavery in the Confederacy 1863–65.
   d. Patrick Cleburne Jan. 2, 1864 Memorial to officers of the Army of Tennessee.
   <u>Main Points:</u>
   1. The Confederacy lacked soldiers
   2. The South lacked supplies.
   3. Slavery had now become a liability
   So…
   Free, train, and arm "courageous" slaves for military service in the Confederate Army, and "guarantee freedom within a reasonable time to every slave in the South who shall remain true to the Confederacy in this war." To conclude, "As between the loss of independence and the loss of slavery, we assume that every patriot will freely give up the latter—give up the Negro slave rather than be a slave himself."

   Initial reactions – silence, contempt, and incredulity among Confederate officers, congressmen, and commentators, but on March 23, 1865, the Confederate government issued General Order #14 which called for the freeing, training, and arming of 200,000 slaves, but by then, way too little, way too late.

4. <u>The End (1864–1865)</u>
   a. Lincoln's re-election and Confederate defeat.
   b. Ratification of the 13th Amendment – Dec. 6, 1865 – Slavery is dead, "except as a punishment for crime whereof the party shall have been duly convicted...."

Addendum II:
Synopsis of the History of the Amerindians and the United States

Conflicts and Policies

From the beginnings of colonization to the tragedy at Wounded Knee, SD in 1890, American policies towards the Amerindians always trended to removal and concentration. Under the best of circumstances, there were many instances of cooperation and friendship between Native Americans and the newcomers. However, cultural differences at a seminal level, precluded true lasting equal coexistence; in other words, one culture would dominate, the other would submit, and over time, the Amerindians would be relegated to the status of a defeated people. There are several factors in this development, the organizational and technological supremacy first of the colonists and then of the new Americans themselves, the sheer and overwhelming numbers of Americans compared to Native Americans, especially after 1800, and finally the inability of the Amerindians to unite against a common foe; indeed, in-fighting among the various tribes substantially weakened Native Americans in the face of an ever more powerful American presence. At each stage of this historical development, colonial and then United States government policies were punctuated with violence which conformed to a general, recurring pattern:

A. New treaties are ratified between the U.S. government and various tribes "guaranteeing " new tribal boundaries.

B. American settlers venture into these tribal regions lured by gold, fertile farm lands, and commercial wealth in general.

C. Scattered and undermanned American military units are unwilling and/or unable to stop American citizens from violating these treaties and entering Amerindian territories.

D. Massacres and wars precipitated by both sides result.

E. American authorities subsequently heightened military and political efforts to bring the Amerindians "under control." The end result of this policy? Tribes of Amerindians are put onto reservations controlled by the American military.

F. New treaties would be ratified, and the process began anew.

<u>Addendum III</u>
<u>The Constitution – A Synopsis</u>

<u>Introduction</u> – 226 years ago today, the main text of the United States Constitution lay completed, the work of 55 tired, bickering, and brilliant "Founding Fathers" who had labored at the task since May 25th. Initially their intent was to revise the existing constitution, the Articles of Confederation, our governing document since 1781. That document, despite some successes, proved inadequate to the needs of the new nation. Instead, over the next 3 1/2 months, they engineered a governmental counter-revolution. The document they created was and is a collection of compromises, some extraordinarily successful in their composition and application, and others inherently flawed in design. Nonetheless, our Constitution is a compendium of most of the enlightened political ideals of that time; limited and divided government, separation of powers, checks and balances, and popular sovereignty, being some of the most important. No similar comprehensive written design for a national government existed anywhere on earth at the time, and 2 1/4 centuries later, it's duration and success are still unparalleled in human history. So, in an abbreviated form, what is this Constitution which set the political groundwork for the evolution of the most prosperous and powerful nation which has ever existed?

<u>The 7 Articles</u> – The original text of the Constitution is only a few pages long and contains just 7 distinct Articles which outline the powers of the various branches of the federal government, define some of the obligations, limitations, and powers held by the states, the amendment and ratification process, and the supremacy of the Constitution and the federal government in general.

<u>Article I</u> stipulates the makeup and powers of the Legislative Branch, the Congress. This is the longest single Article in the Constitution, which spells out how many Representatives and Senators are to be allowed from each state, age and citizenship qualifications, the length of elected terms, and specific rights and duties assigned to each house, including provision for impeachment of federal officials. The most striking part of Article I, Section 8 gives Congress 17 specific powers, including tax authority (including a de facto prohibition on federal income taxes), borrowing authority, the power to declare war (a hot button issue currently) and to raise and fund the armed forces, and the power to establish federal courts. Section 8 concludes with the controversial "Necessary and Proper Clause" which gives Congress the right to pass laws which facilitate the execution of the previous 17 powers. (You might also refer to this as the "end-justifies-the means" clause!)

   Also, Article I places restrictions on states in regards to currency, taxation of exports, and relations with foreign nations. The Article also deals with slavery, although not by name, with the infamous "3/5 Compromise (slaves to count as 3/5 of a person for federal taxation and representation purposes), and the overseas slave trade (Congress could not prohibit the trade until 1808, which it subsequently did).

Article II defines the powers of the Executive Branch, especially the President, including the qualifications and election of presidents' (the electoral college), the Commander-In-Chief provision, vast appointment and removal authority, and the power to negotiate treaties with foreign nations, subject to the Senate's approval. What is not specifically spelled out in Article II are the extremely important powers of Executive Order and Executive Agreement. Executive orders are directives issued by the president, usually to various government agencies (a.k.a. the Bureaucracy) with the force of law, held to be so by the Supreme Court and the acquiescence of Congress. Executive agreements are between the president and foreign nations, also with the force of law or treaties. The constitutional basis for this seems to emanate from the simple statement "he shall take care that the laws be faithfully executed" from Article II, Sec. 3, Cl. 5. Considering the importance of executive orders and agreements historically, for example, internment during World War II (#9066) or the desegregation of the armed forces in 1948 (#9981), this is a significant "inferred" power indeed.

Article III – details the qualifications, terms, duties, and jurisdiction of the Supreme Court and the federal judiciary. Widely perceived by the Founders as the weakest branch of the federal government, an argument can be made that it has become perhaps the most powerful as the virtual final arbiter of the Constitution and federal, state, and local laws. This evolution stems primarily from three sources: 1) Article VI (Clause 2) which states "This Constitution, and Laws of the United States which shall be made in Pursuance thereof; and all Treaties made, or which shall be made, under the Authority of the United States , shall be the supreme Law of the Land;…" a.k.a. The "Supremacy" Clause.
2) The case of *Marbury v. Madison* (1803) in which the Supreme Court established the precedent of deciding if federal laws were constitutional (valid) or unconstitutional (invalid) known as judicial review – which subsequently extended to state laws and state court decisions. 3) The 14th Amendment which continued the expansion of federal oversight of state and local laws through a doctrine referred to as "incorporation." The end result in plain language is that the federal judiciary, especially the Supreme Court can decide the legality of virtually any law brought to it, and nullify laws that do not pass its constitutional interpretation, and that can occur with a simple 5–4 majority vote today. By the way, the only constitutional way an unpopular Supreme Court decision can be changed or voided is to wait for another Supreme Court ruling in the future to overturn it (*Plessy* and *Brown* for instance), or amend the Constitution, not the easiest process!

Article IV - this is the "Full Faith and Credit" segment of the Constitution. Put simply, each state must recognize the official acts of the others in regards to citizens in civil matters (drivers licenses are the easiest example). But there can be complications when the various states' laws or constitutions conflict, for example (as of 2014) same-sex marriages. 19 states allow some form of same sex unions, 31 prohibit them, and 2 make no reference to sexual orientation. Eventually, a same sex married couple will move into a state which does not recognize their marital status. The result will be a Constitution-based challenge in the federal courts; over time, as this is a national issue, the question of same sex marriages will be decided either by a Supreme Court ruling (or non-ruling) or an amendment to the Constitution.

<u>Article V</u> – speaking of amendments, Article V, provides the methods for changing (or amending) the Constitution. This is one of the least familiar major sections of the Constitution, as amendments are somewhat rarely approved, 27 in 226 years, the last one 21 years ago. Contrary to the popular wisdom, neither Congress nor the President has the power to ratify amendments; the States do. The traditional way amendments are submitted to the states is through Congress. Article V begins, "The Congress, whenever two thirds of
both Houses shall deem it necessary, shall propose Amendments to this Constitution…"
although states can propose them as well. Ratification or adoption of an amendment however requires 3/4 of the states approval; today 38 states. Article V serves as a reminder that the Founders respected certain exclusive rights and powers that only the states possess.

<u>Article VII</u> – As previously mentioned Article VI deals with the supremacy of the Constitution and federal law over state and local laws. Article VII, however, dealing with the ratification of this Constitution, seems to more logically follow Article V, but why? The answer again is the States. According to Article VII, the Constitution would only go into effect when 9 of the original 13 states approved it through specially selected conventions, <u>not</u> some form of popular vote. So, once again, even the power to establish the Constitution and indeed the United States under it devolved to the States. This was no easy task, as many of the states had serious and legitimate grievances with the new document. Nonetheless, by late June of 1788, 9 states had ratified the Constitution, but the nation was far from complete without Virginia, New York, North Carolina, and Rhode Island in the fold and they appeared intransigent in their opposition, but why? The Constitution, in its original form carried a Bill of Rights, <u>not for citizens,</u> but for the federal government itself. The entire document lists all the powers of the government, but what about the "unalienable rights" of the people, to quote Jefferson in the Declaration of Independence?! Ten states' constitutions had bills of rights for their citizens, why not the new national government? Eventually a compromise was reached, ratify the Constitution, and one of the first orders of business for the first congress would be the drafting of amendments to accomplish that end. The last state to ratify, Rhode Island, did so in 1790, and the first 10 amendments, the Bill of Rights written by James Madison, was approved by the Congress and sent to the states. Collectively, they were adopted Dec. 15, 1791, a date which should be commemorated for its own historical merits.

   The Bill of Rights is actually a Bill of Limitations on the federal government, a list of "thou shalt not's" in regards to citizens. Consider the first five words of the 1st Amendment: "Congress shall make no law…", and goes on to safeguard freedoms of religion, speech, press, assembly, and petition. The list goes on; the most significant include the right of citizens to bear arms, no unreasonable search and seizure, extensive rights of the accused, no cruel or unusual punishment, no denial of rights not included in the Constitution, and a recognition of the rights of the states. While these rights have never been absolute, The Bill of Rights provide the best protections citizens have against unwanted or oppressive intrusions by the federal government. Indeed, imagine the Constitution and the nation without the inclusion of the Bill of Rights!

Upon completion of the Constitution, Benjamin Franklin wrote to George Washington, "I consent, Sir, to this Constitution, because I expect no better, and because I am not sure it is not the best. The opinions I have had of its errors, I sacrifice to the public good." In that equivocal but cautiously optimistic statement, Franklin perhaps summed up over two centuries of history under the Constitution; the "public good" of hundreds of millions has indeed been served, although tempered by "errors" within the document and the actions of Americans upon them.

Addendum IV:
The States' Rights Argument

A. What Are States' Rights?

Generally speaking, states' rights connotes the right of a state to enact laws and regulations exclusive to that state with little or no interference or oversight from the federal government. In other words, an ordinance, statute, law, or state constitutional provision or amendment which only applies to North Carolina which should not be subject to supervision, alteration, or repeal by any branch of the federal government. Historically, the states maintained exclusive power over their inhabitants health, safety, welfare, education, and morals, the so-called <u>police powers</u>.

B. Is There Any Constitutional Justification Or Basis For States' Rights?

Definitely. There are several antecedents in our laws and history, but for arguments sake, there are three of primary importance:

1. The 13 original states existed <u>prior</u> to the Constitution and were recognized specifically as sovereign and independent by Great Britain in the Treaty of Paris which recognized the United States of America as a new nation. Also, the original governing document of the United States of America, the *Articles of Confederation*, began its preamble by listing all of the States separately, a significant difference from the *Constitution of the United States of America* which starts with "We the People of the United States..." (See Section C)

2. Ratification (approval) of the Constitution went through each state in separate conventions, not through any general vote of the entire U.S. population. For example, North Carolina, which ratified in 1789 and Rhode Island, which ratified in 1790, were <u>not</u> part of the United States when George Washington became our first president, even though they were 2 of the original 13 colonies and 13 original states as organized in 1776–77.

3. The structure of the Constitution guarantees and respects the integrity, identity, and rights of the states as exemplified by:
   a. the structure of the Senate - Each state is guaranteed two Senators, regardless of population, and as originally structured, the Senate was the more powerful of the two Houses of Congress, hence the *"Upper House."* (Article I, Sec. 3, Cl. 1)
   b. the Electoral College - which reserved to the States the election of presidents. Although overshadowed by the popular vote (first instituted in 1824), the Electoral College still retains this power as evidenced by 4 presidential contests in which the winner of the popular vote lost, most recently in 2000. (Article II, Sec. 2, Cl. 2) See Appendix II for more details.

c. the Amendment process - only the states, not the Congress, President, or Supreme Court, have the ability to formally amend the Constitution, requiring ¾ approval (38 states today) to do so. (Article V)

d. the 10th Amendment (1791) which states "The powers not delegated (given) to the United States by the Constitution nor prohibited by it to the States are reserved to the states respectively, or to the people." This is the *Reserved Powers* Amendment.

4. Extra-Constitutional arguments and actions of note include the *Virginia and Kentucky Resolutions of 1798*, John C. Calhoun's "Theory of Nullification", and the Secession Movement of 1860–61 of 11 Southern States, all resting on the inviolability of certain state prerogatives.

C. <u>What Are The Major Arguments Refuting These States' Rights Postulations?</u> The basis for limitations on states' rights, the supremacy of the federal government, and the indissolubility of the Union stem from three sources:

1. Romantic pronouncements of a permanent union in which the Preamble to the Constitution, "We the people of the United States," is used as a justification for the national government's supremacy over the individual states. In other words, we are one people as opposed to citizens of various states within the Union. Daniel Webster's speech to the Senate on Jan. 26th 1831 (The "Second Reply to Hayne") stands as the most eloquent expression of national union and national supremacy. However, when delivering his peroration, Webster probably knew that when the Preamble was originally drafted, it stated "We the people" and then listed each state separately. The Founders changed this because they thought that some of the states might, in fact, not ratify the Constitution, which was indeed the case!

2. Supreme Court decisions based on Article VI of the Constitution, the Supremacy Clause ("The Constitution, and the laws of the United States <u>which shall be in pursuance thereof</u>...shall be the supreme law of the land." The three most important of these cases are *Fletcher v. Peck* in 1810, in which the Court gave itself the power to overturn state laws, *McCulloch v. Maryland* in 1819, where it claimed that the national government and its creations were supreme to the states and *Cohens v. Virginia* in 1821, where the court asserted its right to reverse state court decisions. It is both interesting and revealing that a branch of the federal government assumed for itself and the federal government in general these momentous powers at the expense of the states. It is also interesting that two of the most important of the Founders, Thomas Jefferson and James Madison (the "Father of the Constitution and the Bill of Rights"), declared in the VA and KY. Resolutions of 1798 that the states themselves had the right to question the constitutionality of federal laws.

3. Northern victory in the War Between The States (a.k.a. the Civil War), the highly questionable passage of the 14th Amendment, and numerous 20th century Supreme Court decisions delivered crippling blows to states' rights in practice (*Roth, Mapp, Engel, Miranda, Swann, Furman, Roe, Roper*, and *McDonald* for example).

Appendix I

U.S. Population (1790–1860)

1790 - 3,929,214

1800 - 5,308,483 (35.1% increase from previous decade)

1810 - 7,239,881 (36.4%)

1820 - 9,638,453 (33.1%)

1830 - 12,866,020 (33.5%)

1840 - 17,069,453 (32.7%)

1850 - 23,191,876 (35.9%)

1860 - 31,443,321 (35.6%)

Appendix II

Synopsis of the Electoral College

A. – What is it? – A group of 538 (today) American citizens from each of the 50 states and Washington, D.C. that are either elected or appointed as electors within each state and Washington, D.C., that actually elect the president and vice president. Each state has a number of electors equal to the total number of Representatives and Senators it has in Congress. Thus, in 2008 for example, California, the most populous state, has 55 electors, North Carolina has 15, and Wyoming, the least populous state, has 3. (Note: 5 other states and Washington, D.C. also have 3.) Although, almost any adult citizen can be an Elector, they are almost always nominated or chosen by each state's Republican and Democratic party organizations.

B. – Why was it established? – The Electoral College was the result of several compromises. In short, the options were direct popular vote, Congressional selection of president, or working through the state legislatures. Very few of the Founders approved of a direct popular vote for president (most notably, Hamilton and Jefferson). A significant number felt the Congress was the logical choice, but opponents pointed out that this would inevitably make the Executive Branch dependant and inferior to the Legislative Branch. Finally, the Founders settled on the Electoral College system as a an acceptable method as it:

1. – Reflected the states, and indirectly the will of the people through their state governments.
2. - Avoided the logistical nightmare of a popular election.
3. - Left the decision of who should be president to the best informed members of the citizenry.
4. - Respected the states with small populations, which could be completely ignored in a popular election.

C. – Why is it still utilized if it negates the voting will of the people? –In reality, the Electors from each state <u>have</u> in the vast majority of our presidential elections voted as the residents of their states. In only 4 elections out of 47 featuring the popular vote (1824, 1876, 1888, 2000) has the Electoral College contradicted the popular vote.

D. – Would a direct popular vote be a better method? – Not necessarily, considering the vast discrepancies in the populations of the 50 states. For example, the bottom 25 states in terms of population have 1/6 of the total U.S. population, while just the top <u>7</u> (Ca., Texas, N.Y., Fla., Ill., Penn., and Ohio collectively account for over 135 million people out of a total population of approximately 310 million. At the municipal level, the top 50 cities population amounts to over 47 million. As of 2004, there were 142 million Americans registered to vote, so consider this: In a popular vote election for president, it would be illogical and detrimental for a presidential candidate to campaign in a majority of the states, let alone all 50, when that candidate could win the election by concentrating all of his or her efforts in the top 10 or 12 states in terms of population. Not only that, the nation's largest cities would also be invaluable for precisely the same reason. That being said, what is the problem?

1. The bottom 35 states in terms of population could be (and would be) virtually ignored not only in terms of the campaign, but in the candidates addressing issues of vital importance to those states. In other words, what candidate would care about states like Nebraska, Wyoming, Alaska, Hawaii, West Virginia, Arkansas, etc... when they would have little or no impact on his/ her election chances. Critics argue that is the case today as candidates concentrate their efforts in about a dozen or so battleground states, but the battleground states change (if only slightly) in every presidential election owing to state and regional vicissitudes, which the parties and their candidates must address.

2. Viable candidates in a popular vote format would increasingly, if not exclusively, be chosen by both parties from the big states. Why? To bolster both their candidates election bids, and to put the party in control of the Executive Branch.

3. Imagine the nightmare of a <u>national</u> recount in a tightly contested election!

4. Third-Party "spoilers" could much more easily affect the outcome of a presidential election. Although not necessarily a negative itself, a Third-Party or Independent candidate who actually won just a plurality of the popular vote, would win the election, meaning a majority of the voters cast votes for the other candidates; an ironic twist to the whole concept of majority rule in a national popular vote!

<u>E.</u> – Has the Electoral College worked effectively throughout history? – As mentioned in category <u>C</u>, on only 4 occasions has the Electoral College overruled the popular vote, but that is not the only measure of its effectiveness. One of the most important reasons the Founders created the Electoral College was to respect the rights of the individual states, a prominent theme throughout the original draft of the Constitution. In other words, the <u>states</u> were given the task of electing the president, so if a majority of states vote for a candidate, it seems perfectly reasonable and representative for that candidate to be elected president. So, has this been the case? Since 1788, there have been 57 presidential elections, the first 9 having no real popular vote. In only <u>two</u> elections out of these 57, has the elected president won less states than the loser. In 1960, Democrat John F. Kennedy won with 23 states, defeating Republican Richard Nixon who carried 25, and in 1976, Democrat Jimmy Carter also won carrying 23 states, while the loser Republican Gerald Ford won 27. On just two other occasions did the winner split the states evenly with the loser; in 1880, both Republican James Garfield and Democrat

Winfield Scott Hancock won 19 states, and in 1848, Whig Zachary Taylor and Democrat Lewis Cass each won 15 states. The winners in the controversial Elections of 1876, 1888, and 2000 did so as well; Republican George W. Bush in 2000 won 30 states, while Democrat Al Gore won 20 and Washington, D.C. By the way, in 2012 President Obama carried 26 states, Republican challenger Mitt Romney, 24.

F. – If not, could it be reformed to be more representative of the voters? The winner-take-all nature of the Electoral College in regards to the states is one of its more controversial aspects; that is, electors are supposed to vote unanimously for the candidate receiving the most popular votes in each state. In a two candidate race, the person winning by even the slimmest majority receives all of the state's electoral votes, which hardly seems representative or reflective of the popular will. Also, in rare instances "renegade electors" vote for candidates who did not carry the state. (Most recently, this has occurred in 1968, 1976, and 1988.) In fact however, 26 of the 50 states have either state laws or formal pledges to the major political parties for the individual electors to cast their vote for a particular candidate. So, what could be done? One proposal is proportional representation.

In this method, a state's electoral votes would be divided by the outcome in each congressional district, with the overall popular vote winner receiving the state's 2 at-large electoral votes. (At present, 2 states, Maine and Nebraska, actually have adopted forms of proportional representation.) More simply illustrated, in 2012, North Carolina has 15 electoral votes because it has 13 Representatives from the state's 13 congressional districts. The other two electors come from North Carolina having 2 U.S. Senators, just as every other state does. So....

Election of 2100 (obviously fictional)

Jones wins 9 congressional districts	= 9 electoral votes
Smith wins 4 congressional districts	= 4 electoral votes
Jones wins the state's overall popular vote	= 2 electoral votes

Total

Jones - 11
Smith - 4

The benefit to such a method is it makes every state a battleground and would most likely minimize any popular vote – electoral vote contradiction. The problem? The amount of time needed to campaign in virtually every state would both increase costs as well as the lengthen the duration of presidential campaigns, the latter a somewhat undesirable prospect for many Americans!

Selected Limited Index

C